DEDIC

This work is dedicated to my family, my mother and father, Ruth and Al, sister and brother, Elise and Hank, who showed me how to be strong and stand up for what I believe in. Thank you for giving me the opportunity to find my way to exactly who I am, and for all those years of irreplaceable warmth and laughter.

And to my children, Ethan and Molly, who constantly shine the Light into my life and help me to see my Self.

I Love you all.

Cosmic Quotient

Copyright © 2011-2012 by Stephanie Azaria, Cosmic Quotient, LLC.
All rights reserved.

Published by COSMIC QUOTIENT, LLC.
www.cosmic-quotient.com

Cosmic Astrology® is a registered trademark of Cosmic Quotient, LLC.

ISBN-13: 978-0-615-50748-4

Cover and layout design by Britt Martin.

Prema Agni® and Rising Star® symbols courtesy of SQ Worldwide.
Night Sky: www.forestwander.com.
Earth: NOAA/NASA GOES Project.

Additional research and proofreading contributed by:
 Megan Downing
 Michelle Flood
 Laura Gordon
 Mara Gordon
 Britt Martin
 Lori Rafalof
 Carolyn Robbins
 Jazmin Ruotolo
 Judith Snyderman

Additional artwork credits:
 Master and goddess altar card images by Matt Rockman: www.RockmanDesign.com.
 Spiral-star drawings by Lori Rafalof.
 Cosmic clock & zodiac glyphs property of www.TheCosmicPath.com.
 Moon phase images: www.spaceplace.nasa.gov.
 World Timezone Map © Crown Copyright. Reproduced by permission of the Controller of Her Majesty's Stationery Office and the UK Hydrographic Office (www.ukho.gov.uk), pg. 20.

Astrological calculations by:
Solar Fire www.alabe.com and Matrix Software www.astrologysoftware.com.

Printed in the United States of America.

TABLE OF CONTENTS

4	ACKNOWLEDGMENTS
5	LINEAGE
	ABOUT STEPHANIE AZARIA
	ABOUT DEREK O'NEILL
	ABOUT SQ
	ABOUT COSMIC QUOTIENT
10	HOW COSMIC ASTROLOGY CAME TO BE
14	HOW TO USE THIS JOURNAL
18	QUICK REFERENCES
	MERCURY RETROGRADE
	TIME CHANGES
	ECLIPSES
19	PLANETARY STATIONS
	CHINESE NEW YEAR
20	WORLD TIME ZONE MAP
21	INTRODUCTION TO COSMIC ASTROLOGY
31	THE COSMIC CLOCK
32	ABOUT THE MASTERS AND GODDESSES
34	THE RAYS
35	NEW PLANETARY RULERSHIPS
	COSMIC DESCRIPTIONS
36	PLANETS
45	ASPECTS
47	THE HOURS
49	MOON PHASES/MOON VOID
51	FIXED STARS
53	ASTEROIDS
55	BLACK HOLES
57	CENTAURS
59	KUIPER BELT OBJECTS
62	STAR GATES
	MONTHLY JOURNAL SECTIONS
65	CAPRICORN (DEC 2011 - JAN 2012)
96	AQUARIUS (JAN - FEB)
129	PISCES (FEB - MAR)
161	ARIES (MAR - ARP)
193	TAURUS (APR - MAY)
226	GEMINI (MAY - JUN)
260	CANCER (JUN - JUL)
295	LEO (JUL - AUG)
328	VIRGO (AUG - SEP)
362	LIBRA (SEP - OCT)
395	SCORPIO (OCT - NOV)
427	SAGITTARIUS (NOV - DEC)
471	CALENDAR YEAR AT A GLANCE
472	DAILY MOON ASPECTARIANS
	MONTHLY EPHEMERIDES
498	KUIPER BELT OBJECTS EPHEMERIS
499	HEALING MODALITIES
504	RESOURCES

ACKNOWLEDGMENTS

This work would not have been possible without the steadfast and devoted participation of my friend, colleague and assistant, **Britt Martin**, to whom I owe a wealth of gratitude. Thank you for your diligence and undying devotion, which has revitalized my faith in human goodness. Thank you for your amazing capacity to help me turn a bunch of words into works of art. Thank you for your unparalleled editing skills and for your honesty and openness, which always comes as a breath of fresh air. Your presence has been a shining Light throughout this process and I could not have done it without you.

Thank you also to my great friend and soul sister **Carolyn Robbins**, who is the best hand holder ever to walk the planet. Your organizational skills and capacity to help me stay grounded and focused have been some of my most valued tools throughout this process.

I would also like to extend a special thank you to the group of 12 students/colleagues and friends who have walked this path with me from the beginning:

Britt Martin, Mara Gordon (research and organization), **Laura Gordon** (research and humor), **Michelle Flood** (all around guiding force and strength), **Megan Downing** (channeling and positivity), **Jazmin Ruotolo** (writing and keeping it young), **Lori Rafalof** (artwork and shining Light), **Judith Snyderman, Nicholas West, Rosemarie Siciliano,** and **Tanya Schneider.**

And I wish to acknowledge **Elena Giordano** and **Alison James** for their contributions along the way.

The contributions of the people above are so much more than I could ever communicate, and without any one of them, this book would not be the same.

To **Linda O'Neill, Master Kuthumi, Master Merlin, Djwal Khul, Archangel Michael**, and all the masters on the clock for your unfailing and ever present guidance from the other realms.

I gratefully acknowledge **Elizabeth Clare Prophet** for her groundbreaking work, *Predict Your Future: The Cosmic Clock* and *The Path To Attainment*.

I want to thank **Philip Sedgwick, Mark Appleman** and **Eric Francis** for their pioneering work in galactic astrology. Your work has inspired me so much.

A special thank you to **Matt Rockman** whose mastery has created the new master pictures and the new expressions of the divine feminine energies of the goddesses. Your work is incomparable.

Another special thank you to **Lori Rafalof** for her beautiful spiral drawings, featured throughout the book, which capture the new energies being put forth so well.

And finally, to my Teacher, **Derek O'Neill**, whose unparalleled Love and guidance shone so brightly that I was able to see my capacities and make good use of them. I devote this book, and everything else I ever do to you and to Source.

LINEAGE

ABOUT STEPHANIE AZARIA

Stephanie Azaria is one of the most well respected pioneers in the world of astrology today. She was drawn to the symbols and power of astrology at the age of nine and has developed her natural talent for channeling the higher perspective over the past four decades. She has studied the science of astrology with some of the greatest minds in the field, including Martin Schulman and Michael Lutin. She has authored various magazine columns across the country and has appeared on numerous websites and radio programs. Her clientele includes leaders in the entertainment, business and spiritual communities.

In 1999 Stephanie created her website, www.TheCosmicPath.com, which has grown over the years and evolved into a very popular, well-loved spot that many thousands of visitors frequent daily. She is the author of The Daily Weather feature on her site, which is a daily blog that connects astrological events with the spiritual transformation that we are all going through together. She has written weekly horoscopes for her site for the entire twelve years of its existence.

Stephanie hosts workshops and regular teleconferences designed to educate people about astrology as it relates to their individual charts, with a focus on assisting her clients toward greater awareness. Her mission has always been to raise consciousness on the planet. Those who attended have called her workshops a profound self-awareness experience. Stephanie lectures all over the world on the impact of astrology on our lives and she teaches astrology at the beginner, intermediate and advanced levels.

Ms. Azaria has been on the path to spiritual awakening for as long as she can remember, and her disciplined seeking led her to her teacher, Derek O'Neill, in 2003. She is a devoted Light worker and spiritual teacher and is committed to spending her life in service to Source. Stephanie has been initiated by Derek as a teacher of the Rising Star Healing System®, a practitioner of the Rising Star and Prema Birthing Modalities®, and a facilitator of the More Truth Will Set You Free Workshops, all of which Derek delivered to the world during the past decade.

Derek O'Neill provided the spark that ignited Stephanie's devotion to what she has come to know as her life work. This mission came in the form of a new system of astrology, which she calls Cosmic Astrology.

ABOUT DEREK O'NEILL

Derek O'Neill is a motivational analyst, renowned psychotherapist, inspirational speaker, and spiritual mentor based in Dublin, Ireland. He is the founder of SQ Worldwide LP, a multifaceted international company that currently includes four sub-divisions, SQ Wellness, SQ Foundation, SQ Retreats and SQ Fortune. Derek is committed to teaching individuals and corporations how to use untapped potential to transform themselves and the world around them. He demonstrates that our highest ideals are in fact essential to our success, happiness and fulfillment.

Derek helps others to discover the possibilities for expansion and growth right here, right now to manifest the life they want. Through motivational workshops, professional coaching and teaching tools such as books and DVDs, Derek shows us how in this moment, we are either using conscious choice to create positive change or unconsciously allowing our choices to be made for us.

DEREK O'NEILL
photo by AMALIA MENDEZ

Derek's message is in alignment with all the tried and tested philosophies throughout history. Believing that it is our moral obligation to utilize the tools we have been given to help humanity - including ideas, experiences, support, and financial resources - Derek leads by example as a successful businessman who is happiest when serving and motivating others. His presence, humor, unconventional leadership, charm, and vast Love are forces to be experienced. He is a way-shower of healing and truth in an era of need.

Derek is also founder of Creacon Lodge Healing Retreat Centre, a spiritual teaching and retreat center in Wexford, Ireland. He holds the position of Supervisor of the Ireland's Association of Hypnotherapists and Psychotherapists, and his popular More Truth Will Set You Free workshops have helped thousands worldwide to free themselves from longstanding obstacles and step into Love, joy and empowerment.

ABOUT SQ

OUR MISSION

To re-awaken all beings in the world to their innate goodness by re-introducing unconditional love to them through our willingness to change and learn through service to others, not just ourselves.

OUR VALUES

The Five fundamental human values of Love, Truth, Peace, Non-violence and Right Conduct, leading to acceptance of the value of diversity and the validity of all points of view.

OUR VISION

To help people understand that by service to others they achieve their own goals.

We as human beings have been gifted with an innate potential to perceive, contemplate and experience the Spirit of one's self and of others. It is our Spiritual Quotient - the SQ - that stands for the ability to use Spirit to guide our thoughts, words and actions in alignment with 5 fundamental human values; Love, Peace, Truth, Right Action and Non-Violence.

SQ Worldwide is a leader in spreading love and truth through higher consciousness and service to humanity. SQ Worldwide is an umbrella organization through which SQ Wellness, SQ Foundation and SQ Fortune serve. All SQ members are catalysts for change.

Together we are transforming lives.

PREMA AGNI®
"FIRE OF DIVINE LOVE"

ABOUT SQ WELLNESS

SQ Wellness is a community of people from all walks of life who embrace the five human values - Love, Truth, Peace, Non-Violence and Right Conduct - as a way of life. SQ Wellness is committed to helping humanity heal through love, compassion and higher consciousness. By learning and applying practical teachings, receiving initiations and becoming trained in powerful healing systems, and participating in transformative spiritual workshops, you will awaken your true potential and open to your authentic self.
www.SQ-Wellness.com

ABOUT SQ FORTUNE

SQ Fortune was created for individuals and corporations around the world who are ready to embrace change in the world of business. It is time to bring the heart and balance back into business and incorporate higher values into the decisions and transactions that fuel the business world. Both corporate and personal integrity have become essential components for successful business, not only for long-term growth and success but for the upliftment of humanity as a whole. Join our initiative to create a new paradigm for a more conscious, cooperative and balanced world.

ABOUT SQ FOUNDATION

SQ Foundation is a not-for-profit organization that serves people and animals in need around the world by providing access to shelter, clean water, food, medicine, clothing, education and much more. With the knowledge that we are one humanity, SQ Foundation promotes selfless service to the world with compassion, leading to lasting change and upliftment for all. Together, we really are transforming the world!
www.SQ-Foundation.org

ABOUT SQ RETREATS

Also known as Creacon Lodge Healing Retreat Centre, is an Irish oasis of relaxation, rejuvenation and healing. Here you can discover who you really are, beyond the stress and illusion of everyday life. The energy of the retreat centre nourishes your soul and helps to awaken within you a loving, serving consciousness. Here you will find peace, quiet, enlightenment, Love and a perfect environment in which to find your way back to your true, joyful self.
www.SQ-Retreats.com

ABOUT COSMIC QUOTIENT

Stephanie Azaria created Cosmic Quotient as a bridge between the emerging new consciousness arising from Cosmic Astrology and the far-reaching mission of SQ-Worldwide that touches lives all over the world. Cosmic Quotient is not a legal part of SQ Worldwide LP, but rather a humanitarian partner devoted to the same vision.

You are invited to explore the SQ websites, join us in a workshop, a healing session, become a member, or simply hold integrity in your life and become a catalyst for positive change. Through self-development (SQ Wellness), participation in charitable activities (SQ Foundation), and the application of integrity in leadership (SQ Fortune), Spiritual Quotient is a lifestyle that can meet you wherever you are on your journey.

The Cosmic Quotient website, **WWW.COSMIC-QUOTIENT.COM**, has been created to help you realize your spiritual quotient to the fullest. Astrology has long been the greatest tool there is for facilitating self-awareness. Stephanie's combined astrological expertise and spiritual focus have produced one of the most powerful self-exploration tools to come along in centuries.

A portion of the proceeds from the sale of this journal will go directly to SQ Foundation to support their service to people and animals in need around the world.

HOW COSMIC ASTROLOGY CAME TO BE

According to Stephanie

In October of 2007 I was visiting Creacon Lodge Healing Retreat Centre in New Ross, Ireland, which is my favorite place in the world, and I was offering an impromptu lecture on 'Astrology and 2012' in the meditation hall. There were about 30 people present. Toward the end of my talk many interesting questions were being asked and out of the corner of my eye I spotted my teacher, Derek O'Neill, sitting on the stairs that lead into the meditation hall. I had not seen him sitting there earlier, but in the moment I saw him I became aware that he had been there the entire time.

Derek asked me if I had ever done a 'conception' chart. I told him I had, but that it was a whole other field of astrology and that becoming proficient at that kind of reading would take some doing. In my own mind I was dismissing the option, but Derek said, "Well, it's a field of astrology I'd like to see. And when your teacher's up Uranus, you'd better listen."

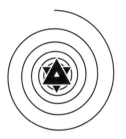

It was comical, as Derek often is when driving a truth home to his students, and in that moment I was aware that I was being asked to do something I could not ignore. I was not yet fully aware that I was being handed my mission, or that I was embarking on the journey that would make sense out of my whole lifetime.

I looked into conception charts, learned to do them proficiently, and realized very quickly that a conception chart is created for a heliocentric being. That is, for a person not living on Earth, but on the Sun. That intrigued me. I have always been a channel, and the messages started coming fast.

I have long been deeply connected to the Ascended Masters, and many of you may be familiar with them too. They are great souls who have lived many human lives, cleared their karmic debts, (also known as the misqualified, fear-based denser energies we all create while we live these lives in separate bodies) while they lived in human form, and after they transitioned to the other side in each of their last lifetimes, they moved fully into a higher level of consciousness, so much so that the physical experience no longer serves them. At the same time they agreed to serve humanity on its journey toward this same level of enlightenment. Tuning into the Ascended Masters has taught me that all of humanity is on its way to enlightenment, which to my mind is simply the 'lightening up' or 'de-densifying' of the quantum energy field we each exist in and have made more and more dense with our fear-based choices over our many lifetimes.

With the guidance of the masters, I was shown that all souls on this planet come into this solar system by way of the Sun, and then head for Earth to have a physical experience. There is a chart that can be constructed for the purpose of delineating the soul's conception. This conception chart is created out of some very ancient rules, delivered to the world by Hermes in his *Emerald Tablet*. Contrary to popular belief, the conception chart is not created for some arbitrary date 9 months before birth, but is determined by a very particular formula that is related to the Moon's cycle. Makes sense, doesn't it? Moon, conception? This was getting exciting. My research moved swiftly, because although I did not realize it at the time, I had a major appointment with destiny. I was led to three very interesting and divergent new astrological concepts, put forth by different astrologers, all of whom were referring to their ideas as 'galactic' astrology.

To me, galactic astrology speaks to the shift that happens when we shift our consciousness, switching the backdrop of our experience from the solar system to the galaxy we live in. From this perspective the planets seem less important and the stars and other galaxies out there come much more fully into view. Through study, contemplation and much meditation, I have come to realize that the cosmos is our own projection of our spiritual body... it is our consciousness, our quantum energy field, turned inside out so we can know ourselves better. God separated Itself from Itself so it could know its Self better. God is One. We are One. We are Source living in separate bodies so we can know our selves better. There is so much to study, so much to take in.

I gathered a group of students and colleagues, 12 in all, and asked them to join me on this journey to forge a whole new system of astrology, which I had begun to realize would become necessary as

MOON RISING FROM OUR
GROUP TRIP TO MT. SHASTA, 2008.
photo by MARA GORDON

humanity is raising its consciousness. Everyone signed on. We worked and studied, explored and researched, and began to come up with a system for reading the awakened (5D) person. Back then, we had to do a powerful meditation when we got together just to be able to access the information we were bringing in.

We were forging the system, working diligently, when I headed to Ireland for Derek's weeklong workshop in Dublin in June 2008. A lot of people attend these intensive weeklong workshops and everyone wants the chance to talk with Derek one on one. I did not expect to have the opportunity to walk with the teacher in Glendalough that summer, though it was in my prayers. Glendalough is also one of my most treasured places in the world, and it was there that we walked together and Derek told me to stop studying and start channeling. He said the masters were trying to send the system through and I was blocking it with all my mental activity.

It was in that moment that I realized I was not creating the system; I was being utilized as a facilitator and channel to bring it through. In that same conversation Derek told me that the system belongs to the Ascended Masters and that when it was ready, he (Derek) would take it back and then it would be given to the world. For me, this is a great blessing and I am honored and humbled to be given this mission. I have been an astrologer all my life, and I can remember being an astrologer in other lifetimes as well. Astrology is what I do. The bringing in of a system of astrology that can help humanity travel to the next level of its journey is so much more than I ever dreamed I would be able to do. But here I AM.

I went home and reported what Derek said to me to the group. Everyone heard it and within a couple of weeks one of the women, Megan Downing, showed up at one of our meetings with a book by Elizabeth Clare Prophet, called *The Path to Attainment*. In that book there is a small chapter about the cosmic clock, which is an astrological system that Ms. Prophet was given when she too was nine years old - by Mother Mary. The system was skeletal, bare bones, but it spoke to all of us. This cosmic clock is presided over by the Ascended Masters and is put forth as a powerful way back to Source. I knew we were on to something.

We learned about another entire book by Elizabeth Clare Prophet dedicated to this system, called *Predict Your Future: The Cosmic Clock*. We all got a copy and started to learn about this new system,

which has nothing to do with what we were doing originally, or so we thought. The book offers very little astrological information, and though Elizabeth Clare Prophet and her husband, Mark Prophet were referred to as 'the messengers' by the Ascended Masters, the language in the book was a lot like Shakespeare. Fortunately I studied Shakespeare in college and with a little focus managed to grasp what was being put forth in the book.

We eventually perceived the full-blown system, fleshed it out, channeled it in its entirety and it is now ready to use as a method that helps the 3D human, living in a separate body, to transmute the law of cause and effect and expand the consciousness into the unity oriented 5D. We have developed a healing modality associated with Cosmic Astrology and we call it the Cosmic Path of Initiations. You will find much more about this healing system in the back of this journal.

I feel blessed to bring this system to you. I spent 28 years as a nurse, all the while doing readings on the side. 12 years ago in 1999 I found the courage, with the help of an angel or two, to leave behind the nursing and step fully into the work I am passionate about. The point is, no matter what the job, I have always been a healer and a guide, as well as a pioneer. Breaking new ground, going first, trying something new is my thing. And here I AM.

And here it is.

Cosmic Astrology: it is my gift to my teacher and, thanks to him, to the world.

Love to each of you,
Stephanie Azaria

HOW TO USE THIS JOURNAL

This journal offers a tool for navigating your path to higher consciousness. It is designed to facilitate daily writing and reflection. Journaling is a valuable conscious discipline that can greatly accelerate your journey toward greater self-awareness.

Welcome to Cosmic Quotient's 2012 Daily Journal.

This journal is unlike any other ever published because it introduces Cosmic Astrology, a new astrological consciousness, to the world. The new system is designed to help accelerate your self-realization process. The choice to approach life from a Love-based perspective is a conscious discipline, above all else. Stephanie Azaria, who has served as the main vehicle for developing Cosmic Astrology, has long believed that astrology has two major purposes: first, to help you understand yourself better, and second, to help bring you to the here and now by telling you exactly what time it is. As humanity expands into a 5D multidimensional reality, time and space take on new meaning, and astrology, representing the cosmos, helps us to navigate this vast frontier and our growing self-awareness.

The wheel becomes a clock.
image from thecosmicpath.com

The most significant purpose of Cosmic Astrology is that it introduces a vital 'correction' that can be applied to the original system through the birth chart. The wheel becomes a clock, and the signs now run clockwise, beginning at the 12 o'clock hour (the Midheaven) on the Winter Solstice (0 Capricorn). The cosmic year begins here (see the Introduction to Cosmic Astrology) and the months are arranged in sequential sections by sign. To use the new system, this astrological clock is placed directly over the natal chart.

Everything in this new system has been shifted to reflect a new consciousness. The 12 signs have been moved out of the animal kingdom, as reflected by the zodiac, and given an entirely new meaning. These changes are listed at the beginning of each monthly section, along with many other important changes and previously unrealized factors that relate to the signs in Cosmic Astrology. The opening page to each section describes in a nutshell how to experience these 12 new 'aspects of consciousness.'

YOU WILL FIND
THE FOLLOWING INFORMATION ABOUT THE SIGNS:

The sign's **GLYPH** and its new **HIGHER PURPOSE** that awakens the heart.

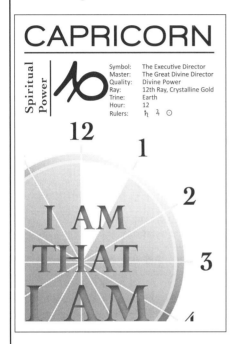

The new archetypal **SYMBOL** for the 5D consciousness.

The Ascended **MASTER** who is the permanent avatar (greatest expression) of each sign.

The **QUALITY** of consciousness represented by the sign.

The **RAY** associated with the sign

The **TRINE** or sacred geometry associated with the sign.

The **HOUR** assigned to the sign on the cosmic clock.

New planetary **RULERS**, the traditional, the affinity, and the 5D.

The sign's **MANTRA.**

Additionally, you will find another full page dedicated to further unveiling the sign's higher purpose according to Cosmic Astrology.

To assist in further aligning our new consciousness with the cosmos that reflects it, the journal features other celestial objects, some familiar and some brand new, that are becoming much more significant to our experience here on Earth. These objects include:

ASTEROIDS
CENTAURS
BLACK HOLES
FIXED STARS
AND MORE….

Before the datebook begins you will find the resources you need to help you understand the new astrology, the daily astrological weather and everything else that appears in the book. Use the **QUICK REFERENCE GUIDE** to understand the glyphs in the **SYMBOL LEGEND**. The guide also includes:

> PLANETARY STATIONS OF THE YEAR
> 2012 ECLIPSE DATES
> MERCURY RETROGRADE CYCLES
> AND MORE...

At the top of each daily journal page you will find the essentials of a classical date book, fleshed out with more modern valuable astrological information such as:

Daily **MOON PHASE IMAGES**.

The **DAILY ASTROLOGICAL ASPECTS**, including the Moon sign and void of course Moon, listed along with the lunar aspect that generates the void.

MAJOR PLANETARY EVENTS for the day such as stations, ingresses, and retrograde motion.

FULL MOON and **NEW MOON** information, along with eclipses when relevant.

Major planetary aspects are listed along with other **RELEVANT OBJECT ACTIVITY**.

STAR GATES formed by the numerology of the day, month, and year.

SPECIAL EVENTS like eclipses and holidays are noted on the bottom left of the page.

A **QUOTE** from a great person to be used for inspiration, contemplation or meditation.

Space for **JOURNALING** and **SCHEDULING** daily activities is provided every day.

**ALL ASPECTS ARE LISTED IN EASTERN TIME,
SO A TIME ZONE MAP IS PROVIDED
TO MAKE CONVERSION EASIER.**

A separate package of **24 BRAND NEW 5X7 ALTAR CARDS**, depicting the Ascended Masters who preside over each sign and the goddesses, or feminine aspects, associated with each sign is included with the journal. The Ascended Masters are assigned to their respective signs for all eternity and the completely new images we offer evoke the essence and multifaceted qualities of these beings and the consciousness they represent. They are designed to be placed on your altar for the month to help you connect with the mastery of each sign within you.

As this is an introduction to Cosmic Astrology, you will find information included that describes the shift from traditional astrology to 5D Cosmic Astrology. The **INTRODUCTION TO COSMIC ASTROLOGY** section describes the basics of the system. A description of the **COSMIC PATH OF INITIATIONS**, the new healing system that utilizes this new astrology and information on **HEALING MODALITIES** that work in tandem with the Cosmic Path of Initiations can be found at the back of the book. There is also an image of the **COSMIC CLOCK** and a description. Please note that while the Cosmic Path of Initiations is highly recommended, the Cosmic Astrology system stands on its own. It is Stephanie's belief that every astrologer and every student of astrology will benefit greatly from this new perspective.

Refer to the **COSMIC DESCRIPTIONS** section to learn more about the meaning of aspects, the planets, Moon phases and all the newly introduced astrological objects. These descriptions are designed to help you understand the significance of these bodies and how to incorporate them into your daily awareness via the aspects and events listed in the datebook.

The **MOON'S ASPECTS** are always important guides in understanding the feeling tone of a day. They are too numerous to list in the daily pages, but there is a handy monthly chart in the back of the book for easy reference.

A **2012 MONTHLY EPHEMERIS** is also included in back of the journal.

It is our greatest wish that this book help facilitate the rapidly expanding awareness that has enveloped humanity at this time. Please feel free to share your comments and ideas for future editions. We can be reached at

COMMENTS@COSMIC-QUOTIENT.COM

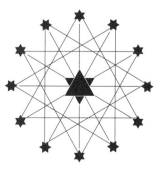

QUICK REFERENCES

All aspects are listed in **Eastern Time**.
See **World Time Zone Map** (pg. 20) for help converting times to your time zone.
Dates written as MM.DD.YY

TIME CHANGES

Daylight begins: 03.11.12
Standard begins: 11.04.12

MERCURY RETROGRADE

R SHADOW BEGINS: 02.27.12
RETROGRADE: 03.12.12 06°♈49'R
STATIONS DIRECT: 04.04.12 23°♓50'
LEAVES D SHADOW: 04.23.12

R SHADOW BEGINS: 06.27.12
RETROGRADE: 07.14.12 12°♌33'R
STATIONS DIRECT: 08.08.12 01°♌26'
LEAVES D SHADOW: 08.22.12

R SHADOW BEGINS: 10.19.12
RETROGRADE: 11.06.12 04°♐18'R
STATIONS DIRECT: 11.26.12 18°♏10'
LEAVES D SHADOW: 12.14.12

2012 ECLIPSES

05.20.12
Annular Solar: 00°♊21'
Time of Max: 7:52p

06.04.12
Partial Lunar: 14°♐14'
Time of Max: 7:03a

11.13.12
Total Solar: 21°♏57'
Time of Max: 5:11p

11.28.12
Penumbral Lunar: 06°♊47'
Time of Max: 9:32a

SYMBOL LEGEND

☉ Sun	♃ Jupiter	☊ North Node	⚸ Black Moon Lilith
☽ Moon	♄ Saturn	☋ South Node	
☿ Mercury	⚷ Chiron	⚳ Ceres	
♀ Venus	♅ Uranus	⚵ Juno	
⊕ Earth	♆ Neptune	⚶ Vesta	
♂ Mars	♇ Pluto	⚴ Pallas	

♈ Aries	♎ Libra	☌ Conjunction 0°	R Retrograde
♉ Taurus	♏ Scorpio	✶ Sextile 60°	D Direct
♊ Gemini	♐ Sagittarius	☐ Square 90°	S Stations
♋ Cancer	♑ Capricorn	△ Trine 120°	→ Enters
♌ Leo	♒ Aquarius	☍ Opposition 180°	voc Void of Course
♍ Virgo	♓ Pisces		

PLANETARY STATIONS

CHINESE NEW YEAR 01.23.12

YEAR OF THE DRAGON

OBJECT	SR/SD	DATE	TIME	DEGREE
☿	SR	03.12.12	3:49A EDT	06°♈49'R
	SD	04.04.12	6:12A EDT	23°♓50'
	SR	07.14.12	10:16P EDT	12°♌33'R
	SD	08.08.12	1:41A EDT	01°♌26'
	SR	11.06.12	6:04P EST	04°♐18'R
	SD	11.26.12	5:48P EST	18°♏10'
♀	SR	05.15.12	10:33A EDT	24°♊00'R
	SD	06.27.12	11:07A EDT	07°♊29'
♂	SR	01.23.12	7:54P EST	23°♍06'R
	SD	04.13.12	11:53P EDT	03°♍41'
♃	SR	10.04.12	9:18A EDT	16°♊23'R
	SD	01.30.13	6:38A EST	06°♊19'
♄	SR	02.07.12	9:03A EST	29°♎30'R
	SD	06.25.12	4:00A EDT	22°♎46'
⚷	SR	06.12.12	1:12A EDT	09°♓45'R
	SD	11.14.12	3:37P EST	04°♓58'
♅	SR	07.13.12	5:49A EDT	08°♈32'R
	SD	12.13.12	7:02A EST	04°♈37'
♆	SR	06.04.12	5:03P EDT	03°♓09'R
	SD	11.11.12	2:52A EST	00°♓22'
♇	SR	04.10.12	12:21P EDT	09°♑34'R
	SD	09.18.12	1:07A EDT	06°♑57'
?	SR	10.31.12	11:46A EDT	03°♋43'R
	SD	02.04.13	3:50A EST	19°♊44'
⚵	SR	07.30.12	6:30P EDT	11°♈29'R
	SD	11.20.12	8:24P EST	22°♓26'
⚶	SR	10.21.12	2:34A EDT	25°♊34'R
	SD	01.27.13	11:52A EST	09°♊50'
✻	SR	03.24.12	7:32P EDT	07°♐06'R
	SD	07.16.12	6:58A EDT	21°♏25'

SD: Stationing, turning Direct.
SR: Stationing, turning Retrograde.

WORLD TIME ZONE MAP

Times provided in this journal are for Eastern Time (ET). Use these conversions to calculate your time compared to Eastern Standard Time.

CENTRAL	MOUNTAIN	PACIFIC	ALASKAN	HAWAIIAN	GMT
Subtract 1hr	Subtract 2hrs	Subtract 3hrs	Subtract 4hrs	Subtract 5hrs	Add 5hrs

PARIS	JERUSALEM	PUTTAPARTHI	HONG KONG	TOKYO
Add 6hrs	Add 7hrs	Add 10.5hrs	Add 13hrs	Add 14hrs

For all other time zones, use the following map to convert times from Universal Time.

STANDARD TIME ZONES
Corrected to January 2011
Zone boundaries are approximate
Daylight Saving Time (*Summer Time*), usually one hour in advance of Standard Time, is kept in some places
Map outline © *Mountain High Maps*
Compiled by HM Nautical Almanac Office

Standard Time = Universal Time − value from table
Universal Time = Standard Time + value from table

	h m		h m		h m
Z	0	N	+1	Q*	+4 30
A	−1	O	+2	R	+5
B	−2	P	+3	S	+6
C	−3	P*	+3 30	T	+7
C*	−3 30	Q	+4	U	+8
D	−4				
D*	−4 30		h m		h m
E	−5	L	−11	V	+9
E*	−5 30	L*	−11 30	V*	+9 30
F	−6	M	−12	X	+10
F*	−6 30	M*	−12 45	X	+11
G	−7	M†	−13	Y	+12
H	−8	M‡	−14		
I	−9				
I*	−9 30				
K	−10				
K*	−10 30			§ No Standard Time legally adopted

INTRODUCTION TO
COSMIC ASTROLOGY

*"This is the teaching of the Stars for the Golden Age.
And it has to be an inner teaching of the Ascended Masters."*
~**Elizabeth Clare Prophet**

Astrology has always been with us. From the beginning of time we have looked to the heavens for guidance and understanding, as a way to make sense of the confusion and chaos that abounds here in the third dimensional physical realm (3D). As far back as we can remember, we have looked out into the universe and found the ring of constellations that we call the zodiac. We have labeled the signs we found there, and assigned meaning to each constellation in the form of animals or people, in most cases, and out of our limited, separate consciousness here on Earth, we have decided that these constellations somehow have influence over us. For centuries we have given them the power to determine our fates, to define our personalities, even to dictate the events of our lives.

And all along, we have processed all data we perceive to be 'outside' of our selves in this same way. We see what is out there, decide that it is a permanent, unchanging, 'timeless' entity, and then invariably we bestow upon it the qualities it needs to determine how our lives will unfold. We do this same thing with people, with places and with all things we interpret to be larger than and outside of our Selves. This has been the inevitable effect of living in physical form (3D), believing in our separateness and feeling isolated and disconnected from the Oneness that is truly our birthright. When we 'fell' into this realm of duality, we were cut off from the Truth of who we are, and we have 'forgotten' that we are the co-creators of our own lives, and ultimately of all that we experience.

The constellations exist because we say they do. If we were to travel out to any

NEWGRANGE, IRELAND
photo by Britt Martin

one of the collections of stars that we refer to as signs of the zodiac, Aries the Ram for example, we would quickly find that the constellation is not there. The stars we perceive to be forming the picture of a ram are, in actuality, nowhere near each other. The constellation is not there at all. The only reason it is in existence is because we believe we see that constellation from our earthly perspective. And if we all see the same picture, then it must be a symbol that exists within the collective consciousness, and it is being projected outward by that collective consciousness.

How did this happen? Why is it that for as far back as we can remember we have seen the same set of symbols forming a circle around our planet, and decided that this would be the backdrop for the experience we are having here on Earth? We see the planets in our solar system traveling through the various signs of the zodiac and we assign meaning to every movement, every nuance of these planetary journeys. We all experience the same planets, the same constellations, and ascribe the same basic meaning to them all, yet we each have a completely different set of personal experiences. Our individual journeys are so diverse and distinct that it is actually impossible to know what others are experiencing.

We each have our own unique connection to Source, to the Creator of 'All That Is,' and our awareness of that connection is what we call our consciousness. There are 6 billion people on this planet and each and every one of us is having a completely different experience. Have you ever wondered how it is possible that the planets and the stars have the ability to homogenize that reality and 'work' for everyone?

With the advent of our expansion into a greater dimension of consciousness (5D), we are beginning to remember

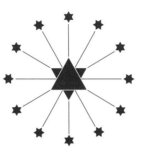

who we are. As we do, it becomes more and more apparent that we are not really separate from anything we perceive and that everything in our perception is our own creation. We are projecting our consciousness onto a blank screen and calling it Life.

As a collective, therefore, we are projecting onto that screen we call the universe, the reflection of what is in our individual being. What else can we be projecting? We can never perceive anything in our world or in our universe that is not already in our consciousness. Those constellations are not separate from us. They ARE us. And so what we perceive 'out there' is not a set of stars placed there to influence us and tell us how to live, but the projection of the inner mechanism of our own consciousness, placed there by us to remind us of the way back home to Source. The zodiac is actually the projection of our own higher consciousness, and if we look at it as our own reflection, we can begin to approach the Truth.

While in 3D, which is the dimension of conscious awareness where we experience our Selves as separate and know time to be linear, we have used our solar system and the zodiac as a way to realize our Selves; and in doing so we have allowed it all to define us. Like everything else, we have given what appears to be outside of us power, and forgotten our own in the process. The system being introduced here, Cosmic Astrology, given originally in skeletal form to Elizabeth

Clare Prophet by Mother Mary, is the ancient system - the correction - that when viewed from unity consciousness is meant to guide us home, to represent not what we can see, but what is beyond our 'physical' sight. Those stars ARE us, and they have been there forever, waiting for us to find our way back to an awakened state.

GLENDALOUGH, IRELAND
photo by Britt Martin

In order to grasp this system, we must consider Christ consciousness and what it is. This has little to do with the organized religion that has come to be associated with Christ. Christ is a rank of consciousness, one that Jesus attained at the end of his earthly life, and one that is available to each and every one of us as we expand into the observer perspective and begin to recall our true origins. That the zodiac is connected to our higher consciousness, to our Christed Selves, becomes an obvious reality, if we look at it closely. The Winter Solstice, when the Sun moves from 29 degrees Sagittarius to 0 degrees Capricorn each year, is the time when the Sun rises at the lowest point in its orbit (in the Northern Hemisphere). It remains there, without moving, for three days, and on Christmas Day, December 25th, the Sun (Son) is resurrected and begins to rise again. That this phenomenon occurs at the same time that we have been told Christ was born is no accident. Nor is it a coincidence that the Sun at the Winter Solstice is conjunct the Galactic Center.

The Galactic Center is thought to be a 'black hole' that exists at the center of our galaxy (when viewed from Earth). It is a void, and from that central point all of creation as we know it emanates. You could call the Galactic Center the greatest dimension of our conscious awareness, or Source. It is the place where the highest aspect of our individual consciousness merges with 'All That Is.' It is the place where our God-Self exists, from the perspective of time and space. Source energy is a completely integrated, unified electromagnetic force. In order for us to experience this power, it must be stepped down to us, or diluted. If we were directly connected to Source from Earth, we could not handle the force of the energy. Source energy is stepped down in many ways, through the Elohim, the Ascended Masters, the Council of 12 (also known as the rays), the angels, and other fully realized beings, some of whom are present in physical form on the planet. From this perspective, the zodiac can be seen to be a very specific hierarchal energy, placed out there by our own consciousness, to step down the power of Source and provide us with a way to get back home.

The signs of the zodiac represent the various aspects of Christ consciousness, which can be thought of as a much higher form of consciousness contained within each of us that serves to connect us to Source. In Cosmic Astrology, the signs of the zodiac are called the solar (soular) hierarchies. The Sun signs can be understood to represent the various aspects of the Sun's (Son's) consciousness. Each soular hierarchy is an aspect of Source that is stepped down so that we can experience it as our Self. The constellations may not actually be there, but they LOOK like they are there, because the energy of each Sun sign exists within us, and each one is an aspect of our higher consciousness. In this new system, these soular hierarchies are given new and expanded designations that relate more fully to the higher aspects of our Selves.

We live in a universe that is based on the number 13. When we lived entirely in 3D, it looked more like a system based on 12. But as our consciousness expands and we remember our Selves, we discover that we exist in Truth at the center of everything we perceive. At the core of all perception is our being, in total union with Source, so the concept of 12 around 1 is born as soon as we enter the 5D experience of unified consciousness and unconditional Love. The Fourth Dimension (4D) served for a very long time as a veil that separated our 3D (separate) Selves from our 5D (unified) experience. We have very recently pierced through and disintegrated the mass consciousness of the collective Fourth Dimension and it no longer exists.

It is a well-known scientific fact that life is made up of spirals. The Golden Ratio, which generates the Fibonacci Spiral of Life, is found at the core of all matter, even in our DNA. We are all individual jivas, or sparks of divine Light, each one of us existing on an eternal energetic spiral that extends from Source to us and from us to Source. This spiral moves us both ways: clockwise toward Source, and counter-clockwise toward Earth. If we were to slice that spiral at the point of birth and death of any incarnation, and we were to look at that slice head on, what we would see is the birth chart for that particular lifetime. That natal chart is the expression of our life at that par-

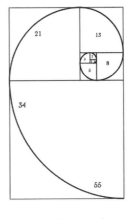

FIBONACCI SPIRAL OF LIFE

drawing by Britt Martin

ticular point in time and space. It looks like a circle because it is. The individual's birth chart is a snapshot of the spiral as it moves counter-clockwise toward the physical 3D plane. It is the map of the movie we are living at that point in time and space.

An entire lifetime translates into a point in time when viewed as a slice of the spiral. The circle is a part of the eternal cycle, and it is expressed here as the birth chart. What has happened here on Earth is that we have gotten stuck on this circle, the karmic wheel of life. We go around and around and around because of the fear-based reactions that are caused by the experience of separation, and these repetitive reactions have made our individual energy fields denser and denser, drawing us back toward the Earth plane with more and more pull. You could think of the law of cause and effect as gravity itself, the very reason we are still here, finding it difficult to get out of this endless revisitation of our actions. This is the force that keeps us bound to the wheel. The Truth is our eternal being is always and forever at the center of the circle. It is here that we experience perfect balance and the harmonious integration of all duality, as well as the power to make the choice that can shift us back toward our Source connection.

The following visualization, from Elizabeth Clare Prophet, can help us to understand:

Imagine yourself standing inside an 'upside down' bell, the round bottom portion of the bell coming up to your solar plexus. If you were to look down, you would see that the 'energy field' contained within the bell, is split into 12 sections, each one representing one of the 12 aspects of higher consciousness.

This energy field can be thought of as our unconscious mind. The unconscious mind carries every iota of karma our soul has ever accrued, and what is more, our soul brings that entire field of unconscious energy into every single incarnation we undertake. We take all of our karma (past actions) with us wherever we are. In order to break the cycle of endless repetition, it is necessary to consciously choose to do so.

In any given moment we are either recreating our past actions or converting their effects and making a different choice. We cannot be doing both, nor can we be doing anything else. The

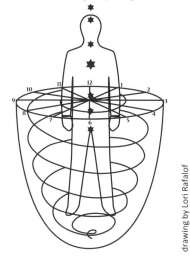

drawing by Lori Rafalof

moment we recognize our Selves to be at the center of all of our existence, at peace with and One with Source, we can reclaim our power to choose and make the conscious effort to change our old habitual patterns instead of perpetuating them. That unconscious energy field in which we live is full of the misqualified energies that have generated the pool of our current circumstances, and in most cases, that pool looks something like a dirty aquarium that needs cleaning.

Each time we engage in an unconscious fear-based response we create some more misqualified energy, and add more density to that pool. The 'correction' provided by the use of Cosmic Astrology brings us consciously to the here and now and focuses us on the fabric of each aspect of our consciousness so that we may choose, with great presence and diligence, to act with disciplined application rather than create more unconscious misqualified energy. With a little focus, we can choose to transform the negative energies we have accrued over all our lifetimes back into Light and Love.

To begin this process, the cosmic clock is superimposed onto the individual birth chart. This makes visible the correction from a counter-clockwise Earth-based experience to the clockwise life that is headed back to Source.

It shifts us to the awareness that all of life is cyclical. We are no longer subjected to the repetitive linear cycles we tend to keep recreating when we are without conscious awareness. In the true zodiac, the map of soular hierarchies of our higher consciousness begins at 0 Capricorn, at the birth of Christ, the re-birth of the Sun. When we look at it as a clock, with 12 hours (formerly known as houses) and 12 qualities of consciousness (formerly called signs), this time going around clockwise, symbolizing and beginning the journey back toward Source, we begin to get the basis for the cosmic system of astrology.

Every one of us travels the same path, starting at 12 o'clock and travelling around the 12 hours, one month at a time, every single year beginning on the birthday. The month and day of birth is placed at the 12 o'clock hour and then each monthly anniversary falls on each successive hour of the clock. On or around that (birth) date each month we enter into the next soular hierarchy, experiencing a particular set of new circumstances, (an initiation), that brings us into the next aspect of our own consciousness. Paying attention to the situations that arise around the date of our birthday each month makes us so much more aware of what needs to be cleared.

The soular hierarchies (signs) are presided over by 12 Ascended Masters. The 12 masters related to the various aspects of consciousness have signed on for this mission forever. They are the hierarchs of each 2,600-year Age in succession. Jesus, for example, is the master on the 2 o'clock hour, the Pisces hour, and he serves as the avatar of the Piscean Age. Each master has an affinity for the specific quality of consciousness that he or she administers to. Each hierarchy has its own purpose, its own master, its own vibration and focus, its own chakra, ray, and divine feminine attribute, and offers us a set of experiences that builds upon our initiation each and every month.

Beginning at the individual birthday, the clock takes each of us successively through three initiations of the spiritual (etheric) body, each one of these three months related to one of the tri-fold flame qualities of Power, Love and Wisdom. The tri-fold flame is located in the heart center, and it represents the qualities of Source that are activating within us as we expand our consciousness into the 5D realm. We then experience three initiations of the mental body, then the emotional, and finally the physical body, before returning again to the 12 o'clock hour at our next birthday. The purpose for going around the clock repetitively is to master our four lower body system in all three aspects of Power, Love and Wisdom, by working sequentially with each soular hierarchy. The clock always tells us what time it is so that we can be fully present and creative with the aspect of consciousness we are in at that moment. This gives us the opportunity to transmute our habitual fear-based reactions back into Love as fully as we possibly can in each sector and ultimately to master that particular aspect of the lower body system we are traveling through.

The four lower bodies and the tri-fold flames of the heart replace the elements and qualities of the older system, as follows:

LOWER BODY	TRI-FOLD FLAME
• Spiritual	• Power
• Mental	• Love
• Emotional	• Wisdom
• Physical	

There is one soular hierarchy, or aspect of higher consciousness that corresponds to each of these combinations:

Capricorn is	SPIRITUAL POWER
Aquarius is	SPIRITUAL LOVE
Pisces is	SPIRITUAL WISDOM
Aries is	MENTAL POWER
Taurus is	MENTAL LOVE
Gemini is	MENTAL WISDOM
Cancer is	EMOTIONAL POWER
Leo is	EMOTIONAL LOVE
Virgo is	EMOTIONAL WISDOM
Libra is	PHYSICAL POWER
Scorpio is	PHYSICAL LOVE
Sagittarius is	PHYSICAL WISDOM

These combinations also correspond to the hours on the clock, formerly known as houses, (please see the section on the hours for more information). We travel around the clock once a year and also once every 12 years. We work with one particular aspect of higher consciousness for an entire year at a time, also working with one particular master to help us focus on one of the four lower bodies and its expression through one of the tri-fold flame qualities. To achieve this we visit each of the twelve hours on the clock, experiencing monthly initiations that relate to our own individual predetermined circumstances around that particular quality or sign. Each month, around our birth date, we have an experience that introduces us to the next soular hierarchy we are entering into. This is called an initiation, because it refers to a circumstance that moves us on to the next leg of our journey. This has always happened, every month since birth, but we have not been paying attention; we have not applied our consciousness to our Selves, and so we have dealt with these initiations unconsciously for the most part, though they have always taken place.

It is amazing to witness these events taking place without fail, and to learn so much about the state of our existence from the initiations we receive. Each month we leave the center of our being to go out to the periphery of our charts – to interact with the outer world, where the illusion or the movie is - and we have an experience that is designed to focus us on the issues that need clearing or the qualities that we need to integrate for the month ahead. By making a conscious choice between a Love or fear-based approach, and taking advantage of the numerous opportunities that present themselves each day, every hour, every minute, if we are paying enough attention, we can consistently make the choice for transmutation. Each journey we take around the wheel provides an opportunity to clear some more of our denser energies, and with diligence and faithful practice it is possible to transform at least 51% of our fear-based circumstances back into Light. This is the amount of transmutation required to expand into 5D at this time. This has not always been true.

Prior to this very powerful transitional time that we are living through, it was necessary to clear 100% of misqualified energies and to leave our physical form in order to achieve ascension. But St. Germaine, who is the greatest embodiment of higher Aquarian consciousness for the new order, went before a group of great beings who oversee life on Earth and petitioned for a special tool for humanity to use in order to help speed up the ascension process. This request was necessary because of the time period we are in. The game of separation and living under the law of cause and effect is ending. The Earth has been promised the gift of ascension herself at the end of the game. In order to help her to achieve this, humanity will have to step down the cosmic energies for her, acting as lightning rods for the Love vibration to penetrate her dense solid ground, created out of the eons of cause and effect energetic. The request for this tool was granted in the 1950's, and we know it as the Violet Flame.

image by Britt Martin

The Violet Flame is a powerful alchemical tool that literally allows us to turn our misqualified, fear-based energies back into the Love that is their original form. It has been called the karmic eraser by the masters. With focus and disciplined use of the Violet Flame, one may easily develop the habit of transmutation. More recently, a second transmutation tool was delivered to the world, when Derek O'Neill channeled the Prema Agni symbol. This symbol, which stands for the 'Fire of Divine Love,' is a powerful neutralizing tool. The use of these two tools together, especially when practiced regularly, can greatly speed up the process of transforming density back into Light.

As we transmute the effects of our habitual fear-based responses, we become less dense and more en-Light-ened. Instead of going around and around the same circle, we find we can choose to spiral up to a new level of conscious awareness each time we cycle around. The more consciously we work with our now exposed misqualified energies, the more fully we return to the center of the wheel to integrate all that we have encountered and transmuted. Then, with this progress under our belts we head out for the periphery again to have our next worldly experience and initiation into the next soular hierarchy of our higher consciousness. With each initiation we bring all that we have achieved with us. As we move around the clock, spiraling from one point to the next, we clear that unconscious pool of dark misqualified energies and lighten it up. This corresponds to the level of enLightenment we are achieving as we go.

The sections that follow provide a deeper understanding of the hours (houses) and shared archetypes (planets) under the new Cosmic Astrology system. The soular hierarchies (signs) are covered throughout the journal. The section on aspects provides some new insights as well.

*May this system grace you
and serve you well on your journey
back to Source.*

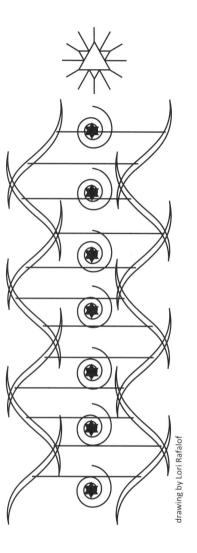

drawing by Lori Rafalof

THE COSMIC CLOCK

Here is a visualization of the cosmic clock, which when placed over the birth chart corrects the way your conscious awareness is directed, allowing you to locate yourself within your own energy field. Use of the cosmic clock instantly restores you to the power to choose a heart-centered approach over the more habitual, unconscious fear-based reaction. The signs go in clockwise order on the clock, whereas in the birth chart they run counter-clockwise. The birth chart is a map of the movie you are living; it tells the counter-clockwise story of your journey downward toward 3D, which is the dimension where separation and the law of cause and effect is perpetuated, keeping you on the seemingly endless Wheel of Life & Death. When the cosmic clock is superimposed on your birth chart and you utilize the system that places you on the clock according to your birth date, you are immediately restored to the 'here and now,' where you can correct your direction through a more disciplined approach. When you make the heart-centered choice, you begin spiraling clockwise back toward Source.

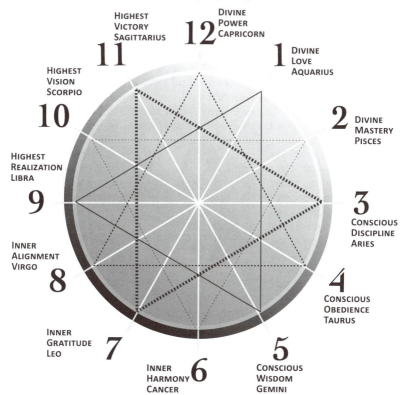

ABOUT THE
MASTERS & GODDESSES

According to Mother Mary (through Elizabeth Clare Prophet) there are 12 Ascended Masters that preside over the various signs on the cosmic clock for all eternity. Jesus, for example, oversees the sign of Pisces, and we all know, because we have just come out of that Age, that Jesus is the avatar, or most significant connection to Source, of the Piscean Era. That reveals that the masters that are assigned to each sign on the clock are the greatest embodiments of higher consciousness for their respective Ages. Some of them are more obscure to us than others, but that is because we are not living in the eras that correspond to those masters. In working with these great beings, however, it has become clear that connecting with all of them facilitates the process of expanding the consciousness in a big way.

The Ascended Masters are beings who have lived on Earth and managed to transmute all their denser misqualified energies and move beyond the third dimension of linear time and separation. Until now, it was imperative to clear 100% of one's gravitational pull toward the Earth plane and bring the cause and effect ratio to a perfect balance before it was possible to move out of this realm of consciousness. It was also required that a soul leave the physical body behind in order to attain that higher perspective. Some of the great beings on the clock are more than Ascended Masters. One or two are Elohim, great beings that have never been embodied in physical form and are very close to Source. The Elohim helped to create the universe as we know it. It is most helpful to connect deeply with the master that presides over each of the signs. The signs can now be seen as the aspects of consciousness that each of us contains within our quantum energy fields. By making conscious contact with the master that embodies each sign, we are able to connect with the highest aspects of our selves. A great place to start is to make a deliberate connection with the master that oversees your own Sun sign.

As we were fleshing out the Cosmic Astrology system, we became aware of the need to find the feminine expression of each aspect of higher consciousness to go along with the creative/active/male expressions that are identified by the masters. At this point in human evolution, there is no male experience without the balanced female, and so each of the soular signs has been assigned a feminine counterpart, an inner/responsive/intuitive expression, known as the 12 Goddesses. These higher feminine energies represent the part of your being that allows the qualities of any soular sign to manifest fully at the heart center. Inside the void

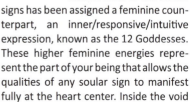

that is the domain of the divine feminine, you can find and connect with these goddesses to help you realize your Self in an integrated (masculine/feminine) way. Whichever quality of consciousness you are moving through at any given time cannot manifest fully within you if this feminine aspect is not activated. To help bring this energy through, meditate on the goddess's presence and the energies she manifests within you. The more fully you can connect with these feminine aspects of your being, the more integrated your consciousness becomes. Begin with the goddess who expresses the feminine energies of your own Sun sign.

THE MASTER AND GODDESS THAT PRESIDE OVER EACH SIGN:

CAPRICORN
Great Divine Director
Goddess of Rebirth & Regeneration

AQUARIUS
St. Germaine
Goddess of Harmonic Resonance

PISCES
Jesus
Goddess of the Rainbow

ARIES
Helios
Goddess of Light

TAURUS
Godfre
Goddess of Sacred Geometry

GEMINI
El Morya
Goddess of Fluidity

CANCER
Serapis Bey
Goddess of Being

LEO
Lady Liberty
Goddess of Abundance & Magic

VIRGO
Lord Lanto
Goddess of Healing

LIBRA
Mighty Victory
Goddess of Balance

SCORPIO
Mighty Cyclopea
Goddess of Consciousness

SAGITTARIUS
Maitreya
Goddess of Time

The beautiful artwork that comes with this journal provides brand-new depictions of the masters and goddesses that have never been seen before. They are meant to depict the most modern version of each soular hierarchy and to help you connect with the master/goddess energies that have always been contained within yourself. We are providing them for you separately, so you can place them on your altar and make essential conscious contact with each aspect of your mastery or divine feminine being.

THE RAYS

The 12 rays, also known as the Council of 12, are not actual beings, but streams of intelligent Light consciousness that have attributes of color, vibration and other significant qualities which, when taken together, serve to make up our higher consciousness. In fact, the 12 rays actually make up the fabric of our universe. The rays can be considered your own council of 12, each one having a correspondence with a specific soular sign, or quality of consciousness. In fact, the ray evokes the highest aspect of the quality of consciousness it resonates with.

If you call on the number associated with any ray, you will automatically be connected to that ray's vibration. Similarly, if you wear the color that belongs to a ray, or even call that color into your consciousness, you will bring yourself into alignment with its powers.

Additionally, you can vocalize the tone that corresponds to the ray, just as you would 'Om' in a yoga class, to help you connect with the ray's energies. Close your eyes, take a few deep breaths, and allow the sound of the tone to resonate in your chest and throughout your body. Don't be concerned with what it sounds like. Instead, allow your Higher Self to generate the tone that emerges from your being. Your own tone will come through, and that is what is important. It works well to sound the tone in sets of 3, 21, 72 or 108.

HOUR	COLOR	SIGNIFICANCE	TONE
12th	Crystalline Gold	Highest Consciousness	Aay-Aay-Aay
1st	Scarlet Red	Will Power; Innovation	Eee-Eee-Eee
2nd	Aqua Blue/Rose Pink	Love and Wisdom	Eee-Om-Ooo
3rd	Yellow Gold	Divine Male; Focused Effort	Aay-Aah
4th	Emerald Green	Harmony and Balance	Aah-Ooo
5th	Crystalline Orange	Expanding Mind	Eee-Aah
6th	Blue-Violet	Male/Female Unity	Ooo-Ooo-Eee
7th	Violet Flame	Purification and Clearing	Ooo-Eee
8th	Green-Violet	Healing	Aah-Ooo-Eee
9th	Blue-Green	Unconditional Love	Ooo-Aah-Ooo
10th	Opalescent Pearl White	Transmutation	Aah-Om
11th	Peach-Apricot	High-Heart Activation	Aah-Om-Eee

NEW PLANETARY RULERSHIPS

The signs have always been assigned planetary rulers. The ruler of a sign is the planetary archetype that gives a sign its disposition for you personally. So, for example, if you have Taurus rising in your natal birth chart, then Venus, the ruler of Taurus, disposes your personality and your entire life experience. (In the original system of astrology the ascendant represents your outlook on life and the way you bring yourself to the world). In order to understand how your Venusian personality is disposed, you can look for Venus in the birth chart and see where she is and what sign she inhabits. This information goes a long way toward understanding what makes you tick.

In Cosmic Astrology, there are three rulers for each aspect of consciousness (sign). These rulers are the modern rulers, the affinity rulers, and the 5D rulers. The first set of these rulers are the original modern rulers, the ones we have known and worked with in the 3D realm of separation consciousness for thousands of years.

The second set is called the affinity rulers. The cosmic clock features a phenomenon that serves to give the new system much of its definition. If you fold the clock in half along the vertical axis, the 6 o'clock-12 o'clock line, the signs and hours that overlap each other as a result are seen to have an affinity with each other. They are mirror images, and it is here that the meaning of the affinity ruler begins to emerge. Affinities produce polarity-like energies that incline you toward the more expansive perspective of your growing consciousness. Considering the placement of the two affinity rulers for any sign in your own chart can go a long way toward expanding your self-realization process.

	Original	Affinity	5D
Capricorn	♄	♃	☉
Aquarius	♅	♇	♆
Pisces	♆	♀	♃
Aries	♂	⚷	☿
Taurus	♀	☉	⊕
Gemini	☿	☽	♅
Cancer	☽	☿	♀
Leo	☉	♀	☽
Virgo	⚷	♂	♄
Libra	♀	♆	♂
Scorpio	♇	♅	♇ & beyond
Sagittarius	♃	♄	⚷

The 5D rulers are derived from the higher, more soul-oriented essence of each field of consciousness. They become active as we attain a more observer-oriented awareness. For example, Capricorn speaks to our connection with Source, and so the Sun represents the conscious 5D rulership of that area of our being, and it will predispose our highest connection with Source.

COSMIC DESCRIPTIONS

PLANETS

In Cosmic Astrology the entire universe is seen to be projected from our individual quantum energy field. Reality has never really been 'out there,' it is all contained within our being. Everyone experiences the universe differently, because each of us is generating the cosmos from within our own consciousness. The cosmos is the representation of our spiritual body, and its vastness reveals the truth about our Higher Selves, which is that the spiritual Self is the greatest aspect of our existence.

The PLANETS in our solar (soular) system are the collective projections of the archetypal energies that each and every human being contains within the personal quantum energy field. We are all working with the same archetypes, but we experience them and utilize their energies differently because of our karmic circumstances and because we each express a slightly different aspect of the Oneness.

Solar System Montage, NASA JPL

According to Cosmic Astrology, the 12 bodies contained within our soular system express their universal forces through our being. The 5D human has realized that it is not a personality run by the ego, as the 3D consciousness believes, but it can associate with the higher mind, thereby recognizing that the 12 major planetary archetypes are being expressed by everyone. Individual differences no longer generate separation and competition consciousness, but instead are honored and valued.

The soular system itself is an exquisite representation of the Oneness we each express. The Sun in the center, generator of consciousness, which, once realized fully, restores us to life in the highest sense of the word. The Sun is our collective projection of the Son, aka higher (Christ) consciousness. It is the central archetypal force around which everything else exists. When we begin to realize this Truth, the sense of separation and the fear-based reactions that are generated by that belief begin to lose their grip on our consciousness.

THE LOWER FOUR BODY SYSTEM

The planets once known as the personal planets comprise the rulership of the lower four body system in Cosmic Astrology. The Sun and Moon, known as the Lights, are the generators of each individual's consciousness here on Earth. In the new system they rule over, or dispose, the spiritual body, and as the archetypes of duality in its most condensed sense, they comprise the gateway to the Higher Self and all of its vastness. This greater part of our existence waits, with seemingly infinite patience, to be realized and embraced once again (from within).

The other three rulers of the lower four body system, formerly known as the inner planets, are Mercury, ruler of the mental body, Venus, ruler of the emotional body, and Mars, ruler of the physical body. These archetypes, the Messenger, the Goddess of Love and the Great Activator, speak to the basics of our existence - thought, feeling and action, and in the cosmic sense, provide the ways in which our lower selves can find balance and integration in order to achieve the alignment necessary to awaken and raise our consciousness. Mind, heart, body and spirit must balance and find harmony with each other for conscious growth to manifest. Like everything else, it is a slow and steady process, not something that happens all at once. Chiron, the King of the Centaurs, who 'appeared' in our soular system in 1977, has many functions (see the Chiron section below), but one of his main roles is to act as a master healer teacher and help each of us to bring our lower four body systems into this healthy, fully functional alignment.

THE SOCIAL CONSCIOUSNESS

At the center of our soular system, (which represents the network of our consciousness), are the two largest planets we have projected. There is a reason why these two planets are so large. They represent the most vital piece of life on Earth: the social identity. This is the inner/outer function of every consciousness. These social identifiers are located at the center of the soular system, and so represent the relationship between the lower four body system (the individual self) and the universal Oneness we all share. Even more significantly, they represent our own personal experience of this relationship.

Jupiter and Saturn signify the way we connect our individuality to the collective whole, through the development of our objectivity, which is a social process. Objectivity means that we can be aware of the way others perceive us, and we can observe the effects that our actions may have on others. Becoming objective about our individual selves is the great stepping stone toward becoming the great observer, a state of consciousness that is vital to attain if ascension is going to take place.

Jupiter and Saturn together embody the social experience of self that each of us has, and they function to bring our connectedness with others to our awareness in diametrically opposed ways. Through Jupiter, we learn to interact with others based on the experiences of growth, opportunity, childlike exploration and the expansion of consciousness, at every level. Jupiter, as the Great Wise One, teaches expansion into the Higher Self through experiences of freedom and liberation, which take us from the personal self to the experience of connectedness and Oneness with others. Through Saturn, we learn about relationships through such experiences as boundaries, restriction and limitation, oppression, handicap and the need to deal maturely with any difficult circumstance. Saturn, as the Great Teacher, often brings us back to the experience of fear, which always stems from the belief in separation, and offers us the greatest lessons we will ever learn about overcoming the lower self and stepping into authenticity.

With these two planets, we begin to experience our lives in terms of a bigger picture, and so we gain the perspective we need to comprehend the idea that a higher power is at work in our lives.

THE RAINBOW BRIDGE

Discovered in 1977, Chiron, originally thought of as a planetoid or large asteroid, appeared in our soular system, right smack between Saturn and Uranus. Named by astronomers, Chiron is mythologically known as the 'wounded healer,' but upon closer inspection of his story, he can actually be seen to be a master healer teacher, whose love of humanity moved him to take on the human condition, complete with mortality and suffering, and in this way he was able to teach the truth about wellbeing and healing: that in order to be fully functional and whole, one must be willing to take on the human condition. Once completely inhabiting the body, a state so many of us are hesitant to take on, it becomes possible to attain personal mastery, and to undertake the journey from the lower self to the Higher Self.

It is for this reason that Chiron has become known as the rainbow bridge, the connection between Saturn, representing the outer edge of the physical (3D) realm and Uranus, the archetype that awakens us to our higher (5D) Selves. Metaphysically speaking, the pineal gland, which sits behind the third eye, connects to and interacts with the hypothalamus gland, which is located at the base of the brain. This connection becomes active with conscious application, and when it does, one has access to ones Higher Self. Chiron, therefore, is the physical expression and reflection of this process, which began to show itself in human experience in the late 1970's.

THE HIGHER SELF

The 'outer' planets represent the aspects of higher consciousness that belong to every human being on the planet. The energies of these planets are vibrating at a higher frequency, and so their effects are not always immediately obvious. However, whether we are aware of these 'higher' promptings or not, Uranus, Neptune, Pluto and beyond are always at work, delivering us to the experiences that can best remind us of our higher purpose. With their presence, we step onto the path of our own evolu-

**JUPITER, SATURN, URANUS, & NEPTUNE.
NASA JPL**

tion and eventually become aware of the connectedness that exists amongst all of us. In this way we come to know the universal forces that bind us together here on Earth, and understand the power and meaning of our Oneness.

These transpersonal planets represent the profound and eventually undeniable urges that we all experience: the sudden unexpected reversals that generate an uncommon intuitive awareness and bring about awakening (Uranus), the inner confusion and self-doubt that leads to enlightenment (Neptune), the profound experiences of loss and intense struggle that produce the metamorphosis of Self (Pluto and beyond). These planets are slow moving and can take a very long time to manifest their true purposes in our lives, but they function with divine perfection and timing, whether we are conscious and ready to accept them into our lives or not.

The conscious experience of these planetary energies is very different from the unconscious experience, and because these planets represent such evolutionary forces, they can be quite uncomfortable to deal with when we are resisting them. Uranus can produce a jolt or a sudden turn in life that can pull the rug out from under us. This leaves us on our behinds when we were once standing tall, and though that can sting, it is designed to get us to look at our lives from a new perspective, thereby awakening us to new possibilities. Neptune can descend upon us like a mist or a cloud, diminishing our awareness and even blinding us to what is real, and this process magnifies the more we resist it. But the lack of clarity is designed to cause us to walk without our senses to guide us. Faith is a profound experience when Neptune is strongly focused, and eventually we may come to the enlightened realization that because we are creating our realities with our own thoughts and beliefs, we have the power to change those thoughts and thereby change our worlds. Pluto can put us through Hell, taking away what we think we want or need the most, forcing us to learn to let go and surrender to a more potent and All-Knowing greater good. The rebirth that ensues from these dark nights of the soul can truly show us the meaning of personal empowerment. Every day astronomers are identifying celestial bodies that live in our consciousness out beyond Neptune and Pluto. For now these are called Kuiper Belt objects (please see the section on these).

The more conscious we are of the methods by which these universal forces operate, the more decidedly we can progress along the path to higher consciousness and human advancement. When these planets are active, they generally affect large groups of us simultaneously (their actions are generational and collective as well as very VERY personal). The very presence of these forces and our knowledge of them automatically produce a greater awareness, and once we become conscious of that, we know we have stepped onto the evolutionary path and cannot turn back.

SYNOPSIS OF PLANETARY ENERGIES

The planets represent the set of archetypal energies we all contain within us and they produce the experience we have as human beings having a physical incarnation on planet Earth. There are ten primary bodies we refer to as planets in astrology: the Sun, the Moon, Mercury, Venus, Mars, Jupiter, Saturn, Uranus, Neptune and Pluto. In addition to the planets, there are some other very important placements that most astrologers use: the North Node of the Moon, the South Node of the Moon, Chiron and Black Moon Lilith. What follows is a quick description of each planetary archetype:

THE SUN ☉

Represents the energy we use to express our individuality and consciousness at the most individual level, and in the higher sense the Sun represents the higher consciousness that we all contain and that is now being reactivated and rediscovered. The SUN is the great metaphor for the SON, the one creation of Source, which is expressed through each of us, taken collectively. As one of the Lights, the Sun co-rules our lower spiritual body, providing expression for our masculine side, which is fundamentally creative and expressive. Through the Sun we experience our personal power and access our vital life force energy.

THE MOON ☽

Represents our inner response to all our experiences though our feminine, intuitive, emotional nature. The Moon travels through our energy field more swiftly than any other archetype, producing the constantly changing emotional atmosphere that we perceive to be so closely connected to the ocean. The ocean is the main expression of the limitless field of potential on this planet, and this potential is made viable through the emotions (energies in motion) that we feel. The powerful Moon, therefore, establishes our connection with all the other planetary energies. We use its receptive power to process our emotions and feelings. The Moon is co-ruler of the lower spiritual body with the Sun. Together these two bodies represent the most vital forces that produce the experience of life on Earth, and so they are the rulers of the greatest part of our being, the cosmic, or spiritual self.

MERCURY ☿

Represents our mental body, ruling over both the lower mind, with its intellectual nature and the ways in which we are stimulated to learn and develop our own points of view, and the higher mind, which is stimulated by the consciousness of the spiritual self, and is activated by that Light. As the Messenger archetype, Mercury is associated with thoughts, ideas, writing, talking, messages, information, logic and reasoning and all forms of connection. He also disposes the great observer mode in each of us, the part of the mind that connects with the inner guidance mechanism and helps to produce an integrated mind/heart balance that ultimately produces ascension.

VENUS ♀

Represents our emotional body, not to be confused with our emotions. The emotional body is housed in the heart center, and Venus is the archetype that disposes our capacity to Love. On one level, Venus describes what you love, what you are attracted to, who you love and your romantic nature. She is very much about your level of self-worth and self-esteem, which in turn describes your relationship with money and other material comforts, as well as your approach to financial affairs and material possessions. As the Goddess of Love, Venus is one of the two main rulers of the divine feminine within. She has only recently begun to activate the heart center and the high heart center (where we commune with Source), with assistance from the outer planets. The divine feminine is such a vital piece of our existence here on Earth, and we are living in a time when this truth is being restored to our awareness. In the process, we remember Venus, and how vital an archetype she is to the experience of our higher Selves.

MARS ♂

Represents our physical body, and has long been recognized as the generator of our physical strength and stamina, as well as the action we take to make things happen. Mars has described how we go after what we want, and what we will fight for. He generates our inner desires and the ways in which our energy is expressed; for example, whether we are aggressive, assertive, or physically active. This archetype has been associated with our libido and sexual style. Once related to the great warrior within us, Mars has more recently become the great keeper of the physical experience. He was connected to war and fighting for so long because the separation that is generated by taking a physical form generates the fear that produces the false belief in the survival instinct. With Love and peace becoming the more significant focus, Mars now grounds us in our physical being, allowing for the individuality that is so vital to the successful expression of Oneness we have come here to experience.

JUPITER ♃

Represents the expansion of our social consciousness through interaction with the outside world, in the form of people, places and things. Jupiter helps us to understand the meaning of life through our cultural and spiritual pursuits. Through understanding our relevance to others, or of others to our Selves, Jupiter guides us throughout our lives to pursue educational, religious, cultural and spiritual truths. This is where abundance, growth and wisdom become available to us. Jupiter has long been known as the most benefic archetype we have at our fingertips. At the social level, we live our lives according to Jupiter's twelve year cycles, changing very significantly at each 12 year mark. Cosmic Astrology is powerfully based on the twelve year cycle, which corresponds with this planet so profoundly. The wisdom generated by the understanding of these twelve year cycles, which we all experience as rites of passage, is a major key to the consciousness required to move to a higher, more awakened level of awareness.

SATURN ♄

Represents the experience of authority in our lives and teaches us to be more mature and responsible for our actions. All authority is ultimately an inner authority, and in the greatest sense we are all accountable only to ourselves. This is so, because as Saturn teaches, we are always only interacting with our own reflection and so we are treated by others in exactly the same way we treat ourselves. The experience of restriction or limitation through fear and self-doubt is where we tend to repeat mistakes, and therefore feel inadequate or handicapped socially. Saturn constitutes the voice of our conscience and where we tend to feel judged by others. In the end, Saturn teaches us that we are responsible to our own higher conscience. The planet is known as the Great Teacher, fate or karma and Father Time, because it creates lessons in becoming responsible for ourselves through repetitive cycles until we become willing to step into our own authority and express our most authentic Selves. Saturn generates another major 29 ½ year cycle that produces major social rites of passage related to maturity and the level of authority one takes on in the lifetime.

CHIRON ⚷

Chiron is technically a centaur, which is a brand new classification of heavenly bodies, as put forth by today's astronomers. However, Chiron's role is so important at this particular time in human evolution that he is being included in this list of major archetypal energies, better known as the planets. As a creature that is half animal and half man, Chiron embodies the balance of the four lower bodies, and of rational mind and animal instincts, serving to bridge our higher and lower selves. Chiron is, mythologically, a wise teacher and master healer who helps us to uncover the mysteries of our soul's purpose. Chiron, sometimes referred to as the Wounded Healer, represents our deepest misalignments as well as the great self-empowerment we must develop to bring ourselves back into balance. Through the experience of healing our wounds, we ultimately help others do the same, creating powerful relationships with the influences of alignment and transformation. Healing our inner wounds brings the ability to expand past our limiting beliefs to rediscover our divine Selves. As his glyph symbolizes, Chiron is considered a key that unlocks our experience of the outer planets, bringing us to the opportunity to reclaim our higher Selves.

URANUS ♅

Represents the universal force of change, awakening, originality, foresight and a touch of creative genius. It allows us to interact with the dimension of higher consciousness just beyond the individual or social self. This is the first planet that connects us with our own higher consciousness and brings flashes of intuitive foresight, psychic awareness and an element of the future. This archetype, when acting in tandem with the rulers of the individual four body system, produces gifts, talents, and experiences that move us swiftly (and often very suddenly) into the greater experience of the Oneness. For example, the combination of Mercury, ruler of the mental body, with Uranus produces flashes of originality and insight that are singular and rare. Mercury/Uranus makes the internet possible, taking us from the capacity to make a phone call or write a letter (Mercury) to the place where we can be connected with the entire world in an instant. Such is the function of Uranus, the Great Awakener.

NEPTUNE ♆

Represents those overwhelming, larger than life passages that find us grappling with confusion, escapism, delusion and deception, but that invariably lead to crystal clear understanding, conscious awareness and compassion. This is the area where we tend to be the most idealistic and romantic about our lives. We are often led by Neptune, ruler of the ocean - the limitless field of potential - into prolonged passages that are tunnel-like, where all of reality tends to disappear, everything that was once defined loses its substance, and we feel we are left to walk along through a long, dark tunnel, without knowing what has happened. We take this journey, because there is no way to go back once we are on the path to evolution, and we learn all about faith and trust. By allowing the Light to emerge from within, we get glimpses of our universal Oneness and we learn that we create our own reality out of all that we believe. We learn that we all have this capacity and we learn to trust ourselves and Source. This is the universal force that produces enlightenment.

PLUTO ♇

Represents the gateway to the greater consciousness we are all poised to enter into. The Great Rebirther invariably takes us to the place where we must let go and surrender to a higher power in order to experience our own personal power. We experience an overwhelming force that is way beyond our control and causes a loss, change or new beginning. The Pluto experience makes us feel that something happens TO us, and we have no choice but to accept it and go on. This is the universal force of death, rebirth and metamorphosis. Because death is a physical experience and does not exist beyond the physical realm, Pluto is the gatekeeper to the next greater realm of consciousness. When Pluto was 'demoted' a few years ago, he was collectively made to go through his own metamorphosis, and now that he has done so, it is no longer necessary to perceive him solely as the 'Lord of the Underworld.' He can now be seen as the gatekeeper to a whole new realm of bodies just like him located in the Kuiper Belt, beyond Pluto's orbit.

NODES ☊ / ☋

The Moon's North and South Nodes can be considered two of the most significant points in any birth chart, and in Cosmic Astrology they represent the doorways through which the soul moves into and out of any incarnation. The Nodes are always exactly opposite each other, creating a polarity that exists in every life, and around which all important relationships and events take place. Everything we ever do in our lifetime is either karmic (a result of the past) or dharmic (evolving us toward the future); the law of cause and effect is always in play. In any given moment we are either reacting to our past or creating our future. We cannot be doing both and we are always choosing one path over the other.

The Moon's South Node can be called the doorway to the soul's past. It is a point that feels very much like gravity, because the energies of past actions are condensed there. When we move toward that point it often feels unavoidable, as though we are being pulled toward the events happening there. Sometimes we feel excited, because it feels so familiar, sometimes we can't understand our own attraction. That point is where everything we have ever done generates its effects on our current life.

The Moon's North Node can be called the door to one's evolution. When we move toward that portal, we feel its importance, though it can sometimes feel like digging a tunnel with a spoon. Moving toward the future that our Higher Self has chosen to access requires a nose to the grindstone type of diligence. Still, we want to move in the direction of our lifework, and we often will stick with it beyond any reason or understanding.

The Moon's nodes are always exactly opposite each other and they are created out of a combination of the Sun and Moon's orbits and the way in which the Earth gets involved with them. Since the Sun and Moon rule over the spiritual body in Cosmic Astrology, it is easy to see how this nodal polarity speaks to the soul's purpose in any birth chart, or map of the movie a soul is experiencing at any given time here on Earth.

BLACK MOON LILITH ⚸

Black Moon Lilith (BML) is actually a calculated geometrical point along the Moon's elliptical orbit around the Earth. In the simplest of descriptions, it is a point along the Moon's orbit farthest from the Earth. It is easier to grasp the essential meaning of the Black Moon Lilith if you consider that it is very much like the Moon's reflection. When you look at the Moon through a telescope, the reflection tends to bounce around, because the earth is actually bouncing. This bouncy reflection can be located at one degree one day and pretty far away the next. This is very much in tune with the true movement of the Black Moon. Before the divine feminine returned to the planet in force, the Black Moon Lilith represented the place where the feminine energies were pent up or deeply suppressed within us. But these days, with full access to the feminine aspect of our being, the Black Moon Lilith points to the location within our own energy field where the divine feminine is most easily contacted.

ASPECTS

Each planet has an energy or function that is specific to it and that we can connect with psychologically, emotionally, physically or spiritually. We live in a solar (soular) system that contains 12 main planets, (including the Earth we live on), the Sun and Moon, which are the vital forces of our consciousness, and other bodies and significant points that are especially relevant at this point in human evolution. Each of us wields all of these energies, and each of us utilizes them and responds to them in our own unique way.

The planets are forever moving and combining with each other to produce the more complicated energies that we work with on a day-to-day basis. All of astrology (and each of the aspects) is based on the 360 degrees of the circle that forms the zodiac. Everything is mathematically connected to everything else. Every time two planets combine to dissect the circle in an exact or inexact way, an aspect is formed.

An aspect is a relationship between two planets that is always based on the number that creates the connection between them. For example, if we take the number 2, we cut the circle in half, and an opposition is formed. If we divide the 360 degree circle by 3, we get 120 degrees, which yields the trine aspect. It is not surprising that 360 is a fascinating and complex number that can be divided, evenly and sometimes not exactly, by every number from 1 to 12. Every single division produces a meaningful aspect, and in Cosmic Astrology nothing is less important than anything else. Everything has meaning that is divinely planned.

However, for the sake of brevity, which is the purpose of this introductory journal, we will take a closer look only at those connections that are known as the Ptolemaic or major aspects: the conjunction (1), the opposition (2), the trine (3), the square (4), and the sextile (6). These are the aspects that produce the most dynamic relationships. If we draw them in the center of a circle, they yield familiar shapes, such as the triangle and the square, and there is no mistake about the sacred geometry of the circle.

The Cosmic Astrology system recognizes that energies we once referred to as 'good' or 'bad' are actually all part of the same Oneness, and that without the tendency to judge a situation, we are always being offered exactly what is required for our expansion and enlightenment.

This journal displays these major aspects, as they occur on a daily basis. All the other aspects, also very important connections, will be covered in the interactive *Cosmic Astrology Workbook* that is my next project and that puts forth the entire system of Cosmic Astrology.

Here is a short description of the essence of each of the major aspects:

CONJUNCTION ☌

Occurs when two planets are 0 degrees apart, at the same degree and in the same sign.

A conjunction is considered the most powerful astrological aspect. The planets involved in the conjunction are together, united as one. While a conjunction tends to produce a harmonious relationship, its quality depends on the planets involved as it intensifies the mutual effects of those archetypes. For example, the union of the Sun with Venus or Jupiter would produce an expansive and positive experience, whereas a conjunction involving Mars, Saturn, Uranus or Pluto would likely produce a life lesson or a challenging circumstance that forces our attention.

SEXTILE ✶

Occurs when two planets are 60 degrees from each other or two signs apart.

The sextile connection produces a harmonious relationship that coaxes the flow of creative energies to reveal themselves, generating all kinds of possibilities. These in turn move us significantly toward the attainment of our goals, but we must make a conscious effort to achieve them. A sextile yields productivity, compatibility and easy communication between the two planetary energies involved.

SQUARE □

Occurs when two planets are 90 degrees from each other or three signs apart.

Planets in a square aspect are almost always of the same tri fold flame energetic, i.e. Power (Aries, Cancer, Libra, Capricorn), Love (Taurus, Leo, Scorpio, Aquarius), and Wisdom signs (Gemini, Virgo, Sagittarius, Pisces) are in a square relationship to each other. The energy of the square tends to be stressful, creating tension and/or inner conflict. At the same time, this relationship will eventually become a source of energy for those who accept the challenges and are determined to overcome limitations. The square is literally a building block, which can just be a block or a resource to build from. Much evolution and growth can be obtained when conscious and illuminated choices are made. When you have mastered a square, growth and new levels of greatness result.

TRINE △

Occurs when two planets are 120 degrees from each other or four signs apart.

A harmonious relationship exists between the two planets that trine each other. There is an ease of expression because the aspects of consciousness involved share the same element, i.e. Fire (Aries, Leo, Sagittarius), Air (Gemini, Libra, Aquarius), Earth (Taurus, Virgo, Capricorn) and Water signs (Cancer, Scorpio, Pisces) trine each other. Trines are a source of creative and natural talent. Traditionally, this aspect is considered to be highly beneficial, though excessive trines in a person's life can tend to have negative characteristics, because too much ease can make you weak or complacent.

However, when you work to apply your consciousness to the energy of the trine, great momentum can occur, blessings and miracles can appear, special innate gifts and talents can be revealed and great progress can be made.

OPPOSITION ☍

Occurs when two planets are 180 degrees from each other or six signs apart.

The opposition produces a relationship of great polarity, which can generate confrontation, conflict and tension. Though challenging, this aspect can be a great energetic power source when channeled constructively and with consciousness. In an opposition the planets tend to reflect off each other, mirror one another. You can master the polarity generated by realizing that the opposition is merely a reflection of your self. This aspect brings your awareness to your relationships, which also act as your mirrors. It is always a challenge to transcend the duality of self and other, by reclaiming that which is perceived to be 'out there.' Mastery of this aspect leads to self-realization.

THE HOURS

The Cosmic Astrology system is based on the cosmic clock, a series of 12 hours, which begin at the Midheaven (MC) and run clockwise, exactly like a clock, overlaid onto the natal birth chart. This produces a way to consciously locate yourself at any point in time. Conscious awareness produces the ability to know where you are, and this 'presence' is what restores you to the power to choose a heart-centered, loving approach to your experience. Choosing Love is the way to transmute your lower, more fear-based energies and ascend.

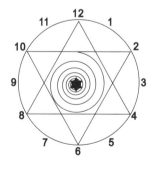

In the older system of astrology, the houses are described as the different areas of your life experience. You are thought to exist at the center of the birth chart. You then repeatedly choose to leave that center and go visit any one of these houses in order to have an experience in the world. It has been believed that the presence of a planet in one of your houses, natally or by transit, somehow compels you to go there. But the truth is you are always at the center of your being and you never leave to go anywhere.

You live inside a four body system that is best depicted as a quantum energy field. This field is made up of the four bodies, spiritual, mental, emotional and physical, as well as the tri-fold aspects of our new heart chakra, Power, Love and Wisdom. Each year, on your own individual birthday, you begin a journey around the clock, beginning at the Midheaven, the 12 o'clock hour. On your birthday every year you agree to take on a certain set of circumstances at the highest level of your being, the place where you are one with Source.

You travel around the clock, one month at a time, one hour at a time, in the same exact way at the same exact time every year, and the purpose of this journey is twofold. First, you are meant to integrate the experience you take on at your birthday fully into the lower four body system, taking it from the highest aspect of Self, where you are connected to Source, all the way to the physical self, where you manifest the results of your integration efforts into the physical world.

Secondly, each hour relates to a particular lower body system and a specific aspect of the tri-fold flame. The 12 o'clock hour, for example, is the hour of Spiritual Power. Each angle of the clock moves you into the experience of another lower body system. Each of you has your own very specific journey around the clock that is repeated each year (and also in twelve year cycles). By applying your conscious awareness to this journey, it is possible to locate yourself within your own energy field at all times. This conscious awareness is what makes the ascension process possible, because it restores you to the power to choose Love.

What follows is a list of the hours on the clock, the lower body/tri-fold flame aspect associated with it, the aspect of consciousness (sign) that naturally presides over each hour, and the old system house it shares an affinity with:

	HOUR	SIGN	HOUSE
12	Spiritual Power	Capricorn	9
1	Spiritual Love	Aquarius	8
2	Spiritual Wisdom	Pisces	7
3	Mental Power	Aries	6
4	Mental Love	Taurus	5
5	Mental Wisdom	Gemini	4
6	Emotional Power	Cancer	3
7	Emotional Love	Leo	2
8	Emotional Wisdom	Virgo	1
9	Physical Power	Libra	12
10	Physical Love	Scorpio	11
11	Physical Wisdom	Sagittarius	10

MOON PHASES

The Moon's phases describe the relationship between the Sun and the Moon at any given time. The Sun and Moon, rulers of the spiritual body, are known as the Lights, and they are the generators of your consciousness. The way the Sun and the Moon relate to each other is described by a series of aspects known as the Moon's phases. The Sun Moon connection speaks greatly to your individual life purpose. The Moon's phases have everything to do with the state of your consciousness at any given time. The phases are specific and repeat themselves monthly, beginning with a new Moon, culminating at the full Moon, and then returning full circle to the new Moon again.

An important element related to the Moon is called the 'void of course' Moon. The Moon moves through a sign every 60 hours or so (give or take a few hours), and a void occurs when the Moon makes her last major aspect to any of the other planets before entering a new sign. A void can last anywhere from one minute to the full two and a half days. When the Moon is not in aspect to any other planet it is prime time for communing with the feminine within. It is the perfect opportunity to let go of the world and just allow it all to show itself for what it is. The void is inner communion time, and the quality of that period, especially when it is prolonged, takes on the flavor of the last aspect the Moon makes and the archetypal energies of the planet she connects with.

NEW MOON:	waxing 0°- 45°
CRESCENT:	waxing 45°- 90°
FIRST QUARTER:	waxing 90°-135°
GIBBOUS:	waxing 135°- 180°
FULL MOON:	waning 180°-135°
DISSEMINATING:	waning 135°-90°
LAST QUARTER:	waning 90°-45°
BALSAMIC:	waning 45°-0°

NEW MOON
Birth, New beginnings.
The new Moon occurs each month when the Moon and the Sun come together. Invisible in the sky at this time, the Moon merges with the Sun and is energized by its life force, according to the sign they are traveling through together. The new Moon brings the moment when the seed of a new beginning takes hold and all possibilities become viable.

CRESCENT
Incubation, Nurture.

Nurture the new seeds you have planted. Take steps toward your dreams and new ideas, but go quietly, gently. They are still fragile and just about to break ground. Get quiet and listen to what is needed to nurture your new projects or desires.

FIRST QUARTER
Commitment, Affirmation.

The 1st quarter Moon appears as a half Moon in the sky. You are on the path that the seeds of the new Moon have created. It is now time to re-affirm your wishes and make a choice, a commitment to align yourself with the new growth that is emerging. Once this commitment is made, the seed begins to grow according to your choices.

GIBBOUS
Integrate, Adapt.

Your seedlings are growing and the world around you starts to take notice. You may feel support and/or resistance. This is the time to stay true to yourself, but not rigid. Integrate your new garden into your already existing reality.

FULL MOON
Blossoming, Clarity.

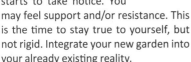

The seeds you planted on the new Moon are now blooming. Things initiated at the new Moon will culminate in some way at the full Moon. Take responsibility for your manifestations and you will gain clarity on how to nurture, change or release your creations for the next cycle.

DISSEMINATING
Share, Connect.

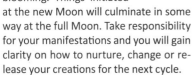

Share the harvest you have created. It will come in many forms, but most of all in the wisdom you have gained from this process. Share insights and listen to what others have learned. Take stock of what you have and where you want to go.

LAST QUARTER
Release, Let go.

The last quarter Moon reveals to us what is no longer needed. From now until the next new Moon, clear the decks, tie up lose ends and release what no longer holds any value. Pull the weeds and prepare the soil for the next cycle. Will you continue to nurture what has manifested from the seeds you planted on the last new Moon? Or you will plant new seeds? It is your garden, your life and the possibilities are endless.

BALSAMIC
Oneness, Faith.

You are re-entering into the void, becoming one with all that is once again so that you can plant new seeds at the new Moon. It may feel like a small death. If you have any fear it simply means you are resisting your connection to Source. Take a deep breath, and let it all go. Allow yourself to feel your connectedness with those around you as well as the Earth herself. Rest in the void, it is almost time to be born again.

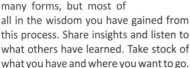

FIXED STARS

When we shift into the view of the observer, we are able to see the bigger picture so much more clearly. Recognizing that we are living within the zodiac and the solar (soular) system that contains our 10 planets is like looking in the mirror and seeing only a face, without taking into account the rest of our body. The fixed stars are so called because they are far enough away to appear as though they are not moving. Of course, they are. There is nothing in the universe that is not moving. But if a star moves one degree over the course of an entire human lifetime, it qualifies as a fixed star.

The fixed stars have been a part of our consciousness for a long time. They have names and we are familiar with many of them. They actually represent whole constellations, or in some cases galaxies, and it is important, once again, to expand out our vision in order to be able to perceive the essence and meaning of any fixed star. Fixed stars are often the brightest stars in a planetary picture (constellation) or a cluster of many stars (a galaxy).

If we think in 5D, realizing that all is one and nothing is separate from anything else, it becomes easy to see that the planets in our soular system reflect the various archetypes traveling around in our minds, while the fixed stars represent much larger concepts or realizations, and serve as landmarks in the mirrored reflections of our Selves. They exist in the higher dimensions of our consciousness, and though we can 'see' them in 3D, they do not take on any real meaning until we perceive them from a higher perspective. Their significance is far less personal, way more collective than the planets, and it is possible to meditate on them and connect very deeply with all that they convey.

The following is a list of major fixed stars to familiarize yourself with, but these are by no means the complete list. The Alpha star of any constellation is a major 5D connection in the Cosmic Astrology system. There is not enough space in this introductory journal to go into the meanings of these stars, but you are urged to contemplate them. Connect with them individually in your consciousness and you will begin to remember the essence of each keeper of our higher realms. The fixed stars will be covered at length in the *Cosmic Astrology Workbook* that will deliver the entire system, to be published in 2013.

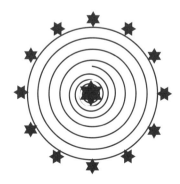

THE ROYAL STARS
Formalhaut, Aldebaran, Regulus and Antares

These stars represent the important turning points of the equinoxes and solstices. They are known as the Archangel Stars and are gatekeepers of the four angles.

VEGA: 15° ♑ 29'
Alpha star of the constellation Lyra.

ALTAIR: 01° ♒ 57'
Alpha star of the constellation Aquila, the Eagle.

FOMALHAUT: 04° ♓ 02'
Alpha star of Piscis Austrinus, the Southern Fish. Royal Star associated with the South.

DENEB ADIGE: 05° ♓ 30'
Alpha star of the constellation Cygnus, the Swan.

ALPHERATZ: 14° ♈ 29'
Alpha star of the constellation Andromeda.

MIRACH: 00° ♉ 35'
Beta star of the constellation Andromeda.

HAMAL: 07° ♉ 50'
Alpha star of the constellation Aries.

SCHEDIR: 07° ♉ 58'
Alpha star of the constellation Cassiopeia.

ALCYONE: 00° ♊ 10'
A binary star system in the constellation Taurus. It is the brightest star in the Pleiades star cluster.

ALDEBARAN: 09° ♊ 58'
Alpha star in the constellation Taurus. Royal Star associated with the East.

RIGEL: 17° ♊ 01'
Beta star of the constellation Orion, the Hunter.

POLARIS: 28° ♊ 45'
Alpha star of the constellation Ursa Minor, the Little Bear.

BETELGEUSE: 28° ♊ 56'
Alpha star of the constellation Orion, the Hunter.

SIRIUS: 14° ♋ 16'
The binary alpha star system of the constellation Canis Major, the Greater Dog (aka the Dog Star).

CASTOR: 20° ♋ 25'
The binary alpha star system of the constellation Gemini.

POLLUX: 23° ♋ 24'
Beta star of the constellation Gemini.

DUBHE: 15° ♌ 23'
Alpha star of the constellation Ursa Major, the Greater Bear (aka the Big Dipper).

REGULUS: 00° ♍ 01'
The alpha star system of the constellation Leo. Royal Star associated with the North.

THUBAN: 07° ♍ 38'
Alpha star of the constellation Draco, the Dragon's Tail.

SPICA: 24° ♎ 01'
The binary alpha star of the constellation Virgo.

ARCTURUS: 24° ♎ 24'
Alpha star of the constellation Bootes.

ANTARES: 09° ♐ 57'
The binary alpha star of the constellation Scorpio. Royal Star associated with the West.

RASALHAGUE: 22° ♐ 37
Alphas star of the constellation Ophiuchus, the Snake Charmer.

ASTEROIDS

There is a region in our solar (soular) system located between the orbits of Mars and Jupiter that contains nearly 400,000 objects classified as asteroids. This 'asteroid belt' has an orbit all its own, which suggests the remains of a once upon a time planet. The asteroids have almost unanimously been thought of as feminine in their energies, and in the new Cosmic Astrology system they can be recognized as the all-important, most immediately accessible, fragments of our feminine consciousness. Considering our recently restored access to the divine feminine here on Earth, it makes sense that the remnants of her existence are fragmented and in need of realignment. The influence of the asteroids is more specific than that of a

regular planet and so the incorporation of them into our awareness adds important definition and fullness to our understanding of our soul signature. At this point we are gathering and reclaiming all these pieces and reabsorbing them back into our energy field. The healing they offer plays a pivotal part in our return to wholeness and our reconnection to our Higher Self. They are the key elements of the divine feminine principle that holds the balance in our lower four body system.

The following four asteroids are thought to be the most influential of all the bodies in the asteroid belt. Ceres was recently given an upgrade, and the scientific community of astronomers is now classifying her as a dwarf planet. Esoterically speaking, this is very revealing good news, because it indicates that the collective consciousness is ready and willing to accept the divine feminine archetype back into the mainstream consciousness. These four asteroids can be thought of to represent the most popular and well-known streams of modern human consciousness, but every single asteroid, all 400,000 of them, holds a bit of our fragmented feminine being, and ultimately requires reintegration. No doubt this is an ongoing process that in true 'feminine' fashion will occur naturally over time, now that it has begun.

CERES ⚳

Ceres is the main representative of the 'Mother' energy. She brings up your mother issues and reveals the nature of your own instincts to nurture and protect. The specifics she adds to the natal (3D) birth chart relate to your response to loss, separation, and any kind of emotional devastation that your lower self struggles with because of a perceived lack of nurturing or protection. In Cosmic Astrology, she has to do with the tri-fold flame aspect of Physical Power. Ceres works to restore your connection to the mystery and power of Mother Nature. Here archetypal energies promote a deep, intuitive and transformational mothering instinct influencing the quality of consciousness in the hour where she appears. Her presence points out the place where you will go the distance to reclaim what is rightfully yours: a secure, supported, and celebrated divine child within.

JUNO ⚵

Juno imparts to us the archetype of 'The Partner.' Juno gives definition to the fear-based ways in which you seek fulfillment outside of yourself, specifically through relationships and partnerships. Her placement in the natal birth chart reveals imbalances in your confidence and self-esteem, how you project those insecurities onto other people, and where you struggle to see and appreciate yourself clearly. In Cosmic Astrology, Juno's influence shifts to the quality of Emotional Power and indicates how you show up for yourself in life, because with an expanded consciousness you are already aware that any partnership reflects your masculine/feminine energetic balance. Juno's placement on the cosmic clock defines where fear-based patterns of jealousy, neediness, and attachment especially need clearing, which when healed allows a great alliance and commitment to emerge with that aspect of consciousness.

PALLAS ATHENA ⚴

Pallas provides the female 'spiritual warrior' archetype. In the natal birth chart, Pallas gives definition to your father issues and points out how perceived weakness or defenselessness has wounded your capacity to follow your intuition and trust yourself (and therefore anyone else). On the cosmic clock, Pallas bestows the tri-fold flame quality of Mental Power, as in higher consciousness, and shows you the way to rely on loving thought rather than brute force to heal and rectify grievances. Pallas supports the clearing of the fear-based energies that create mental chatter, selfishness, and lack of courage. Her placement in the hours on the cosmic clock is where an aptitude for higher consciousness lies, realized or not, and where a core motivation to pursue Truth drives you toward the realization of that expanded consciousness.

VESTA ⚶

Vesta represents the life giving 'fire within.' She influences the direction of your kundalini life-force energy and in the 3D birth chart provides a window into fear-based patterns related to sex and sexuality, including how you might give away or misuse your body, or abuse your primal creative impulses. With an expanded consciousness, Vesta takes on the energy of creation, devotion, and passion, distinguishing your capacity to serve tirelessly and selflessly. In Cosmic Astrology the presence of Vesta is the empowered creative force within that lights your path of service for the greater good of all. Her placement on the cosmic clock corresponds to Spiritual Power, which serves to shift and clear the ways in which you disempower yourself. "Love all, serve all" becomes the motivational force for realizing Vesta's archetypal energy.

BLACK HOLES

It is important to note that when scientists put their focus on a new classification of bodies in the cosmos, the collective consciousness is expressing its readiness to integrate the meaning of those new objects into itself. Black holes are becoming more and more crucial, because humanity is ready to embrace what they represent. We cannot recognize anything in physical form that is not in our consciousness in the first place, and once named, we have the capacity to gain depth and understanding about an object we perceive that we did not have before. The danger is always in too much definition, because a finite understanding tends to eliminate the possibility for added dimension and conscious awareness. Since we are working with objects in the cosmos, which represents our spiritual body, it is never a good idea to assume we know everything about anything we find there. Understanding the cosmos is an intuitive art, and the intuition knows that there is always more to what we perceive, and that, in fact, the Truth is limitless. What follows is the beginning of an intuitive understanding about black holes.

Black holes are pockets in the universe (representing our spiritual body) where we have hidden parts of ourselves. Each black hole takes you through a specific alchemical process by drawing to you events, situations and people that push you into the unknown, providing the opportunity to reconnect with that missing part of yourself. You emerge from an encounter with a black hole forever changed, and much closer to who you really are. A great deal of faith and trust is required when working with a black hole. Because they are perceived to move very slowly, they remain in the same place in your chart for your entire lifetime. A black hole becomes much more of a focus when you are moving through the hour or trine where it lives, or when you have a natal planetary placement aspecting the point where a black hole resides. The nature of the aspect will define your relationship with the process brought on by the black hole.

The Great Attractor and the Galactic Center are two of the most significant black holes in our known universe. We have already successfully brought them into our field of awareness, and a brief description of them follows.

Below that is a list of some of the other black holes, with their zodiacal degrees, that have already been named and that we have therefore begun to integrate into our consciousness at this time. These black holes will be fleshed out further in the forthcoming *Cosmic Astrology Workbook*.

GREAT ATTRACTOR: 13°/14° ♐

The Great Attractor is that place outside of us where we think all the answers lie. If we could only have that one unattainable thing, then we could be happy, complete. That beautiful point in the sky, and in our charts, hears our cries for wholeness and gently whispers, 'but YOU are that one unattainable thing.' Like Dorothy in the Wizard of Oz you have always had the power to go home.

GALACTIC CENTER: 26°/27° ♐

The Galactic Center is at the heart of the Milky Way. It is the beginning and end of the journey. It is the cosmic womb, which birthed our system and will reclaim it in the far distant future. Where ever this black hole is in your chart is where you directly connect with Source.

DURGA: 04°/05° ♑

HEL: 19° ♑

KYBELE & ATTIS: 11°/12° ♒ and 12°/13° ♒

HEKATE: 27°/28° ♒

QUETZALCOATL: 28° ♓

KORE/PERSEPHONE: 26°/27° ♈

EURYDICE: 16° ♉

PARVATI: 04° ♋

KALI: 28° ♋

MERLIN: 02°/03° ♌

CERNUNNOS: 09° ♌

TIAMAT: 06°/07° ♍

APSU: 09° ♍

ADONIS: 01° ♎

NEMESIS: 13° ♎

PELE: 28°/29° ♎

DIONYSOS: 06°/07° ♏

OSIRIS, ISIS, HORUS: 03°/04°/05° ♐

INANNA & ERESHKIGAL: 17°/18° ♐ and 18°/19° ♐

CENTAURS

Centaurs are the newest group of celestial objects, so designated because they cannot be classified as planets, asteroids, or comets. They behave differently in their orbital patterns than everything else, but are still part of our solar (soular) system. One of the criteria for this new type of object is that all centaurs make contact with at least two of the outer planets: Jupiter, Saturn, Uranus, Neptune, or Pluto. The emergence of centaurs in our soular system is clear evidence that we have moved beyond previously known frontiers in consciousness.

The centaurs, taken collectively, represent a dormant and subsequently shadowy aspect of our feminine nature. Feminine aspects of our being just ARE, and it is a part of our purpose in living on this planet at this time to retrieve these feminine energies and allow them to re-emerge. All centaurs serve to escort us from a lower to a higher consciousness. They provide the keys to this transition by helping us to recollect, reawaken, or release hidden and untapped potential through the healing they provide. This restores us to our higher instinctual nature. Realignment is always a part of the process. Centaurs represent the energies that assist us in moving beyond the older constructs of our awareness by bridging seemingly disparate parts of ourselves.

Chiron has come to be known as the king of centaurs. He plays such an important role in our lower four body alignment process that he has come to be recognized as the ruler of Virgo. All centaurs, however, have an affinity with Sagittarius, an aspect of our consciousness long symbolized by the centaur. On the cosmic clock the connection makes sense, as Sagittarius represents the victory of the Higher Self over the lower self. Centaurs can bring forth the dark side of feminine energy and consequently produce some intense experiences, but their main purpose is to help us embrace the long dormant feminine aspect within, which ultimately serves to neutralize the intensity. What follows is a brief introduction to a few of the main centaurs:

ASBOLUS

Asbolus is "The Seer" and, like the other centaurs, is intimately involved in helping you restore your instincts and intuitive faculties. Challenges involving survival through the use of common sense instincts and seeing with more than your eyes are key experiences associated with this centaur. Asbolus presides over the process of healing emotional patterns that involve suffering due to unfair situations and any bitterness or separation that results. He helps you to move out of victim consciousness and brings you to the realization that every potentially life-threatening experience is intended to get you to trust yourself more absolutely.

CHARIKLO

Chariklo invites realizations about intimacy and personal boundaries by assisting in the healing of wounds that are inflicted during painful relationship events. When you are hurt, you instinctively shield yourself from further wounding. But putting up unconscious blocks makes it impossible to experience intimacy, because you are no longer allowing yourself to be fully shared and known. Through Chariklo's action, your own relationship patterns are tested, which produces a healing process that serves to clear co-dependency and gender related belief systems. Chariklo's influence helps to work through conditional and self-destructive behavior patterns in relationships, correcting and evolving your motivation to serve by taking it to the highest level: Love all, serve all.

NESSUS

Nessus exposes ANCIENT patterns of violence and abuse in your lower four body system that are profoundly linked to your familial and ancient lineage. These patterns are deeply ingrained and require considerable, concerted effort to uncover and transcend, often drawing to you harsh or jolting experiences. But transcendence is the higher octave of Nessus. As with any healing, you must face and embrace the dark and disowned parts of yourself to be totally at peace. Nessus triggers these kinds of experiences to help you face the 'devil' and finish the game, allowing the Higher Self to triumph over the lower self.

PHOLUS

Contact with Pholus can put you in touch with your multi-dimensionality and your potential for transpersonal or quantum healing – the kind of release that happens seemingly out of nowhere, but faster than the speed of Light and across generations. True to the shadow feminine nature of the centaurs, Pholus activates a strong unconscious pull to rectify an issue that is felt deeply, but is vast and therefore somewhat elusive. Once an issue is opened up and activated, it quickly becomes hard to ignore, and so resolution is essential before further progress can be made. The problem isn't necessarily personal, the activated issue is often a familial fear-based pattern of fragmentation that appears as a distraction to prevent a true focus on your life path. Patterns of addiction surface, especially toward food, because these are common reactions to the fragmentation Pholus can cause – food addiction is a self-soothing response that must be redirected and released.

HYLONOME

This centaur represents a wild or passionate attachment pattern that can be so blinding that senseless acts of suffering and grief ensue. The release of shame and insurmountable sorrow are possible with the consciousness Hylonome brings, often through personal sacrifice. The Buddhist practice Tonglen is a great representation of the healing awareness available with Hylonome. It involves connecting with and embracing your sorrow, so as to overcome the fear associated with the pain of suffering. The ultimate healing is freedom from the desire for pleasure.

KUIPER BELT OBJECTS

The Kuiper Belt is a region of our solar (soular) system that lies beyond the known planets, extending from the orbit of Neptune all the way out about 25 au (an astronomical unit (au) = the mean distance between the Earth and the Sun). It was discovered by astronomers in 1992. In Cosmic Astrology, the Kuiper Belt represents the new field of consciousness that we are moving into and scientists are continually discovering new objects in this field. Pluto has been named the first Kuiper Belt object. The rapid succession of discoveries within the Kuiper Belt over the last 10 years is an announcement from the collective consciousness that we have successfully expanded our awareness and found our way into another realm of our consciousness. Pluto with his capacity to put us through complete rebirth and metamorphosis is now the gatekeeper to our new multidimensionality.

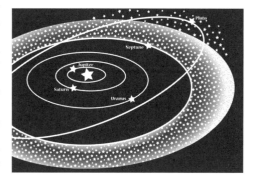

drawing by Lori Rafalof

The objects in the Kuiper Belt and beyond (because there is already much much more) all relate to our multidimensionality and therefore to the quantum field that we live in. These are energies that are beyond the known planetary archetypes of ancient mythologies and preside over a level of consciousness that we are only just beginning to resonate with, even though they are named after ancient beings. (After all, nothing is really new, is it? It is all right here, right now, and it is all completed already). Whenever a new body is discovered in the vastness of our soular system (consciousness) we assign a name, which carries an ancient mythological meaning, to help us begin to grasp the essence of that new attribute of our awareness. It will take some time for us to fully recognize the essential meaning of these objects. However, it is already evident that they have to do with cosmic order rather than personal order. Like the asteroids and centaurs, Kuiper Belt objects are shepparding us toward a new frontier of enlightenment. Neptune, the planet of enlightenment, after all controls the orbital pattern of Kuiper Belt objects.

The planetary archetypes and masters on the cosmic clock have been in our consciousness for a long time and guide us toward re-embodying the qualities of consciousness they represent, but it seems likely that these Kuiper Belt objects denote the larger guiding laws of the universe that are behind all of the archetypes we have known for the past 12,000 years. Since all Kuiper Belt objects move very slowly, their influence in the birth chart is not as specific and personal as the other planets in our soular system. On the cosmic clock they loom larger. These are supervisory superconscious paradigm-creating energies that are part of the magnetic pull of the newly awakening divine feminine prototype.

ORCUS: orbit 248.01 yrs

Named after the Etruscan god of the Underworld, this dwarf planet bears striking resemblance to Pluto. These two bodies travel at nearly the same speed and in a similar path around the Sun, but when Pluto is closest to the Sun, Orcus is at its farthest point from the Sun and vice versa, creating a polarity. They travel in opposition to each other much like the Moon's Nodes. They are like soular nodes and together represent a model of the 'Oneness' of polarity. Orcus is the energy behind the transcendence of polarity consciousness.

QUAOAR: orbit 283.84 yrs

Pronounced Kwah-o-whar, this Kuiper Belt object has an orbit that is nearly a perfect circle. Named after a cosmic creator god from the native Californian tribe, the Tongvas, this being brought spirit into form through dance and song. Like Eris, there is a connection to the cosmic law of resonance as it pertains to manifestation. With Quaoar, there is importance in the perfection of the circle and the feminine devotional expression or essence (femin-essence) of joy and Light.

VARUNA: orbit 284.65 yrs

The name Varuna comes from the ancient Sanskrit tome, Rig Veda, which depicts Varuna as a sky god who presides over the celestial ocean and cosmic law, where order is born out of chaos. As a huge overseeing energetic, Varuna relates to the evolution of 'the observer' perspective that enables healthy detachment from the drama of the lower self and ultimately heightens your sensory faculties and non-verbal communication ability.

HAUMEA: orbit 285.31yrs

Haumea is an unusual Kuiper Belt object due to its oblong shape, which causes it to spin rapidly end over end, and is surrounded by smaller ice chunks that were likely once pieces of her much larger body. The Hawaiian fertility, childbirth, and rebirth goddess, Haumea, is said to have been a woman, married to a god, whose children sprang from different parts of her body. Haumea relates to the fluidity of manifestation when thought is unhampered by the interference of the lower mind.

MAKEMAKE: orbit 309 yrs

From the Polynesian people of Rapa Nui (Easter Island) comes the myth of Makemake (MAH-kay MAH-kay), the main creator god of humanity, of fertility and chief of a bird-man cult. It calls forth personal empowerment and its related struggle, whose goal is to bring you full circle from the journey through the lower four bodies back to the memory that you created it all in the first place. This consciousness restores your response-ability to choose Love over limitation and reclaim the Self as the creator.

ERIS: orbit 556.65 yrs

Eris is named after the Roman goddess of discord and strife. The discovery of Eris triggered the reclassification of many objects in our soular system, a huge disruption in the world of astronomy and astrology, instigating the shift of Pluto to dwarf planet and much more. Eris relates to laws of harmonics and resonance, where lower vibrating frequencies adjust in the presence of a higher vibrating frequency. Discord produces a change in vibration that is unfamiliar and is therefore initially unsettling. Eris is a feminine version of Uranus and an 'all-seeing' energetic that creates purposeful disruption.

SEDNA: orbit about 11,000 yrs

Sedna is the slowest moving and farthest orbiting object known (as of 2011), traveling so far beyond the Kuiper Belt that her discovery tripled the size of our soular system. Sedna's orbit is highly elongated and eccentric, taking almost 12,000 years to complete a cycle around the Sun, linking her to the precession of the equinoxes. Her namesake is derived from an Inuit myth about a woman whose harsh story and eventual dismemberment created the creatures of the ocean. The 5D consciousness of Sedna is not unlike the otherworldly, diverse and fertile aquatic life of the dark, cold Arctic Sea. Here the dark divine feminine in the energy field of the unconscious is returning to our attention as the *re-memberment* of the Divine Mother. She is an enigmatic reminder that there is always something beyond our perception.

STAR GATES

Star Gates are like combination locks that deliver the keys and codes that we require for our evolutionary journey. A Star Gate is an information highway, a powerful stream of Light that carries knowledge and wisdom from Source through our crown chakras to our lower four body system. Like most combination locks, a Star Gate is revealed when numbers align. The entire universe is made of numbers. Numbers are the fabric of our existence, and when these numbers come together in certain specific ways, a Star Gate opens and we are given access to all that it has to offer. We may or may not be conscious of the Star Gate, but the more aware we are the more we can receive.

When you 'happen' to glance at a clock and it says 11:11, 5:55, or some other alignment of numbers that you just seem to notice all the time, that is a Star Gate that is opening for you personally. We all experience 11:11, for example, on the clock, twice a day, but not all of us are so attuned to that combination that we just happen to catch it. Clocks, buildings, dates, billboards - Star Gates are everywhere, offering access to the universal consciousness all the time.

Star Gates have always existed, of course, but we have only recently become conscious enough to avail ourselves of them. Digital clocks helped. But like everything else, it is hard to say which came first, the digital read out or the consciousness that is able to utilize it.

So how do they work? We exist here in 3D on a horizontal, linear plane. The universal consciousness exists on the vertical axis. At the center of this cross, we can access the heart, the core of our own being, which is truly where the 'mind' emanates from. The 'mind' is a quantum energy field we each live inside of. When the numbers align, the Star Gate opens and a major stream of Light consciousness flows freely from Source through our crown chakras and into the very cells and DNA of our being. Even when we are not conscious the Star Gate is there, but it takes conscious awareness to access it. And once conscious, all it takes is openness.

When Star Gates open, it is in our highest interest to avail our Selves of them. Stillness, willingness, faith and discipline are important and helpful. Hidden Star Gates exist also, and they are in many ways more powerful than regular ones, because they are more esoteric, more metaphysically attuned, deeper, more edgy and profound. When you add numbers and they do not repeat until you add them again you have a 'Hidden' Star Gate. For example, when you add a

'9' to any number it yields the original number. September 4 is 9+4 = 13, which added together again is a '4.' This is a Hidden 4:4 Star Gate.

Star Gates carry with them the meaning of the numbers attached to them. Here is a very simple list, to help you understand what is being offered on the days when Star Gates are present:

1
New beginnings, personal power or empowerment.

2
Partnership, duality, the mirrored self.

3
Manifestation, the bringing of thought into physical form.

4
Work, discipline, the doors that open as a result of effort put in.

5
Creativity, humanity, communication.

6
Divine feminine, allowing, surrender, compassion and unconditional love.

7
The spiritual realm, the esoteric, the hidden elements.

8
Achievement, acknowledgment, fruits of work well done.

9
Completion, end of a cycle.

10
The same as one, but with the energy of Source thrown in.

11
Personal mastery.

12
Universal qualities.

When Star Gates are active, do your best to open yourself up to them. Light is energy and energy changes everything. Star Gates change your DNA and ultimately your consciousness. Gather your information while you can.

CAPRICORN

Spiritual Power

Symbol: The Executive Director
Master: The Great Divine Director
Quality: Divine Power
Ray: 12th Ray, Crystalline Gold
Trine: Earth
Hour: 12
Rulers: ♄ ♃ ☉

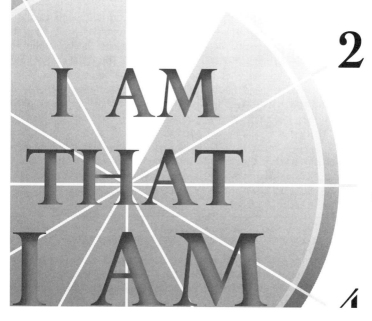

I AM THAT I AM

Spiritual Power

12 O'Clock Hour
Main Purpose:

To perfect the quality of our connection to Source and to access the highest authority within.

DECEMBER 22 - JANUARY 19

The constellations that surround the Earth provide the backdrop for our day-to-day experience. We call this the zodiac, or the Sun signs, which in Cosmic Astrology can be recognized as Son signs, or the various aspects of our higher consciousness. These qualities are the key to our awakening process. The Sun/Son is the center of our solar/soular system. Every year at the Winter Solstice the Sun rises at its lowest point in the sky (in the Northern Hemisphere), remaining at this low point for three days until, on Christmas Day, it begins to rises a little higher each day, until it reaches its highest point, at the Summer Solstice. This is the familiar story of the Sun/Son that has been with us from the beginning. Thus, Cosmic Astrology begins at the Winter Solstice, Capricorn, which is called the 12 o'clock hour in the new system. We follow the Sun's journey, beginning at this 12 o'clock hour, every year.

The resurrection of the Son in Capricorn is the beginning of Cosmic Astrology. At the highest level of our being we are all one with Source. Capricorn represents **Divine Power**, the part of our spiritual body where this connection exists. This aspect of our higher consciousness is recognizable as the Great Divine Director. Within this aspect of our consciousness we access the Executive Director within, taking the leap from the goat that spends his life climbing to the top of the mountain into the one who has achieved the goal. At the 12 o'clock hour, which corresponds to the Midheaven, or the top of the birth chart, exists the place where we access the Great Divine Director within.

Wherever Capricorn is in your birth chart, you have the greatest capacity to connect with the highest level of authority that you contain. This is the area of your consciousness that knows itself to have the command to create its experience; it is where you are highly empowered. If you have chosen the Capricorn identity for this lifetime, it is your evolutionary purpose to explore the principle of your own authority and empowerment for the entire course of your lifetime, and to activate it and take responsibility for it.

FAMOUS CAPRICORNS

Muhammed Ali, John Edgar Hoover, Mother Meera, Jeanne Dixon, Joe Frazier, Janis Joplin, Henri Matisse, Dolly Parton, Elvis Presley, Denzel Washington, Carlos Castaneda, Sir Isaac Newton, JRR Tolkien, Paramahansa Yogananda, Martin Luther King Jr., Jim Carrey, Ramana Maharshi

Spiritual Power

THURSDAY
12.22.2011

Balsamic

☽ IN ♏
☽ →♐: 7:03A
☽ VOC: 4:48A-7:03A {☉ □ ♆}
♃ IS R
☿ IN D SHADOW
☉→♑: 12:30A

☉ △ ♃ 00°♑/♉ 9:33A
☉ □ ♅ 01°♑/♈ 5:10P

4:4 STAR GATE/HIDDEN 11:11 STAR GATE

"I must govern the clock, not be governed by it."
                                              Golda Meir

8 AM	2 PM
9 AM	3 PM
10 AM	4 PM
11 AM	5 PM
12 PM	6 PM
1 PM	7 PM

Winter Solstice
Yule
First Day of Hanukkah

All times Eastern Standard Time

Spiritual Power

FRIDAY
12.23.2011

Balsamic

☽ IN ♐: ALL DAY
☽ VOC: NO
♃ IS R
☿ IN D SHADOW
HIDDEN 3:3 STAR GATE

☉ ✶ ♄ 02° ♑/♓ 12:49P

"Example is leadership."
Albert Schweitzer

8ᴬᴹ	2ᴾᴹ
9ᴬᴹ	3ᴾᴹ
10ᴬᴹ	4ᴾᴹ
11ᴬᴹ	5ᴾᴹ
12ᴾᴹ	6ᴾᴹ
1ᴾᴹ	7ᴾᴹ

December 2011

S	M	T	W	T	F	S
				1	2	3
4	5	6	7	8	9	10
11	12	13	14	15	16	17
18	19	20	21	22	23	24
25	26	27	28	29	30	31

January 2012

S	M	T	W	T	F	S
1	2	3	4	5	6	7
8	9	10	11	12	13	14
15	16	17	18	19	20	21
22	23	24	25	26	27	28
29	30	31				

Spiritual Power

SATURDAY
12.24.2011

New Moon

DEC

☽ IN ♐
☽ → ♑: 8:47A
☽ VOC: 5:03A - 8:47A {☽ ✶ ♄}
♃ IS STATIONING {D}
☿ IN D SHADOW
HIDDEN 4:4 STAR GATE

NEW MOON {☽ ☌ ☉}: 1:06P
02° ♑ 34'

> *"You are stronger than you think."*
> Linda O'Neill

8 AM	2 PM
9 AM	3 PM
10 AM	4 PM
11 AM	5 PM
12 PM	6 PM
1 PM	7 PM

All times Eastern Standard Time

Spiritual Power

SUNDAY
12.25.2011

New Moon

☽ IN ♑: ALL DAY
☽ VOC: NO
♃ STATION: 5:08P
♃ TURNS D: 0° ♉
☿ IN D SHADOW
HIDDEN 11:11 STAR GATE

> *"The Universe does not give you anything that you are not ready for."*
> Derek O'Neill

8ᴬᴹ	**2**ᴾᴹ
9ᴬᴹ	**3**ᴾᴹ
10ᴬᴹ	**4**ᴾᴹ
11ᴬᴹ	**5**ᴾᴹ
12ᴾᴹ	**6**ᴾᴹ
1ᴾᴹ	**7**ᴾᴹ

Christmas Day

S	M	T	W	T	F	S	S	M	T	W	T	F	S
December 2011			1	2	3		1	2	3	4	5	6	7
4	5	6	7	8	9	10	8	9	10	11	12	13	14
11	12	13	14	15	16	17	15	16	17	18	19	20	21
18	19	20	21	22	23	24	22	23	24	25	26	27	28
25	26	27	28	29	30	31	29	30	31		January 2012		

Spiritual Power

MONDAY
12.26.2011

Crescent

DEC

☽ IN ♑
☽ → ♒: 12:15P
☽ VOC: 8:36A - 12:15P { ☽ □ ♄ }
♃ HAS STATIONED {D}
☿ IN D SHADOW
ALL PLANETS ARE IN D MOTION
11:11 STAR GATE/HIDDEN 3:3 STAR GATE

"You cannot see me from where I look at myself."
Francesca Woodman

8^{AM}	2^{PM}
9^{AM}	3^{PM}
10^{AM}	4^{PM}
11^{AM}	5^{PM}
12^{PM}	6^{PM}
1^{PM}	7^{PM}

Kwanza Begins
Boxing Day

All times Eastern Standard Time

Spiritual Power

TUESDAY
12.27.2011

Crescent

☽ in ♒: All Day
☽ voc: No
☿ in ☽ Shadow
All Planets are in D Motion
Hidden 3:3/4:4/7:7 Star Gate

☿ ☌ ☊ 14° ♐ 8:39a
♀ ☍ ☋ 14° ♐/♊ 8:39a

> *"Now is the moment. Now is the time."*
> Archangel Gabriel

8ᴀᴍ	2ᴘᴍ
9ᴀᴍ	3ᴘᴍ
10ᴀᴍ	4ᴘᴍ
11ᴀᴍ	5ᴘᴍ
12ᴘᴍ	6ᴘᴍ
1ᴘᴍ	7ᴘᴍ

S	M	T	W	T	F	S	S	M	T	W	T	F	S
December 2011			1	2	3	1	2	3	4	5	6	7
4	5	6	7	8	9	10	8	9	10	11	12	13	14
11	12	13	14	15	16	17	15	16	17	18	19	20	21
18	19	20	21	22	23	24	22	23	24	25	26	27	28
25	26	27	28	29	30	31	29	30	31		January 2012		

Spiritual Power

WEDNESDAY
12.28.2011

Crescent

DEC

☽ IN ♒
☽ →♓: 6:46P
☽ VOC: 4:31P - 6:46P { ☽ ☍ ♆ }
☿ IN D SHADOW
ALL PLANETS ARE IN D MOTION
4:4 STAR GATE

> *"Conscience is God present in man."*
> Victor Hugo

8ᴀᴍ	2ᴘᴍ
9ᴀᴍ	3ᴘᴍ
10ᴀᴍ	4ᴘᴍ
11ᴀᴍ	5ᴘᴍ
12ᴘᴍ	6ᴘᴍ
1ᴘᴍ	7ᴘᴍ

All times Eastern Standard Time

Spiritual Power

THURSDAY
12.29.2011

Crescent

☽ in ♓: All Day
☽ voc: No
☿ in ☽ Shadow
All Planets are in D Motion
11:11 Star Gate/Hidden 5:5 Star Gate

☉ ☌ ♇ 07° ♑   2:42a

"What you are comes to you."
Ralph Waldo Emerson

8ᴀᴍ	2ᴘᴍ
9ᴀᴍ	3ᴘᴍ
10ᴀᴍ	4ᴘᴍ
11ᴀᴍ	5ᴘᴍ
12ᴘᴍ	6ᴘᴍ
1ᴘᴍ	7ᴘᴍ

S	M	T	W	T	F	S	S	M	T	W	T	F	S
December 2011			1	2	3	1	2	3	4	5	6	7
4	5	6	7	8	9	10	8	9	10	11	12	13	14
11	12	13	14	15	16	17	15	16	17	18	19	20	21
18	19	20	21	22	23	24	22	23	24	25	26	27	28
25	26	27	28	29	30	31	29	30	31		January 2012		

Spiritual Power

FRIDAY
12.30.2011

Crescent

☽ IN ♓: ALL DAY
☽ VOC: 8:38A - MIDNIGHT { ☽ ☍ ♂ }
☿ IN D SHADOW
ALL PLANETS ARE IN D MOTION
3:3 STAR GATE

"When the solution is simple, God is answering."
Albert Einstein

8ᴀᴍ	**2**ᴘᴍ
9ᴀᴍ	**3**ᴘᴍ
10ᴀᴍ	**4**ᴘᴍ
11ᴀᴍ	**5**ᴘᴍ
12ᴘᴍ	**6**ᴘᴍ
1ᴘᴍ	**7**ᴘᴍ

All times Eastern Standard Time

Spiritual Power

SATURDAY
12.31.2011

Crescent

☽ IN ♓
☽ →♈: 4:48A
☽ VOC: MIDNIGHT - 4:48A
☿ IN D SHADOW
ALL PLANETS ARE IN D MOTION
4:4 STAR GATE/HIDDEN 11:11 STAR GATE

♀ ✶ ☊ 14°♒/♐ 9:56P
♀ △ ☋ 14°♒/♊ 9:56P

"Act as if what you do makes a difference. It does."
William James

8ᴬᴹ	2ᴾᴹ
9ᴬᴹ	3ᴾᴹ
10ᴬᴹ	4ᴾᴹ
11ᴬᴹ	5ᴾᴹ
12ᴾᴹ	6ᴾᴹ
1ᴾᴹ	7ᴾᴹ

New Year's Eve

S	M	T	W	T	F	S	S	M	T	W	T	F	S
December 2011				1	2	3	1	2	3	4	5	6	7
4	5	6	7	8	9	10	8	9	10	11	12	13	14
11	12	13	14	15	16	17	15	16	17	18	19	20	21
18	19	20	21	22	23	24	22	23	24	25	26	27	28
25	26	27	28	29	30	31	29	30	31		January 2012		

SUNDAY
01.01.2012

First Quarter

JAN

☽ IN ♈: ALL DAY
☽ VOC: NO
☿ LEAVES ☽ SHADOW
ALL PLANETS ARE IN ☽ MOTION
1:1 STAR GATE

☿ ☐ ♂ 20°♐/♍ 1:06A

> *"When we realize that there is no difference between pleasure and pain, we become enlightened."*
>
> Derek O'Neill

8ᴬᴹ	**2**ᴾᴹ
9ᴬᴹ	**3**ᴾᴹ
10ᴬᴹ	**4**ᴾᴹ
11ᴬᴹ	**5**ᴾᴹ
12ᴾᴹ	**6**ᴾᴹ
1ᴾᴹ	**7**ᴾᴹ

New Year's Day
Kwanzaa Ends

All times Eastern Standard Time

Spiritual Power

MONDAY
01.02.2012

First Quarter

☽ IN ♈
☽ → ♉: 5:16P
☽ VOC: 3:06P - 5:16P { ☽ ✶ ♆ }
ALL PLANETS ARE IN D MOTION

> *"I believe that what people call God is something in all of us."*
>
> John Lennon

8 AM	2 PM
9 AM	3 PM
10 AM	4 PM
11 AM	5 PM
12 PM	6 PM
1 PM	7 PM

S	M	T	W	T	F	S		S	M	T	W	T	F	S
1	2	3	4	5	6	7	February 2012			1	2	3	4
8	9	10	11	12	13	14	5	6	7	8	9	10	11
15	16	17	18	19	20	21	12	13	14	15	16	17	18
22	23	24	25	26	27	28	19	20	21	22	23	24	25
29	30	31		January 2012			26	27	28	29			

Spiritual Power

TUESDAY
01.03.2012

First Quarter

☽ IN ♉: ALL DAY
☽ VOC: NO
ALL PLANETS ARE IN D MOTION

"I am what I choose to become."

Carl Jung

8 AM	2 PM
9 AM	3 PM
10 AM	4 PM
11 AM	5 PM
12 PM	6 PM
1 PM	7 PM

All times Eastern Standard Time

WEDNESDAY
01.04.2012

First Quarter

Spiritual Power

☽ IN ♉: ALL DAY
☽ VOC: NO
ALL PLANETS ARE IN D MOTION
5:5 STAR GATE

"Don't believe anything I say, find out for yourself."

Derek O'Neill

8 AM	2 PM
9 AM	3 PM
10 AM	4 PM
11 AM	5 PM
12 PM	6 PM
1 PM	7 PM

January 2012

S	M	T	W	T	F	S
1	2	3	4	5	6	7
8	9	10	11	12	13	14
15	16	17	18	19	20	21
22	23	24	25	26	27	28
29	30	31				

February 2012

S	M	T	W	T	F	S
			1	2	3	4
5	6	7	8	9	10	11
12	13	14	15	16	17	18
19	20	21	22	23	24	25
26	27	28	29			

Spiritual Power

THURSDAY
01.05.2012

Gibbous

JAN

☽ IN ♉
☽ →♊: 5:44A
☽ VOC: 3:46A - 5:44A { ☽ □ ♆ }
ALL PLANETS ARE IN D MOTION
5:5 STAR GATE

"Each one prays to God according to his own light."
Mahatma Gandhi

8 AM	2 PM
9 AM	3 PM
10 AM	4 PM
11 AM	5 PM
12 PM	6 PM
1 PM	7 PM

All times Eastern Standard Time

FRIDAY
01.06.2012

Spiritual Power 10

Gibbous

☽ IN ♊: ALL DAY
☽ VOC: NO
ALL PLANETS ARE IN D MOTION
5:5/6:6 STAR GATE

"Heaven means to be one with God."
Confucius

8AM	**2**PM
9AM	**3**PM
10AM	**4**PM
11AM	**5**PM
12PM	**6**PM
1PM	**7**PM

Epiphany

S	M	T	W	T	F	S		S	M	T	W	T	F	S
1	2	3	4	5	6	7	February 2012			1	2	3	4
8	9	10	11	12	13	14		5	6	7	8	9	10	11
15	16	17	18	19	20	21		12	13	14	15	16	17	18
22	23	24	25	26	27	28		19	20	21	22	23	24	25
29	30	31		January 2012				26	27	28	29			

Spiritual Power

SATURDAY
01.07.2012

Gibbous

JAN

☽ IN ♊
☽ → ♋: 4:05P
☽ VOC: 2:52P - 4:05P { ☽ ☌ ☿ }
ALL PLANETS ARE IN D MOTION

☿ ✶ ♄   29°♐/♎ 3:13A
☿ ✶ ♆   29°♐/♒ 10:15A

> *"We see the brightness of*
> *a new page where everything yet can happen."*
> — Rainer Maria Rilke

8ᴀᴍ	2ᴘᴍ
9ᴀᴍ	3ᴘᴍ
10ᴀᴍ	4ᴘᴍ
11ᴀᴍ	5ᴘᴍ
12ᴘᴍ	6ᴘᴍ
1ᴘᴍ	7ᴘᴍ

All times Eastern Standard Time

Spiritual Power

SUNDAY
01.08.2012

Gibbous

☽ IN ♋: ALL DAY
☽ VOC: NO
☿ →♑: 1:34A
ALL PLANETS ARE IN D MOTION
5:5 STAR GATE

☿ △ ♃ 01° ♑/♉ 1:05P
☿ □ ♅ 01° ♑/♈ 6:23P

"Shift your focus from what you want to what God wants."
— Derek O'Neill

8 AM	2 PM
9 AM	3 PM
10 AM	4 PM
11 AM	5 PM
12 PM	6 PM
1 PM	7 PM

S	M	T	W	T	F	S	S	M	T	W	T	F	S
1	2	3	4	5	6	7	February 2012		1	2	3	4
8	9	10	11	12	13	14	5	6	7	8	9	10	11
15	16	17	18	19	20	21	12	13	14	15	16	17	18
22	23	24	25	26	27	28	19	20	21	22	23	24	25
29	30	31		January 2012			26	27	28	29			

Spiritual Power

MONDAY
01.09.2012

Full Moon

JAN

☽ IN ♋
☽ → ♌: 11:35P
☽ VOC: 9:25P - 11:35P { ☽ □ ♄ }
ALL PLANETS ARE IN D MOTION
HIDDEN 1:1/5:5/6:6 STAR GATE

FULL MOON { ☽ ☍ ☉ }: 2:30A
18° ♋26'

☿ ✶ ♃ 02° ♑/♓ 4:13P

"You are very powerful, provided you know how powerful you are."

Yogi Bhajan

8ᴀᴍ	2ᴘᴍ
9ᴀᴍ	3ᴘᴍ
10ᴀᴍ	4ᴘᴍ
11ᴀᴍ	5ᴘᴍ
12ᴘᴍ	6ᴘᴍ
1ᴘᴍ	7ᴘᴍ

All times Eastern Standard Time

Spiritual Power

TUESDAY
01.10.2012

Full Moon

☽ IN ♌: ALL DAY
☽ VOC: NO
ALL PLANETS ARE IN D MOTION
1:1 STAR GATE

> *"It takes courage to grow up and turn out to be who you really are."*
>
> e.e. Cummings

8 AM	2 PM
9 AM	3 PM
10 AM	4 PM
11 AM	5 PM
12 PM	6 PM
1 PM	7 PM

S	M	T	W	T	F	S	S	M	T	W	T	F	S
1	2	3	4	5	6	7	February 2012		1	2	3	4
8	9	10	11	12	13	14	5	6	7	8	9	10	11
15	16	17	18	19	20	21	12	13	14	15	16	17	18
22	23	24	25	26	27	28	19	20	21	22	23	24	25
29	30	31		January 2012			26	27	28	29			

Spiritual Power

WEDNESDAY 01.11.2012

Full Moon

☽ IN ♌: ALL DAY
☽ VOC: NO
ALL PLANETS ARE IN D MOTION
12:12 STAR GATE

"Truth is my God. Non-violence is the means of realizing Him."

Mohandas Gandhi

8ᴀᴍ	2ᴘᴍ
9ᴀᴍ	3ᴘᴍ
10ᴀᴍ	4ᴘᴍ
11ᴀᴍ	5ᴘᴍ
12ᴘᴍ	6ᴘᴍ
1ᴘᴍ	7ᴘᴍ

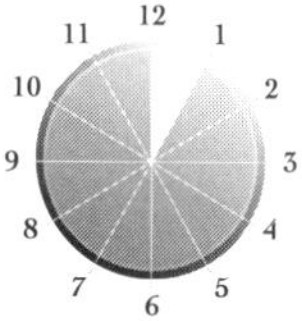

All times Eastern Standard Time

Spiritual Power

THURSDAY
01.12.2012

Disseminating

☽ in ♌
☽ → ♍: 4:44A
☽ voc: 3:23A - 4:44A { ☽ ☍ ♆ }
ALL PLANETS ARE IN D MOTION
12:12 STAR GATE

☉ △ ♂ 22°♑/ ♍ 11:46P

> *"What God intended for you goes far beyond anything you can imagine."*
>
> Oprah Winfrey

8AM	**2**PM
9AM	**3**PM
10AM	**4**PM
11AM	**5**PM
12PM	**6**PM
1PM	**7**PM

S	M	T	W	T	F	S	S	M	T	W	T	F	S
1	2	3	4	5	6	7	February 2012		1	2	3	4
8	9	10	11	12	13	14	5	6	7	8	9	10	11
15	16	17	18	19	20	21	12	13	14	15	16	17	18
22	23	24	25	26	27	28	19	20	21	22	23	24	25
29	30	31		January 2012			26	27	28	29			

Spiritual Power

FRIDAY
01.13.2012

Disseminating

☽ IN ♍: ALL DAY
☽ VOC: 8:58P - MIDNIGHT { ☽ △ ☉ }
ALL PLANETS ARE IN D MOTION
5:5 STAR GATE

♀ △ ♄ 29°♒/♎ 4:05A
☿ ☌ ♇ 08°♑   8:03A
♀ ☌ ♆ 29°♒   10:17A

"God has entrusted me with myself."

Epictetus

8ᴀᴍ	2ᴘᴍ
9ᴀᴍ	3ᴘᴍ
10ᴀᴍ	4ᴘᴍ
11ᴀᴍ	5ᴘᴍ
12ᴘᴍ	6ᴘᴍ
1ᴘᴍ	7ᴘᴍ

All times Eastern Standard Time

Spiritual Power

SATURDAY
01.14.2012

Disseminating

☽ IN ♍
☽ → ♎: 8:28A
☽ VOC: MIDNIGHT - 8:28A
♀ → ♓: 12:47A
ALL PLANETS ARE IN D MOTION
5:5 STAR GATE

♀ ✶ ♃   01° ♓/♉ 9:47P

"God helps those who help themselves."
Benjamin Franklin

8ᴀᴍ	2ᴘᴍ
9ᴀᴍ	3ᴘᴍ
10ᴀᴍ	4ᴘᴍ
11ᴀᴍ	5ᴘᴍ
12ᴘᴍ	6ᴘᴍ
1ᴘᴍ	7ᴘᴍ

S	M	T	W	T	F	S	S	M	T	W	T	F	S
1	2	3	4	5	6	7	February 2012		1	2	3	4
8	9	10	11	12	13	14	5	6	7	8	9	10	11
15	16	17	18	19	20	21	12	13	14	15	16	17	18
22	23	24	25	26	27	28	19	20	21	22	23	24	25
29	30	31		January 2012			26	27	28	29			

Spiritual Power

SUNDAY
01.15.2012

Disseminating

☽ IN ♎: ALL DAY
☽ VOC: NO
ALL PLANETS ARE IN D MOTION
HIDDEN 12:12 STAR GATE

> *"Churches are not built on rock or sand;*
> *churches are built on you."*
>
> Derek O'Neill

8ᴀᴍ	2ᴘᴍ
9ᴀᴍ	3ᴘᴍ
10ᴀᴍ	4ᴘᴍ
11ᴀᴍ	5ᴘᴍ
12ᴘᴍ	6ᴘᴍ
1ᴘᴍ	7ᴘᴍ

All times Eastern Standard Time

Spiritual Power

MONDAY
01.16.2012

Last Quarter

☽ in ♎
☽ → ♏: 11:34a
☽ voc: 10:29a - 11:34a { ☽ △ ♆ }
ALL PLANETS ARE IN D MOTION
HIDDEN 12:12 STAR GATES

♀ ☌ ☿ 03°♓   6:12a

"The highest revelation is that God is in every man."
Ralph Waldo Emerson

8ᴬᴹ	2ᴾᴹ
9ᴬᴹ	3ᴾᴹ
10ᴬᴹ	4ᴾᴹ
11ᴬᴹ	5ᴾᴹ
12ᴾᴹ	6ᴾᴹ
1ᴾᴹ	7ᴾᴹ

Martin Luther King Jr. Day

S	M	T	W	T	F	S
1	2	3	4	5	6	7
8	9	10	11	12	13	14
15	16	17	18	19	20	21
22	23	24	25	26	27	28
29	30	31				

January 2012

S	M	T	W	T	F	S
February 2012		1	2	3	4	
5	6	7	8	9	10	11
12	13	14	15	16	17	18
19	20	21	22	23	24	25
26	27	28	29			

Spiritual Power

TUESDAY
01.17.2012

Last Quarter

☽ IN ♏: ALL DAY
☽ VOC: NO
ALL PLANETS ARE IN D MOTION
5:5 STAR GATE

> *"To be truly happy you must recognize who you are with nothing."*
>
> Gangaji

8 AM	2 PM
9 AM	3 PM
10 AM	4 PM
11 AM	5 PM
12 PM	6 PM
1 PM	7 PM

All times Eastern Standard Time

Spiritual Power

WEDNESDAY
01.18.2012

Last Quarter

☽ IN ♏
☽ →♐: 2:29P
☽ VOC: 1:31P - 2:29P { ☽ □ ♆ }
ALL PLANETS ARE IN D MOTION
5:5 STAR GATE

> *"Strength, courage and wisdom, it's been inside of me all along."*
>
> India Arie

8 AM	2 PM
9 AM	3 PM
10 AM	4 PM
11 AM	5 PM
12 PM	6 PM
1 PM	7 PM

S	M	T	W	T	F	S	S	M	T	W	T	F	S
1	2	3	4	5	6	7	February 2012		1	2	3	4
8	9	10	11	12	13	14	5	6	7	8	9	10	11
15	16	17	18	19	20	21	12	13	14	15	16	17	18
22	23	24	25	26	27	28	19	20	21	22	23	24	25
29	30	31		January 2012			26	27	28	29			

Spiritual Power

THURSDAY
01.19.2012

Last Quarter

☽ IN ♐: ALL DAY
☽ VOC: NO
ALL PLANETS ARE IN D MOTION
1:1 STAR GATE

> *"Life stands for
> Look Inside For Everything."*
>
> Derek O'Neill

8AM	**2**PM
9AM	**3**PM
10AM	**4**PM
11AM	**5**PM
12PM	**6**PM
1PM	**7**PM

All times Eastern Standard Time

AQUARIUS

Spiritual Love

Symbol: The Great Awakener
Master: St. Germaine
Quality: Divine Love
Ray: 1st Ray, Scarlet Red
Trine: Air
Hour: 1
Rulers: ♅ ♇ ♆

12 1 2 3 4

I AM ONE WITH ALL

Spiritual Love

1 O'Clock Hour
Main Purpose:
Where you work with the experience of Oneness and your capacity to Love your Self as Source Loves.

JANUARY 20 - FEBRUARY 18

In Cosmic Astrology, Aquarius is the sign of **Divine Love**, where Love is experienced as unconditional and endlessly abundant. Here you learn to access this higher Love and direct it toward your Self, the way Source does. This aspect of your consciousness then, is about recognizing and loving the highest aspect of your Self. In this part of your consciousness you are always expanding into your capacity to be the Love you are. Aquarius is the sign of the Great Awakener, and the soul capable of waking humanity is already awakened. In Aquarius we have moved from the 3D water bearer archetype, who pours consciousness out to humanity, to the 5D Great Awakener who is fully conscious and understands that Love is all there is.

Under this new cosmic system, Aquarius is a part of the conscious energy field that relates to Spiritual Love. It is expressed in the 1 o'clock hour, which corresponds to the 8th house of the birth chart, where sharing one's Self as freely and fully as possible is the higher purpose. In the 8th house we all experience the depth of sharing, but when the cosmic purpose comes into play, all experience is about the Self. Great transformation occurs in this aspect of consciousness, which is overseen by the great St. Germaine and his Violet Flame. Alchemy is a natural occurrence here.

Wherever Aquarius is in your birth chart you have the potential to allow your heart its fullest expression. This is the area of your consciousness that knows how vital it is to Love and be Loved; it is where you are highly motivated to share your truth openly. If your Sun sign is Aquarius, you have chosen the Aquarius identity for your lifetime and it is your evolutionary purpose to learn to Love yourself completely by working to take down the defenses that cause you to hide your authentic Self from the world. You are here to learn to have an experience of true intimacy by allowing all that you are to be seen and shared.

FAMOUS AQUARIANS

Justin Timberlake, Abraham Lincoln, Yoko Ono, Sir Francis Bacon, Alfred Adler, Neil Diamond, Christian Dior, Mia Farrow, Farrah Fawcett, Peter Gabriel, Benny Hill, Jimmy Hoffa, Wolfgang A. Mozart, Paul Newman, Jack Nicklaus, Leontyne Price, Vanessa Redgrave, Galileo, John Travolta, Oprah Winfrey, Thomas Edison

Spiritual Love

FRIDAY
01.20.2012

Balsamic

☽ IN ♐
☽ →♑: 5:40P
☽ VOC: 4:49P - 5:40P { ☽ ✶ ♆ }
☉ → ♒: 11:10A
ALL PLANETS ARE IN D MOTION
3:3 STAR GATE

♀ ✶ ♇ 08°♓/♑ 3:32P

"The most terrifying thing is to accept oneself completely."
                                                    Carl Jung

8 AM	2 PM
9 AM	3 PM
10 AM	4 PM
11 AM	5 PM
12 PM	6 PM
1 PM	7 PM

All times Eastern Standard Time

Spiritual Love

SATURDAY
01.21.2012

Balsamic

☽ in ♑: All Day ☉ ✶ ♅ 01° ♒/ ♈ 8:20p
☽ voc: no
All Planets are in D Motion
3:3 Star Gate

"He that falls in love with himself will have no rivals."

Benjamin Franklin

8ᴀᴍ	2ᴘᴍ
9ᴀᴍ	3ᴘᴍ
10ᴀᴍ	4ᴘᴍ
11ᴀᴍ	5ᴘᴍ
12ᴘᴍ	6ᴘᴍ
1ᴘᴍ	7ᴘᴍ

S	M	T	W	T	F	S		S	M	T	W	T	F	S
1	2	3	4	5	6	7		February 2012		1	2	3	4
8	9	10	11	12	13	14		5	6	7	8	9	10	11
15	16	17	18	19	20	21		12	13	14	15	16	17	18
22	23	24	25	26	27	28		19	20	21	22	23	24	25
29	30	31		January 2012				26	27	28	29			

Spiritual Love

SUNDAY
01.22.2012

Balsamic

JAN

☽ IN ♑
☽ → ♒: 9:53P
☽ VOC: 8:38P - 9:53P { ☽ □ ♄ }
ALL PLANETS ARE IN D MOTION
5:5 STAR GATE

☉ □ ♃ 02°♒/ ♉ 1:35A

"There is only one teacher, the teacher within."

Derek O'Neill

8ᴀᴍ	**2**ᴘᴍ
9ᴀᴍ	**3**ᴘᴍ
10ᴀᴍ	**4**ᴘᴍ
11ᴀᴍ	**5**ᴘᴍ
12ᴘᴍ	**6**ᴘᴍ
1ᴘᴍ	**7**ᴘᴍ

All times Eastern Standard Time

Spiritual Love

MONDAY
01.23.2012

New Moon

☽ IN ♒: ALL DAY
☽ VOC: NO
♂ STATION: 7:54P
♂ TURNS R: 23° ♍
5:5 STAR GATE

NEW MOON { ☽ ☌ ☉ }: 2:39A
02° ♒42'

☿ △ ♂ 23° ♑/ ♍ 6:15A

> *"You yourself, as much as anybody in the entire universe, deserve your love and affection."*
>
> Gautama Buddha

8ᴬᴹ	2ᴾᴹ
9ᴬᴹ	3ᴾᴹ
10ᴬᴹ	4ᴾᴹ
11ᴬᴹ	5ᴾᴹ
12ᴾᴹ	6ᴾᴹ
1ᴾᴹ	7ᴾᴹ

Chinese New Year: Dragon

S	M	T	W	T	F	S		S	M	T	W	T	F	S
1	2	3	4	5	6	7		February 2012		1	2	3	4	
8	9	10	11	12	13	14		5	6	7	8	9	10	11
15	16	17	18	19	20	21		12	13	14	15	16	17	18
22	23	24	25	26	27	28		19	20	21	22	23	24	25
29	30	31		January 2012				26	27	28	29			

Spiritual Love

TUESDAY
01.24.2012

New Moon

☽ IN ♒: ALL DAY ♂ IS R ♀ □ ☊ 13°♓/♐ 7:08P
☽ VOC: NO ♀ □ ☋ 13°♓/♊ 7:08P
12:12 STAR GATE

"The privilege of a lifetime is being who you are."

Joseph Campbell

8ᴀᴍ	2ᴘᴍ
9ᴀᴍ	3ᴘᴍ
10ᴀᴍ	4ᴘᴍ
11ᴀᴍ	5ᴘᴍ
12ᴘᴍ	6ᴘᴍ
1ᴘᴍ	7ᴘᴍ

All times Eastern Standard Time

WEDNESDAY
01.25.2012

Spiritual Love

Crescent

☽ IN ♒   ♂ IS R
☽ →♓: 4:11A
☽ VOC: 3:33A - 4:11A { ☽ ☍ ♆ }
HIDDEN 12:12 STAR GATE

"I don't like myself, I'm crazy about myself."

Mae West

8AM	**2**PM
9AM	**3**PM
10AM	**4**PM
11AM	**5**PM
12PM	**6**PM
1PM	**7**PM

S	M	T	W	T	F	S		S	M	T	W	T	F	S
1	2	3	4	5	6	7	February 2012			1	2	3	4
8	9	10	11	12	13	14		5	6	7	8	9	10	11
15	16	17	18	19	20	21		12	13	14	15	16	17	18
22	23	24	25	26	27	28		19	20	21	22	23	24	25
29	30	31		January 2012				26	27	28	29			

Spiritual Love

THURSDAY
01.26.2012

Crescent

JAN

☽ IN ♓: ALL DAY   ♂ IS R
☽ VOC: 11:52P - MIDNIGHT { ☽ ☍ ♂ }
HIDDEN 5:5 STAR GATE

"Whatever you are doing, love yourself for doing it.
Whatever you are feeling, love yourself for feeling it."

Thaddeus Golas

8ᴬᴹ	**2**ᴾᴹ
9ᴬᴹ	**3**ᴾᴹ
10ᴬᴹ	**4**ᴾᴹ
11ᴬᴹ	**5**ᴾᴹ
12ᴾᴹ	**6**ᴾᴹ
1ᴾᴹ	**7**ᴾᴹ

All times Eastern Standard Time

Spiritual Love

FRIDAY
01.27.2012

Crescent

☽ IN ♓ ♂ IS R ☿ □ ♄ 29°♑/♎ 4:19A
☽ →♈: 1:28P
☽ VOC: MIDNIGHT - 1:28P
☿ →♒: 1:12P
HIDDEN 5:5 STAR GATE

"I celebrate myself, and sing myself."
— Walt Whitman

8 AM	2 PM
9 AM	3 PM
10 AM	4 PM
11 AM	5 PM
12 PM	6 PM
1 PM	7 PM

S	M	T	W	T	F	S	S	M	T	W	T	F	S
1	2	3	4	5	6	7	February 2012		1	2	3	4
8	9	10	11	12	13	14	5	6	7	8	9	10	11
15	16	17	18	19	20	21	12	13	14	15	16	17	18
22	23	24	25	26	27	28	19	20	21	22	23	24	25
29	30	31		January 2012			26	27	28	29			

Spiritual Love

SATURDAY
01.28.2012

Crescent

☽ IN ♈: ALL DAY 　　　♂ IS R 　　　☿ ✶ ♅ 02°♒/♈ 1:26P
☽ VOC: NO 　　　　　　　　　　　　☿ □ ♃ 02°♒/♉ 11:08P
1:1 STAR GATE

"Nobody can make you feel inferior without your consent."

Eleanor Roosevelt

8ᴬᴹ	2ᴾᴹ
9ᴬᴹ	3ᴾᴹ
10ᴬᴹ	4ᴾᴹ
11ᴬᴹ	5ᴾᴹ
12ᴾᴹ	6ᴾᴹ
1ᴾᴹ	7ᴾᴹ

All times Eastern Standard Time

Spiritual Love

SUNDAY
01.29.2012

Crescent

☽ IN ♈: ALL DAY   ♂ IS R
☽ VOC: NO
☿ →♐: 9:13A
1:1 STAR GATE

> "Our purpose in life is to offer all we are to ourself, through ourself, by ourself, and to know ourself for who we are."
>
> Derek O'Neill

8 AM	2 PM
9 AM	3 PM
10 AM	4 PM
11 AM	5 PM
12 PM	6 PM
1 PM	7 PM

S	M	T	W	T	F	S	S	M	T	W	T	F	S
1	2	3	4	5	6	7	February 2012		1	2	3	4
8	9	10	11	12	13	14	5	6	7	8	9	10	11
15	16	17	18	19	20	21	12	13	14	15	16	17	18
22	23	24	25	26	27	28	19	20	21	22	23	24	25
29	30	31		January 2012			26	27	28	29			

Spiritual Love

MONDAY
01.30.2012

Crescent

JAN

☽ IN ♈ ♂ IS R
☽ → ♉: 1:28A
☽ VOC: 1:08A - 1:28A { ☽ ✷ ♆ }
3:3 STAR GATE

> "When people believe in themselves they have
> the first secret of success."
>
> Norman Vincent Peale

8ᴀᴍ	2ᴘᴍ
9ᴀᴍ	3ᴘᴍ
10ᴀᴍ	4ᴘᴍ
11ᴀᴍ	5ᴘᴍ
12ᴘᴍ	6ᴘᴍ
1ᴘᴍ	7ᴘᴍ

All times Eastern Standard Time

Spiritual Love

TUESDAY
01.31.2012

First Quarter

☽ IN ♉: ALL DAY
☽ VOC: NO
5:5 STAR GATE

♂ IS R

"I tore myself away from the safe comfort of certainties through my love for truth - and truth rewarded me."

Simone de Beauvoir

8ᴀᴍ	2ᴘᴍ
9ᴀᴍ	3ᴘᴍ
10ᴀᴍ	4ᴘᴍ
11ᴀᴍ	5ᴘᴍ
12ᴘᴍ	6ᴘᴍ
1ᴘᴍ	7ᴘᴍ

S	M	T	W	T	F	S		S	M	T	W	T	F	S
February 2012			1	2	3	4		March 2012				1	2	3
5	6	7	8	9	10	11		4	5	6	7	8	9	10
12	13	14	15	16	17	18		11	12	13	14	15	16	17
19	20	21	22	23	24	25		18	19	20	21	22	23	24
26	27	28	29					25	26	27	28	29	30	31

Spiritual Love

WEDNESDAY
02.01.2012

First Quarter

☽ IN ♉
♂ IS R
☉ ✶ ☊ 12°♒/♐ 4:48P

☽ →♊: 2:14P
☉ △ ☋ 12°♒/♊ 4:48P

☽ VOC: 2:05P - 2:14P { ☽ □ ♆ }
♀ ☍ ♂ 23°♓/♍ 6:41P

3:3 STAR GATE

"It's not your job to like me...it's MINE!"
                              Byron Katie

8ᴀᴍ	2ᴘᴍ
9ᴀᴍ	3ᴘᴍ
10ᴀᴍ	4ᴘᴍ
11ᴀᴍ	5ᴘᴍ
12ᴘᴍ	6ᴘᴍ
1ᴘᴍ	7ᴘᴍ

Imbolic
St. Brigid's Day
Candlemas

All times Eastern Standard Time

Spiritual Love

THURSDAY
02.02.2012

First Quarter

☽ in ♊: All Day
☽ voc: no
2:2 Star Gate

♂ is R

"Yours is the energy that makes your world. There are no limitations to the self except those you believe in."

Jane Roberts

8 AM	2 PM
9 AM	3 PM
10 AM	4 PM
11 AM	5 PM
12 PM	6 PM
1 PM	7 PM

Groundhog Day

	S	M	T	W	T	F	S
February 2012				1	2	3	4
	5	6	7	8	9	10	11
	12	13	14	15	16	17	18
	19	20	21	22	23	24	25
	26	27	28	29			

	S	M	T	W	T	F	S
March 2012					1	2	3
	4	5	6	7	8	9	10
	11	12	13	14	15	16	17
	18	19	20	21	22	23	24
	25	26	27	28	29	30	31

Spiritual Love

FRIDAY
02.03.2012

First Quarter

☽ IN ♊: ALL DAY
☽ VOC: NO
♆ →♓: 2:03P
3:3/5:5 STAR GATE

♂ IS R

☿ ✶ ♌ 12°♒/♐ 11:13P
☿ △ ☊ 12°♒/♊ 11:13P

FEB

"Love is the outreach of self toward completion."
Ralph W. Sockman

8ᴬᴹ	2ᴾᴹ
9ᴬᴹ	3ᴾᴹ
10ᴬᴹ	4ᴾᴹ
11ᴬᴹ	5ᴾᴹ
12ᴾᴹ	6ᴾᴹ
1ᴾᴹ	7ᴾᴹ

All times Eastern Standard Time

Spiritual Love

SATURDAY
02.04.2012

Gibbous

☽ in ♊︎   ♂ is R

☽ → ♋︎: 1:03A
☽ voc: 12:06P - 1:03A { ☽ △ ♄ }
♄ is stationing {R}

> *"The greatest magnifying glasses in the world are a man's own eyes when they look upon his own person."*
>
> Alexander Pope

8AM	2PM
9AM	3PM
10AM	4PM
11AM	5PM
12PM	6PM
1PM	7PM

S	M	T	W	T	F	S
February 2012			1	2	3	4
5	6	7	8	9	10	11
12	13	14	15	16	17	18
19	20	21	22	23	24	25
26	27	28	29			

S	M	T	W	T	F	S
March 2012				1	2	3
4	5	6	7	8	9	10
11	12	13	14	15	16	17
18	19	20	21	22	23	24
25	26	27	28	29	30	31

Spiritual Love

SUNDAY
02.05.2012

Gibbous

☽ IN ♋: ALL DAY   ♂ IS R
☽ VOC: NO
♄ IS STATIONING {R}
5:5 STAR GATE/HIDDEN 5:5 STAR GATE

"Whatever you are doing that brings you love, give it away."

Derek O'Neill

8AM	**2**PM
9AM	**3**PM
10AM	**4**PM
11AM	**5**PM
12PM	**6**PM
1PM	**7**PM

All times Eastern Standard Time

Spiritual Love

MONDAY
02.06.2012

Gibbous

☽ IN ♋
☽ →♌: 8:24A
☽ VOC: 7:31A - 8:24A { ☽ □ ♄ }
♄ IS STATIONING {R}

♂ IS R

"Your chances of success in any undertaking can always be measured by your belief in yourself."

Robert Collier

8ᴀᴍ	2ᴘᴍ
9ᴀᴍ	3ᴘᴍ
10ᴀᴍ	4ᴘᴍ
11ᴀᴍ	5ᴘᴍ
12ᴘᴍ	6ᴘᴍ
1ᴘᴍ	7ᴘᴍ

S	M	T	W	T	F	S	S	M	T	W	T	F	S
February 2012			1	2	3	4	March 2012				1	2	3
5	6	7	8	9	10	11	4	5	6	7	8	9	10
12	13	14	15	16	17	18	11	12	13	14	15	16	17
19	20	21	22	23	24	25	18	19	20	21	22	23	24
26	27	28	29				25	26	27	28	29	30	31

Spiritual Love

TUESDAY
02.07.2012

Full Moon

☽ IN ♌: ALL DAY   ♂ IS R   FULL MOON { ☽ ☍ ☉ }: 4:54P
☽ VOC: NO   18° ♌ 32'
♄ STATIONS: 9:03A
♄ TURNS R: 29° ♎   ☉ ☌ ☿ 18° ♒   04:02A
7:7 STAR GATE/HIDDEN 5:5 STAR GATE

FEB

> *"It is our privilege and our adventure to discover our own special light."*
>
> — Mary Dunbar

8 AM	2 PM
9 AM	3 PM
10 AM	4 PM
11 AM	5 PM
12 PM	6 PM
1 PM	7 PM

All times Eastern Standard Time

Spiritual Love

WEDNESDAY
02.08.2012

Full Moon

☾ IN ♌   ♂ IS R
☾ → ♍: 12:33P
☾ VOC: 11:42A - 12:33P { ☾ ✶ ♄ }
♄ HAS STATIONED {R}
♀ → ♈: 1:01A

> *"Appreciation and self-love are the most important tools that you could ever nurture."*
>
> Abraham

8 AM	2 PM
9 AM	3 PM
10 AM	4 PM
11 AM	5 PM
12 PM	6 PM
1 PM	7 PM

Parinirvana
Nirvana Day
Tu Bishvat

S	M	T	W	T	F	S
February 2012			1	2	3	4
5	6	7	8	9	10	11
12	13	14	15	16	17	18
19	20	21	22	23	24	25
26	27	28	29			

S	M	T	W	T	F	S
March 2012				1	2	3
4	5	6	7	8	9	10
11	12	13	14	15	16	17
18	19	20	21	22	23	24
25	26	27	28	29	30	31

Spiritual Love

≈≈ **THURSDAY**
02.09.2012

Full Moon

FEB

☽ IN ♍: ALL DAY
☽ VOC: NO
HIDDEN 2:2/5:5 STAR GATE

♄ IS R
♂ IS R

♀ ☌ ♅ 02°♈ 9:29P

*"Compare not yourself with anybody
else lest you spoil God's curriculum."*
Rabbi Israel ben Eliezer

8ᴬᴹ	2ᴾᴹ
9ᴬᴹ	3ᴾᴹ
10ᴬᴹ	4ᴾᴹ
11ᴬᴹ	5ᴾᴹ
12ᴾᴹ	6ᴾᴹ
1ᴾᴹ	7ᴾᴹ

All times Eastern Standard Time

Spiritual Love

FRIDAY
02.10.2012

Full Moon

☽ IN ♍
☽ →♎: 2:54P
☽ VOC: 12:12A - 2:54P { ☽ ☌ ♂ }
12:12 STAR GATE

♄ IS R
♂ IS R

*"The snow goose need not bathe to make itself white.
Neither need you do anything but be yourself."*

Lao-Tzu

8ᴬᴹ	2ᴾᴹ
9ᴬᴹ	3ᴾᴹ
10ᴬᴹ	4ᴾᴹ
11ᴬᴹ	5ᴾᴹ
12ᴾᴹ	6ᴾᴹ
1ᴾᴹ	7ᴾᴹ

S	M	T	W	T	F	S		S	M	T	W	T	F	S
February 2012			1	2	3	4	March 2012					1	2	3
5	6	7	8	9	10	11		4	5	6	7	8	9	10
12	13	14	15	16	17	18		11	12	13	14	15	16	17
19	20	21	22	23	24	25		18	19	20	21	22	23	24
26	27	28	29					25	26	27	28	29	30	31

Spiritual Love

SATURDAY
02.11.2012

Disseminating

☽ IN ♎: ALL DAY
☽ VOC: NO

♄ IS R
♂ IS R

> *"Self-love is the basis of all love."*
> — Thomas Traherne

8ᴀᴍ	2ᴘᴍ
9ᴀᴍ	3ᴘᴍ
10ᴀᴍ	4ᴘᴍ
11ᴀᴍ	5ᴘᴍ
12ᴘᴍ	6ᴘᴍ
1ᴘᴍ	7ᴘᴍ

All times Eastern Standard Time

Spiritual Love

SUNDAY
02.12.2012

Disseminating

☽ IN ♎
☽ →♏: 5:01P
☽ VOC: 4:09P - 5:01P { ☽ ☌ ♄ }
♀ →♓: 12:05A
12:12 STAR GATE

♄ IS R
♂ IS R

> *"Too many people overvalue what they are not and undervalue what they are."*
>
> Malcolm S. Forbes

8ᴀᴍ	2ᴘᴍ
9ᴀᴍ	3ᴘᴍ
10ᴀᴍ	4ᴘᴍ
11ᴀᴍ	5ᴘᴍ
12ᴘᴍ	6ᴘᴍ
1ᴘᴍ	7ᴘᴍ

S	M	T	W	T	F	S	S	M	T	W	T	F	S
February 2012			1	2	3	4	March 2012				1	2	3
5	6	7	8	9	10	11	4	5	6	7	8	9	10
12	13	14	15	16	17	18	11	12	13	14	15	16	17
19	20	21	22	23	24	25	18	19	20	21	22	23	24
26	27	28	29				25	26	27	28	29	30	31

Spiritual Love

MONDAY
02.13.2012

Disseminating

☽ IN ♏: ALL DAY   ♄ IS R   ☿ △ ♄ 29°♒/♎ 1:44P
☽ VOC: NO   ♂ IS R
☿ →♓: 8:38P

HIDDEN 2:2 STAR GATE

"Where love is, there God is also."
Mohandas Gandhi

8ᴀᴍ	2ᴘᴍ
9ᴀᴍ	3ᴘᴍ
10ᴀᴍ	4ᴘᴍ
11ᴀᴍ	5ᴘᴍ
12ᴘᴍ	6ᴘᴍ
1ᴘᴍ	7ᴘᴍ

All times Eastern Standard Time

Spiritual Love

TUESDAY
02.14.2012

Last Quarter

☽ IN ♏
☽ →♐: 7:56P
☽ VOC: 12:04P - 7:56P { ☽ □ ☉ }
5:5 STAR GATE

♄ IS R
♂ IS R

☿ ☌ ♆ 00°♓ 1:47A
♃ ✶ ☍ 05°♉/♓ 8:41P

"The way you treat yourself sets the standard for others."
Sonya Friedman

8 AM	2 PM
9 AM	3 PM
10 AM	4 PM
11 AM	5 PM
12 PM	6 PM
1 PM	7 PM

Valentine's Day

S	M	T	W	T	F	S
February 2012			1	2	3	4
5	6	7	8	9	10	11
12	13	14	15	16	17	18
19	20	21	22	23	24	25
26	27	28	29			

S	M	T	W	T	F	S
March 2012				1	2	3
4	5	6	7	8	9	10
11	12	13	14	15	16	17
18	19	20	21	22	23	24
25	26	27	28	29	30	31

Spiritual Love

WEDNESDAY
02.15.2012

Last Quarter

FEB

☽ IN ♐: ALL DAY
☽ VOC: NO
2:2 STAR GATE

♄ IS R
♂ IS R

♀ □ ♇ 09°♈/♑ 1:32P

"By being yourself, you put something wonderful in the world that was not there before."

Edwin Elliot

8AM	**2**PM
9AM	**3**PM
10AM	**4**PM
11AM	**5**PM
12PM	**6**PM
1PM	**7**PM

All times Eastern Standard Time

Spiritual Love

THURSDAY
02.16.2012

Last Quarter

☽ IN ♐: ALL DAY
☽ VOC: 11:03P - MIDNIGHT { ☽ ✷ ♄ }
HIDDEN 5:5/12:12 STAR GATE

♄ IS R
♂ IS R

☿ ☌ ♇ 05°♓ 9:14A
☿ ✷ ♃ 05°♓/♉ 11:07A

"You are as amazing as you let yourself be."
Elizabeth Alraune

8AM	**2**PM
9AM	**3**PM
10AM	**4**PM
11AM	**5**PM
12PM	**6**PM
1PM	**7**PM

S	M	T	W	T	F	S		S	M	T	W	T	F	S
February 2012			1	2	3	4		March 2012				1	2	3
5	6	7	8	9	10	11		4	5	6	7	8	9	10
12	13	14	15	16	17	18		11	12	13	14	15	16	17
19	20	21	22	23	24	25		18	19	20	21	22	23	24
26	27	28	29					25	26	27	28	29	30	31

Spiritual Love

FRIDAY
02.17.2012

Last Quarter

FEB

☽ IN ♐
☽ → ♑: 12:03A
☽ VOC: MIDNIGHT - 12:03A

♄ IS R
♂ IS R

♀ △ ☊ 11° ♈/♐ 2:10P
♀ ✶ ☋ 11° ♈/♐ 2:10P

"There is a divine and infinite potential within every soul."

K. Allen Kay

8ᴀᴍ	2ᴘᴍ
9ᴀᴍ	3ᴘᴍ
10ᴀᴍ	4ᴘᴍ
11ᴀᴍ	5ᴘᴍ
12ᴘᴍ	6ᴘᴍ
1ᴘᴍ	7ᴘᴍ

All times Eastern Standard Time

Spiritual Love

SATURDAY
02.18.2012

Last Quarter

☽ IN ♐: ALL DAY
☽ VOC: NO
HIDDEN 2:2/5:5 STAR GATE

♄ IS R
♂ IS R

☉ △ ♄ 29°♒/♎ 11:02P
☿ ✶ ♇ 09°♓/♑ 4:23P

"When you show self-compassion, it expands outwards."
Derek O'Neill

8AM	**2**PM
9AM	**3**PM
10AM	**4**PM
11AM	**5**PM
12PM	**6**PM
1PM	**7**PM

S	M	T	W	T	F	S	S	M	T	W	T	F	S
February 2012			1	2	3	4	March 2012				1	2	3
5	6	7	8	9	10	11	4	5	6	7	8	9	10
12	13	14	15	16	17	18	11	12	13	14	15	16	17
19	20	21	22	23	24	25	18	19	20	21	22	23	24
26	27	28	29				25	26	27	28	29	30	31

PISCES

Spiritual Wisdom

♓

Symbol: The Ocean of Consciousness
Master: Jesus
Quality: Divine Mastery
Ray: 2nd Ray, Rose-Pink/Aqua-Blue
Trine: Water
Hour: 2
Rulers: ♆ ♀ ♃

12 1 2 3 4

I AM THE CREATOR

Spiritual Wisdom

2 O'Clock Hour
Main Purpose:

Where you work on expanding into universal consciousness.

FEBRUARY 19 – MARCH 19

Pisces is the sign of **Divine Mastery**, and it is here that you learn to be all that you are meant to be. In this part of your energy field you can find the inner territory that you have not had access to before. You go above and beyond, deeper and deeper still; and eventually realize that your inner landscape is as limitless as the cosmos appears to be. In the Cosmic Astrology system, Pisces represents the ocean of consciousness, which is an infinite field of possibilities. You must explore the vastness of your being on a continual basis if you are to have the experience of Knowing your Self. It is here in the Piscean aspect of your consciousness that you fathom all that you are. You encounter your self-imposed limitations and learn to go beyond them to experience your limitless Self. It is here that the 3D duality of the two fishes swimming in opposite directions becomes the entire ocean in which the duality exists. This is where integrating duality becomes possible.

Pisces is the 2 o'clock hour on the cosmic clock, and it corresponds to the 7th house of the birth chart. The 7th house is where you experience your significant relationships, which provide the mirror for you to Self-realize, that is to understand that everything 'out there' is a reflection of your own consciousness. Relationships provide the opportunity to transcend duality at all times. This is the true beginning of Mastery, to take responsibility for all that you experience and come to know your Self according to what you Create.

Wherever Pisces is in your birth chart you must find the freedom to go deeply into your own core motivations to realize yourself more fully than ever before. Pisces is often referred to as 'selfless,' because it is difficult for the sign of universal consciousness to locate its self in the Oneness of everything. Yet that is exactly what this field of consciousness offers. If your Sun sign is Pisces it is your soul's intention to explore all the limitless uncharted territory that you contain within you, without doubting your greatness or holding too tightly to your past. You are here to master your Self by knowing your Self as fully as possible.

FAMOUS PISCEANS

Elizabeth Taylor, Tammy Faye Bakker, Drew Barrymore, Alexander Graham Bell, W.H. Auden, Glenn Close, Kurt Cobain, Albert Einstein, Chaz Bono, Ron L. Hubbard, Quincy Jones, Ted Kennedy, Jane Goodall, Rupert Murdoch, Steve Jobs, George Harrison, Nicolaus Copernicus, Rudolf Nureyev, Johnny Cash

Spiritual Wisdom ♓

SUNDAY
02.19.2012

Balsamic

☽ IN ♑
☽ →♒: 5:28A
☽ VOC: 4:22A - 5:28A {☽ □ ♄}
☉ →♓: 1:18A
12:12 STAR GATE

♄ IS R
♂ IS R

☉ ☌ ♆ 01° ♓ 3:41P
☿ □ ☊ 11° ♓/♐ 6:36P
♀ □ ☋ 11° ♓/♊ 6:36P

FEB

> "The only way to empower yourself
> is to be absolutely honest."
>
> Derek O'Neill

8ᴀᴍ	2ᴘᴍ
9ᴀᴍ	3ᴘᴍ
10ᴀᴍ	4ᴘᴍ
11ᴀᴍ	5ᴘᴍ
12ᴘᴍ	6ᴘᴍ
1ᴘᴍ	7ᴘᴍ

All times Eastern Standard Time

MONDAY
02.20.2012

Balsamic

☽ IN ♒: ALL DAY
☽ VOC: NO
2:2 STAR GATE

♄ IS R
♂ IS R

"If you surrender to the wind, you can ride it."
— Toni Morrison

8ᴀᴍ	**2**ᴘᴍ
9ᴀᴍ	**3**ᴘᴍ
10ᴀᴍ	**4**ᴘᴍ
11ᴀᴍ	**5**ᴘᴍ
12ᴘᴍ	**6**ᴘᴍ
1ᴘᴍ	**7**ᴘᴍ

President's Day
Maha Shivratri

S	M	T	W	T	F	S		S	M	T	W	T	F	S
1	2	3	4	5	6	7		February 2012		1	2	3	4	
8	9	10	11	12	13	14		5	6	7	8	9	10	11
15	16	17	18	19	20	21		12	13	14	15	16	17	18
22	23	24	25	26	27	28		19	20	21	22	23	24	25
29	30	31		January 2012				26	27	28	29			

Spiritual Wisdom ♓

TUESDAY
02.21.2012

New Moon

☽ IN ♒
☽ →♓: 12:31P
☽ VOC: 11:17A - 12:31P { ☽ △ ♄ }
3:3/5:5 Star Gate

♄ IS R
♂ IS R

NEW MOON { ☽ ☌ ☉ }: 5:35P
02° ♓42'

"The important thing is this: To be able at any moment to sacrifice that which we are for what we could become."
— Charles DuBois

8 AM	2 PM
9 AM	3 PM
10 AM	4 PM
11 AM	5 PM
12 PM	6 PM
1 PM	7 PM

Fat Tuesday
Mardi Gras
Shrove Tuesday

All times Eastern Standard Time

Spiritual Wisdom

WEDNESDAY
02.22.2012

New Moon

☽ IN ♓: ALL DAY
☽ VOC: 9:24P - MIDNIGHT { ☽ ☌ ♂ }
HIDDEN 2:2 STAR GATE

♄ IS R
♂ IS R

"Be kind to your shadow."
Rebecca Lawless

8AM	**2**PM
9AM	**3**PM
10AM	**4**PM
11AM	**5**PM
12PM	**6**PM
1PM	**7**PM

Ash Wednesday

S	M	T	W	T	F	S
1	2	3	4	5	6	7
8	9	10	11	12	13	14
15	16	17	18	19	20	21
22	23	24	25	26	27	28
29	30	31		January 2012		

S	M	T	W	T	F	S
February 2012		1	2	3	4
5	6	7	8	9	10	11
12	13	14	15	16	17	18
19	20	21	22	23	24	25
26	27	28	29			

Spiritual Wisdom ♓

THURSDAY
02.23.2012

New Moon

☽ IN ♓ ♄ IS R ☿ ☍ ♂ 17° ♓/♍ 6:25A
☽ →♈: 9:48P ♂ IS R
☽ VOC: MIDNIGHT - 9:48P
HIDDEN 5:5/12:12 STAR GATE

> *"I would not waste my life in friction when it could be turned into momentum."*
> Frances Willard

8 AM	2 PM
9 AM	3 PM
10 AM	4 PM
11 AM	5 PM
12 PM	6 PM
1 PM	7 PM

All times Eastern Standard Time

FRIDAY
02.24.2012

Crescent

☽ IN ♈: ALL DAY ♄ IS R ☉ ☌ ☿ 05°♓ 4:06A
☽ VOC: NO ♂ IS R
HIDDEN 2:2 STAR GATE

"Time you enjoy wasting, is not wasted."
John Lennon

8ᴬᴹ	2ᴾᴹ
9ᴬᴹ	3ᴾᴹ
10ᴬᴹ	4ᴾᴹ
11ᴬᴹ	5ᴾᴹ
12ᴾᴹ	6ᴾᴹ
1ᴾᴹ	7ᴾᴹ

S	M	T	W	T	F	S	S	M	T	W	T	F	S
1	2	3	4	5	6	7	February 2012		1	2	3	4
8	9	10	11	12	13	14	5	6	7	8	9	10	11
15	16	17	18	19	20	21	12	13	14	15	16	17	18
22	23	24	25	26	27	28	19	20	21	22	23	24	25
29	30	31		January 2012			26	27	28	29			

SATURDAY
02.25.2012

Crescent

☽ IN ♈: ALL DAY
☽ VOC: NO
⚷ → ♈: 2:05P
HIDDEN 5:5/12:12 STAR GATE

♄ IS R
♂ IS R

☉ ✶ ♃ 06°♓/♉ 5:32A

> "Am I not destroying my enemies when
> I make friends of them?"
>
> — Abraham Lincoln

8 AM	2 PM
9 AM	3 PM
10 AM	4 PM
11 AM	5 PM
12 PM	6 PM
1 PM	7 PM

All times Eastern Standard Time

Spiritual Wisdom

SUNDAY
02.26.2012

Crescent

☽ IN ♈
♄ IS R
☽ →♉: 9:29A
♂ IS R
☽ VOC: 7:51A - 9:29A { ☽ ☍ ♄ }
2:2 STAR GATE

"As long as you are prepared to accept the consequences of your actions you are enlightened."

Derek O'Neill

8 AM	2 PM
9 AM	3 PM
10 AM	4 PM
11 AM	5 PM
12 PM	6 PM
1 PM	7 PM

S	M	T	W	T	F	S	S	M	T	W	T	F	S
1	2	3	4	5	6	7	February 2012		1	2	3	4
8	9	10	11	12	13	14	5	6	7	8	9	10	11
15	16	17	18	19	20	21	12	13	14	15	16	17	18
22	23	24	25	26	27	28	19	20	21	22	23	24	25
29	30	31		January 2012			26	27	28	29			

Spiritual Wisdom ♓

MONDAY
02.27.2012

Crescent

☽ IN ♉: ALL DAY
☽ VOC: NO
☿ → R SHADOW: 23° ♓
HIDDEN 2:2/5:5 STAR GATE

♄ IS R
♂ IS R

"It wasn't raining when Noah built the ark."
Howard Ruff

8ᴀᴍ	2ᴘᴍ
9ᴀᴍ	3ᴘᴍ
10ᴀᴍ	4ᴘᴍ
11ᴀᴍ	5ᴘᴍ
12ᴘᴍ	6ᴘᴍ
1ᴘᴍ	7ᴘᴍ

All times Eastern Standard Time

Spiritual Wisdom

TUESDAY
02.28.2012

Crescent

☽ IN ♉
☽ →♊: 10:27P
☽ VOC: 2:45P - 10:27P {☽ ⚹ ☿}
☿ IN R SHADOW
3:3 STAR GATE/HIDDEN 3:3 STAR GATE

♄ IS R
♂ IS R

☉ ⚹ ♇ 09°♓/♑ 2:15A
☉ □ ☊ 09°♓/♐ 11:34A
☉ □ ☋ 09°♓/♊ 11:34A

"It is every man's obligation to put back into the world at least the equivalent of what he takes out of it."

Albert Einstein

8ᴀᴍ	2ᴘᴍ
9ᴀᴍ	3ᴘᴍ
10ᴀᴍ	4ᴘᴍ
11ᴀᴍ	5ᴘᴍ
12ᴘᴍ	6ᴘᴍ
1ᴘᴍ	7ᴘᴍ

S	M	T	W	T	F	S		S	M	T	W	T	F	S
1	2	3	4	5	6	7	February 2012		1	2	3	4
8	9	10	11	12	13	14		5	6	7	8	9	10	11
15	16	17	18	19	20	21		12	13	14	15	16	17	18
22	23	24	25	26	27	28		19	20	21	22	23	24	25
29	30	31		January 2012				26	27	28	29			

WEDNESDAY
02.29.2012

Spiritual Wisdom ♓

Crescent

☽ IN ♊: ALL DAY
☽ VOC: NO
☿ IN R SHADOW
2:2 STAR GATE

♄ IS R
♂ IS R

"Self-suggestion makes you master of yourself."
W. Clement Stone

8ᴀᴍ	2ᴘᴍ
9ᴀᴍ	3ᴘᴍ
10ᴀᴍ	4ᴘᴍ
11ᴀᴍ	5ᴘᴍ
12ᴘᴍ	6ᴘᴍ
1ᴘᴍ	7ᴘᴍ

Leap Year

All times Eastern Standard Time

THURSDAY
03.01.2012

First Quarter

☽ IN ♊: ALL DAY
☽ VOC: NO
⚥ IN R SHADOW

♄ IS R
♂ IS R

"Faith is the bird that feels the light and sings when the dawn is still dark."

Rabindranath Tagore

8ᴬᴹ	2ᴾᴹ
9ᴬᴹ	3ᴾᴹ
10ᴬᴹ	4ᴾᴹ
11ᴬᴹ	5ᴾᴹ
12ᴾᴹ	6ᴾᴹ
1ᴾᴹ	7ᴾᴹ

S	M	T	W	T	F	S	S	M	T	W	T	F	S
March 2012			1	2	3	1	2	3	4	5	6	7
4	5	6	7	8	9	10	8	9	10	11	12	13	14
11	12	13	14	15	16	17	15	16	17	18	19	20	21
18	19	20	21	22	23	24	22	23	24	25	26	27	28
25	26	27	28	29	30	31	29	30				April 2012	

Spiritual Wisdom ♓

FRIDAY
03.02.2012

First Quarter

☽ IN ♊
☽ →♋: 10:08A
☽ VOC: 8:13A - 10:08A { ☽ △ ♄ }
☿ IN R SHADOW
☿ →♈: 6:41A
5:5 STAR GATE

♄ IS R
♂ IS R

MAR

> *"Be pleasant until ten o'clock in the morning and the rest of the day will take care of itself."*
>
> Elbert Hubbard

8ᴀᴍ	2ᴘᴍ
9ᴀᴍ	3ᴘᴍ
10ᴀᴍ	4ᴘᴍ
11ᴀᴍ	5ᴘᴍ
12ᴘᴍ	6ᴘᴍ
1ᴘᴍ	7ᴘᴍ

All times Eastern Standard Time

SATURDAY
03.03.2012

First Quarter

☽ IN ♋: ALL DAY
☽ VOC: NO
☿ IN R SHADOW
3:3 STAR GATE

♄ IS R
♂ IS R

☉ ☍ ♂ 14° ♓/ ♍ 3:10P

> *"I make the most of all that comes and
> the least of all that goes."*
>
> Sara Teasdale

8ᴬᴹ	2ᴾᴹ
9ᴬᴹ	3ᴾᴹ
10ᴬᴹ	4ᴾᴹ
11ᴬᴹ	5ᴾᴹ
12ᴾᴹ	6ᴾᴹ
1ᴾᴹ	7ᴾᴹ

S	M	T	W	T	F	S	S	M	T	W	T	F	S
March 2012				1	2	3	1	2	3	4	5	6	7
4	5	6	7	8	9	10	8	9	10	11	12	13	14
11	12	13	14	15	16	17	15	16	17	18	19	20	21
18	19	20	21	22	23	24	22	23	24	25	26	27	28
25	26	27	28	29	30	31	29	30				April 2012	

Spiritual Wisdom ♓

SUNDAY 03.04.2012

Gibbous

☽ IN ♋
☽ →♌: 6:17P
☽ VOC: 5:17P - 6:17P {☽ □ ♀}
☿ IN R SHADOW
HIDDEN 12:12 STAR GATE

♄ IS R
♂ IS R

♀ ☍ ♄ 29°♈/♎ 6:18A

MAR

"Don't try to change the world, change yourself."
Derek O'Neill

8ᴀᴍ	2ᴘᴍ
9ᴀᴍ	3ᴘᴍ
10ᴀᴍ	4ᴘᴍ
11ᴀᴍ	5ᴘᴍ
12ᴘᴍ	6ᴘᴍ
1ᴘᴍ	7ᴘᴍ

All times Eastern Standard Time

Spiritual Wisdom

MONDAY
03.05.2012

Gibbous

☽ IN ♌: ALL DAY
☽ VOC: NO
♀ →♉: 5:25A
☿ IN R SHADOW
5:5 STAR GATE

♄ IS R
♂ IS R

☿ ☌ ♅ 03°♈   6:35A

"We all walk in the dark and each of us must learn to turn on his or her own light."

Earl Nightingale

....

....

....

....

....

....

....

....

8ᴬᴹ	2ᴾᴹ
9ᴬᴹ	3ᴾᴹ
10ᴬᴹ	4ᴾᴹ
11ᴬᴹ	5ᴾᴹ
12ᴾᴹ	6ᴾᴹ
1ᴾᴹ	7ᴾᴹ

S	M	T	W	T	F	S		S	M	T	W	T	F	S
March 2012				1	2	3		1	2	3	4	5	6	7
4	5	6	7	8	9	10		8	9	10	11	12	13	14
11	12	13	14	15	16	17		15	16	17	18	19	20	21
18	19	20	21	22	23	24		22	23	24	25	26	27	28
25	26	27	28	29	30	31		29	30				April 2012	

Spiritual Wisdom ♓

TUESDAY
03.06.2012

Gibbous

☽ IN ♌
☽ → ♍: 10:27p
☽ VOC: 8:27p - 10:27p {☽ ✶ ♄}
☿ IN R SHADOW
HIDDEN 5:5 STAR GATE

♄ IS R
♂ IS R

♀ ✶ ♆ 01° ♉ / ♓ 7:25a

MAR

"Don't worry. Be happy."
Meher Baba

8ᴀᴍ	2ᴘᴍ
9ᴀᴍ	3ᴘᴍ
10ᴀᴍ	4ᴘᴍ
11ᴀᴍ	5ᴘᴍ
12ᴘᴍ	6ᴘᴍ
1ᴘᴍ	7ᴘᴍ

All times Eastern Standard Time

Spiritual Wisdom

WEDNESDAY
03.07.2012

Gibbous

☽ IN ♍: ALL DAY
☽ VOC: NO
☿ IN R SHADOW
HIDDEN 12:12 STAR GATE

♄ IS R
♂ IS R

"Only one who devotes himself to a cause with his whole strength and soul can be a true master."

Albert Einstein

8ᴀᴍ	2ᴘᴍ
9ᴀᴍ	3ᴘᴍ
10ᴀᴍ	4ᴘᴍ
11ᴀᴍ	5ᴘᴍ
12ᴘᴍ	6ᴘᴍ
1ᴘᴍ	7ᴘᴍ

S	M	T	W	T	F	S	S	M	T	W	T	F	S
March 2012				1	2	3	1	2	3	4	5	6	7
4	5	6	7	8	9	10	8	9	10	11	12	13	14
11	12	13	14	15	16	17	15	16	17	18	19	20	21
18	19	20	21	22	23	24	22	23	24	25	26	27	28
25	26	27	28	29	30	31	29	30				April 2012	

Spiritual Wisdom

THURSDAY
03.08.2012

Full Moon

☽ IN ♍
☽ →♎: 11:51P
☽ VOC: 4:40A - 11:51P { ☽ ☍ ☉ }
☿ IN R SHADOW
HIDDEN 8:8 STAR GATE

♄ IS R
♂ IS R

FULL MOON { ☽ ☍ ☉ }: 4:40A
18° ♍13'

MAR

"If fear is cultivated it will become stronger, if faith is cultivated it will achieve mastery."

John Paul Jones

8ᴬᴹ	2ᴾᴹ
9ᴬᴹ	3ᴾᴹ
10ᴬᴹ	4ᴾᴹ
11ᴬᴹ	5ᴾᴹ
12ᴾᴹ	6ᴾᴹ
1ᴾᴹ	7ᴾᴹ

Purim

FRIDAY
03.09.2012

Full Moon

☽ IN ♎: ALL DAY
☽ VOC: NO
☿ IN R SHADOW
3:3/5:5 STAR GATE

♄ IS R
♂ IS R

"Make somebody happy today. Mind your own business."
Ann Landers

8ᴀᴍ	2ᴘᴍ
9ᴀᴍ	3ᴘᴍ
10ᴀᴍ	4ᴘᴍ
11ᴀᴍ	5ᴘᴍ
12ᴘᴍ	6ᴘᴍ
1ᴘᴍ	7ᴘᴍ

S	M	T	W	T	F	S	S	M	T	W	T	F	S
March 2012				1	2	3	1	2	3	4	5	6	7
4	5	6	7	8	9	10	8	9	10	11	12	13	14
11	12	13	14	15	16	17	15	16	17	18	19	20	21
18	19	20	21	22	23	24	22	23	24	25	26	27	28
25	26	27	28	29	30	31	29	30				April 2012	

Spiritual Wisdom

SATURDAY
03.10.2012

Full Moon

☽ in ♎: All Day   ♄ is R   ♀ ✶ ☊ 06°♉/ ♓ 9:28P
☽ voc: 10:09P - Midnight {☽ ☌ ♄}   ♂ is R
☿ in R Shadow

MAR

> *"You've got to do your own growing, no matter how tall your grandfather was."*
>
> Irish Proverb

8ᴬᴹ	2ᴾᴹ
9ᴬᴹ	3ᴾᴹ
10ᴬᴹ	4ᴾᴹ
11ᴬᴹ	5ᴾᴹ
12ᴾᴹ	6ᴾᴹ
1ᴾᴹ	7ᴾᴹ

All times Eastern Standard Time

Spiritual Wisdom

SUNDAY
03.11.2012

Disseminating

☽ IN ♎
☽ →♏: 12:24A
☽ VOC: MIDNIGHT - 12:24A
☿ IS STATIONING {R}
5:5 STAR GATE

♄ IS R
♂ IS R

"Trauma separates you into three parts: 'I,' 'me' and the 'experience.' Eliminate the 'I' and the 'me,' and you will be in your heart forever."

Derek O'Neill

8ᴀᴍ	2ᴘᴍ
9ᴀᴍ	3ᴘᴍ
10ᴀᴍ	4ᴘᴍ
11ᴀᴍ	5ᴘᴍ
12ᴘᴍ	6ᴘᴍ
1ᴘᴍ	7ᴘᴍ

Daylight Savings Time Begins - 2:00am (North America)

S	M	T	W	T	F	S
March 2012			1	2	3
4	5	6	7	8	9	10
11	12	13	14	15	16	17
18	19	20	21	22	23	24
25	26	27	28	29	30	31

S	M	T	W	T	F	S
1	2	3	4	5	6	7
8	9	10	11	12	13	14
15	16	17	18	19	20	21
22	23	24	25	26	27	28
29	30					April 2012

Spiritual Wisdom

MONDAY
03.12.2012

Disseminating

☽ IN ♏
☽ VOC: 2:30P - MIDNIGHT { ☽ △ ♄ }
☿ STATION: 3:49A
☿ TURNS R: 07° ♈
12:12 STAR GATE

♄ IS R
♂ IS R

"When you throw dirt, you lose ground."
　　　　　　　　　　　　　　　　Texan Proverb

8ᴬᴹ	2ᴾᴹ
9ᴬᴹ	3ᴾᴹ
10ᴬᴹ	4ᴾᴹ
11ᴬᴹ	5ᴾᴹ
12ᴾᴹ	6ᴾᴹ
1ᴾᴹ	7ᴾᴹ

All times Eastern Daylight Time

Spiritual Wisdom

TUESDAY
03.13.2012

Disseminating

☽ in ♏
☽ →♐: 2:54a
☽ voc: Midnight - 2:54a
☿ has Stationed {R}
Hidden 12:12 Star Gate

♄ is R
♂ is R

♃ △ ♇ 09°♉/♑ 12:43a
♀ △ ♇ 09°♉/♑ 9:27p

> *"A man is rich in proportion to the number*
> *of things he can afford to let alone."*
>
> Henry David Thoreau

8ᴀᴍ	2ᴘᴍ
9ᴀᴍ	3ᴘᴍ
10ᴀᴍ	4ᴘᴍ
11ᴀᴍ	5ᴘᴍ
12ᴘᴍ	6ᴘᴍ
1ᴘᴍ	7ᴘᴍ

S	M	T	W	T	F	S	S	M	T	W	T	F	S
March 2012				1	2	3					1	2	3
4	5	6	7	8	9	10	8	9	10	11	12	13	14
11	12	13	14	15	16	17	15	16	17	18	19	20	21
18	19	20	21	22	23	24	22	23	24	25	26	27	28
25	26	27	28	29	30	31	29	30				April 2012	

Spiritual Wisdom ♓

WEDNESDAY
03.14.2012

Disseminating

☽ IN ♐: ALL DAY
☽ VOC: NO
5:5 STAR GATE/HIDDEN 5:5 STAR GATE

♄ IS R
♂ IS R
☿ IS R

♀ ☌ ♃ 09°♉ 1:54A
♀ △ ♂ 09°♉/♍ 3:27A
♂ △ ♃ 09°♍/♉ 5:51A
♂ △ ♇ 09°♍/♑ 8:24P

MAR

"Look at everything as though you were seeing it either for the first or last time."
Betty Smith

8ᴀᴍ	2ᴘᴍ
9ᴀᴍ	3ᴘᴍ
10ᴀᴍ	4ᴘᴍ
11ᴀᴍ	5ᴘᴍ
12ᴘᴍ	6ᴘᴍ
1ᴘᴍ	7ᴘᴍ

All times Eastern Daylight Time

THURSDAY
03.15.2012

Last Quarter

☽ IN ♐
☽ →♑: 6:24A
☽ VOC: 3:34A - 6:24A { ☽ ✶ ♄ }
HIDDEN 5:5 STAR GATE

♄ IS R
♂ IS R
☿ IS R

*"The black moment is the moment when
the real message of transformation is going to come.
At the darkest moment comes the light."*

Joseph Campbell

8ᴀᴍ	2ᴘᴍ
9ᴀᴍ	3ᴘᴍ
10ᴀᴍ	4ᴘᴍ
11ᴀᴍ	5ᴘᴍ
12ᴘᴍ	6ᴘᴍ
1ᴘᴍ	7ᴘᴍ

S	M	T	W	T	F	S	S	M	T	W	T	F	S
March 2012			1	2	3	1	2	3	4	5	6	7
4	5	6	7	8	9	10	8	9	10	11	12	13	14
11	12	13	14	15	16	17	15	16	17	18	19	20	21
18	19	20	21	22	23	24	22	23	24	25	26	27	28
25	26	27	28	29	30	31	29	30				April 2012	

Spiritual Wisdom

FRIDAY
03.16.2012

Last Quarter

☽ IN ♑: ALL DAY
☽ VOC: NO
HIDDEN 12:12 STAR GATE

♄ IS R
♂ IS R
☿ IS R

"Don't compromise yourself. You're all you've got."
Janis Joplin

8 AM	2 PM
9 AM	3 PM
10 AM	4 PM
11 AM	5 PM
12 PM	6 PM
1 PM	7 PM

All times Eastern Daylight Time

Spiritual Wisdom

SATURDAY
03.17.2012

Last Quarter

☽ IN ♑
☽ →♒: 12:11A
☽ VOC: 9:00A - 12:11A { ☽ □ ♄ }
8:8 STAR GATE

♄ IS R
♂ IS R
☿ IS R

"If I could know me, I could know the universe."
                                        Shirley MacLaine

8^{AM}	2^{PM}
9^{AM}	3^{PM}
10^{AM}	4^{PM}
11^{AM}	5^{PM}
12^{PM}	6^{PM}
1^{PM}	7^{PM}

St. Patrick's Day

S	M	T	W	T	F	S	S	M	T	W	T	F	S
March 2012				1	2	3	1	2	3	4	5	6	7
4	5	6	7	8	9	10	8	9	10	11	12	13	14
11	12	13	14	15	16	17	15	16	17	18	19	20	21
18	19	20	21	22	23	24	22	23	24	25	26	27	28
25	26	27	28	29	30	31	29	30				April 2012	

Spiritual Wisdom

SUNDAY
03.18.2012

Last Quarter

☽ IN ♒: ALL DAY
☽ VOC: NO
3:3/5:5 STAR GATE

♄ IS R
♂ IS R
♀ IS R

☿ ☌ ♅ 04°♈ 1:24P

"When you help another by word or deed you change the world for the better."

Derek O'Neill

8ᴀᴍ	2ᴘᴍ
9ᴀᴍ	3ᴘᴍ
10ᴀᴍ	4ᴘᴍ
11ᴀᴍ	5ᴘᴍ
12ᴘᴍ	6ᴘᴍ
1ᴘᴍ	7ᴘᴍ

All times Eastern Daylight Time

MONDAY
03.19.2012

Balsamic

☽ IN ♒
☽ →♓: 8:05P
☽ VOC: 4:31P - 8:05P { ☽ △ ♄ }

♄ IS R
♂ IS R
☿ IS R

♂ □ ☊ 08°♍/♐ 2:24P
♂ □ ☋ 08°♍/♊ 2:24P

"Life is not about waiting for the storms to pass...
It's about learning how to dance in the rain."

Vivian Greene

8ᴀᴍ	2ᴘᴍ
9ᴀᴍ	3ᴘᴍ
10ᴀᴍ	4ᴘᴍ
11ᴀᴍ	5ᴘᴍ
12ᴘᴍ	6ᴘᴍ
1ᴘᴍ	7ᴘᴍ

Spiritual Wisdom

S	M	T	W	T	F	S	S	M	T	W	T	F	S
March 2012				1	2	3	1	2	3	4	5	6	7
4	5	6	7	8	9	10	8	9	10	11	12	13	14
11	12	13	14	15	16	17	15	16	17	18	19	20	21
18	19	20	21	22	23	24	22	23	24	25	26	27	28
25	26	27	28	29	30	31	29	30					April 2012

ARIES

Mental Power

Symbol: The Divine Spark of Creation
Master: Helios
Quality: Conscious Discipline
Ray: 3rd Ray, Yellow Gold
Trine: Fire
Hour: 3
Rulers: ♂ ☿ ☿

Mental Power ♈

3 O'Clock Hour
Main Purpose:

Where you bring the Light of spirit in to activate the higher mind.

MARCH 20 - APRIL 18

In Cosmic Astrology, Aries is the sign of **Conscious Discipline**, where you diligently choose to make all your thoughts Loving. This is the first of three signs that encompass the mental body. In the new system, the mental body refers to the higher consciousness, which every human is equipped with, and can access once the lower self is triumphed over. This is the area of your energy field where your Christ consciousness dwells. In 3D astrology, Aries started it all by kicking off the zodiac, which is 3D animal-related. But in Cosmic Astrology it is Capricorn and the spiritual connection to Source that begins our journey. Aries is the Divine Spark of Creation in 5D astrology, a quantum leap from the Ram's reality. Like much in the 3D world, Aries has been so misunderstood as to disempower its function. No wonder it became known as the warrior!

This Aries quality of consciousness can now be seen as the place where we bring the Higher Self into the human experience, by disciplining the thought process and choosing only loving words and thoughts. As we begin to experience the world we create out of this disciplined thinking, we realize our Selves as the co-creators of our world. The Aries consciousness is expressed in the 3 o'clock hour, which corresponds to the 6th house of the birth chart. Here we work with great focus to bring our Selves into alignment, mind, heart, body and spirit. In 5D it is essential to make the connection between spirit and mind first. "In the beginning was the Word...."

Wherever Aries is in your birth chart you are empowered to bring your higher consciousness on line, and to activate the creator function within you as a result. This is a place where some struggle and conflict is inevitable, because it is essential to break through the cocoon of self-absorption, which was the Aries focus for so long. Here it becomes essential to move the self past the experience of separation and aloneness, in order to become the leader who is unafraid to create out of a more unified consciousness. If your sun Sign is Aries, you are here to learn to bring the Light of the Sun (Son) into your being and shine brightly as the great leader you are.

FAMOUS ARIES

Maya Angelou, Hugh Hefner, Marlon Brando, Elton John, Billie Holiday, Celine Dion, Stephen Sondheim, Vincent Van Gogh, Ram Dass, Kofi Annan, Elizabeth C. Prophet, David Blane, Leonardo Da Vinci, Quentin Tarantino

Mental Power # TUESDAY
03.20.2012

Balsamic

☽ IN ♓: ALL DAY
☽ VOC: NO
☉ → ♈: 1:14A
5:5 STAR GATE

♄ IS R
♂ IS R
☿ IS R

"Sunshine is my quest."
Winston Churchill

8 AM	2 PM
9 AM	3 PM
10 AM	4 PM
11 AM	5 PM
12 PM	6 PM
1 PM	7 PM

Spring Equinox
Ostara

All times Eastern Daylight Time

Mental Power

WEDNESDAY
03.21.2012

Balsamic

☽ IN ♓: ALL DAY   ♄ IS R   ☉ ☌ ☿ 02° ♈   3:21P
☽ VOC: 4:39A - MIDNIGHT { ☽ ✶ ♀ }   ♂ IS R
3:3/12:12 STAR GATE   ☿ IS R

"Conflict is the beginning of consciousness."

M. Esther Harding

8ᴀᴍ	2ᴘᴍ
9ᴀᴍ	3ᴘᴍ
10ᴀᴍ	4ᴘᴍ
11ᴀᴍ	5ᴘᴍ
12ᴘᴍ	6ᴘᴍ
1ᴘᴍ	7ᴘᴍ

S	M	T	W	T	F	S	S	M	T	W	T	F	S
March 2012				1	2	3	1	2	3	4	5	6	7
4	5	6	7	8	9	10	8	9	10	11	12	13	14
11	12	13	14	15	16	17	15	16	17	18	19	20	21
18	19	20	21	22	23	24	22	23	24	25	26	27	28
25	26	27	28	29	30	31	29	30				April 2012	

THURSDAY
03.22.2012

New Moon

☽ IN ♓
☽ → ♈: 5:57A
☽ VOC: MIDNIGHT - 5:57A
HIDDEN 12:12 STAR GATE

♄ IS R
♂ IS R
☿ IS R

NEW MOON { ☽ ☌ ☉}: 10:37A
02° ♈ 22'

♂ ☍ ⚷ 07° ♍/ ♓ 11:21A

> *"Man cannot remake himself without suffering;*
> *he is both the marble and the sculptor."*
>
> Dr. Alexis Carrel

8 AM	2 PM
9 AM	3 PM
10 AM	4 PM
11 AM	5 PM
12 PM	6 PM
1 PM	7 PM

All times Eastern Daylight Time

FRIDAY
03.23.2012

New Moon

☽ IN ♈: ALL DAY   ♄ IS R   ♆ □ ☊ 07°♓/♐ 3:12P
☽ VOC: NO   ♂ IS R   ♆ □ ☋ 07°♓/♊ 3:12P
☿ →♓: 9:22A   ♀ IS R

5:5 STAR GATE/HIDDEN 5:5 STAR GATE

"There is no life without consciousness; there is no consciousness without life."

Annie Besant

8ᴬᴹ	2ᴾᴹ
9ᴬᴹ	3ᴾᴹ
10ᴬᴹ	4ᴾᴹ
11ᴬᴹ	5ᴾᴹ
12ᴾᴹ	6ᴾᴹ
1ᴾᴹ	7ᴾᴹ

S	M	T	W	T	F	S	S	M	T	W	T	F	S
March 2012			1	2	3	1	2	3	4	5	6	7
4	5	6	7	8	9	10	8	9	10	11	12	13	14
11	12	13	14	15	16	17	15	16	17	18	19	20	21
18	19	20	21	22	23	24	22	23	24	25	26	27	28
25	26	27	28	29	30	31	29	30				April 2012

Mental Power

SATURDAY
03.24.2012

New Moon

☽ IN ♈
☽ →♉: 5:43P
☽ VOC: 1:17P - 5:43P { ☽ ☍ ♄ }
♆ STATION: 7:32P
♆ TURNS R: 07° ♐
HIDDEN 5:5 STAR GATE

♄ IS R
♂ IS R
☿ IS R

☉ ☌ ♅ 04°♈   2:20P

> "There are two kinds of light: the glow that illumines,
> and the glare that obscures."
>
> James Thurber

8 AM	2 PM
9 AM	3 PM
10 AM	4 PM
11 AM	5 PM
12 PM	6 PM
1 PM	7 PM

All times Eastern Daylight Time

Mental Power

SUNDAY
03.25.2012

Crescent

☽ IN ♉: ALL DAY
☽ VOC: NO
☿ HAS STATIONED {R}
HIDDEN 12:12 STAR GATE

♄ IS R
♂ IS R
☿ IS R

*"What you are conscious of always changes.
What you are not conscious of doesn't."*

Derek O'Neill

8ᴬᴹ	2ᴾᴹ
9ᴬᴹ	3ᴾᴹ
10ᴬᴹ	4ᴾᴹ
11ᴬᴹ	5ᴾᴹ
12ᴾᴹ	6ᴾᴹ
1ᴾᴹ	7ᴾᴹ

S	M	T	W	T	F	S	S	M	T	W	T	F	S
March 2012				1	2	3	1	2	3	4	5	6	7
4	5	6	7	8	9	10	8	9	10	11	12	13	14
11	12	13	14	15	16	17	15	16	17	18	19	20	21
18	19	20	21	22	23	24	22	23	24	25	26	27	28
25	26	27	28	29	30	31	29	30				April 2012	

Mental Power

♈

MONDAY
03.26.2012

Crescent

☽ IN ♉: ALL DAY
☽ VOC: NO
8:8 STAR GATE

♄ IS R
♆ IS R
♂ IS R
☿ IS R

☉ △ ☊ 07°♈/♐ 6:52P
☉ ✶ ☋ 07°♈/♊ 6:52P

"He not busy being born is busy dying."

Bob Dylan

8ᴬᴹ	2ᴾᴹ
9ᴬᴹ	3ᴾᴹ
10ᴬᴹ	4ᴾᴹ
11ᴬᴹ	5ᴾᴹ
12ᴾᴹ	6ᴾᴹ
1ᴾᴹ	7ᴾᴹ

All times Eastern Daylight Time

Mental Power

TUESDAY
03.27.2012

Crescent

☽ IN ♉
☽ →♊: 6:43A
☽ VOC: 12:34A - 6:43A { ☽ ✶ ☿ }
3:3/5:5 STAR GATE

♄ IS R
✶ IS R
♂ IS R
☿ IS R

"Consciousness is the glory of creation."

James Broughton

8ᴀᴍ	2ᴘᴍ
9ᴀᴍ	3ᴘᴍ
10ᴀᴍ	4ᴘᴍ
11ᴀᴍ	5ᴘᴍ
12ᴘᴍ	6ᴘᴍ
1ᴘᴍ	7ᴘᴍ

S	M	T	W	T	F	S	S	M	T	W	T	F	S
March 2012				1	2	3	1	2	3	4	5	6	7
4	5	6	7	8	9	10	8	9	10	11	12	13	14
11	12	13	14	15	16	17	15	16	17	18	19	20	21
18	19	20	21	22	23	24	22	23	24	25	26	27	28
25	26	27	28	29	30	31	29	30				April 2012	

Mental Power

WEDNESDAY
03.28.2012

Crescent

☽ IN ♊: ALL DAY
☽ VOC: NO

♄ IS R
⚸ IS R
♂ IS R
☿ IS R

MAR

> *"The universal intelligence that we call God or Consciousness is everywhere and in all things."*
>
> Wayne Dyer

8 AM	2 PM
9 AM	3 PM
10 AM	4 PM
11 AM	5 PM
12 PM	6 PM
1 PM	7 PM

All times Eastern Daylight Time

Mental Power

THURSDAY
03.29.2012

Crescent

☽ IN ♊
☽ →♋: 7:07P
☽ VOC: 2:04P - 7:07P { ☽ △ ♄ }
5:5 Star Gate

♄ IS R
♆ IS R
♂ IS R
☿ IS R

☉ □ ♇ 09°♈/♑ 3:55P
☿ ⚹ ♀ 25°♓/♉ 1:43P

"Consciousness is our only reprieve from Time."

Mason Cooley

8ᴬᴹ	2ᴾᴹ
9ᴬᴹ	3ᴾᴹ
10ᴬᴹ	4ᴾᴹ
11ᴬᴹ	5ᴾᴹ
12ᴾᴹ	6ᴾᴹ
1ᴾᴹ	7ᴾᴹ

March 2012

S	M	T	W	T	F	S
				1	2	3
4	5	6	7	8	9	10
11	12	13	14	15	16	17
18	19	20	21	22	23	24
25	26	27	28	29	30	31

S	M	T	W	T	F	S
1	2	3	4	5	6	7
8	9	10	11	12	13	14
15	16	17	18	19	20	21
22	23	24	25	26	27	28
29	30					

April 2012

Mental Power

FRIDAY
03.30.2012

First Quarter

☽ IN ♋: ALL DAY
☽ VOC: NO
3:3 STAR GATE

♄ IS R
⚷ IS R
♂ IS R
☿ IS R

"The only mistake that we can make as human beings is to be asleep, unaware of ourselves."

Guy Finley

8 AM	2 PM
9 AM	3 PM
10 AM	4 PM
11 AM	5 PM
12 PM	6 PM
1 PM	7 PM

All times Eastern Daylight Time

Mental Power

SATURDAY
03.31.2012

First Quarter

☽ IN ♋: ALL DAY
☽ VOC: NO
HIDDEN 12:12 STAR GATE

♄ IS R
♆ IS R
♂ IS R
☿ IS R

"Each of us can manifest a field of consciousness that transcends space, time, and linear causality."

Stanislav Grof

8ᴬᴹ	2ᴾᴹ
9ᴬᴹ	3ᴾᴹ
10ᴬᴹ	4ᴾᴹ
11ᴬᴹ	5ᴾᴹ
12ᴾᴹ	6ᴾᴹ
1ᴾᴹ	7ᴾᴹ

S	M	T	W	T	F	S	S	M	T	W	T	F	S
March 2012			1	2	3	1	2	3	4	5	6	7
4	5	6	7	8	9	10	8	9	10	11	12	13	14
11	12	13	14	15	16	17	15	16	17	18	19	20	21
18	19	20	21	22	23	24	22	23	24	25	26	27	28
25	26	27	28	29	30	31	29	30				April 2012	

SUNDAY
04.01.2012

First Quarter

☽ IN ♋
☽ →♌: 4:35A
☽ VOC: 12:20A - 4:35A { ☽ ✶ ♀ }
5:5 Star Gate/Hidden 1:1 Star Gate

♄ IS R
♆ IS R
♂ IS R
☿ IS R

Mental Power

APR

*"If you are in your mind, it is you.
If you are out of your mind, it is God."*

Derek O'Neill

8ᴬᴹ	2ᴾᴹ
9ᴬᴹ	3ᴾᴹ
10ᴬᴹ	4ᴾᴹ
11ᴬᴹ	5ᴾᴹ
12ᴾᴹ	6ᴾᴹ
1ᴾᴹ	7ᴾᴹ

April Fools Day
Palm Sunday

All times Eastern Daylight Time

Mental Power

MONDAY
04.02.2012

First Quarter

☽ IN ♌: ALL DAY
☽ VOC: NO
HIDDEN 2:2 STAR GATE

♄ IS R
♆ IS R
♂ IS R
☿ IS R

"Wherever you go, no matter what the weather, always bring your own sunshine."

Anthony J. D'Angelo

8ᴀᴍ	2ᴘᴍ
9ᴀᴍ	3ᴘᴍ
10ᴀᴍ	4ᴘᴍ
11ᴀᴍ	5ᴘᴍ
12ᴘᴍ	6ᴘᴍ
1ᴘᴍ	7ᴘᴍ

S	M	T	W	T	F	S	S	M	T	W	T	F	S
1	2	3	4	5	6	7	May		1	2	3	4	5
8	9	10	11	12	13	14	6	7	8	9	10	11	12
15	16	17	18	19	20	21	13	14	15	16	17	18	19
22	23	24	25	26	27	28	20	21	22	23	24	25	26
29	30			April 2012			27	28	29	30	31		2012

Mental Power ♈

TUESDAY
04.03.2012

Gibbous

☽ IN ♌
☽ →♍: 9:53A
☽ VOC: 9:47A - 9:53A { ☽ □ ♀ }
♀ →♊: 11:18A
☿ IS STATIONING {D}
3:3 STAR GATE

♄ IS R
⚷ IS R
♂ IS R

"Life is consciousness."
Emmet Fox

8ᴀᴍ	2ᴘᴍ
9ᴀᴍ	3ᴘᴍ
10ᴀᴍ	4ᴘᴍ
11ᴀᴍ	5ᴘᴍ
12ᴘᴍ	6ᴘᴍ
1ᴘᴍ	7ᴘᴍ

All times Eastern Daylight Time

Mental Power

WEDNESDAY
04.04.2012

Gibbous

☽ IN ♍: ALL DAY
☽ VOC: NO
☿ STATION: 6:12A
☿ TURNS D: 24° ♓

♄ IS R
♆ IS R
♂ IS R

4:4 STAR GATE/HIDDEN 4:4 STAR GATE

> *"My sense of identity broke down and was replaced by something that is very hard to put into words. Awareness, Consciousness."*
>
> Eckhart Tolle

8ᴀᴍ	2ᴘᴍ
9ᴀᴍ	3ᴘᴍ
10ᴀᴍ	4ᴘᴍ
11ᴀᴍ	5ᴘᴍ
12ᴘᴍ	6ᴘᴍ
1ᴘᴍ	7ᴘᴍ

S	M	T	W	T	F	S		S	M	T	W	T	F	S
1	2	3	4	5	6	7	May		1	2	3	4	5
8	9	10	11	12	13	14		6	7	8	9	10	11	12
15	16	17	18	19	20	21		13	14	15	16	17	18	19
22	23	24	25	26	27	28		20	21	22	23	24	25	26
29	30			April 2012				27	28	29	30	31		2012

Mental Power

THURSDAY
04.05.2012

Gibbous

☽ IN ♍
☽ →♎: 11:33A
☽ VOC: 1:38A - 11:33A { ☽ ☌ ☿ }
☿ HAS STATIONED {D}
5:5 STAR GATE/HIDDEN 5:5 STAR GATE

♄ IS R
♅ IS R
♂ IS R

♀ □ ♆ 02°♊/♓ 9:49A

APR

> *"God is not found in places.*
> *God is found in consciousness."*
>   Joel Goldsmith

8ᴀᴍ	2ᴘᴍ
9ᴀᴍ	3ᴘᴍ
10ᴀᴍ	4ᴘᴍ
11ᴀᴍ	5ᴘᴍ
12ᴘᴍ	6ᴘᴍ
1ᴘᴍ	7ᴘᴍ

Mahavir Jayanthi

All times Eastern Daylight Time

FRIDAY
04.06.2012

Full Moon

☽ IN ♎: ALL DAY
☽ VOC: NO
☿ IN D SHADOW
HIDDEN 6:6 STAR GATE

♄ IS R
♆ IS R
♂ IS R

FULL MOON { ☽ ☌ ☉ }: 3:19P
17° ♎23'

> *"Enlightenment is not imagining figures of light,
> but making the darkness conscious."*
>
> Carl Jung

8ᴀᴍ	2ᴘᴍ
9ᴀᴍ	3ᴘᴍ
10ᴀᴍ	4ᴘᴍ
11ᴀᴍ	5ᴘᴍ
12ᴘᴍ	6ᴘᴍ
1ᴘᴍ	7ᴘᴍ

Good Friday

S	M	T	W	T	F	S		S	M	T	W	T	F	S
1	2	3	4	5	6	7	May			1	2	3	4	5
8	9	10	11	12	13	14		6	7	8	9	10	11	12
15	16	17	18	19	20	21		13	14	15	16	17	18	19
22	23	24	25	26	27	28		20	21	22	23	24	25	26
29	30			April 2012				27	28	29	30	31		2012

Mental Power

SATURDAY
04.07.2012

Full Moon

☽ IN ♎
☽ →♏: 11:18A
☽ VOC: 6:16A - 11:18A { ☽ ☌ ♄ }
♇ IS STATIONING {R}
☿ IN D SHADOW
HIDDEN 12:12/7:7 STAR GATE

♄ IS R
♆ IS R
♂ IS R

♀ □ ♂ 04°♊/♍ 9:36P

APR

> *"Voluntary endeavor is the only*
> *qualification for spiritual perfection."*
>
> C. Bhaktivedanta Swami

8ᴀᴍ	2ᴘᴍ
9ᴀᴍ	3ᴘᴍ
10ᴀᴍ	4ᴘᴍ
11ᴀᴍ	5ᴘᴍ
12ᴘᴍ	6ᴘᴍ
1ᴘᴍ	7ᴘᴍ

First Day of Passover

All times Eastern Daylight Time

Mental Power

SUNDAY
04.08.2012

Full Moon

☽ IN ♏: ALL DAY
☽ VOC: NO
♇ IS STATIONING {R}
☿ IN D SHADOW

♄ IS R
⚹ IS R
♂ IS R

12:12 STAR GATE/HIDDEN 8:8 STAR GATE

"We all have two minds. The first is the thinking mind. The other is consciousness."

Derek O'Neill

8ᴀᴍ	2ᴘᴍ
9ᴀᴍ	3ᴘᴍ
10ᴀᴍ	4ᴘᴍ
11ᴀᴍ	5ᴘᴍ
12ᴘᴍ	6ᴘᴍ
1ᴘᴍ	7ᴘᴍ

Easter

S	M	T	W	T	F	S	S	M	T	W	T	F	S
1	2	3	4	5	6	7	May		1	2	3	4	5
8	9	10	11	12	13	14	6	7	8	9	10	11	12
15	16	17	18	19	20	21	13	14	15	16	17	18	19
22	23	24	25	26	27	28	20	21	22	23	24	25	26
29	30			April 2012			27	28	29	30	31		2012

Mental Power ♈

MONDAY
04.09.2012

Disseminating

☽ IN ♏
☽ →♐: 11:13A
☽ VOC: 2:56A - 11:13A { ☽ △ ☿ }
♇ IS STATIONING {R}
? →♐: 11:12A
☿ IN D SHADOW

♄ IS R
♆ IS R
♂ IS R

♀ ✶ ♅ 05°♊/♈ 12:51P

4:4/5:5 STAR GATE/HIDDEN 9:9 STAR GATE

> *"The spiritual is the parent of the practical."*
> Thomas Carlyle

8ᴀᴍ	2ᴘᴍ
9ᴀᴍ	3ᴘᴍ
10ᴀᴍ	4ᴘᴍ
11ᴀᴍ	5ᴘᴍ
12ᴘᴍ	6ᴘᴍ
1ᴘᴍ	7ᴘᴍ

All times Eastern Daylight Time

Mental Power

TUESDAY
04.10.2012

Disseminating

☽ IN ♐: ALL DAY
☽ VOC: NO
♇ STATION: 12:21P
♇ TURNS R: 10° ♑
☿ IN D SHADOW
5:5 STAR GATE/HIDDEN 1:1 STAR GATE

♄ IS R
⚴ IS R
♂ IS R

♀ ☍ ☊ 06°♊/♐ 2:24A
♀ ☌ ☋ 06°♊ 2:24A

> *"Life will give you whatever experience is most helpful for the evolution of consciousness."*
>
> Eckhart Tolle

8ᴬᴹ	**2**ᴾᴹ
9ᴬᴹ	**3**ᴾᴹ
10ᴬᴹ	**4**ᴾᴹ
11ᴬᴹ	**5**ᴾᴹ
12ᴾᴹ	**6**ᴾᴹ
1ᴾᴹ	**7**ᴾᴹ

S	M	T	W	T	F	S	S	M	T	W	T	F	S
1	2	3	4	5	6	7	May		1	2	3	4	5
8	9	10	11	12	13	14	6	7	8	9	10	11	12
15	16	17	18	19	20	21	13	14	15	16	17	18	19
22	23	24	25	26	27	28	20	21	22	23	24	25	26
29	30			April 2012			27	28	29	30	31		2012

Mental Power

WEDNESDAY
04.11.2012

Disseminating

☽ IN ♐
☽ → ♑: 1:02P
☽ VOC: 9:06A - 1:02P { ☽ ✶ ♄ }
♇ HAS STATIONED {R}
☿ IN D SHADOW
HIDDEN 2:2 STAR GATE

♄ IS R
⚴ IS R
♂ IS R

APR

> *"The journey of a thousand miles begins with a single step."*
>
> Lao Tse

8^{AM}	2^{PM}
9^{AM}	3^{PM}
10^{AM}	4^{PM}
11^{AM}	5^{PM}
12^{PM}	6^{PM}
1^{PM}	7^{PM}

All times Eastern Daylight Time

Mental Power

THURSDAY
04.12.2012

Disseminating

☽ IN ♑: ALL DAY ♇ IS R ♀ □ ☋ 08°♊/♓ 6:06P
☽ VOC: NO ♄ IS R
☿ IN D SHADOW ✴ IS R
12:12 STAR GATE/HIDDEN 3:3 ♂ IS R

*"The foundations of a person
are not in matter but in spirit."*
Ralph Waldo Emerson

8ᴀᴍ	2ᴘᴍ
9ᴀᴍ	3ᴘᴍ
10ᴀᴍ	4ᴘᴍ
11ᴀᴍ	5ᴘᴍ
12ᴘᴍ	6ᴘᴍ
1ᴘᴍ	7ᴘᴍ

S	M	T	W	T	F	S		S	M	T	W	T	F	S
1	2	3	4	5	6	7	May		1	2	3	4	5
8	9	10	11	12	13	14		6	7	8	9	10	11	12
15	16	17	18	19	20	21		13	14	15	16	17	18	19
22	23	24	25	26	27	28		20	21	22	23	24	25	26
29	30			April 2012				27	28	29	30	31		2012

Mental Power

FRIDAY
04.13.2012

Last Quarter

☽ IN ♑
☽ →♒: 5:47P
☽ VOC: 1:04P - 5:47P { ☽ ✶ ☿ }
♂ STATION: 11:53P
♂ TURNS D: 04° ♍
☿ IN D SHADOW
4:4 STAR GATE/HIDDEN 4:4 STAR GATE

♇ IS R
♄ IS R
⚳ IS R

APR

> *"Consciousness is an end in itself.
> There is nowhere to get to."*
> — D. H. Lawrence

8ᴀᴍ	2ᴘᴍ
9ᴀᴍ	3ᴘᴍ
10ᴀᴍ	4ᴘᴍ
11ᴀᴍ	5ᴘᴍ
12ᴘᴍ	6ᴘᴍ
1ᴘᴍ	7ᴘᴍ

All times Eastern Daylight Time

Mental Power

SATURDAY
04.14.2012

Last Quarter

☽ IN ♒: ALL DAY
☽ VOC: NO
♂ HAS STATIONED {D}
☿ IN D SHADOW
5:5 STAR GATE/HIDDEN 5:5 STAR GATE

♇ IS R
♄ IS R
⚹ IS R

"When you get into a spiritual approach to life, you are not trying to get someplace else."

Wayne Dyer

8ᴀᴍ	**2**ᴘᴍ
9ᴀᴍ	**3**ᴘᴍ
10ᴀᴍ	**4**ᴘᴍ
11ᴀᴍ	**5**ᴘᴍ
12ᴘᴍ	**6**ᴘᴍ
1ᴘᴍ	**7**ᴘᴍ

S	M	T	W	T	F	S	S	M	T	W	T	F	S
1	2	3	4	5	6	7	May		1	2	3	4	5
8	9	10	11	12	13	14	6	7	8	9	10	11	12
15	16	17	18	19	20	21	13	14	15	16	17	18	19
22	23	24	25	26	27	28	20	21	22	23	24	25	26
29	30			April 2012			27	28	29	30	31		2012

Mental Power

SUNDAY
04.15.2012

Last Quarter

☽ IN ♒: ALL DAY
☽ VOC: 6:41P - MIDNIGHT { ☽ ✶ ☉ }
☿ IN D SHADOW
HIDDEN 6:6 STAR GATE

♇ IS R
♄ IS R
♆ IS R

☉ ☍ ♄ 26° ♈/♎ 2:26P

"Enlightenment is not the end, it is the beginning."
Derek O'Neill

8ᴬᴹ	2ᴾᴹ
9ᴬᴹ	3ᴾᴹ
10ᴬᴹ	4ᴾᴹ
11ᴬᴹ	5ᴾᴹ
12ᴾᴹ	6ᴾᴹ
1ᴾᴹ	7ᴾᴹ

All times Eastern Daylight Time

Mental Power

MONDAY
04.16.2012

Last Quarter

☽ IN ♒
☽ →♓: 1:37A
☽ VOC: MIDNIGHT - 1:37A
☿ →♈: 6:42P
☿ IN D SHADOW
HIDDEN 7:7/12:12 STAR GATE

♇ IS R
♄ IS R
⚳ IS R

♅ △ ☊ 06°♈/♐ 12:56P
♅ ✶ ☊ 06°♈/♊ 12:56P

"Consciousness and meditation are methods where you can actually obtain 'God' perception."

George Harrison

8ᴀᴍ	2ᴘᴍ
9ᴀᴍ	3ᴘᴍ
10ᴀᴍ	4ᴘᴍ
11ᴀᴍ	5ᴘᴍ
12ᴘᴍ	6ᴘᴍ
1ᴘᴍ	7ᴘᴍ

S	M	T	W	T	F	S	S	M	T	W	T	F	S
1	2	3	4	5	6	7	May		1	2	3	4	5
8	9	10	11	12	13	14	6	7	8	9	10	11	12
15	16	17	18	19	20	21	13	14	15	16	17	18	19
22	23	24	25	26	27	28	20	21	22	23	24	25	26
29	30			April 2012			27	28	29	30	31		2012

Mental Power ♈

TUESDAY
04.17.2012

Last Quarter

☽ in ♓
☽ voc: 10:34a - Midnight {☽ ✷ ♃}
☿ in D Shadow
Hidden 8:8/12:12 Star Gate

♇ is R
♄ is R
⛢ is R

APR

> "You have to be whole: rich in the body, rich in science; rich in meditation, rich in consciousness."
>
> Osho

8ᴀᴍ	2ᴘᴍ
9ᴀᴍ	3ᴘᴍ
10ᴀᴍ	4ᴘᴍ
11ᴀᴍ	5ᴘᴍ
12ᴘᴍ	6ᴘᴍ
1ᴘᴍ	7ᴘᴍ

All times Eastern Daylight Time

WEDNESDAY
04.18.2012

Balsamic

Mental Power

☽ in ♓
☽ →♈: 11:58a
☽ voc: Midnight - 11:58a
☿ in D Shadow

♇ is R
♄ is R
⚴ is R

4:4/5:5/9:9 Star Gate/Hidden 9:9 Star Gate

> *"Man has the unquestionable ability to elevate his life by a conscious endeavor."*
>
> Henry David Thoreau

8ᴀᴍ	2ᴘᴍ
9ᴀᴍ	3ᴘᴍ
10ᴀᴍ	4ᴘᴍ
11ᴀᴍ	5ᴘᴍ
12ᴘᴍ	6ᴘᴍ
1ᴘᴍ	7ᴘᴍ

S	M	T	W	T	F	S	S	M	T	W	T	F	S
1	2	3	4	5	6	7	May		1	2	3	4	5
8	9	10	11	12	13	14	6	7	8	9	10	11	12
15	16	17	18	19	20	21	13	14	15	16	17	18	19
22	23	24	25	26	27	28	20	21	22	23	24	25	26
29	30			April 2012			27	28	29	30	31		2012

TAURUS

Mental Love

Symbol: The Tree of Life
Master: Godfre
Quality: Conscious Obedience
Ray: 4th Ray, Emerald Green
Trine: Earth
Hour: 4
Rulers: ♀ ☉ ⊕

I AM PRESENT

Mental Love

4 O'Clock Hour
Main Purpose:

Where you work to tune into your inner guidance and learn to trust it.

APRIL 19 – MAY 19

In Cosmic Astrology, Taurus is the sign of **Conscious Obedience**, an area of consciousness that resonates with the pink Love plume of the threefold flame within the heart. The Love energy requires a steadfast devotion. Here, in the mental body, you become more and more aware of the need to balance thought with emotion, mind with heart. As you travel through this part of your energy field you are compelled to develop an unwavering focus on your inner guidance mechanism, and to learn to obey it so well that it ultimately dictates your every move. The more you tune into your inner voice, the more you understand it to be emanating from your heart. Taurus was once known as the Bull, a solid, sturdy immovable force that can charge in anger when provoked. This is not a fitting energetic for the 5D human. Taurus is more like the Tree of Life in the new perspective, because it is always firmly rooted in the ground (the heart in 5D), and by trusting in its core connection, it slowly learns to reach higher and believe in infinite possibilities.

Taurus corresponds to the 4 o'clock hour in Cosmic Astrology, once known as the 5th house. This aspect of consciousness is connected to the mental body, but it is very much connected to the emotional Self for the first time. The 5th house has its creative potentials, but the heart becomes the place where all creation comes from in the Taurus energetic. All of our potential becomes so much more accessible when we allow our Selves to be guided by the inner voice and follow our hearts.

Wherever Taurus is in your birth chart you must learn to overcome inner resistance, which is the result of past actions, and trust in your own inner voice. Trusting your instincts, your intuitive faculties, is the main objective here. If Taurus is your Sun sign, you have chosen the Taurus identity for your entire lifetime and it is your evolutionary purpose to overcome core stuckness and allow your soul to grow into its greater potential.

FAMOUS TAURUS

Barbra Streisand, Charlotte Bronte, Tony Blair, Martha Graham, Karl Marx, George Lucas, Queen Elizabeth II, David Beckham, Audrey Hepburn, Katharine Hepburn, Jiddu Krishnamurti, Jack Nicholson, Duke Ellington, Bertrand Russell, Bono, Dante Alighieri, Enya, Sigmund Freud, Vladimir Nabokov

Mental Love

THURSDAY
04.19.2012

Balsamic

☽ IN ♈: ALL DAY
☽ VOC: NO
☿ IN D SHADOW
☉→♉: 12:12P
5:5 STAR GATE/HIDDEN 1:1 STAR GATE

♇ IS R
♄ IS R
⯝ IS R

"Let Love Rule."
Lenny Kravitz

8 AM	2 PM
9 AM	3 PM
10 AM	4 PM
11 AM	5 PM
12 PM	6 PM
1 PM	7 PM

All times Eastern Daylight Time

FRIDAY
04.20.2012

Balsamic

Mental Love

☽ IN ♈: ALL DAY
☽ VOC: 3:34P - MIDNIGHT { ☽ ☍ ♄ }
☿ IN D SHADOW
HIDDEN 2:2 STAR GATE

♇ IS R
♄ IS R
♆ IS R

"Leave the city of your comfort, go into the wilderness of your intuition, and you will discover yourself."

Alan Alda

8ᴬᴹ	2ᴾᴹ
9ᴬᴹ	3ᴾᴹ
10ᴬᴹ	4ᴾᴹ
11ᴬᴹ	5ᴾᴹ
12ᴾᴹ	6ᴾᴹ
1ᴾᴹ	7ᴾᴹ

S	M	T	W	T	F	S	S	M	T	W	T	F	S
1	2	3	4	5	6	7	May		1	2	3	4	5
8	9	10	11	12	13	14	6	7	8	9	10	11	12
15	16	17	18	19	20	21	13	14	15	16	17	18	19
22	23	24	25	26	27	28	20	21	22	23	24	25	26
29	30			April 2012			27	28	29	30	31		2012

Mental
Love

SATURDAY
04.21.2012

New Moon

☽ IN ♈
☽ →♉: 12:05A
☽ VOC: MIDNIGHT - 12:05A
☿ IN D SHADOW
HIDDEN 3:3/12:12 STAR GATE

♇ IS R
♄ IS R
⚴ IS R

NEW MOON { ☽ ☌ ☉ }: 3:18A
01° ♉35'

☿ △ ☊ 05°♈/♐ 10:46P
☿ ⚹ ☋ 05°♈/♊ 10:46P

APR

"Live your beliefs and you can turn the world around."
                                        Henry David Thoreau

8ᴀᴍ	2ᴘᴍ
9ᴀᴍ	3ᴘᴍ
10ᴀᴍ	4ᴘᴍ
11ᴀᴍ	5ᴘᴍ
12ᴘᴍ	6ᴘᴍ
1ᴘᴍ	7ᴘᴍ

All times Eastern Daylight Time

Mental Love

SUNDAY
04.22.2012

New Moon

☽ IN ♉: ALL DAY
☽ VOC: 1:10P - MIDNIGHT { ☽ ☌ ♃ }
☿ IN D SHADOW
4:4 STAR GATE/HIDDEN 4:4 STAR GATE

♇ IS R
♄ IS R
⚹ IS R

☉ ✶ ♆ 03°♉/♓ 5:18A
☿ ☌ ♅ 06°♈   4:29P

"We all go everywhere looking for something that is inside us."

Derek O'Neill

8ᴀᴍ	2ᴘᴍ
9ᴀᴍ	3ᴘᴍ
10ᴀᴍ	4ᴘᴍ
11ᴀᴍ	5ᴘᴍ
12ᴘᴍ	6ᴘᴍ
1ᴘᴍ	7ᴘᴍ

Earth Day

S	M	T	W	T	F	S	S	M	T	W	T	F	S
1	2	3	4	5	6	7	May		1	2	3	4	5
8	9	10	11	12	13	14	6	7	8	9	10	11	12
15	16	17	18	19	20	21	13	14	15	16	17	18	19
22	23	24	25	26	27	28	20	21	22	23	24	25	26
29	30			April 2012			27	28	29	30	31		2012

Mental
Love

MONDAY
04.23.2012

Crescent

☽ IN ♉
☽ →♊: 1:05P
☽ VOC: MIDNIGHT - 1:05P
☿ LEAVES ☽ SHADOW
5:5 STAR GATE/HIDDEN 5:5 STAR GATE

♇ IS R
♄ IS R
⚹ IS R

☉ △ ♂ 04°♉/♍ 8:59P

APR

> *"Your treasure house is within; it contains all you'll ever need."*
>
> Hui-Hai

8 AM	2 PM
9 AM	3 PM
10 AM	4 PM
11 AM	5 PM
12 PM	6 PM
1 PM	7 PM

All times Eastern Daylight Time

Mental Love

TUESDAY
04.24.2012

Crescent

☽ IN ♊: ALL DAY
☽ VOC: NO
HIDDEN 6:6 STAR GATE

♇ IS R
♄ IS R
⚸ IS R

> *"If you love everything, you will perceive the divine mystery in things."*
>
> Fyodor Dostoyevsky

8ᴀᴍ	2ᴘᴍ
9ᴀᴍ	3ᴘᴍ
10ᴀᴍ	4ᴘᴍ
11ᴀᴍ	5ᴘᴍ
12ᴘᴍ	6ᴘᴍ
1ᴘᴍ	7ᴘᴍ

S	M	T	W	T	F	S		S	M	T	W	T	F	S
1	2	3	4	5	6	7	May		1	2	3	4	5
8	9	10	11	12	13	14		6	7	8	9	10	11	12
15	16	17	18	19	20	21		13	14	15	16	17	18	19
22	23	24	25	26	27	28		20	21	22	23	24	25	26
29	30			April 2012				27	28	29	30	31		2012

Mental
Love

WEDNESDAY
04.25.2012

Crescent

☽ IN ♊: ALL DAY
☽ VOC: 4:31P - MIDNIGHT { ☽ △ ♄ }
HIDDEN 7:7/12:12 STAR GATE

♇ IS R
♄ IS R
⚵ IS R

☿ □ ♇ 09°♈/♑ 10:51A

APR

> *"Faith is belief in what we do not see; and its reward is to see what we believe."*
>
> St. Augustine

8ᴀᴍ	2ᴘᴍ
9ᴀᴍ	3ᴘᴍ
10ᴀᴍ	4ᴘᴍ
11ᴀᴍ	5ᴘᴍ
12ᴘᴍ	6ᴘᴍ
1ᴘᴍ	7ᴘᴍ

All times Eastern Daylight Time

Mental Love

THURSDAY
04.26.2012

Crescent

☽ IN ♊
☽ →♋: 1:42A
☽ VOC: MIDNIGHT - 1:42A
HIDDEN 8:8/12:12 STAR GATE

♇ IS R
♄ IS R
⚸ IS R

"Often you have to rely on intuition."
Bill Gates

8ᴀᴍ	2ᴘᴍ
9ᴀᴍ	3ᴘᴍ
10ᴀᴍ	4ᴘᴍ
11ᴀᴍ	5ᴘᴍ
12ᴘᴍ	6ᴘᴍ
1ᴘᴍ	7ᴘᴍ

Yom HaAtzma'ut

S	M	T	W	T	F	S	S	M	T	W	T	F	S
1	2	3	4	5	6	7	May		1	2	3	4	5
8	9	10	11	12	13	14	6	7	8	9	10	11	12
15	16	17	18	19	20	21	13	14	15	16	17	18	19
22	23	24	25	26	27	28	20	21	22	23	24	25	26
29	30			April	2012		27	28	29	30	31		2012

Mental
Love

FRIDAY
04.27.2012

Crescent

☽ IN ♋: ALL DAY
☽ VOC: NO
HIDDEN 4:4/5:5/9:9 STAR GATE

♇ IS R
♄ IS R
♆ IS R

"Intuition is a spiritual faculty and does not explain, but simply points the way."

Florence Scovel Shinn

8^{AM}	2^{PM}
9^{AM}	3^{PM}
10^{AM}	4^{PM}
11^{AM}	5^{PM}
12^{PM}	6^{PM}
1^{PM}	7^{PM}

All times Eastern Daylight Time

Mental
Love

SATURDAY
04.28.2012

Crescent

☽ IN ♋
☽ →♌: 12:10P
☽ VOC: 3:05A - 12:10P {☽ □ ♄}
HIDDEN 1:1/5:5 STAR GATE

♇ IS R
♄ IS R
⚴ IS R

☉ ✶ ♃ 09°♉/♓ 1:52P

"It is through science that we prove, but through intuition that we discover."

Henri Poincare

8ᴀᴍ	**2**ᴘᴍ
9ᴀᴍ	**3**ᴘᴍ
10ᴀᴍ	**4**ᴘᴍ
11ᴀᴍ	**5**ᴘᴍ
12ᴘᴍ	**6**ᴘᴍ
1ᴘᴍ	**7**ᴘᴍ

S	M	T	W	T	F	S	S	M	T	W	T	F	S
1	2	3	4	5	6	7	May		1	2	3	4	5
8	9	10	11	12	13	14	6	7	8	9	10	11	12
15	16	17	18	19	20	21	13	14	15	16	17	18	19
22	23	24	25	26	27	28	20	21	22	23	24	25	26
29	30			April 2012			27	28	29	30	31		2012

Mental Love

SUNDAY
04.29.2012

First Quarter

☽ IN ♌: ALL DAY
☽ VOC: NO
HIDDEN 11:11 STAR GATE

♇ IS R
♄ IS R
⚷ IS R

☉ △ ♇ 09°♉/♑ 5:34p

"Motivation is much more important than action."

Derek O'Neill

8ᴀᴍ	2ᴘᴍ
9ᴀᴍ	3ᴘᴍ
10ᴀᴍ	4ᴘᴍ
11ᴀᴍ	5ᴘᴍ
12ᴘᴍ	6ᴘᴍ
1ᴘᴍ	7ᴘᴍ

All times Eastern Daylight Time

Mental
Love

MONDAY
04.30.2012

First Quarter

☽ IN ♌
☽ →♍: 7:02P
☽ VOC: 10:17A - 7:02P {☽ ✶ ♄}
⚵ →♉: 7:02P
HIDDEN 3:3/12:12 STAR GATE

♇ IS R
♄ IS R
⚷ IS R

♂ □ ☊ 05°♍/♐ 7:30P
♂ □ ☋ 05°♍/♊ 7:30P

"Trust yourself. You know more than you think you do."
Benjamin Spock

8ᴀᴍ	2ᴘᴍ
9ᴀᴍ	3ᴘᴍ
10ᴀᴍ	4ᴘᴍ
11ᴀᴍ	5ᴘᴍ
12ᴘᴍ	6ᴘᴍ
1ᴘᴍ	7ᴘᴍ

S	M	T	W	T	F	S	S	M	T	W	T	F	S
1	2	3	4	5	6	7	May		1	2	3	4	5
8	9	10	11	12	13	14	6	7	8	9	10	11	12
15	16	17	18	19	20	21	13	14	15	16	17	18	19
22	23	24	25	26	27	28	20	21	22	23	24	25	26
29	30			April 2012			27	28	29	30	31		2012

Mental Love

TUESDAY
05.01.2012

First Quarter

☽ IN ♍: ALL DAY
☽ VOC: NO
5:5 STAR GATE

♇ IS R
♄ IS R
⚹ IS R

MAY

"Just as a candle cannot burn without fire, men cannot live without a spiritual life."
Gautama Buddha

8ᴀᴍ	2ᴘᴍ
9ᴀᴍ	3ᴘᴍ
10ᴀᴍ	4ᴘᴍ
11ᴀᴍ	5ᴘᴍ
12ᴘᴍ	6ᴘᴍ
1ᴘᴍ	7ᴘᴍ

Beltane
May Day

All times Eastern Daylight Time

Mental
Love

WEDNESDAY
05.02.2012

Gibbous

☽ in ♍
☽ →♎: 10:04p
☽ voc: 6:58a - 10:04p { ☽ □ ♀ }
5:5/12:12 Star Gate

♇ is R
♄ is R
⚹ is R

"I allow my intuition to lead my path."

Manuel Puig

8ᴀᴍ	2ᴘᴍ
9ᴀᴍ	3ᴘᴍ
10ᴀᴍ	4ᴘᴍ
11ᴀᴍ	5ᴘᴍ
12ᴘᴍ	6ᴘᴍ
1ᴘᴍ	7ᴘᴍ

	S	M	T	W	T	F	S	S	M	T	W	T	F	S
	May		1	2	3	4	5	June 2012					1	2
	6	7	8	9	10	11	12	3	4	5	6	7	8	9
	13	14	15	16	17	18	19	10	11	12	13	14	15	16
	20	21	22	23	24	25	26	17	18	19	20	21	22	23
	27	28	29	30	31		2012	24	25	26	27	28	29	30

Mental Love

THURSDAY
05.03.2012

Gibbous

☽ IN ♎: ALL DAY
☽ VOC: NO
5:5 STAR GATE

♇ IS R
♄ IS R
⚸ IS R

☿ ✶ ♀ 22°♉/♊ 11:01P

MAY

"Instinct is untaught ability."

Bain

8ᴀᴍ	2ᴘᴍ
9ᴀᴍ	3ᴘᴍ
10ᴀᴍ	4ᴘᴍ
11ᴀᴍ	5ᴘᴍ
12ᴘᴍ	6ᴘᴍ
1ᴘᴍ	7ᴘᴍ

All times Eastern Daylight Time

Mental Love

FRIDAY
05.04.2012

Gibbous

☽ IN ♎
☽ →♏: 10:20P
☽ VOC: 2:02P - 10:20P {☽ ☌ ♄}
5:5 STAR GATE

♇ IS R
♄ IS R
⚹ IS R

"Listen to your intuition.
It will tell you everything you need to know."

Anthony J. D'Angelo

8ᴀᴍ	2ᴘᴍ
9ᴀᴍ	3ᴘᴍ
10ᴀᴍ	4ᴘᴍ
11ᴀᴍ	5ᴘᴍ
12ᴘᴍ	6ᴘᴍ
1ᴘᴍ	7ᴘᴍ

	S	M	T	W	T	F	S	S	M	T	W	T	F	S
May		1	2	3	4	5	June 2012					1	2
	6	7	8	9	10	11	12	3	4	5	6	7	8	9
	13	14	15	16	17	18	19	10	11	12	13	14	15	16
	20	21	22	23	24	25	26	17	18	19	20	21	22	23
	27	28	29	30	31		2012	24	25	26	27	28	29	30

Mental Love

SATURDAY
05.05.2012

Full Moon

☽ IN ♏: ALL DAY
☽ VOC: NO
5:5:5 TRIPLE STAR GATE

♇ IS R
♄ IS R
⚷ IS R

FULL MOON { ☽ ☍ ☉ }: 11:35P
16° ♏01'

☿ ☍ ♄ 25° ♉/ ♎ 9:07P

*"Follow your instincts.
That's where true wisdom manifests itself."*

Oprah Winfrey

8 AM	2 PM
9 AM	3 PM
10 AM	4 PM
11 AM	5 PM
12 PM	6 PM
1 PM	7 PM

Cinco de Mayo

All times Eastern Daylight Time

SUNDAY
05.06.2012

Full Moon

☽ IN ♏
☽ →♐: 9:39P
☽ VOC: 8:15A - 9:39P { ☽ ☌ ♃ }
5:5 STAR GATE

♇ IS R
♄ IS R
⚹ IS R

"Don't ask for guidance on the Internet.
Go on the Inner-Net."

Derek O'Neill

8ᴀᴍ	2ᴘᴍ
9ᴀᴍ	3ᴘᴍ
10ᴀᴍ	4ᴘᴍ
11ᴀᴍ	5ᴘᴍ
12ᴘᴍ	6ᴘᴍ
1ᴘᴍ	7ᴘᴍ

Wesak Moon
Buddha Purnima
Saga Dawa

S	M	T	W	T	F	S	S	M	T	W	T	F	S
May		1	2	3	4	5	June 2012					1	2
6	7	8	9	10	11	12	3	4	5	6	7	8	9
13	14	15	16	17	18	19	10	11	12	13	14	15	16
20	21	22	23	24	25	26	17	18	19	20	21	22	23
27	28	29	30	31		2012	24	25	26	27	28	29	30

Mental Love

MONDAY
05.07.2012

Full Moon

☽ IN ♐: ALL DAY
☽ VOC: NO
5:5/12:12 STAR GATE

♇ IS R
♄ IS R
✤ IS R

MAY

"You must trust the small voice inside you which tells you exactly what to say, what to decide."

Ingrid Bergman

8ᴬᴹ	2ᴾᴹ
9ᴬᴹ	3ᴾᴹ
10ᴬᴹ	4ᴾᴹ
11ᴬᴹ	5ᴾᴹ
12ᴾᴹ	6ᴾᴹ
1ᴾᴹ	7ᴾᴹ

May Day (Ireland)

Mental
Love

TUESDAY
05.08.2012

Full Moon

☽ IN ♐
☽ →♑: 10:00P
☽ VOC: 9:34P - 10:00P { ☽ △ ☿ }
5:5 STAR GATE

♇ IS R
♄ IS R
⚴ IS R

*"He who knows others is learned; he
who knows himself is wise."*

Lao-tzu

8ᴬᴹ	2ᴾᴹ
9ᴬᴹ	3ᴾᴹ
10ᴬᴹ	4ᴾᴹ
11ᴬᴹ	5ᴾᴹ
12ᴾᴹ	6ᴾᴹ
1ᴾᴹ	7ᴾᴹ

S	M	T	W	T	F	S	S	M	T	W	T	F	S
May		1	2	3	4	5	June 2012					1	2
6	7	8	9	10	11	12	3	4	5	6	7	8	9
13	14	15	16	17	18	19	10	11	12	13	14	15	16
20	21	22	23	24	25	26	17	18	19	20	21	22	23
27	28	29	30	31		2012	24	25	26	27	28	29	30

Mental Love

WEDNESDAY
05.09.2012

Disseminating

☽ IN ♐: ALL DAY
☽ VOC: NO
☿ →♉: 1:14A
5:5 STAR GATE

♇ IS R
♄ IS R
⚸ IS R

"All great men are gifted with intuition. They know without reasoning or analysis, what they need to know."

Alexis Carrel

8ᴬᴹ	2ᴾᴹ
9ᴬᴹ	3ᴾᴹ
10ᴬᴹ	4ᴾᴹ
11ᴬᴹ	5ᴾᴹ
12ᴾᴹ	6ᴾᴹ
1ᴾᴹ	7ᴾᴹ

All times Eastern Daylight Time

Mental Love

THURSDAY
05.10.2012

Disseminating

☽ IN ♌: ALL DAY
☽ VOC: 3:11P - MIDNIGHT {☽ □ ♄}
5:5 STAR GATE

♇ IS R
♄ IS R
⚷ IS R

☿ ✶ ♆   03°♉/♓ 5:59P

"All men should strive to learn before they die, what they are running from, and to, and why."

James Thurber

8ᴀᴍ	2ᴘᴍ
9ᴀᴍ	3ᴘᴍ
10ᴀᴍ	4ᴘᴍ
11ᴀᴍ	5ᴘᴍ
12ᴘᴍ	6ᴘᴍ
1ᴘᴍ	7ᴘᴍ

Lag B'Omer

S	M	T	W	T	F	S	S	M	T	W	T	F	S
May		1	2	3	4	5	June 2012					1	2
6	7	8	9	10	11	12	3	4	5	6	7	8	9
13	14	15	16	17	18	19	10	11	12	13	14	15	16
20	21	22	23	24	25	26	17	18	19	20	21	22	23
27	28	29	30	31		2012	24	25	26	27	28	29	30

Mental Love

FRIDAY
05.11.2012

Disseminating

☽ in ♑
☽ →♒: 1:03a
☽ voc: Midnight - 1:03a
5:5 Star Gate

♇ is R
♄ is R
⚴ is R

MAY

*"The more you trust your intuition,
the more empowered you become, the stronger
you become, and the happier you become."*

Gisele Bundchen

8ᴀᴍ	2ᴘᴍ
9ᴀᴍ	3ᴘᴍ
10ᴀᴍ	4ᴘᴍ
11ᴀᴍ	5ᴘᴍ
12ᴘᴍ	6ᴘᴍ
1ᴘᴍ	7ᴘᴍ

All times Eastern Daylight Time

Mental Love

SATURDAY
05.12.2012

Last Quarter

☽ IN ♒: ALL DAY
☽ VOC: 8:52P - MIDNIGHT {☽ △ ♄}
5:5 STAR GATE

♇ IS R
♄ IS R
⛢ IS R

☿ ✶ ♇ 09°♓/♑ 10:07A

*"The universe is a single atom:
the convergence of science and spirituality."*
14th Dalai Lama

....
....
....
....
....
....
....
....

8ᴀᴍ	2ᴘᴍ
9ᴀᴍ	3ᴘᴍ
10ᴀᴍ	4ᴘᴍ
11ᴀᴍ	5ᴘᴍ
12ᴘᴍ	6ᴘᴍ
1ᴘᴍ	7ᴘᴍ

	S	M	T	W	T	F	S	S	M	T	W	T	F	S
May			1	2	3	4	5	June 2012					1	2
	6	7	8	9	10	11	12	3	4	5	6	7	8	9
	13	14	15	16	17	18	19	10	11	12	13	14	15	16
	20	21	22	23	24	25	26	17	18	19	20	21	22	23
	27	28	29	30	31		2012	24	25	26	27	28	29	30

Mental Love

SUNDAY
05.13.2012

Last Quarter

☽ IN ♒
☽ →♓: 7:42A
☽ VOC: MIDNIGHT - 7:42A
5:5 STAR GATE

♇ IS R
♄ IS R
⚹ IS R

☉ ☌ ♃ 23°♉ 9:23A
☿ △ ♂ 08°♉/♍ 4:54P

MAY

> "No one is stuck. No one is ever stuck. Things change all the time, whether we want them to or not."
>
> Derek O'Neill

8ᴬᴹ	2ᴾᴹ
9ᴬᴹ	3ᴾᴹ
10ᴬᴹ	4ᴾᴹ
11ᴬᴹ	5ᴾᴹ
12ᴾᴹ	6ᴾᴹ
1ᴾᴹ	7ᴾᴹ

Mother's Day

All times Eastern Daylight Time

Mental Love

MONDAY
05.14.2012

Last Quarter

☽ IN ♓: ALL DAY
☽ VOC: NO
♀ IS STATIONING {R}
5:5:5 TRIPLE STAR GATE

♇ IS R
♄ IS R
♆ IS R

☿ △ ♇ 09°♉/♑ 4:09A
☿ ✶ ♃ 09°♉/♓ 5:07A

> *"Every time you don't follow your inner guidance,*
> *you feel a loss of energy, loss of power,*
> *a sense of spiritual deadness."*
>
> Shakti Gawain

8 AM	2 PM
9 AM	3 PM
10 AM	4 PM
11 AM	5 PM
12 PM	6 PM
1 PM	7 PM

Mental Love

TUESDAY
05.15.2012

Last Quarter

☽ in ♓
☽ →♈: 5:45p
☽ voc: 7:59a - 5:45p {☽ ✶ ☉}
♀ Station: 10:33a
♀ turns R: 24° ♊
5:5 Star Gate

♇ is R
♄ is R
⚷ is R

MAY

"To the question of your life, you are the only answer.
To the problems of your life, you are the only solution."
Joe Cordare

8ᴀᴍ	2ᴘᴍ
9ᴀᴍ	3ᴘᴍ
10ᴀᴍ	4ᴘᴍ
11ᴀᴍ	5ᴘᴍ
12ᴘᴍ	6ᴘᴍ
1ᴘᴍ	7ᴘᴍ

All times Eastern Daylight Time

WEDNESDAY
05.16.2012

Last Quarter

Mental Love

☽ IN ♈: ALL DAY
☽ VOC: NO
♀ HAS STATIONED {R}
5:5/12:12 STAR GATE

♇ IS R
♄ IS R
⯝ IS R

♂ △ ♇ 09°♍/♑ 12:26P

> *"Our appointment with life takes place in the present moment. And the venue is right where we are right now."*
> — Gautama Buddha

8ᴬᴹ	**2**ᴾᴹ
9ᴬᴹ	**3**ᴾᴹ
10ᴬᴹ	**4**ᴾᴹ
11ᴬᴹ	**5**ᴾᴹ
12ᴾᴹ	**6**ᴾᴹ
1ᴾᴹ	**7**ᴾᴹ

S	M	T	W	T	F	S	S	M	T	W	T	F	S
May		1	2	3	4	5	June 2012					1	2
6	7	8	9	10	11	12	3	4	5	6	7	8	9
13	14	15	16	17	18	19	10	11	12	13	14	15	16
20	21	22	23	24	25	26	17	18	19	20	21	22	23
27	28	29	30	31		2012	24	25	26	27	28	29	30

Mental Love

THURSDAY
05.17.2012

Last Quarter

☽ IN ♈: ALL DAY
☽ VOC: 5:44P - MIDNIGHT { ☽ ☍ ♄ }
5:5 STAR GATE

♇ IS R
♄ IS R
⚹ IS R
♀ IS R

♂ ☍ ☿ 09°♍/♓ 2:57A

MAY

"Wisdom is knowing what to do next; virtue is doing it."
David Star Jordan

8ᴬᴹ	2ᴾᴹ
9ᴬᴹ	3ᴾᴹ
10ᴬᴹ	4ᴾᴹ
11ᴬᴹ	5ᴾᴹ
12ᴾᴹ	6ᴾᴹ
1ᴾᴹ	7ᴾᴹ

All times Eastern Daylight Time

Mental Love

FRIDAY
05.18.2012

Balsamic

☽ IN ♈
☽ →♉: 6:03A
☽ VOC: MIDNIGHT - 6:03A
☿ →♈: 12:18A
5:5 STAR GATE

♇ IS R
♄ IS R
⚹ IS R
♀ IS R

"True happiness is when the love that is within us finds expression in external activities."

Mother Amma

8AM	**2**PM
9AM	**3**PM
10AM	**4**PM
11AM	**5**PM
12PM	**6**PM
1PM	**7**PM

S	M	T	W	T	F	S	S	M	T	W	T	F	S
May		1	2	3	4	5	June 2012					1	2
6	7	8	9	10	11	12	3	4	5	6	7	8	9
13	14	15	16	17	18	19	10	11	12	13	14	15	16
20	21	22	23	24	25	26	17	18	19	20	21	22	23
27	28	29	30	31		2012	24	25	26	27	28	29	30

Mental Love

SATURDAY
05.19.2012

Balsamic

☽ IN ♉: ALL DAY
☽ VOC: NO
5:5 STAR GATE

♇ IS R
♄ IS R
⚹ IS R
♀ IS R

"Faith is power to believe and power to see."

Prentice Mulford

8ᴀᴍ	2ᴘᴍ
9ᴀᴍ	3ᴘᴍ
10ᴀᴍ	4ᴘᴍ
11ᴀᴍ	5ᴘᴍ
12ᴘᴍ	6ᴘᴍ
1ᴘᴍ	7ᴘᴍ

All times Eastern Daylight Time

GEMINI

Mental Wisdom

Symbol: The Diamond
Master: El Morya
Quality: Conscious Wisdom
Ray: 5th Ray, Crystalline Orange
Trine: Air
Hour: 5
Rulers: ☿ ☽ ♅

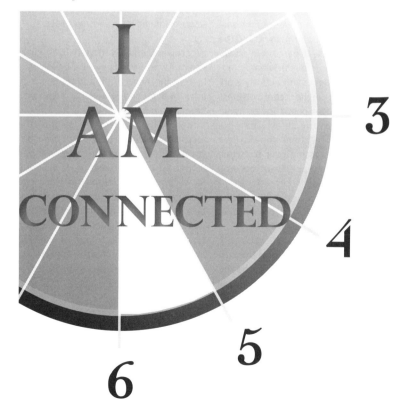

I AM CONNECTED

5 O'Clock Hour
Main Purpose:

Where you allow Love and only Love to generate all of your thoughts.

MAY 20 – JUNE 19

Gemini is the sign of **Conscious Wisdom**, where the experience of loving with the mind becomes a reality, and the integrated mind/heart can be realized. This is the part of your energy field that completes the experience of the mental body, the higher consciousness, and every year the journey through this sector delivers you to the experience of your emotional body. The awareness of the mind and the heart are ever present here. It is essential to become conscious of what is motivating your thoughts and actively work to express your higher consciousness instead of your fear-based lower mind. When you consciously detach from habitual fear-based reactions you discover the power of expressing your true Self. In Cosmic Astrology, the Twins become the Diamond. That is, the perception that was based on duality in the lower mind becomes the multifaceted brilliance of the diamond (die-mind) in 5D.

Gemini is the 5 o'clock hour on the cosmic clock, which corresponds to the 4th house of the birth chart. The 4th house represents one's root system, the motivational forces that move you to become all that you become in the world. The core of any motive is belief, and what is belief but a thought backed up by an emotion? This Gemini hour is where we truly can experience the power of the mind/heart connection in a realized way. Wisdom is always the result of coming from a consciously integrated mind and heart.

Wherever Gemini is in your birth chart you must work to resolve any imbalances in the mind, heart, body and spirit as they arise by consciously aligning mind with heart. When this balance is achieved, the throat chakra activates and becomes the focus for speaking your Truth. The discovery of expressing your authentic self follows. If your Sun sign is Gemini you have chosen this lifetime to transcend the duality of thought and emotion, first by experiencing each in all their intensity, and then, by utilizing your great capacity for understanding duality to transcend it. In your lifetime you have the opportunity to use your voice to speak your Truth.

FAMOUS GEMINI

John F. Kennedy, Bob Hope, Bob Dylan, Paul McCartney, Marilyn Monroe, Helena Bonham-Carter, Igor Stravinsky, Miles Davis, Che Guevara, Henry Kissinger, William Butler Yeats, Jacques-Yves Costeau, Prince, Donald Trump, Venus Williams, Johnny Depp, Cole Porter, Derek O'Neill

SUNDAY
05.20.2012

New Moon

☽ IN ♉
☽ →♊: 7:05P
☽ VOC: 8:35A - 7:05P { ☽ ☌ ♃ }
☉ →♊: 11:15A
5:5 Star Gate

♇ IS R
♄ IS R
⚹ IS R
♀ IS R

NEW MOON { ☽ ☌ ☉ }: 7:47P
00° ♊ 21'
ANNULAR SOLAR ECLIPSE

"Love is the answer. Now what is the question?"
Derek O'Neill

8 AM	2 PM
9 AM	3 PM
10 AM	4 PM
11 AM	5 PM
12 PM	6 PM
1 PM	7 PM

All times Eastern Daylight Time

MONDAY
05.21.2012

New Moon

☽ IN ♊: ALL DAY
☽ VOC: NO
5:5 STAR GATE

♇ IS R
♄ IS R
⛢ IS R
♀ IS R

"There is no God higher than Truth."
Mahatma Gandhi

8ᴀᴍ	2ᴘᴍ
9ᴀᴍ	3ᴘᴍ
10ᴀᴍ	4ᴘᴍ
11ᴀᴍ	5ᴘᴍ
12ᴘᴍ	6ᴘᴍ
1ᴘᴍ	7ᴘᴍ

Victoria Day

S	M	T	W	T	F	S
May		1	2	3	4	5
6	7	8	9	10	11	12
13	14	15	16	17	18	19
20	21	22	23	24	25	26
27	28	29	30	31		2012

S	M	T	W	T	F	S
June 2012					1	2
3	4	5	6	7	8	9
10	11	12	13	14	15	16
17	18	19	20	21	22	23
24	25	26	27	28	29	30

Mental Wisdom

TUESDAY
05.22.2012

New Moon

☽ IN ♊︎   ♇ IS R   ☿ ☌ ♃ 25°♉︎   1:58A
☽ VOC: 6:50P - MIDNIGHT { ☽ △ ♄ }   ♄ IS R
5:5 STAR GATE   ⚹ IS R
     ♀ IS R

"Climb the mountains and get their good tidings."
                                              John Muir

8ᴬᴹ	2ᴾᴹ
9ᴬᴹ	3ᴾᴹ
10ᴬᴹ	4ᴾᴹ
11ᴬᴹ	5ᴾᴹ
12ᴾᴹ	6ᴾᴹ
1ᴾᴹ	7ᴾᴹ

All times Eastern Daylight Time

Mental Wisdom

WEDNESDAY
05.23.2012

Crescent

☽ IN ♊
☽ →♋: 7:31A
☽ VOC: MIDNIGHT - 7:31A
5:5:5 TRIPLE STAR GATE

♇ IS R
♄ IS R
⚹ IS R
♀ IS R

☉ □ ♆ 03°♋/♓ 4:55P

"Turn your wounds into wisdom."
Oprah Winfrey

8 AM	2 PM
9 AM	3 PM
10 AM	4 PM
11 AM	5 PM
12 PM	6 PM
1 PM	7 PM

S	M	T	W	T	F	S		S	M	T	W	T	F	S
May		1	2	3	4	5		June 2012					1	2
6	7	8	9	10	11	12		3	4	5	6	7	8	9
13	14	15	16	17	18	19		10	11	12	13	14	15	16
20	21	22	23	24	25	26		17	18	19	20	21	22	23
27	28	29	30	31		2012		24	25	26	27	28	29	30

Mental Wisdom

THURSDAY
05.24.2012

Crescent

☽ IN ♋: ALL DAY
☽ VOC: NO
☿ →♊: 7:12A
5:5 STAR GATE

♇ IS R
♄ IS R
⚹ IS R
♀ IS R

MAY

"The only true wisdom is in knowing you know nothing."
Socrates

8ᴀᴍ	2ᴘᴍ
9ᴀᴍ	3ᴘᴍ
10ᴀᴍ	4ᴘᴍ
11ᴀᴍ	5ᴘᴍ
12ᴘᴍ	6ᴘᴍ
1ᴘᴍ	7ᴘᴍ

All times Eastern Daylight Time

Mental Wisdom

FRIDAY
05.25.2012

Crescent

☽ IN ♋
☽ →♌: 6:11p
☽ VOC: 10:33a - 6:11p {☽ ✶ ♃}
5:5 Star Gate

♇ IS R
♄ IS R
⚷ IS R
♀ IS R

☉ ☍ ☊ 05°Ⅱ/♐ 5:33p
☉ ☌ ☋ 05°Ⅱ   5:33p
☿ □ ♆ 03°Ⅱ/♓ 5:37p

> *"Instinct is intelligence incapable of self-consciousness."*
> — John Sterling

8ᴀᴍ	2ᴘᴍ
9ᴀᴍ	3ᴘᴍ
10ᴀᴍ	4ᴘᴍ
11ᴀᴍ	5ᴘᴍ
12ᴘᴍ	6ᴘᴍ
1ᴘᴍ	7ᴘᴍ

S	M	T	W	T	F	S
May		1	2	3	4	5
6	7	8	9	10	11	12
13	14	15	16	17	18	19
20	21	22	23	24	25	26
27	28	29	30	31		2012

S	M	T	W	T	F	S
June 2012					1	2
3	4	5	6	7	8	9
10	11	12	13	14	15	16
17	18	19	20	21	22	23
24	25	26	27	28	29	30

Mental Wisdom

SATURDAY
05.26.2012

Crescent

☽ IN ♌: ALL DAY
☽ VOC: NO
5:5/12:12 STAR GATE

♇ IS R
♄ IS R
⚴ IS R
♀ IS R

☿ ☍ ☊ 05°Ⅱ/♐ 2:48P
☿ ☌ ☋ 05°Ⅱ 2:48P

MAY

"There is no Truth. There is only the truth within each moment."

Ramana Maharshi

8ᴀᴍ	2ᴘᴍ
9ᴀᴍ	3ᴘᴍ
10ᴀᴍ	4ᴘᴍ
11ᴀᴍ	5ᴘᴍ
12ᴘᴍ	6ᴘᴍ
1ᴘᴍ	7ᴘᴍ

All times Eastern Daylight Time

SUNDAY
05.27.2012

Crescent

Mental Wisdom

☽ IN ♌: ALL DAY
☽ VOC: 8:54P - MIDNIGHT { ☽ □ ♃ }
5:5 STAR GATE

♇ IS R
♄ IS R
♆ IS R
♀ IS R

☉ ☌ ☿ 07°♊ 7:40A
☿ ✶ ♅ 08°♊/♈ 5:33P

"Information is what you find in books. Knowledge is what you have experienced."

Derek O'Neill

8ᴀᴍ	2ᴘᴍ
9ᴀᴍ	3ᴘᴍ
10ᴀᴍ	4ᴘᴍ
11ᴀᴍ	5ᴘᴍ
12ᴘᴍ	6ᴘᴍ
1ᴘᴍ	7ᴘᴍ

Shavuot

S	M	T	W	T	F	S
May		1	2	3	4	5
6	7	8	9	10	11	12
13	14	15	16	17	18	19
20	21	22	23	24	25	26
27	28	29	30	31		2012

S	M	T	W	T	F	S
June 2012					1	2
3	4	5	6	7	8	9
10	11	12	13	14	15	16
17	18	19	20	21	22	23
24	25	26	27	28	29	30

Mental Wisdom

MONDAY
05.28.2012

First Quarter

☽ IN ♌
☽ →♍: 2:06A
☽ VOC: MIDNIGHT - 2:06A
5:5 STAR GATE

♇ IS R
♄ IS R
⚷ IS R
♀ IS R

☉ ✶ ♅ 08°♊/♈ 12:04P
☿ □ ♂ 10°♊/♓ 4:59P

"Spiritual force is stronger than material force; thoughts rule the world."

Ralph Waldo Emerson

8ᴬᴹ	2ᴾᴹ
9ᴬᴹ	3ᴾᴹ
10ᴬᴹ	4ᴾᴹ
11ᴬᴹ	5ᴾᴹ
12ᴾᴹ	6ᴾᴹ
1ᴾᴹ	7ᴾᴹ

Memorial Day

All times Eastern Daylight Time

Mental Wisdom

TUESDAY
05.29.2012

First Quarter

☽ IN ♍: ALL DAY
☽ VOC: NO
5:5 STAR GATE

♇ IS R
♄ IS R
⚹ IS R
♀ IS R

"The wise teacher does not bid you to enter the house of his wisdom but rather leads you to the threshold of your mind."

Kahlil Gibran

8 AM	2 PM
9 AM	3 PM
10 AM	4 PM
11 AM	5 PM
12 PM	6 PM
1 PM	7 PM

S	M	T	W	T	F	S
May		1	2	3	4	5
6	7	8	9	10	11	12
13	14	15	16	17	18	19
20	21	22	23	24	25	26
27	28	29	30	31		2012

S	M	T	W	T	F	S
June 2012					1	2
3	4	5	6	7	8	9
10	11	12	13	14	15	16
17	18	19	20	21	22	23
24	25	26	27	28	29	30

Mental Wisdom

WEDNESDAY
05.30.2012

First Quarter

☽ IN ♍
☽ →♎: 6:46A
☽ VOC: 1:50A - 6:46A { ☽ △ ♃ }
♆ IS STATIONING {R}
5:5 STAR GATE

♇ IS R
♄ IS R
⚸ IS R
♀ IS R

☉ □ ⚷   10° ♊/♓ 1:05P
☿ □ ♂   14° ♊/♍ 8:20P

"If you cannot find the truth right where you are, where else do you expect to find it?"

                                                            Dogen

8 AM	2 PM
9 AM	3 PM
10 AM	4 PM
11 AM	5 PM
12 PM	6 PM
1 PM	7 PM

All times Eastern Daylight Time

Mental Wisdom

THURSDAY
05.31.2012

First Quarter

☽ IN ♎: ALL DAY
☽ VOC: 9:31P - MIDNIGHT { ☽ ☌ ♄ }
♆ IS STATIONING {R}
5:5 STAR GATE

♇ IS R
♄ IS R
⚷ IS R
♀ IS R

"Truth, like gold, is to be obtained not by its growth, but by washing away from it all that is not gold."

Leo Tolstoy

8AM	**2**PM
9AM	**3**PM
10AM	**4**PM
11AM	**5**PM
12PM	**6**PM
1PM	**7**PM

S	M	T	W	T	F	S		S	M	T	W	T	F	S
May		1	2	3	4	5	June 2012						1	2
6	7	8	9	10	11	12	3	4	5	6	7	8	9
13	14	15	16	17	18	19	10	11	12	13	14	15	16
20	21	22	23	24	25	26	17	18	19	20	21	22	23
27	28	29	30	31		2012	24	25	26	27	28	29	30

Mental Wisdom

FRIDAY
06.01.2012

Gibbous

☽ IN ♎
☽ →♏: 8:32A
☽ VOC: MIDNIGHT - 8:32A
♆ IS STATIONING {R}
HIDDEN 12:12 STAR GATE

♇ IS R
♄ IS R
✷ IS R
♀ IS R

☿ ☌ ♀ 18°♊ 4:31P

> "That man has reached immortality who is disturbed by nothing material."
>
> Swami Vivekananda

JUN

8 AM	2 PM
9 AM	3 PM
10 AM	4 PM
11 AM	5 PM
12 PM	6 PM
1 PM	7 PM

All times Eastern Daylight Time

Mental Wisdom

SATURDAY
06.02.2012

Gibbous

☽ IN ♏: ALL DAY
☽ VOC: NO
♆ IS STATIONING {R}

♇ IS R
♄ IS R
⚴ IS R
♀ IS R

"Little minds are tamed and subdued by misfortune; but great minds rise above them."

Washington Irving

8ᴬᴹ	**2**ᴾᴹ
9ᴬᴹ	**3**ᴾᴹ
10ᴬᴹ	**4**ᴾᴹ
11ᴬᴹ	**5**ᴾᴹ
12ᴾᴹ	**6**ᴾᴹ
1ᴾᴹ	**7**ᴾᴹ

S	M	T	W	T	F	S	S	M	T	W	T	F	S
June 2012					1	2	1	2	3	4	5	6	7
3	4	5	6	7	8	9	8	9	10	11	12	13	14
10	11	12	13	14	15	16	15	16	17	18	19	20	21
17	18	19	20	21	22	23	22	23	24	25	26	27	28
24	25	26	27	28	29	30	29	30	31			July	2012

SUNDAY
06.03.2012

Gibbous

☽ IN ♏
☽ →♐: 8:33A
☽ VOC: 5:30A - 8:33A { ☽ ☍ ♃ }
♆ IS STATIONING {R}
5:5 STAR GATE

♇ IS R
♄ IS R
⚹ IS R
♀ IS R

☿ △ ♄ 23°Ⅱ/♎ 10:38P

JUN

"All questions come from the ego."
Derek O'Neill

8ᴀᴍ	**2**ᴘᴍ
9ᴀᴍ	**3**ᴘᴍ
10ᴀᴍ	**4**ᴘᴍ
11ᴀᴍ	**5**ᴘᴍ
12ᴘᴍ	**6**ᴘᴍ
1ᴘᴍ	**7**ᴘᴍ

All times Eastern Daylight Time

MONDAY
06.04.2012

Full Moon

☽ IN ♐: ALL DAY
☽ VOC: NO
♆ STATION: 5:03P
♆ TURNS R: 03° ♓
6:6 STAR GATE

♇ IS R
♄ IS R
⚹ IS R
♀ IS R

FULL MOON { ☽ ☍ ☉ }: 7:12A
14° ♐ 14'
PARTIAL LUNAR ECLIPSE

♀ □ ♂ 16° ♊/♍ 8:28P

"Our deepest fear is not that we are inadequate.
Our deepest fear is that we are powerful beyond measure."

Marianne Williamson

8ᴀᴍ	2ᴘᴍ
9ᴀᴍ	3ᴘᴍ
10ᴀᴍ	4ᴘᴍ
11ᴀᴍ	5ᴘᴍ
12ᴘᴍ	6ᴘᴍ
1ᴘᴍ	7ᴘᴍ

S	M	T	W	T	F	S
June 2012					1	2
3	4	5	6	7	8	9
10	11	12	13	14	15	16
17	18	19	20	21	22	23
24	25	26	27	28	29	30

S	M	T	W	T	F	S
1	2	3	4	5	6	7
8	9	10	11	12	13	14
15	16	17	18	19	20	21
22	23	24	25	26	27	28
29	30	31			July	2012

Mental Wisdom

TUESDAY
06.05.2012

Full Moon

☽ IN ♐
☽ →♑: 8:32A
☽ VOC: 1:08A - 8:32A { ☽ ☌ ☿ }
♆ HAS STATIONED {R}
5:5 STAR GATE

♇ IS R
♄ IS R
⚴ IS R
♀ IS R

☉ ☌ ♀   16° ♊   9:09P

JUN

"A conclusion is the place where you get tired of thinking."

Arthur Block

8ᴬᴹ	2ᴾᴹ
9ᴬᴹ	3ᴾᴹ
10ᴬᴹ	4ᴾᴹ
11ᴬᴹ	5ᴾᴹ
12ᴾᴹ	6ᴾᴹ
1ᴾᴹ	7ᴾᴹ

All times Eastern Daylight Time

WEDNESDAY
06.06.2012

Full Moon

☽ IN ♑: ALL DAY
☽ VOC: NO
6:6 STAR GATE

♇ IS R
♆ IS R
♄ IS R
⯰ IS R
♀ IS R

"If I don't have wisdom, I can teach you only ignorance."

Leo Buscaglia

8ᴀᴍ	2ᴘᴍ
9ᴀᴍ	3ᴘᴍ
10ᴀᴍ	4ᴘᴍ
11ᴀᴍ	5ᴘᴍ
12ᴘᴍ	6ᴘᴍ
1ᴘᴍ	7ᴘᴍ

S	M	T	W	T	F	S	S	M	T	W	T	F	S
June 2012					1	2	1	2	3	4	5	6	7
3	4	5	6	7	8	9	8	9	10	11	12	13	14
10	11	12	13	14	15	16	15	16	17	18	19	20	21
17	18	19	20	21	22	23	22	23	24	25	26	27	28
24	25	26	27	28	29	30	29	30	31			July 2012	

THURSDAY
06.07.2012

Disseminating

☽ IN ♑
☽ →♒: 10:17A
☽ VOC: 8:38A - 10:17A {☽ △ ♃}
☿ →♋: 7:16A

♇ IS R
♆ IS R
♄ IS R
⛢ IS R
♀ IS R

☉ □ ♂ 18°♊/♍ 10:30P

"Be careful of your thoughts; they may become words at any moment."

Lara Gassen

8ᴬᴹ	2ᴾᴹ
9ᴬᴹ	3ᴾᴹ
10ᴬᴹ	4ᴾᴹ
11ᴬᴹ	5ᴾᴹ
12ᴾᴹ	6ᴾᴹ
1ᴾᴹ	7ᴾᴹ

All times Eastern Daylight Time

Mental Wisdom

FRIDAY
06.08.2012

Disseminating

☽ IN ♒: ALL DAY
☽ VOC: NO
⚷ IS STATIONING {R}
5:5 STAR GATE

♇ IS R
♆ IS R
♄ IS R
⛢ IS R
♀ IS R

☿ △ ♆ 03°♋/♓ 9:49P

"It will never be possible by pure reason to arrive at some absolute truth."

Werner Heisenberg

8 AM	2 PM
9 AM	3 PM
10 AM	4 PM
11 AM	5 PM
12 PM	6 PM
1 PM	7 PM

	S	M	T	W	T	F	S		S	M	T	W	T	F	S
June 2012						1	2		1	2	3	4	5	6	7
	3	4	5	6	7	8	9		8	9	10	11	12	13	14
	10	11	12	13	14	15	16		15	16	17	18	19	20	21
	17	18	19	20	21	22	23		22	23	24	25	26	27	28
	24	25	26	27	28	29	30		29	30	31			July 2012	

Mental Wisdom

SATURDAY
06.09.2012

Disseminating

☽ IN ♒
☽ →♓: 3:22P
☽ VOC: 2:33P - 3:22P {☽ ☐ ♃}
☿ IS STATIONING {R}
5:5/6:6 STAR GATE

♇ IS R
♆ IS R
♄ IS R
⚴ IS R
♀ IS R

"The world cares very little about what a man or woman knows; it is what the man or woman is able to do that counts."

Booker T. Washington

8ᴀᴍ	2ᴘᴍ
9ᴀᴍ	3ᴘᴍ
10ᴀᴍ	4ᴘᴍ
11ᴀᴍ	5ᴘᴍ
12ᴘᴍ	6ᴘᴍ
1ᴘᴍ	7ᴘᴍ

All times Eastern Daylight Time

SUNDAY
06.10.2012

Disseminating

☽ IN ♓: ALL DAY
☽ VOC: NO
⚷ IS STATIONING {R}
6:6 STAR GATE

♇ IS R
♆ IS R
♄ IS R
⚹ IS R
♀ IS R

> *"Flowers are great teachers. They don't care whether God is looking at them or not. They just are."*
>
> Derek O'Neill`

8ᴀᴍ	**2**ᴘᴍ
9ᴀᴍ	**3**ᴘᴍ
10ᴀᴍ	**4**ᴘᴍ
11ᴀᴍ	**5**ᴘᴍ
12ᴘᴍ	**6**ᴘᴍ
1ᴘᴍ	**7**ᴘᴍ

S	M	T	W	T	F	S	S	M	T	W	T	F	S
June 2012					1	2	1	2	3	4	5	6	7
3	4	5	6	7	8	9	8	9	10	11	12	13	14
10	11	12	13	14	15	16	15	16	17	18	19	20	21
17	18	19	20	21	22	23	22	23	24	25	26	27	28
24	25	26	27	28	29	30	29	30	31			July 2012	

MONDAY
06.11.2012

Last Quarter

Mental Wisdom

☽ IN ♓: ALL DAY
☽ VOC: 6:41A - MIDNIGHT {☽ □ ☉}
♃ →♊: 1:22P
☿ IS STATIONING {R}

♇ IS R
♆ IS R
♄ IS R
⚹ IS R
♀ IS R

☿ □ ♅ 08°♋/♈ 1:41P
☿ ☍ ♇ 09°♋/♑ 9:04P

"Silence is the speech of the spiritual seeker."
                              Sri Sathya Sai Baba

JUN

8ᴀᴍ	2ᴘᴍ
9ᴀᴍ	3ᴘᴍ
10ᴀᴍ	4ᴘᴍ
11ᴀᴍ	5ᴘᴍ
12ᴘᴍ	6ᴘᴍ
1ᴘᴍ	7ᴘᴍ

All times Eastern Daylight Time

|Mental Wisdom|  | **TUESDAY**
06.12.2012 |
Last Quarter |

☽ IN ♓
☽ → ♈: 12:21A
☽ VOC: MIDNIGHT - 12:21A
♄ STATION: 1:12A
♄ TURNS R: 10° ♓
5:5 STAR GATE

♇ IS R
♆ IS R
♄ IS R
⚹ IS R
♀ IS R

☿ △ ♄ 10°♋/♓ 11:08A
☉ △ ♄ 23°♊/♎ 8:12P

"Seek to become more aware of what causes
anger and separation, and what overcomes them.
Learn to live compassionately and mindfully."

Thich Nhat Hanh

8ᴀᴍ	2ᴘᴍ
9ᴀᴍ	3ᴘᴍ
10ᴀᴍ	4ᴘᴍ
11ᴀᴍ	5ᴘᴍ
12ᴘᴍ	6ᴘᴍ
1ᴘᴍ	7ᴘᴍ

June 2012

S	M	T	W	T	F	S
					1	2
3	4	5	6	7	8	9
10	11	12	13	14	15	16
17	18	19	20	21	22	23
24	25	26	27	28	29	30

S	M	T	W	T	F	S
1	2	3	4	5	6	7
8	9	10	11	12	13	14
15	16	17	18	19	20	21
22	23	24	25	26	27	28
29	30	31				

July 2012

Mental Wisdom

WEDNESDAY
06.13.2012

Last Quarter

☽ IN ♈: ALL DAY
☽ VOC: 11:09A - MIDNIGHT {☽ ⚹ ☉}
☿ HAS STATIONED {R}

♇ IS R
♆ IS R
♄ IS R
⚳ IS R
♀ IS R

JUN

> *"Explaining puzzling or difficult things isn't necessary, in order to know beyond a shadow of a doubt that love is always present."*
>
> The Universe (Mike Dooley)

8^{AM}	2^{PM}
9^{AM}	3^{PM}
10^{AM}	4^{PM}
11^{AM}	5^{PM}
12^{PM}	6^{PM}
1^{PM}	7^{PM}

All times Eastern Daylight Time

Mental Wisdom

MONDAY
06.14.2012

Last Quarter

☽ IN ♈
☽ →♉: 12:22P
☽ VOC: MIDNIGHT - 12:22P
5:5 STAR GATE

♇ IS R
♆ IS R
⚷ IS R
♄ IS R
♅ IS R
♀ IS R

"God grant me the courage not to give up what I think is right, even though I think it is hopeless."

Chester W. Nimitz

8ᴬᴹ	2ᴾᴹ
9ᴬᴹ	3ᴾᴹ
10ᴬᴹ	4ᴾᴹ
11ᴬᴹ	5ᴾᴹ
12ᴾᴹ	6ᴾᴹ
1ᴾᴹ	7ᴾᴹ

Flag Day (USA)

S	M	T	W	T	F	S	S	M	T	W	T	F	S
June 2012					1	2	1	2	3	4	5	6	7
3	4	5	6	7	8	9	8	9	10	11	12	13	14
10	11	12	13	14	15	16	15	16	17	18	19	20	21
17	18	19	20	21	22	23	22	23	24	25	26	27	28
24	25	26	27	28	29	30	29	30	31			July 2012	

Mental Wisdom

FRIDAY
06.15.2012

Last Quarter

☽ IN ♉: ALL DAY
☽ VOC: NO
6:6 STAR GATE

♇ IS R
♆ IS R
⚷ IS R
♄ IS R
⯺ IS R
♀ IS R

"We should realize that man has not only a mind which conceives thoughts, but also a heart which can put them into practice."

Sri Sathya Sai Baba

JUN

8ᴀᴍ	2ᴘᴍ
9ᴀᴍ	3ᴘᴍ
10ᴀᴍ	4ᴘᴍ
11ᴀᴍ	5ᴘᴍ
12ᴘᴍ	6ᴘᴍ
1ᴘᴍ	7ᴘᴍ

All times Eastern Daylight Time

Mental Wisdom

SATURDAY
06.16.2012

Balsamic

☽ IN ♉: ALL DAY
☽ VOC: 8:08A - MIDNIGHT {☽ △ ♂}

♇ IS R
♆ IS R
⚷ IS R
♄ IS R
⚵ IS R
♀ IS R

♀ □ ⚷ 10° ♊/ ♓ 5:23P

"Always keep an open mind and a compassionate heart."

Phil Jackson

8AM	2PM
9AM	3PM
10AM	4PM
11AM	5PM
12PM	6PM
1PM	7PM

June 2012

S	M	T	W	T	F	S
					1	2
3	4	5	6	7	8	9
10	11	12	13	14	15	16
17	18	19	20	21	22	23
24	25	26	27	28	29	30

S	M	T	W	T	F	S
1	2	3	4	5	6	7
8	9	10	11	12	13	14
15	16	17	18	19	20	21
22	23	24	25	26	27	28
29	30	31				

July 2012

Mental Wisdom

SUNDAY
06.17.2012

Balsamic

☽ IN ♉
☽ →♊: 1:24ᴀ
☽ VOC: MIDNIGHT - 1:24ᴀ
5:5 STAR GATE

♇ IS R
♆ IS R
♅ IS R
♄ IS R
⚹ IS R
♀ IS R

"We all have two minds. The first is the thinking mind. The other is consciousness."

Derek O'Neill

8ᴀᴍ	2ᴘᴍ
9ᴀᴍ	3ᴘᴍ
10ᴀᴍ	4ᴘᴍ
11ᴀᴍ	5ᴘᴍ
12ᴘᴍ	6ᴘᴍ
1ᴘᴍ	7ᴘᴍ

Father's Day

All times Eastern Daylight Time

MONDAY
06.18.2012

Balsamic

Mental Wisdom

☽ IN ♊: ALL DAY
☽ VOC: NO
6:6/5:5 STAR GATE

♇ IS R
♆ IS R
⚷ IS R
♄ IS R
⯰ IS R
♀ IS R

"There is a wisdom of the head, and a wisdom of the heart."
Charles Dickens

8ᴬᴹ	2ᴾᴹ
9ᴬᴹ	3ᴾᴹ
10ᴬᴹ	4ᴾᴹ
11ᴬᴹ	5ᴾᴹ
12ᴾᴹ	6ᴾᴹ
1ᴾᴹ	7ᴾᴹ

S	M	T	W	T	F	S	S	M	T	W	T	F	S
June 2012					1	2	1	2	3	4	5	6	7
3	4	5	6	7	8	9	8	9	10	11	12	13	14
10	11	12	13	14	15	16	15	16	17	18	19	20	21
17	18	19	20	21	22	23	22	23	24	25	26	27	28
24	25	26	27	28	29	30	29	30	31			July 2012	

TUESDAY
06.19.2012

Mental Wisdom

New Moon

☽ IN ♊
☽ →♋: 1:33P
☽ VOC: 11:02A - 1:33P { ☽ ☌ ☉ }
6:6 STAR GATE

♇ IS R
♆ IS R
⚷ IS R
♄ IS R
⯡ IS R
♀ IS R

NEW MOON { ☽ ☌ ☉ }: 11:02A
28°♊43'

> *"A good head and a good heart are always a formidable combination."*
> Nelson Mandela

8ᴬᴹ	2ᴾᴹ
9ᴬᴹ	3ᴾᴹ
10ᴬᴹ	4ᴾᴹ
11ᴬᴹ	5ᴾᴹ
12ᴾᴹ	6ᴾᴹ
1ᴾᴹ	7ᴾᴹ

All times Eastern Daylight Time

CANCER

Emotional Power

Symbol: The Divine Mother
Master: Serapis Bey
Quality: Inner Harmony
Ray: 6th Ray, Blue-Violet
Trine: Water
Hour: 6
Rulers: ☽ ☿ ♀

I AM LOVE

Emotional Power

6 O'Clock Hour
Main Purpose:

Where you allow yourself to feel your emotions (energies-in-motion).

JUNE 20 - JULY 21

Cancer is the sign of Emotional Power in Cosmic Astrology, and the emotions are possibly the most misunderstood aspect of our being. If we compare our emotional selves to the water on the planet, we can discover the true relationship of our feelings with our physical bodies. Water comprises 70% of the planet AND 70% of our bodies. The water on the planet is mostly contained within the ocean, which is the greatest metaphor for our universal consciousness. The rivers on the planet carry the water back to the ocean. Water flows freely everywhere on Earth. This is what our emotions are meant to do. When we allow ourselves the full force of our emotions, without judging them or holding on to them, they take us back to the core of our being. Cancer is called **Inner Harmony** in this new system. Allowing your Self to feel all your emotions is the ultimate expression of this aspect of consciousness. The Crab becomes the Divine Mother energy, the core of all nurturing and heartfelt experience.

Cancer is the 6 o'clock hour, corresponding to the 3rd house of the birth chart. The 3rd house is where you communicate your knowledge and speak your Truth. This is not possible without mind/heart integration. In this portion of your energy field you allow your feelings free reign. They arise from the core of your being (your heart) and bring you through to the crown chakra where you commune with Source. Because we live in duality, fully half of our emotions are 'down.' Getting used to allowing the ups and downs of our emotions will allow us to move past the fear-based responses we tend to develop, and our emotional power is released.

Wherever Cancer is in your birth chart you are meant to feel your feelings to the fullest. Typically there are issues around doing so, but that is the very purpose of this placement... to move yourself past the fears that keep your emotions blocked, like a dam in the river, and release yourself from the dis-ease that results. If your Sun sign is Cancer you are here to learn to put your feelings first, to nurture your Self fully and realize your capacity to do the same for others. Letting your Self just BE is where your truest mastery lies.

FAMOUS CANCERS

George W. Bush, Princess Diana, Richard Branson, 14th Dalai Lama, Tom Hanks, Ringo Starr, Ernest Hemingway, Estee Lauder, Meryl Streep, Helen Keller, Nelson Mandela, Mary McAleese, Oscar Hammerstein II, R. Buckminster Fuller

Emotional Power

WEDNESDAY
06.20.2012

New Moon

☽ IN ♋: ALL DAY
☽ VOC: NO
☉ → ♋: 7:09P

♇ IS R
♆ IS R
♅ IS R
♄ IS R
⚹ IS R
♀ IS R

☿ □ ♄ 23°♋/♎ 12:05P
♀ ⚹ ♅ 08°♊/♈ 8:55P

JUN

"Harmony is pure love, for love is complete agreement."

Lope de Vega

8 AM	2 PM
9 AM	3 PM
10 AM	4 PM
11 AM	5 PM
12 PM	6 PM
1 PM	7 PM

Summer Solstice
Litha

All times Eastern Daylight Time

Emotional Power

THURSDAY
06.21.2012

New Moon

☽ IN ♋
☽ →♌: 11:47P
☽ VOC: 12:48P - 11:47P { ☽ ☍ ☿ }
5:5/ 6:6 STAR GATE

♇ IS R
♆ IS R
♅ IS R
♄ IS R
♆ IS R
♀ IS R

☿ ✶ ♂ 24°♋/♍ 6:14A

"He who lives in harmony with himself lives in harmony with the universe."

Marcus Aurelius

8ᴀᴍ	2ᴘᴍ
9ᴀᴍ	3ᴘᴍ
10ᴀᴍ	4ᴘᴍ
11ᴀᴍ	5ᴘᴍ
12ᴘᴍ	6ᴘᴍ
1ᴘᴍ	7ᴘᴍ

S	M	T	W	T	F	S	S	M	T	W	T	F	S
June 2012					1	2	1	2	3	4	5	6	7
3	4	5	6	7	8	9	8	9	10	11	12	13	14
10	11	12	13	14	15	16	15	16	17	18	19	20	21
17	18	19	20	21	22	23	22	23	24	25	26	27	28
24	25	26	27	28	29	30	29	30	31			July 2012	

Emotional Power		# FRIDAY ## 06.22.2012

Crescent

☽ IN ♌: ALL DAY
☽ VOC: NO
♄ IS STATIONING {D}
6:6 STAR GATE

♇ IS R
♆ IS R
⚷ IS R
♄ IS R
⯓ IS R
♀ IS R

"The way is not in the sky. The way is in the heart."
                                           Gautama Buddha

....

....

....

....

....

....

....

....

8ᴬᴹ	2ᴾᴹ
9ᴬᴹ	3ᴾᴹ
10ᴬᴹ	4ᴾᴹ
11ᴬᴹ	5ᴾᴹ
12ᴾᴹ	6ᴾᴹ
1ᴾᴹ	7ᴾᴹ

All times Eastern Daylight Time

Emotional Power

SATURDAY
06.23.2012

Crescent

☽ IN ♌: ALL DAY
☽ VOC: 6:26P - MIDNIGHT {☽ ✶ ♄}
♄ IS STATIONING {D}
5:5 STAR GATE

♇ IS R
♆ IS R
⚷ IS R
♄ IS R
⚴ IS R
♀ IS R

☉ △ ♆ 03°♋/♓ 11:54P

*"Grace has been defined as the outward
expression of the inward harmony of the soul."*

William Hazlitt

8ᴬᴹ	2ᴾᴹ
9ᴬᴹ	3ᴾᴹ
10ᴬᴹ	4ᴾᴹ
11ᴬᴹ	5ᴾᴹ
12ᴾᴹ	6ᴾᴹ
1ᴾᴹ	7ᴾᴹ

S	M	T	W	T	F	S	S	M	T	W	T	F	S
June 2012					1	2	1	2	3	4	5	6	7
3	4	5	6	7	8	9	8	9	10	11	12	13	14
10	11	12	13	14	15	16	15	16	17	18	19	20	21
17	18	19	20	21	22	23	22	23	24	25	26	27	28
24	25	26	27	28	29	30	29	30	31			July 2012	

Emotional Power

SUNDAY
06.24.2012

Crescent

☽ IN ♌
☽ →♍: 8:42A
☽ VOC: MIDNIGHT - 8:42A
♄ IS STATIONING {D}
6:6 STAR GATE

♇ IS R
♆ IS R
♊ IS R
♄ IS R
⚹ IS R
♀ IS R

♅ □ ♇ 08°♈/♑ 5:14A

"If you want to feel safe, you have to find the truth, which is that part of you that is aware, and is immortal."

Derek O'Neill

8ᴀᴍ	2ᴘᴍ
9ᴀᴍ	3ᴘᴍ
10ᴀᴍ	4ᴘᴍ
11ᴀᴍ	5ᴘᴍ
12ᴘᴍ	6ᴘᴍ
1ᴘᴍ	7ᴘᴍ

All times Eastern Daylight Time

Emotional Power

MONDAY
06.25.2012

Crescent

☽ IN ♍: ALL DAY
☽ VOC: NO
♄ STATION: 4:00A
♄ TURNS D: 23° ♎
☿ → ♌: 10:24P

♇ IS R
♆ IS R
⛢ IS R
⚴ IS R
♀ IS R

♃ □ ♆   03°♊/♓ 3:56A

"Harmony is one phase of the law whose spiritual expression is love."

James Allen

8ᴬᴹ	2ᴾᴹ
9ᴬᴹ	3ᴾᴹ
10ᴬᴹ	4ᴾᴹ
11ᴬᴹ	5ᴾᴹ
12ᴾᴹ	6ᴾᴹ
1ᴾᴹ	7ᴾᴹ

S	M	T	W	T	F	S	S	M	T	W	T	F	S
June 2012					1	2	1	2	3	4	5	6	7
3	4	5	6	7	8	9	8	9	10	11	12	13	14
10	11	12	13	14	15	16	15	16	17	18	19	20	21
17	18	19	20	21	22	23	22	23	24	25	26	27	28
24	25	26	27	28	29	30	29	30	31			July 2012	

Emotional Power

TUESDAY
06.26.2012

Crescent

☽ IN ♍
☽ →♎: 1:15P
☽ VOC: 6:53A - 1:15P {☽ ☌ ♂}
♄ HAS STATIONED {D}
♀ IS STATIONING {D}
5:5 STAR GATE

♇ IS R
♆ IS R
⚷ IS R
⚵ IS R
♀ IS R

> *"Each and every master has heard the call
> and attained harmony with heaven and earth."*
>
> Morihei Ueshiba

8ᴀᴍ	2ᴘᴍ
9ᴀᴍ	3ᴘᴍ
10ᴀᴍ	4ᴘᴍ
11ᴀᴍ	5ᴘᴍ
12ᴘᴍ	6ᴘᴍ
1ᴘᴍ	7ᴘᴍ

All times Eastern Daylight Time

Emotional Power

WEDNESDAY
06.27.2012

First Quarter

☽ IN ♎: ALL DAY
☽ VOC: NO
♀ STATION: 11:07A
♀ TURNS D: 07° ♊
☿ → R SHADOW
5:5/6:6 STAR GATE

♇ IS R
♆ IS R
⚷ IS R
⚳ IS R

> *"Happiness is not a matter of intensity but of balance, order, rhythm and harmony."*
>
> Thomas Merton

8 AM	2 PM
9 AM	3 PM
10 AM	4 PM
11 AM	5 PM
12 PM	6 PM
1 PM	7 PM

S	M	T	W	T	F	S	S	M	T	W	T	F	S
June 2012					1	2	1	2	3	4	5	6	7
3	4	5	6	7	8	9	8	9	10	11	12	13	14
10	11	12	13	14	15	16	15	16	17	18	19	20	21
17	18	19	20	21	22	23	22	23	24	25	26	27	28
24	25	26	27	28	29	30	29	30	31			July 2012	

Emotional Power

THURSDAY
06.28.2012

First Quarter

☽ IN ♎
☽ →♏: 4:32p
☽ VOC: 4:22A - 4:32P { ☽ ☌ ♄ }
♀ HAS STATIONED {D}
☿ IN R SHADOW
6:6 STAR GATE

♇ IS R
♆ IS R
⚷ IS R
⯰ IS R

> *"My only true harmony lies deep within my soul, wherever that is. I know that somehow I am in tune with the universe."*
>
> Mercedes McCambridge

8^{AM}	2^{PM}
9^{AM}	3^{PM}
10^{AM}	4^{PM}
11^{AM}	5^{PM}
12^{PM}	6^{PM}
1^{PM}	7^{PM}

All times Eastern Daylight Time

Emotional Power

FRIDAY
06.29.2012

First Quarter

- ☽ in ♏: All Day
- ☽ voc: No
- ☿ in R Shadow
- **11:11 Star Gate**

- ♇ is R
- ♆ is R
- ♄ is R
- ⚷ is R

- ☉ ☍ ♇ 08°♋/♑ 11:02a
- ☿ ✶ ♃ 04°♌/♊ 11:37a
- ☉ □ ♅ 08°♋/♈ 4:10p

"When you are at one with the universe, the universe replies with total acceptance."

Mr. Prophet

8ᴬᴹ	2ᴾᴹ
9ᴬᴹ	3ᴾᴹ
10ᴬᴹ	4ᴾᴹ
11ᴬᴹ	5ᴾᴹ
12ᴾᴹ	6ᴾᴹ
1ᴾᴹ	7ᴾᴹ

S	M	T	W	T	F	S
June 2012					1	2
3	4	5	6	7	8	9
10	11	12	13	14	15	16
17	18	19	20	21	22	23
24	25	26	27	28	29	30

S	M	T	W	T	F	S
1	2	3	4	5	6	7
8	9	10	11	12	13	14
15	16	17	18	19	20	21
22	23	24	25	26	27	28
29	30	31				July 2012

Emotional Power

SATURDAY
06.30.2012

Gibbous

☽ IN ♏
☽ →♐: 6:04p
☽ VOC: 3:46p - 6:04p { ☽ ⚹ ♂ }
☿ IN R SHADOW
5:5 STAR GATE

♇ IS R
♆ IS R
⚷ IS R
⚴ IS R

☿ △ ☊ 05°♌/♐ 5:20A
☿ ⚹ ☋ 05°♌/♊ 5:20A
☉ △ ⚷ 09°♋/♓ 8:23P

> "Life at its best is a creative synthesis of opposites in fruitful harmony."
>
> Martin Luther King, Jr.

JUN

8ᴀᴍ	2ᴘᴍ
9ᴀᴍ	3ᴘᴍ
10ᴀᴍ	4ᴘᴍ
11ᴀᴍ	5ᴘᴍ
12ᴘᴍ	6ᴘᴍ
1ᴘᴍ	7ᴘᴍ

All times Eastern Daylight Time

Emotional Power

SUNDAY
07.01.2012

Gibbous

☽ IN ♐: ALL DAY
☽ VOC: NO
☿ IN R SHADOW

♇ IS R
♆ IS R
⚷ IS R
⯝ IS R

"If you learn to breathe, you will be given everything."

Derek O'Neill

8ᴬᴹ	2ᴾᴹ
9ᴬᴹ	3ᴾᴹ
10ᴬᴹ	4ᴾᴹ
11ᴬᴹ	5ᴾᴹ
12ᴾᴹ	6ᴾᴹ
1ᴾᴹ	7ᴾᴹ

S	M	T	W	T	F	S	S	M	T	W	T	F	S
1	2	3	4	5	6	7	August 2012		1	2	3	4
8	9	10	11	12	13	14	5	6	7	8	9	10	11
15	16	17	18	19	20	21	12	13	14	15	16	17	18
22	23	24	25	26	27	28	19	20	21	22	23	24	25
29	30	31		July 2012			26	27	28	29	30	31	

Emotional Power		**MONDAY** **07.02.2012**	

Gibbous

☽ IN ♐
☽ →♑: 6:51P
☽ VOC: 6:21P - 6:51P { ☽ □ ♂ }
☿ IN R SHADOW
5:5 STAR GATE

♇ IS R
♆ IS R
⚷ IS R
⯝ IS R

♃ ☍ ☊ 05°♊/♐ 8:09P
♃ ☌ ☋ 05°♊   8:09P

> "Happiness happens when you fit with your life, when you fit
> so harmoniously that whatsoever you are doing is your joy."
>
> Osho

JUL

8ᴬᴹ	2ᴾᴹ
9ᴬᴹ	3ᴾᴹ
10ᴬᴹ	4ᴾᴹ
11ᴬᴹ	5ᴾᴹ
12ᴾᴹ	6ᴾᴹ
1ᴾᴹ	7ᴾᴹ

Canada Day

All times Eastern Daylight Time

Emotional Power

TUESDAY
07.03.2012

Full Moon

☽ IN ♑: ALL DAY
☽ VOC: NO
♂ → ♎: 8:31A
☿ IN R SHADOW
3:3 STAR GATE

♇ IS R
♆ IS R
⚷ IS R
⚸ IS R

FULL MOON { ☽ ☌ ☉ }: 2:52P
12° ♑ 14'

"When we pay attention to nature's music, we find that everything on the earth contributes to its harmony."

Hazrat Inayat Khan

8ᴬᴹ	2ᴾᴹ
9ᴬᴹ	3ᴾᴹ
10ᴬᴹ	4ᴾᴹ
11ᴬᴹ	5ᴾᴹ
12ᴾᴹ	6ᴾᴹ
1ᴾᴹ	7ᴾᴹ

Asala-Dharma Day

S	M	T	W	T	F	S
1	2	3	4	5	6	7
8	9	10	11	12	13	14
15	16	17	18	19	20	21
22	23	24	25	26	27	28
29	30	31			July 2012	

August 2012	S	M	T	W	T	F	S
				1	2	3	4
	5	6	7	8	9	10	11
	12	13	14	15	16	17	18
	19	20	21	22	23	24	25
	26	27	28	29	30	31	

Emotional Power

WEDNESDAY
07.04.2012

Full Moon

☽ IN ♋
☽ →♒: 8:26P
☽ VOC: 8:25A - 8:26P {☽ □ ♄}
☿ IN R SHADOW
7:7 STAR GATE

♇ IS R
♆ IS R
⚷ IS R
⯛ IS R

☿ ✶ ♀ 08°♌/♊ 9:26A
☿ △ ♅ 08°♌/♈ 1:53P
♀ ✶ ♅ 08°♊/♈ 10:36P

> *"No dis-ease can interrupt the Eternal Flow of my Harmony."*
> — Darshan Baba

JUL

8ᴀᴍ	2ᴘᴍ
9ᴀᴍ	3ᴘᴍ
10ᴀᴍ	4ᴘᴍ
11ᴀᴍ	5ᴘᴍ
12ᴘᴍ	6ᴘᴍ
1ᴘᴍ	7ᴘᴍ

Independence Day (USA)

All times Eastern Daylight Time

Emotional Power

THURSDAY
07.05.2012

Full Moon

☽ IN ♒: ALL DAY
☽ VOC: NO
☿ IN R SHADOW
12:12 STAR GATE

♇ IS R
♆ IS R
⚷ IS R
⚶ IS R

> *"The trees and plants show respect*
> *for each other by the way they live in harmony.*
> *This also applies to the animal kingdom."*
>
> — Masuru Emoto

8AM	**2**PM
9AM	**3**PM
10AM	**4**PM
11AM	**5**PM
12PM	**6**PM
1PM	**7**PM

S	M	T	W	T	F	S		S	M	T	W	T	F	S
1	2	3	4	5	6	7	August 2012			1	2	3	4
8	9	10	11	12	13	14		5	6	7	8	9	10	11
15	16	17	18	19	20	21		12	13	14	15	16	17	18
22	23	24	25	26	27	28		19	20	21	22	23	24	25
29	30	31			July 2012		26	27	28	29	30	31	

Emotional Power

FRIDAY
07.06.2012

Full Moon

☽ IN ♒: ALL DAY
☽ VOC: 11:49A - MIDNIGHT { ☽ △ ♄ }
☿ IN R SHADOW

♇ IS R
♆ IS R
⚷ IS R
⯰ IS R

"Truth is inner harmony."
Walther Rathenau

JUL

8ᴀᴍ	2ᴘᴍ
9ᴀᴍ	3ᴘᴍ
10ᴀᴍ	4ᴘᴍ
11ᴀᴍ	5ᴘᴍ
12ᴘᴍ	6ᴘᴍ
1ᴘᴍ	7ᴘᴍ

All times Eastern Daylight Time

Emotional Power

SATURDAY
07.07.2012

Disseminating

☽ IN ♒
☽ →♓: 12:29A
☽ VOC: MIDNIGHT - 12:29A
☿ IN R SHADOW
7:7/5:5 STAR GATE

♇ IS R
♆ IS R
⚷ IS R
♅ IS R

♀ □ ☋   09°♊/♓ 9:51P

> *"You have to make peace with yourself. The key is to find the harmony in what you have."*
> Naomi Watts

8ᴀᴍ	2ᴘᴍ
9ᴀᴍ	3ᴘᴍ
10ᴀᴍ	4ᴘᴍ
11ᴀᴍ	5ᴘᴍ
12ᴘᴍ	6ᴘᴍ
1ᴘᴍ	7ᴘᴍ

S	M	T	W	T	F	S	S	M	T	W	T	F	S
1	2	3	4	5	6	7	August 2012		1	2	3	4
8	9	10	11	12	13	14	5	6	7	8	9	10	11
15	16	17	18	19	20	21	12	13	14	15	16	17	18
22	23	24	25	26	27	28	19	20	21	22	23	24	25
29	30	31		July 2012			26	27	28	29	30	31	

Emotional Power

SUNDAY
07.08.2012

Disseminating

☽ IN ♓
☽ VOC: 6:59A - MIDNIGHT { ☽ △ ☉ }
♅ IS STATIONING {R}
☿ IN R SHADOW

♇ IS R
♆ IS R
⚷ IS R
♆ IS R

> "God hid in the place he knew we would never look. He hid in our hearts."
>
> Derek O'Neill

8ᴀᴍ	2ᴘᴍ
9ᴀᴍ	3ᴘᴍ
10ᴀᴍ	4ᴘᴍ
11ᴀᴍ	5ᴘᴍ
12ᴘᴍ	6ᴘᴍ
1ᴘᴍ	7ᴘᴍ

All times Eastern Daylight Time

Emotional Power

MONDAY
07.09.2012

Disseminating

☾ IN ♓
☾ →♈: 8:13A
☾ VOC: MIDNIGHT - 8:13A
♅ IS STATIONING {R}
☿ IN R SHADOW
5:5/7:7 STAR GATE

♇ IS R
♆ IS R
⚷ IS R
⚸ IS R

*"Happiness is when what you think, what you say,
and what you do are in harmony."*

Mahatma Gandhi

8ᴬᴹ	2ᴾᴹ
9ᴬᴹ	3ᴾᴹ
10ᴬᴹ	4ᴾᴹ
11ᴬᴹ	5ᴾᴹ
12ᴾᴹ	6ᴾᴹ
1ᴾᴹ	7ᴾᴹ

S	M	T	W	T	F	S	S	M	T	W	T	F	S
1	2	3	4	5	6	7	August 2012		1	2	3	4
8	9	10	11	12	13	14	5	6	7	8	9	10	11
15	16	17	18	19	20	21	12	13	14	15	16	17	18
22	23	24	25	26	27	28	19	20	21	22	23	24	25
29	30	31		July 2012			26	27	28	29	30	31	

Emotional Power

TUESDAY
07.10.2012

Last Quarter

☽ IN ♈: ALL DAY
☽ VOC: NO
♅ IS STATIONING {R}
☿ IN R SHADOW

♇ IS R
♆ IS R
⚷ IS R
⯰ IS R

"The secret of success is to be in harmony with existence, to be always calm to let each wave of life wash us a little farther up the shore."

Cyril Connolly

8ᴬᴹ	2ᴾᴹ
9ᴬᴹ	3ᴾᴹ
10ᴬᴹ	4ᴾᴹ
11ᴬᴹ	5ᴾᴹ
12ᴾᴹ	6ᴾᴹ
1ᴾᴹ	7ᴾᴹ

All times Eastern Daylight Time

Emotional Power

WEDNESDAY
07.11.2012

Last Quarter

☽ IN ♈
☽ →♉: 7:30P
☽ VOC: 5:23A - 7:30P {☽ ☌ ♄}
♅ IS STATIONING {R}
☿ IN R SHADOW
5:5/7:7 STAR GATE

♇ IS R
♆ IS R
⚷ IS R
⚴ IS R

♂ ✶ ☊ 04°♎/♐ 12:46A
♂ △ ☋ 04°♎/♊ 12:46A

> *"Grace has been defined as the outward expression of the inward harmony of the soul."*
>
> William Hazlitt

8ᴀᴍ	**2**ᴘᴍ
9ᴀᴍ	**3**ᴘᴍ
10ᴀᴍ	**4**ᴘᴍ
11ᴀᴍ	**5**ᴘᴍ
12ᴘᴍ	**6**ᴘᴍ
1ᴘᴍ	**7**ᴘᴍ

S	M	T	W	T	F	S	S	M	T	W	T	F	S
1	2	3	4	5	6	7	August 2012		1	2	3	4	
8	9	10	11	12	13	14	5	6	7	8	9	10	11
15	16	17	18	19	20	21	12	13	14	15	16	17	18
22	23	24	25	26	27	28	19	20	21	22	23	24	25
29	30	31		July 2012			26	27	28	29	30	31	

Emotional Power

THURSDAY
07.12.2012

Last Quarter

☽ IN ♉: ALL DAY
☽ VOC: NO
♅ IS STATIONING {R}
☿ IN R SHADOW
12:12 STAR GATE

♇ IS R
♆ IS R
♃ IS R
⚷ IS R

"Beauty is being in harmony with what you are."
Peter Nivlo Zarlenga

8 AM	2 PM
9 AM	3 PM
10 AM	4 PM
11 AM	5 PM
12 PM	6 PM
1 PM	7 PM

All times Eastern Daylight Time

Emotional Power

FRIDAY
07.13.2012

Last Quarter

☽ IN ♉
☽ VOC: 3:45P - MIDNIGHT { ☽ ✶ ☉ }
♅ STATION: 5:49A
♅ TURNS R: 04° ♈
☿ IS STATIONING {R}
5:5/7:7 STAR GATE

♇ IS R
♆ IS R
⚷ IS R
⚳ IS R

*"A persistent simplification of life creates
an inner and outer well-being that places harmony in one's life."*

Peace Pilgrim

8ᴀᴍ	2ᴘᴍ
9ᴀᴍ	3ᴘᴍ
10ᴀᴍ	4ᴘᴍ
11ᴀᴍ	5ᴘᴍ
12ᴘᴍ	6ᴘᴍ
1ᴘᴍ	7ᴘᴍ

S	M	T	W	T	F	S	S	M	T	W	T	F	S
1	2	3	4	5	6	7	August 2012		1	2	3	4
8	9	10	11	12	13	14	5	6	7	8	9	10	11
15	16	17	18	19	20	21	12	13	14	15	16	17	18
22	23	24	25	26	27	28	19	20	21	22	23	24	25
29	30	31		July 2012			26	27	28	29	30	31	

SATURDAY
07.14.2012

Emotional Power

Last Quarter

☽ IN ♉
☽ →♊: 8:26A
☽ VOC: MIDNIGHT - 8:26A
♅ HAS STATIONED {R}
☿ STATION: 10:16P
☿ TURNS R: 13° ♌
5:5/12:12 STAR GATE

♇ IS R
♆ IS R
⚷ IS R
⯝ IS R

☿ ✶ ♀   13°♌/♊ 6:41P

> *"Love can attain
> what the intellect cannot fathom."*
>
> Meher Baba

8ᴀᴍ	2ᴘᴍ
9ᴀᴍ	3ᴘᴍ
10ᴀᴍ	4ᴘᴍ
11ᴀᴍ	5ᴘᴍ
12ᴘᴍ	6ᴘᴍ
1ᴘᴍ	7ᴘᴍ

All times Eastern Daylight Time

Emotional Power

SUNDAY
07.15.2012

Last Quarter

☽ IN ♊: ALL DAY
☽ VOC: NO
♇ IS STATIONING {D}
♀ HAS STATIONED {R}
5:5/12:12 STAR GATE

♇ IS R
♆ IS R
♅ IS R
⚷ IS R
⯝ IS R

☉ □ ♄   23°♋/ ♎ 12:14A

"If you give your heart with love, there is no being on the planet that can harm you."

Derek O'Neill

....
....
....
....
....
....
....
....

8ᴀᴍ	2ᴘᴍ
9ᴀᴍ	3ᴘᴍ
10ᴀᴍ	4ᴘᴍ
11ᴀᴍ	5ᴘᴍ
12ᴘᴍ	6ᴘᴍ
1ᴘᴍ	7ᴘᴍ

S	M	T	W	T	F	S	S	M	T	W	T	F	S
1	2	3	4	5	6	7	August 2012		1	2	3	4
8	9	10	11	12	13	14	5	6	7	8	9	10	11
15	16	17	18	19	20	21	12	13	14	15	16	17	18
22	23	24	25	26	27	28	19	20	21	22	23	24	25
29	30	31		July 2012			26	27	28	29	30	31	

Emotional Power

MONDAY
07.16.2012

Balsamic

☽ IN ♊
☽ →♋: 8:31P
☽ VOC: 6:56A - 8:31P { ☽ △ ♄ }
⚹ STATION: 6:58A
⚹ TURNS D: 21° ♏

5:5/7:7 STAR GATE

♇ IS R
♆ IS R
♅ IS R
⚷ IS R
☿ IS R

"When I let go of what I am, I become what I might be."
                                                    Lao Tzu

JUL

8ᴀᴍ	2ᴘᴍ
9ᴀᴍ	3ᴘᴍ
10ᴀᴍ	4ᴘᴍ
11ᴀᴍ	5ᴘᴍ
12ᴘᴍ	6ᴘᴍ
1ᴘᴍ	7ᴘᴍ

All times Eastern Daylight Time

Emotional Power

TUESDAY
07.17.2012

Balsamic

☽ IN ♋: ALL DAY
☽ VOC: NO
⚳ HAS STATIONED {D}

♇ IS R
♆ IS R
♅ IS R
⚷ IS R
☿ IS R

♂ △ ♃ 08°♎/♊ 8:38A
♂ □ ♇ 08°♎/♑ 4:26P

"A beautiful thing is never perfect."
Egyptian Proverb

8ᴀᴍ	2ᴘᴍ
9ᴀᴍ	3ᴘᴍ
10ᴀᴍ	4ᴘᴍ
11ᴀᴍ	5ᴘᴍ
12ᴘᴍ	6ᴘᴍ
1ᴘᴍ	7ᴘᴍ

S	M	T	W	T	F	S	S	M	T	W	T	F	S
1	2	3	4	5	6	7	August 2012		1	2	3	4
8	9	10	11	12	13	14	5	6	7	8	9	10	11
15	16	17	18	19	20	21	12	13	14	15	16	17	18
22	23	24	25	26	27	28	19	20	21	22	23	24	25
29	30	31			July 2012		26	27	28	29	30	31	

Emotional Power

WEDNESDAY
07.18.2012

Balsamic

☽ IN ♋: ALL DAY
☽ VOC: NO
5:5/7:7 STAR GATE

♇ IS R
♆ IS R
♅ IS R
⚷ IS R
⚵ IS R

♂ ☍ ♅ 08° ♎ / ♈ 10:55P

"And forget not that the earth delights to feel your bare feet and the winds long to play with your hair."
Kahlil Gibran

8ᴀᴍ	2ᴘᴍ
9ᴀᴍ	3ᴘᴍ
10ᴀᴍ	4ᴘᴍ
11ᴀᴍ	5ᴘᴍ
12ᴘᴍ	6ᴘᴍ
1ᴘᴍ	7ᴘᴍ

All times Eastern Daylight Time

Emotional Power

THURSDAY
07.19.2012

New Moon

☽ IN ♋
☽ →♌: 6:13A
☽ VOC: 12:24A - 6:13A { ☽ ☌ ☉ }

♇ IS R
♆ IS R
♅ IS R
⚷ IS R
♀ IS R

NEW MOON { ☽ ☌ ☉ }: 12:24A
26° ♋55'

"The best thing one can do when it's raining is to let it rain."
Henry Wadsworth Longfellow

8ᴬᴹ	2ᴾᴹ
9ᴬᴹ	3ᴾᴹ
10ᴬᴹ	4ᴾᴹ
11ᴬᴹ	5ᴾᴹ
12ᴾᴹ	6ᴾᴹ
1ᴾᴹ	7ᴾᴹ

S	M	T	W	T	F	S		S	M	T	W	T	F	S
1	2	3	4	5	6	7	August 2012			1	2	3	4
8	9	10	11	12	13	14		5	6	7	8	9	10	11
15	16	17	18	19	20	21		12	13	14	15	16	17	18
22	23	24	25	26	27	28		19	20	21	22	23	24	25
29	30	31			July 2012			26	27	28	29	30	31	

Emotional Power

FRIDAY
07.20.2012

New Moon

☽ IN ♌: ALL DAY
☽ VOC: NO
5:5/7:7 STAR GATE

♇ IS R
♆ IS R
♅ IS R
⚷ IS R
☿ IS R

"In compassion lies the world's true strength."
Gautama Buddha

8ᴀᴍ	2ᴘᴍ
9ᴀᴍ	3ᴘᴍ
10ᴀᴍ	4ᴘᴍ
11ᴀᴍ	5ᴘᴍ
12ᴘᴍ	6ᴘᴍ
1ᴘᴍ	7ᴘᴍ

Ramadan begins

All times Eastern Daylight Time

Emotional Power

SATURDAY
07.21.2012

Crescent

☽ IN ♌
☽ →♍: 1:24P
☽ VOC: 1:17A - 1:24P { ☽ ✷ ♄ }

♇ IS R
♆ IS R
♅ IS R
⚷ IS R
☿ IS R

"We will only understand the miracle of life fully when we allow the unexpected to happen."

Paulo Coelho

8ᴬᴹ	2ᴾᴹ
9ᴬᴹ	3ᴾᴹ
10ᴬᴹ	4ᴾᴹ
11ᴬᴹ	5ᴾᴹ
12ᴾᴹ	6ᴾᴹ
1ᴾᴹ	7ᴾᴹ

S	M	T	W	T	F	S	S	M	T	W	T	F	S
1	2	3	4	5	6	7	August 2012		1	2	3	4
8	9	10	11	12	13	14	5	6	7	8	9	10	11
15	16	17	18	19	20	21	12	13	14	15	16	17	18
22	23	24	25	26	27	28	19	20	21	22	23	24	25
29	30	31		July 2012			26	27	28	29	30	31	

LEO

Emotional Love

Symbol: The Life Force
Master: Lady Liberty
Quality: Inner Gratitude
Ray: 7th Ray, Violet Flame
Trine: Fire
Hour: 7
Rulers: ☉ ♀ ☽

I AM RADIANT

Emotional Power

7 O'Clock Hour
Main Purpose:

Where you spread positivity by giving of yourself selflessly.

JULY 22 – AUGUST 21

In Cosmic Astrology, Leo is the sign of ***Inner Gratitude***. It is the place where you learn to recognize the positivity in anything and everything you experience. There is a blessing to every situation you encounter, as it is all part of the Divine Plan. Knowing this is the beginning of joy, because it frees you from the need to understand and to control your world. Once we are emotionally attuned to the perfection of the Divine Plan we begin to generate a positivity that is contagious, much like the Sun shining brightly in the middle of the day. Assuming a positive approach empowers you and everyone whose life you touch. This is true service. The Lion becomes the heart, the core of every situation, affirming life and Love and the goodness of all things.

Leo is the 7 o'clock hour, corresponding to the 2nd house of the birth chart. In the 2nd house you develop your values and your level of self-worth. Beginning with a positive outlook and a belief that 'it's all good' is a strong basis for the kind of self-esteem that generates abundance, not only for the self, but for anyone around you. Gratitude is the foundation of happiness and joy, and these become possible when we move beyond self-centeredness to the awareness of the bigger picture. Only then can we become central to the picture, the way the Sun is the center of everything.

Wherever Leo is in your birth chart you are challenged to move beyond self-focus to the greater awareness of the perfection of the Divine Plan. The Leo area of your energy field is where you ultimately offer your Light in service to others. If that Light is colored with self-importance it is not delivering all that it can. Here is where we learn that everything has a silver lining, and knowing this and learning to locate that positivity is all it takes to be a powerful force for good in the world. If your Sun sign is Leo you have chosen to learn the value of service in this lifetime by coming to realize that being loving is the highest form of giving there is.

FAMOUS LEOS

Jacqueline Kennedy Onassis, Halle Berry, Madonna, Bill Clinton, Martha Stewart, Lucille Ball, Whitney Houston, Percy B. Shelly, Robert Redford, Gene Roddenberry, Helena Blavatski, George B. Shaw, Carl G. Jung, Yves St. Laurent, Sri Aurobindo, Fidel Castro, Coco Chanel, Napoleon Bonaparte, Barack Obama

Emotional Love

SUNDAY
07.22.2012

Crescent

☽ IN ♍: ALL DAY
☽ VOC: 8:44P - MIDNIGHT {☽ □ ♀}
☉ → ♌: 6:01A
HIDDEN 7:7 STAR GATE

♇ IS R
♆ IS R
♅ IS R
⚷ IS R
⚴ IS R

♃ ✷ ♅ 08°♊/♈ 12:04A
☿ ✷ ♂ 10°♌/♎ 6:55A

> *"When you are serving someone,*
> *think how grateful you are, not how lucky they are."*
> — Derek O'Neill

8ᴀᴍ	2ᴘᴍ
9ᴀᴍ	3ᴘᴍ
10ᴀᴍ	4ᴘᴍ
11ᴀᴍ	5ᴘᴍ
12ᴘᴍ	6ᴘᴍ
1ᴘᴍ	7ᴘᴍ

All times Eastern Daylight Time

Emotional Love | ♌

MONDAY
07.23.2012

Crescent

☽ IN ♍
☽ →♎: 6:38P
☽ VOC: MIDNIGHT - 6:38P
5:5 STAR GATE

♇ IS R
♆ IS R
♅ IS R
⚷ IS R
⚥ IS R

"Give light, and the darkness will disappear of itself."
Desiderius Erasmus

8ᴬᴹ	2ᴾᴹ
9ᴬᴹ	3ᴾᴹ
10ᴬᴹ	4ᴾᴹ
11ᴬᴹ	5ᴾᴹ
12ᴾᴹ	6ᴾᴹ
1ᴾᴹ	7ᴾᴹ

S	M	T	W	T	F	S
1	2	3	4	5	6	7
8	9	10	11	12	13	14
15	16	17	18	19	20	21
22	23	24	25	26	27	28
29	30	31			July 2012	

	S	M	T	W	T	F	S
August 2012				1	2	3	4
	5	6	7	8	9	10	11
	12	13	14	15	16	17	18
	19	20	21	22	23	24	25
	26	27	28	29	30	31	

Emotional Love

TUESDAY
07.24.2012

Crescent

☽ IN ♎: ALL DAY
☽ VOC: NO

♇ IS R
♆ IS R
♅ IS R
⚷ IS R
☿ IS R

♃ □ ♄ 09°♊/♓ 9:09A
☿ ✶ ♃ 09°♌/♊ 3:15P

"If the only prayer you said in your whole life was, 'thank you,' that would suffice."

Meister Eckhart

JUL

8ᴬᴹ	2ᴾᴹ
9ᴬᴹ	3ᴾᴹ
10ᴬᴹ	4ᴾᴹ
11ᴬᴹ	5ᴾᴹ
12ᴾᴹ	6ᴾᴹ
1ᴾᴹ	7ᴾᴹ

All times Eastern Daylight Time

Emotional Love ♌

WEDNESDAY
07.25.2012

Crescent

☽ IN ♎
☽ →♏: 10:29P
☽ VOC: 11:22A - 10:29P { ☽ ☌ ♄ }
7:7 STAR GATE

♇ IS R
♆ IS R
♅ IS R
⚷ IS R
♀ IS R

☿ △ ♅ 08°♌/♈ 9:28A
☉ △ ☊ 03°♌/♐ 12:28P
☉ ✶ ☋ 03°♌/♊ 12:28P

"Gratitude is the fairest blossom which springs from the soul."
Henry Ward Beecher

8ᴀᴍ	2ᴘᴍ
9ᴀᴍ	3ᴘᴍ
10ᴀᴍ	4ᴘᴍ
11ᴀᴍ	5ᴘᴍ
12ᴘᴍ	6ᴘᴍ
1ᴘᴍ	7ᴘᴍ

S	M	T	W	T	F	S
	1	2	3	4	5	6	7
8	9	10	11	12	13	14
15	16	17	18	19	20	21
22	23	24	25	26	27	28
29	30	31			July 2012	

S	M	T	W	T	F	S
August 2012			1	2	3	4
5	6	7	8	9	10	11
12	13	14	15	16	17	18
19	20	21	22	23	24	25
26	27	28	29	30	31	

Emotional Love

THURSDAY
07.26.2012

First Quarter

☽ IN ♏
☽ VOC: 11:38A - MIDNIGHT { ☽ □ ☿ }

♇ IS R
♆ IS R
♅ IS R
⚷ IS R
☿ IS R

"Gratitude unlocks the fullness of life.
It turns what we have into enough, and more."

Melody Beattie

JUL

8ᴬᴹ	2ᴾᴹ
9ᴬᴹ	3ᴾᴹ
10ᴬᴹ	4ᴾᴹ
11ᴬᴹ	5ᴾᴹ
12ᴾᴹ	6ᴾᴹ
1ᴾᴹ	7ᴾᴹ

All times Eastern Daylight Time

Emotional Love

 ♌

FRIDAY
07.27.2012

First Quarter

☽ IN ♏: ALL DAY
☽ VOC: ALL DAY
7:7/5:5 STAR GATE

♇ IS R
♆ IS R
♅ IS R
⚷ IS R
☿ IS R

*"When eating bamboo sprouts,
remember the man who planted them."*

Chinese Proverb

8 AM	2 PM
9 AM	3 PM
10 AM	4 PM
11 AM	5 PM
12 PM	6 PM
1 PM	7 PM

July 2012

S	M	T	W	T	F	S
1	2	3	4	5	6	7
8	9	10	11	12	13	14
15	16	17	18	19	20	21
22	23	24	25	26	27	28
29	30	31				

August 2012

S	M	T	W	T	F	S
			1	2	3	4
5	6	7	8	9	10	11
12	13	14	15	16	17	18
19	20	21	22	23	24	25
26	27	28	29	30	31	

Emotional Love

SATURDAY
07.28.2012

First Quarter

☽ IN ♏
☽ →♐: 1:18A
☽ VOC: MIDNIGHT - 1:18A

♇ IS R
♆ IS R
♅ IS R
⚷ IS R
☿ IS R

☉ ☌ ☿ 06°♌ 3:58P

"Real living is living for others."
Bruce Lee

8ᴀᴍ	2ᴘᴍ
9ᴀᴍ	3ᴘᴍ
10ᴀᴍ	4ᴘᴍ
11ᴀᴍ	5ᴘᴍ
12ᴘᴍ	6ᴘᴍ
1ᴘᴍ	7ᴘᴍ

All times Eastern Daylight Time

Emotional Love

SUNDAY
07.29.2012

Gibbous

☽ IN ♐

☽ VOC: 5:01P - MIDNIGHT { ☽ ✶ ♄ }

♀ IS STATIONING {R}

HIDDEN 5:5 STAR GATE

♇ IS R
♆ IS R
♅ IS R
⚷ IS R
☿ IS R

"The secret to happiness is to want what you have."
Derek O'Neill

8AM	2PM
9AM	3PM
10AM	4PM
11AM	5PM
12PM	6PM
1PM	7PM

Tisha B'av

S	M	T	W	T	F	S
1	2	3	4	5	6	7
8	9	10	11	12	13	14
15	16	17	18	19	20	21
22	23	24	25	26	27	28
29	30	31			July 2012	

S	M	T	W	T	F	S
August 2012			1	2	3	4
5	6	7	8	9	10	11
12	13	14	15	16	17	18
19	20	21	22	23	24	25
26	27	28	29	30	31	

Emotional Love

MONDAY
07.30.2012

Gibbous

☽ IN ♐
☽ →♑: 3:30A
☽ VOC: MIDNIGHT - 3:30A
♀ STATION: 6:30P
♀ TURNS R: 11° ♈

♇ IS R
♆ IS R
♅ IS R
⚷ IS R
☿ IS R

"Gratitude is happiness doubled by wonder."
G.K. Chesterton

8ᴬᴹ	2ᴾᴹ
9ᴬᴹ	3ᴾᴹ
10ᴬᴹ	4ᴾᴹ
11ᴬᴹ	5ᴾᴹ
12ᴾᴹ	6ᴾᴹ
1ᴾᴹ	7ᴾᴹ

All times Eastern Daylight Time

Emotional Love

TUESDAY
07.31.2012

Gibbous

☽ IN ♑: ALL DAY
☽ VOC: 8:30P - MIDNIGHT { ☽ □ ♄ }
♀ HAS STATIONED {R}
HIDDEN 7:7 STAR GATE

♇ IS R
♆ IS R
♅ IS R
⚷ IS R
⚳ IS R

☉ △ ♅ 08°♌/♈ 1:31A
♀ △ ♄ 24°♊/♎ 3:38A

"If you want to turn your life around, try thankfulness."

Gerald Good

8ᴀᴍ	2ᴘᴍ
9ᴀᴍ	3ᴘᴍ
10ᴀᴍ	4ᴘᴍ
11ᴀᴍ	5ᴘᴍ
12ᴘᴍ	6ᴘᴍ
1ᴘᴍ	7ᴘᴍ

S	M	T	W	T	F	S
1	2	3	4	5	6	7
8	9	10	11	12	13	14
15	16	17	18	19	20	21
22	23	24	25	26	27	28
29	30	31			July 2012	

S	M	T	W	T	F	S
August 2012			1	2	3	4
5	6	7	8	9	10	11
12	13	14	15	16	17	18
19	20	21	22	23	24	25
26	27	28	29	30	31	

Emotional Love

WEDNESDAY
08.01.2012

Full Moon

☽ IN ♑
☽ →♒: 5:56A
☽ VOC: MIDNIGHT - 5:56A
5:5 STAR GATE

♇ IS R
♆ IS R
♅ IS R
⚷ IS R
♀ IS R
☿ IS R

FULL MOON { ☽ ☍ ☉}: 11:28P
10° ♒15'

> *"We can only be said to be alive in those moments when our hearts are conscious of our treasures."*
>
> — Thornton Wilder

AUG

8ᴬᴹ	2ᴾᴹ
9ᴬᴹ	3ᴾᴹ
10ᴬᴹ	4ᴾᴹ
11ᴬᴹ	5ᴾᴹ
12ᴾᴹ	6ᴾᴹ
1ᴾᴹ	7ᴾᴹ

Lughnasadh
Lammas

All times Eastern Daylight Time

Emotional Love

THURSDAY
08.02.2012

Full Moon

☽ IN ♒: ALL DAY
☽ VOC: NO

♇ IS R
♆ IS R
♅ IS R
⚷ IS R
♀ IS R
☿ IS R

☉ ✱ ♃ 11° ♌/♊ 5:56A

"There is not a more pleasing exercise of the mind than gratitude."

Joseph Addison

8ᴀᴍ	2ᴘᴍ
9ᴀᴍ	3ᴘᴍ
10ᴀᴍ	4ᴘᴍ
11ᴀᴍ	5ᴘᴍ
12ᴘᴍ	6ᴘᴍ
1ᴘᴍ	7ᴘᴍ

S	M	T	W	T	F	S	S	M	T	W	T	F	S
August 2012			1	2	3	4	September 2012						1
5	6	7	8	9	10	11	2	3	4	5	6	7	8
12	13	14	15	16	17	18	9	10	11	12	13	14	15
19	20	21	22	23	24	25	16	17	18	19	20	21	22
26	27	28	29	30	31		23	24	25	26	27	28	29
							30						

Emotional Love		**FRIDAY** **08.03.2012**	
			Full Moon

☽ IN ♒
☽ →♓: 9:58A
☽ VOC: 3:24A - 9:58A {☽ △ ♀}

♇ IS R
♆ IS R
♅ IS R
⚷ IS R
♀ IS R
☿ IS R

☿ △ ☊ 02°♌/♐ 2:10P
☿ ✶ ☋ 02°♌/♊ 2:10P

"Sometimes when we are generous in small, barely detectable ways it can change someone else's life forever."

Margaret Cho

AUG

8ᴀᴍ	2ᴘᴍ
9ᴀᴍ	3ᴘᴍ
10ᴀᴍ	4ᴘᴍ
11ᴀᴍ	5ᴘᴍ
12ᴘᴍ	6ᴘᴍ
1ᴘᴍ	7ᴘᴍ

All times Eastern Daylight Time

Emotional Love

SATURDAY
08.04.2012

Full Moon

☽ IN ♓: ALL DAY
☽ VOC: NO
12:12 STAR GATE

♇ IS R
♆ IS R
♅ IS R
⚷ IS R
♀ IS R
☿ IS R

♆ □ ☊ 02°♓/♐ 5:00P
♆ □ ☋ 02°♓/♊ 5:00P

"I am a little pencil in the hand of a writing God who is sending a love letter to the world."

Mother Teresa

8ᴀᴍ	2ᴘᴍ
9ᴀᴍ	3ᴘᴍ
10ᴀᴍ	4ᴘᴍ
11ᴀᴍ	5ᴘᴍ
12ᴘᴍ	6ᴘᴍ
1ᴘᴍ	7ᴘᴍ

S	M	T	W	T	F	S	S	M	T	W	T	F	S
August 2012			1	2	3	4	September 2012						1
5	6	7	8	9	10	11	2	3	4	5	6	7	8
12	13	14	15	16	17	18	9	10	11	12	13	14	15
19	20	21	22	23	24	25	16	17	18	19	20	21	22
26	27	28	29	30	31		23	24	25	26	27	28	29
							30						

Emotional
Love

SUNDAY
08.05.2012

Disseminating

☽ IN ♓
☽ →♈: 4:58P
☽ VOC: 1:56P - 4:58P { ☽ □ ♀ }
5:5 STAR GATE

♇ IS R
♆ IS R
♅ IS R
⚷ IS R
♀ IS R
☿ IS R

"When we forget to say thank you we suffer."

Derek O'Neill

8ᴬᴹ	2ᴾᴹ
9ᴬᴹ	3ᴾᴹ
10ᴬᴹ	4ᴾᴹ
11ᴬᴹ	5ᴾᴹ
12ᴾᴹ	6ᴾᴹ
1ᴾᴹ	7ᴾᴹ

All times Eastern Daylight Time

Emotional Love

MONDAY
08.06.2012

Disseminating

☽ IN ♈: ALL DAY
☽ VOC: NO
5:5 STAR GATE

♇ IS R
♆ IS R
♅ IS R
⚷ IS R
♀ IS R
☿ IS R

*"Gratitude helps you to grow and expand;
gratitude brings joy and laughter into your life and into
the lives of all those around you."*

Eileen Caddy

8ᴬᴹ	2ᴾᴹ
9ᴬᴹ	3ᴾᴹ
10ᴬᴹ	4ᴾᴹ
11ᴬᴹ	5ᴾᴹ
12ᴾᴹ	6ᴾᴹ
1ᴾᴹ	7ᴾᴹ

S	M	T	W	T	F	S	S	M	T	W	T	F	S
August 2012			1	2	3	4	September 2012						1
5	6	7	8	9	10	11	2	3	4	5	6	7	8
12	13	14	15	16	17	18	9	10	11	12	13	14	15
19	20	21	22	23	24	25	16	17	18	19	20	21	22
26	27	28	29	30	31		23	24	25	26	27	28	29
							30						

Emotional Love

TUESDAY
08.07.2012

Disseminating

- ☽ IN ♈: ALL DAY
- ☽ VOC: 4:04P - MIDNIGHT { ☽ ☍ ♄ }
- ☿ IS STATIONING {D}
- ♀ → ♋: 9:43A

- ♇ IS R
- ♆ IS R
- ♅ IS R
- ⚷ IS R
- ⚶ IS R

> *"Everything we do should be a result of our gratitude for what God has done for us."*
>
> Lauryn Hill

AUG

8ᴀᴍ	2ᴘᴍ
9ᴀᴍ	3ᴘᴍ
10ᴀᴍ	4ᴘᴍ
11ᴀᴍ	5ᴘᴍ
12ᴘᴍ	6ᴘᴍ
1ᴘᴍ	7ᴘᴍ

All times Eastern Daylight Time

Emotional Love

♌

WEDNESDAY
08.08.2012

Disseminating

☽ IN ♈
☽ →♉: 3:27A
☽ VOC: MIDNIGHT - 3:27A
☿ STATION: 1:41A
☿ TURNS D: 01° ♌
8:8 STAR GATE

♇ IS R
♆ IS R
♅ IS R
♄ IS R
♀ IS R

"The hardest arithmetic to master is that which enables us to count our blessings."
Eric Hoffer

8ᴬᴹ	2ᴾᴹ
9ᴬᴹ	3ᴾᴹ
10ᴬᴹ	4ᴾᴹ
11ᴬᴹ	5ᴾᴹ
12ᴾᴹ	6ᴾᴹ
1ᴾᴹ	7ᴾᴹ

S	M	T	W	T	F	S	S	M	T	W	T	F	S
August 2012		1	2	3	4	September 2012						1
5	6	7	8	9	10	11	2	3	4	5	6	7	8
12	13	14	15	16	17	18	9	10	11	12	13	14	15
19	20	21	22	23	24	25	16	17	18	19	20	21	22
26	27	28	29	30	31		23	24	25	26	27	28	29
							30						

Emotional Love

THURSDAY
08.09.2012

Last Quarter

☽ IN ♉: ALL DAY
☽ VOC: 2:55P - MIDNIGHT {☽ □ ☉}
☿ HAS STATIONED {D}
HIDDEN 8:8/5:5 STAR GATE

♇ IS R
♆ IS R
♅ IS R
♄ IS R
♀ IS R

♀ △ ♆ 02°♋/♓ 6:34P

"There is a treasury of joy within you,
why do you keep knocking door to door?"

Sufi saying

AUG

8ᴀᴍ	2ᴘᴍ
9ᴀᴍ	3ᴘᴍ
10ᴀᴍ	4ᴘᴍ
11ᴀᴍ	5ᴘᴍ
12ᴘᴍ	6ᴘᴍ
1ᴘᴍ	7ᴘᴍ

All times Eastern Daylight Time

Emotional Love

FRIDAY
08.10.2012

Last Quarter

☽ IN ♉
☽ → ♊: 4:10P
☽ VOC: MIDNIGHT - 4:10P
☿ IN D SHADOW
HIDDEN 5:5 STAR GATE

♇ IS R
♆ IS R
♅ IS R
⚷ IS R
♀ IS R

☿ △ ☊ 02° ♌/♐ 11:51P
☿ ✶ ☋ 02° ♌/♊ 11:51P

"Life loves the liver of it."
Maya Angelou

8 AM	2 PM
9 AM	3 PM
10 AM	4 PM
11 AM	5 PM
12 PM	6 PM
1 PM	7 PM

Krishna Janmastami

S	M	T	W	T	F	S
August 2012		1	2	3	4
5	6	7	8	9	10	11
12	13	14	15	16	17	18
19	20	21	22	23	24	25
26	27	28	29	30	31	

S	M	T	W	T	F	S
September 2012						1
2	3	4	5	6	7	8
9	10	11	12	13	14	15
16	17	18	19	20	21	22
23	24	25	26	27	28	29
30						

Emotional Love ♌

SATURDAY
08.11.2012

Last Quarter

☽ IN ♊: ALL DAY
☽ VOC: NO
☿ IN D SHADOW

♇ IS R
♆ IS R
♅ IS R
⚷ IS R
♀ IS R

> "Happiness is the spiritual experience of living every minute with love, grace, and gratitude."
> — Denis Waitley

8ᴀᴍ	2ᴘᴍ
9ᴀᴍ	3ᴘᴍ
10ᴀᴍ	4ᴘᴍ
11ᴀᴍ	5ᴘᴍ
12ᴘᴍ	6ᴘᴍ
1ᴘᴍ	7ᴘᴍ

All times Eastern Daylight Time

Emotional Love

SUNDAY
08.12.2012

Last Quarter

☽ IN ♊: ALL DAY
☽ VOC: 5:49P - MIDNIGHT { ☽ △ ♄ }
☿ IN D SHADOW
HIDDEN 8:8 STAR GATE

♇ IS R
♆ IS R
♅ IS R
⚷ IS R
♀ IS R

*"We need to stop wanting to get out of here
and start to enjoy being here."*

Derek O'Neill

8ᴀᴍ	2ᴘᴍ
9ᴀᴍ	3ᴘᴍ
10ᴀᴍ	4ᴘᴍ
11ᴀᴍ	5ᴘᴍ
12ᴘᴍ	6ᴘᴍ
1ᴘᴍ	7ᴘᴍ

	S	M	T	W	T	F	S
August 2012			1	2	3	4
	5	6	7	8	9	10	11
	12	13	14	15	16	17	18
	19	20	21	22	23	24	25
	26	27	28	29	30	31	

	S	M	T	W	T	F	S
September 2012							1
	2	3	4	5	6	7	8
	9	10	11	12	13	14	15
	16	17	18	19	20	21	22
	23	24	25	26	27	28	29
	30						

Emotional Love

MONDAY
08.13.2012

Last Quarter

☽ IN ♊
☽ →♋: 4:27A
☽ VOC: MIDNIGHT - 4:27A
☿ IN ☽ SHADOW
HIDDEN 8:8 STAR GATE

♇ IS R
♆ IS R
♅ IS R
⚷ IS R
♀ IS R

"Prayers go up and blessings come down."
Yiddish Proverb

AUG

8ᴀᴍ	2ᴘᴍ
9ᴀᴍ	3ᴘᴍ
10ᴀᴍ	4ᴘᴍ
11ᴀᴍ	5ᴘᴍ
12ᴘᴍ	6ᴘᴍ
1ᴘᴍ	7ᴘᴍ

All times Eastern Daylight Time

Emotional Love

TUESDAY
08.14.2012

Last Quarter

☽ IN ♋: ALL DAY
☽ VOC: NO
☿ IN D SHADOW
5:5 STAR GATE

♇ IS R
♆ IS R
♅ IS R
⚷ IS R
♀ IS R

"Not what we say about our blessings, but how we use them, is the true measure of our thanksgiving."

W. T. Purkiser

....
....
....
....
....
....
....
....

8ᴀᴍ	2ᴘᴍ
9ᴀᴍ	3ᴘᴍ
10ᴀᴍ	4ᴘᴍ
11ᴀᴍ	5ᴘᴍ
12ᴘᴍ	6ᴘᴍ
1ᴘᴍ	7ᴘᴍ

S	M	T	W	T	F	S	S	M	T	W	T	F	S
August 2012			1	2	3	4	September 2012						1
5	6	7	8	9	10	11	2	3	4	5	6	7	8
12	13	14	15	16	17	18	9	10	11	12	13	14	15
19	20	21	22	23	24	25	16	17	18	19	20	21	22
26	27	28	29	30	31		23	24	25	26	27	28	29
							30						

Emotional Love

WEDNESDAY
08.15.2012

Balsamic

☽ IN ♋
☽ →♌: 2:04P
☽ VOC: 4:21A 0 2:04P {☽ □ ♄}
☿ IN D SHADOW
HIDDEN 5:5 STAR GATE

♇ IS R
♆ IS R
♅ IS R
⚷ IS R
♀ IS R

♀ ☍ ♇ 07°♋/♑ 5:11A
♂ ☌ ♄ 25°♎ 6:35A

"Gratitude changes the pangs of memory into a tranquil joy."

Dietrich Bonhoeffer

8ᴀᴍ	2ᴘᴍ
9ᴀᴍ	3ᴘᴍ
10ᴀᴍ	4ᴘᴍ
11ᴀᴍ	5ᴘᴍ
12ᴘᴍ	6ᴘᴍ
1ᴘᴍ	7ᴘᴍ

All times Eastern Daylight Time

Emotional Love

THURSDAY
08.16.2012

Balsamic

☽ IN ♌: ALL DAY
☽ VOC: NO
☿ IN D SHADOW

♇ IS R
♆ IS R
♅ IS R
⚷ IS R
♀ IS R

♀ △ ⚷ 08°♋/♓ 12:28A
♀ □ ♅ 08°♋/♈ 2:48A

*"Gratitude is not only the greatest of virtues,
but the parent of all the others."*

Marcus Tullius Cicero

8ᴬᴹ	2ᴾᴹ
9ᴬᴹ	3ᴾᴹ
10ᴬᴹ	4ᴾᴹ
11ᴬᴹ	5ᴾᴹ
12ᴾᴹ	6ᴾᴹ
1ᴾᴹ	7ᴾᴹ

S	M	T	W	T	F	S	S	M	T	W	T	F	S
August 2012			1	2	3	4	September 2012						1
5	6	7	8	9	10	11	2	3	4	5	6	7	8
12	13	14	15	16	17	18	9	10	11	12	13	14	15
19	20	21	22	23	24	25	16	17	18	19	20	21	22
26	27	28	29	30	31		23	24	25	26	27	28	29
							30						

Emotional Love

FRIDAY
08.17.2012

New Moon

☽ IN ♌
☽ →♍: 8:33P
☽ VOC: 1:55P - 8:33P { ☽ ✶ ♂ }
☿ IN D SHADOW
8:8 STAR GATE

♇ IS R
♆ IS R
♅ IS R
⚷ IS R
♀ IS R

NEW MOON { ☽ ☌ ☉ }: 11:54A
25° ♌08'

☉ ✶ ♄ 25°♌/♎ 8:04A

"Gratitude is the sign of noble souls."
Aesop

8ᴀᴍ	2ᴘᴍ
9ᴀᴍ	3ᴘᴍ
10ᴀᴍ	4ᴘᴍ
11ᴀᴍ	5ᴘᴍ
12ᴘᴍ	6ᴘᴍ
1ᴘᴍ	7ᴘᴍ

All times Eastern Daylight Time

Emotional Love

SATURDAY
08.18.2012

New Moon

☽ IN ♍: ALL DAY
☽ VOC: 7:26P - MIDNIGHT { ☽ □ ♃ }
☿ IN D SHADOW
HIDDEN 8:8/5:5 STAR GATE

♇ IS R
♆ IS R
♅ IS R
♄ IS R
♀ IS R

☿ △ ♅ 08°♌/♈ 7:29P

> *"Gratitude is when memory is stored in the heart and not in the mind."*
>
> Lionel Hampton

8ᴬᴹ	2ᴾᴹ
9ᴬᴹ	3ᴾᴹ
10ᴬᴹ	4ᴾᴹ
11ᴬᴹ	5ᴾᴹ
12ᴾᴹ	6ᴾᴹ
1ᴾᴹ	7ᴾᴹ

S	M	T	W	T	F	S	S	M	T	W	T	F	S
August 2012			1	2	3	4	September 2012						1
5	6	7	8	9	10	11	2	3	4	5	6	7	8
12	13	14	15	16	17	18	9	10	11	12	13	14	15
19	20	21	22	23	24	25	16	17	18	19	20	21	22
26	27	28	29	30	31		23	24	25	26	27	28	29
							30						

Emotional Love

SUNDAY
08.19.2012

Crescent

☽ IN ♍: ALL DAY
☽ VOC: ALL DAY
☿ IN D SHADOW

♇ IS R
♆ IS R
♅ IS R
⚷ IS R
♀ IS R

"If you give your heart with love, there is no being on the planet that can harm you."

Derek O'Neill

AUG

8ᴬᴹ	2ᴾᴹ
9ᴬᴹ	3ᴾᴹ
10ᴬᴹ	4ᴾᴹ
11ᴬᴹ	5ᴾᴹ
12ᴾᴹ	6ᴾᴹ
1ᴾᴹ	7ᴾᴹ

Eid-Ul-Fitr (end of Ramadan)

All times Eastern Daylight Time

Emotional Love

MONDAY
08.20.2012

Crescent

☽ IN ♍
☽ →♎: 12:45A
☽ VOC: MIDNIGHT - 12:45A { ☽ ✶ ♂ }
☿ IN D SHADOW

♇ IS R
♆ IS R
♅ IS R
⚷ IS R
♀ IS R

☉ ✶ ♂ 28° ♌/♎ 5:45P

"The essence of all beautiful art, all great art, is gratitude."

Friedrich Nietzsche

8ᴀᴍ	2ᴘᴍ
9ᴀᴍ	3ᴘᴍ
10ᴀᴍ	4ᴘᴍ
11ᴀᴍ	5ᴘᴍ
12ᴘᴍ	6ᴘᴍ
1ᴘᴍ	7ᴘᴍ

S	M	T	W	T	F	S	S	M	T	W	T	F	S
August 2012		1	2	3	4	September 2012							1
5	6	7	8	9	10	11	2	3	4	5	6	7	8
12	13	14	15	16	17	18	9	10	11	12	13	14	15
19	20	21	22	23	24	25	16	17	18	19	20	21	22
26	27	28	29	30	31		23	24	25	26	27	28	29
							30						

Emotional Love

TUESDAY
08.21.2012

Crescent

☽ IN ♎: ALL DAY
☽ VOC: NO
☿ IN D SHADOW
HIDDEN 8:8 STAR GATE

♇ IS R
♆ IS R
♅ IS R
⚷ IS R
♀ IS R

"When you have truly surrendered, there will be no questions."
Derek O'Neill

AUG

8ᴬᴹ	2ᴾᴹ
9ᴬᴹ	3ᴾᴹ
10ᴬᴹ	4ᴾᴹ
11ᴬᴹ	5ᴾᴹ
12ᴾᴹ	6ᴾᴹ
1ᴾᴹ	7ᴾᴹ

All times Eastern Daylight Time

VIRGO

Emotional Wisdom

Symbol: The Master Healer
Master: Lord Lanto
Quality: Inner Alignment
Ray: 8th Ray, Green-Violet
Trine: Earth
Hour: 8
Rulers: ☄ ♂ ♄

I AM IN SERVICE

8 O'Clock Hour
Main Purpose:

Where you work to bring about conscious well-being.

AUGUST 22 – SEPTEMBER 21

In Cosmic Astrology, Virgo is the sign of **Inner Alignment**. It is also the last of the three signs that encompass the emotional body. Conscious well-being is achieved when mind, heart, body and spirit are in balance, and this is not possible without the benefit of emotional wisdom. In this aspect of your energy field you learn to look inside for your answers instead of 'out there.' This happens when we can finally trust that all we experience is perfect and we understand the creative power of a positive attitude. In Virgo, we learn to bring about true healing by bringing the lower four body system in alignment. This is the emergence of integrity. Here we move from the Virgin to the Master Healer/Teacher, which is the natural result of a well-balanced fully aligned individual. Well-being is full functionality that allows you to become the great example for others to learn from.

Virgo is the 8 o'clock hour on the cosmic clock, which corresponds to the 1st house of the birth chart. The connection here is easy to understand. The 5D human is fundamentally involved with the self as a four body system. Carefully tending to your own well-being is a great service to humanity. Well-being generates full functionality, which in turn helps you to know your own capacity fully. This eventually facilitates the awareness that all you are lies within, and every answer you need is contained in your own heart.

Wherever you find Virgo in your birth chart, you are working to bring about healing to facilitate the fullest expression of who you are and what you do. Here you learn to value every part of yourself, particularly the parts you have trouble embracing. If Virgo is your Sun sign, you have chosen to devote your life to personal mastery by carefully tending to your own wellness. Any imbalance, mental, emotional, physical or spiritual can be the vehicle for learning to heal your Self. This, in turn, becomes the Truth you can teach by example.

FAMOUS VIRGOS

Michael Jackson, Sophia Loren, Raquel Welch, Agatha Christie, Warren Buffet, David Copperfield, Greta Garbo, Amy Winehouse, Stephen King, Ken Kesey, Peter Sellers, Oliver Stone, Charlie Sheen, Mother Teresa, D.H. Lawrence, Van Morrison, Dr. Joyce Brothers, Queen Elizabeth I, Lance Armstrong

Emotional Wisdom

WEDNESDAY
08.22.2012

Crescent

☽ IN ♎
☽ →♏: 3:54A
☽ VOC: 3:13A - 3:54A {☽ ✶ ☉}
☿ LEAVES D SHADOW
☉ →♍: 1:07P
HIDDEN 8:8 STAR GATE

♇ IS R
♆ IS R
♅ IS R
⚷ IS R
♀ IS R

☿ ✶ ♃   14° ♌/ ♊   6:56P

> *"Eventually you will come to understand that love heals everything, and love is all there is."*
>
> Gary Zukav

AUG

8ᴀᴍ	2ᴘᴍ
9ᴀᴍ	3ᴘᴍ
10ᴀᴍ	4ᴘᴍ
11ᴀᴍ	5ᴘᴍ
12ᴘᴍ	6ᴘᴍ
1ᴘᴍ	7ᴘᴍ

All times Eastern Daylight Time

Emotional Wisdom

THURSDAY
08.23.2012

Crescent

☽ IN ♏: ALL DAY
☽ VOC: 5:34A - MIDNIGHT {☽ △ ♀}
♂ →♏: 11:24A
5:5 STAR GATE

♇ IS R
♆ IS R
♅ IS R
⚷ IS R
♀ IS R

☉ □ ☊ 00°♍/♐ 12:54A
☉ □ ☋ 00°♍/♊ 12:54A

"When I am simple I am able to be free from pain or hurt even in adverse situations."

Brahma Kumaris

8ᴀᴍ	**2**ᴘᴍ
9ᴀᴍ	**3**ᴘᴍ
10ᴀᴍ	**4**ᴘᴍ
11ᴀᴍ	**5**ᴘᴍ
12ᴘᴍ	**6**ᴘᴍ
1ᴘᴍ	**7**ᴘᴍ

S	M	T	W	T	F	S	S	M	T	W	T	F	S
August 2012			1	2	3	4	September 2012						1
5	6	7	8	9	10	11	2	3	4	5	6	7	8
12	13	14	15	16	17	18	9	10	11	12	13	14	15
19	20	21	22	23	24	25	16	17	18	19	20	21	22
26	27	28	29	30	31		23	24	25	26	27	28	29
							30						

| Emotional Wisdom | ♍ | **FRIDAY**
08.24.2012 |
First Quarter |

☽ IN ♏
☽ →♐: 6:50A
☽ VOC: MIDNIGHT - 6:50A
5:5 STAR GATE

♇ IS R
♆ IS R
♅ IS R
⚷ IS R
♀ IS R

☉ ☍ ♆ 02° ♍/♓ 8:32A

> "Healing is about letting go of everything that isn't you
> and becoming who you are."
>
> Rachel Naomi Remen

8ᴀᴍ	2ᴘᴍ
9ᴀᴍ	3ᴘᴍ
10ᴀᴍ	4ᴘᴍ
11ᴀᴍ	5ᴘᴍ
12ᴘᴍ	6ᴘᴍ
1ᴘᴍ	7ᴘᴍ

All times Eastern Daylight Time

Emotional Wisdom

SATURDAY
08.25.2012

First Quarter

☽ IN ♐: ALL DAY
☽ VOC: NO

♇ IS R
♆ IS R
♅ IS R
⚷ IS R
♀ IS R

"Our sorrows and wounds are healed only when we touch them with compassion."

Gautama Buddha

8ᴀᴍ	2ᴘᴍ
9ᴀᴍ	3ᴘᴍ
10ᴀᴍ	4ᴘᴍ
11ᴀᴍ	5ᴘᴍ
12ᴘᴍ	6ᴘᴍ
1ᴘᴍ	7ᴘᴍ

S	M	T	W	T	F	S	S	M	T	W	T	F	S
August 2012			1	2	3	4	September 2012						1
5	6	7	8	9	10	11	2	3	4	5	6	7	8
12	13	14	15	16	17	18	9	10	11	12	13	14	15
19	20	21	22	23	24	25	16	17	18	19	20	21	22
26	27	28	29	30	31		23	24	25	26	27	28	29
							30						

Emotional Wisdom

 ♍

SUNDAY
08.26.2012

First Quarter

☽ IN ♐
☽ →♑: 9:59A
☽ VOC: 2:39A - 9:59A {☽ ✷ ♄}
8:8 STAR GATE

♇ IS R
♆ IS R
♅ IS R
⚷ IS R
♀ IS R

♂ △ ♆ 02°♏/♓ 2:53A

> "People do not heal because they do not realize what a gift their pain is."
>
> Derek O'Neill

AUG

8^{AM}	2^{PM}
9^{AM}	3^{PM}
10^{AM}	4^{PM}
11^{AM}	5^{PM}
12^{PM}	6^{PM}
1^{PM}	7^{PM}

All times Eastern Daylight Time

Emotional Wisdom

MONDAY
08.27.2012

First Quarter

☽ IN ♍: ALL DAY
☽ VOC: NO
HIDDEN 5:5 STAR GATE

♇ IS R
♆ IS R
♅ IS R
⚷ IS R
♀ IS R

"Healing yourself is connected with healing others."

Yoko Ono

8 AM	2 PM
9 AM	3 PM
10 AM	4 PM
11 AM	5 PM
12 PM	6 PM
1 PM	7 PM

S	M	T	W	T	F	S	S	M	T	W	T	F	S
August 2012			1	2	3	4	September 2012						1
5	6	7	8	9	10	11	2	3	4	5	6	7	8
12	13	14	15	16	17	18	9	10	11	12	13	14	15
19	20	21	22	23	24	25	16	17	18	19	20	21	22
26	27	28	29	30	31		23	24	25	26	27	28	29
							30						

| Emotional Wisdom | ♍ | **TUESDAY**
08.28.2012 |
Gibbous |

☽ IN ♑
☽ →♒: 1:39P
☽ VOC: 6:33A - 1:39P { ☽ □ ♄ }
HIDDEN 5:5 STAR GATE

♇ IS R
♆ IS R
♅ IS R
⚷ IS R
♀ IS R

> *"The greatest healing therapy is friendship and love."*
> Hubert H. Humphrey

8ᴀᴍ	2ᴘᴍ
9ᴀᴍ	3ᴘᴍ
10ᴀᴍ	4ᴘᴍ
11ᴀᴍ	5ᴘᴍ
12ᴘᴍ	6ᴘᴍ
1ᴘᴍ	7ᴘᴍ

All times Eastern Daylight Time

Emotional Wisdom

WEDNESDAY
08.29.2012

Gibbous

☽ IN ♒: ALL DAY
☽ VOC: NO

♇ IS R
♆ IS R
♅ IS R
⚷ IS R
♀ IS R

☉ △ ♇ 07°♍/♑ 8:21P
☿ ✱ ♄ 26°♌/♎ 9:25P

"All healing is first a healing of the heart."
                                     Carl Townsend

8ᴀᴍ	**2**ᴘᴍ
9ᴀᴍ	**3**ᴘᴍ
10ᴀᴍ	**4**ᴘᴍ
11ᴀᴍ	**5**ᴘᴍ
12ᴘᴍ	**6**ᴘᴍ
1ᴘᴍ	**7**ᴘᴍ

Emotional Wisdom

THURSDAY
08.30.2012

Gibbous

☽ IN ♒
☽ →♓: 6:31P
☽ VOC: 1:48P - 6:31P { ☽ ☌ ☿ }
8:8 Star Gate

♇ IS R
♆ IS R
♅ IS R
⚷ IS R
♀ IS R

☉ ☌ ☊ 07°♍/♓ 3:24A

"Smile, breathe and go slowly."
Thich Nhat Hanh

8ᴀᴍ	2ᴘᴍ
9ᴀᴍ	3ᴘᴍ
10ᴀᴍ	4ᴘᴍ
11ᴀᴍ	5ᴘᴍ
12ᴘᴍ	6ᴘᴍ
1ᴘᴍ	7ᴘᴍ

All times Eastern Daylight Time

Emotional Wisdom

FRIDAY
08.31.2012

Full Moon

☽ IN ♓: ALL DAY
☽ VOC: NO
☿ → ♍: 10:32P
HIDDEN 8:8 STAR GATE

♇ IS R
♆ IS R
♅ IS R
⚷ IS R
♀ IS R

FULL MOON { ☽ ☌ ☉ }: 9:58A
08° ♓34'

☿ □ ☊ 29°♌/♏ 6:01P
☿ □ ☋ 29°♌/♉ 6:01P

"Love is infectious and the greatest healing energy."
Sri Sathya Sai Baba

8ᴀᴍ	2ᴘᴍ
9ᴀᴍ	3ᴘᴍ
10ᴀᴍ	4ᴘᴍ
11ᴀᴍ	5ᴘᴍ
12ᴘᴍ	6ᴘᴍ
1ᴘᴍ	7ᴘᴍ

S	M	T	W	T	F	S		S	M	T	W	T	F	S
August 2012			1	2	3	4		September 2012						1
5	6	7	8	9	10	11		2	3	4	5	6	7	8
12	13	14	15	16	17	18		9	10	11	12	13	14	15
19	20	21	22	23	24	25		16	17	18	19	20	21	22
26	27	28	29	30	31			23	24	25	26	27	28	29
								30						

Emotional Wisdom		SATURDAY 09.01.2012	
			Full Moon

☽ IN ♓: ALL DAY
☽ VOC: 4:02P - MIDNIGHT { ☽ △ ♀ }
HIDDEN 1:1/5:5 STAR GATE

♇ IS R
♆ IS R
♅ IS R
⚷ IS R
♀ IS R

☿ ☍ ♆ 01° ♍/♓ 5:16P

"To heal from the inside out is the key."

Wynonna Judd

8 AM	2 PM
9 AM	3 PM
10 AM	4 PM
11 AM	5 PM
12 PM	6 PM
1 PM	7 PM

All times Eastern Daylight Time

Emotional Wisdom

SUNDAY
09.02.2012

Full Moon

☽ IN ♓
☽ →♈: 1:37A
☽ VOC: MIDNIGHT - 1:37A
HIDDEN 2:2/5:5 STAR GATE

♇ IS R
♆ IS R
♅ IS R
⚷ IS R
♀ IS R

*"Whenever you get sick, offer it to God.
God will transform it into love."*

Derek O'Neill

8 AM	2 PM
9 AM	3 PM
10 AM	4 PM
11 AM	5 PM
12 PM	6 PM
1 PM	7 PM

September 2012

S	M	T	W	T	F	S
						1
2	3	4	5	6	7	8
9	10	11	12	13	14	15
16	17	18	19	20	21	22
23	24	25	26	27	28	29
30						

October 2012

S	M	T	W	T	F	S
	1	2	3	4	5	6
7	8	9	10	11	12	13
14	15	16	17	18	19	20
21	22	23	24	25	26	27
28	29	30	31			

Emotional Wisdom ♍

MONDAY
09.03.2012

Full Moon

☽ IN ♈: ALL DAY
☽ VOC: NO
HIDDEN 3:3/5:5 STAR GATE

♇ IS R
♆ IS R
♅ IS R
⚷ IS R
♀ IS R

♀ □ ♄ 26° ♑/♎ 3:43A
♂ ⚹ ♇ 07° ♏/♑ 7:05A
♂ △ ⚷ 07° ♏/♓ 11:12A

*"True silence is the rest of the mind,
and is to the spirit what sleep is to the body,
nourishment and refreshment."*

William Penn

8 AM	2 PM
9 AM	3 PM
10 AM	4 PM
11 AM	5 PM
12 PM	6 PM
1 PM	7 PM

Labor Day

Emotional Wisdom

TUESDAY
09.04.2012

Disseminating

☽ IN ♈
☽ →♉: 11:41A
☽ VOC: 7:06A - 11:41A {☽ □ ♀}
HIDDEN 4:4/5:5 STAR GATE

♇ IS R
♆ IS R
♅ IS R
⚷ IS R
♀ IS R

☿ △ ♇   07°♍/♑ 12:46A
☿ ☍ ⚷   07°♍/♓ 1:37P

"Nature always wears the colors of the spirit."

Ralph Waldo Emerson

8ᴀᴍ	2ᴘᴍ
9ᴀᴍ	3ᴘᴍ
10ᴀᴍ	4ᴘᴍ
11ᴀᴍ	5ᴘᴍ
12ᴘᴍ	6ᴘᴍ
1ᴘᴍ	7ᴘᴍ

S	M	T	W	T	F	S	S	M	T	W	T	F	S
September 2012						1		1	2	3	4	5	6
2	3	4	5	6	7	8	7	8	9	10	11	12	13
9	10	11	12	13	14	15	14	15	16	17	18	19	20
16	17	18	19	20	21	22	21	22	23	24	25	26	27
23	24	25	26	27	28	29	28	29	30	31	October 2012		
30													

Emotional Wisdom

WEDNESDAY
09.05.2012

Disseminating

☽ IN ♉: ALL DAY
☽ VOC: 2:54P - MIDNIGHT {☽ △ ☉}
5:5 STAR GATE/HIDDEN 5:5/9:9

♇ IS R
♆ IS R
♅ IS R
⚷ IS R
♀ IS R

☿ ✶ ♂ 08°♍/♏ 4:06A
♀ △ ☊ 29°♋/♏ 12:50P
♀ ✶ ☋ 29°♋/♉ 12:50P

"Live your life from your heart. Share from your heart. And your story will touch and heal people's souls."

Melody Beattie

8ᴬᴹ	2ᴾᴹ
9ᴬᴹ	3ᴾᴹ
10ᴬᴹ	4ᴾᴹ
11ᴬᴹ	5ᴾᴹ
12ᴾᴹ	6ᴾᴹ
1ᴾᴹ	7ᴾᴹ

All times Eastern Daylight Time

Emotional Wisdom

THURSDAY
09.06.2012

Disseminating

☽ IN ♉: ALL DAY
☽ VOC: ALL DAY
♀ →♌: 10:48A
HIDDEN 6:6/5:5 STAR GATE

♇ IS R
♆ IS R
♅ IS R
⚷ IS R
♀ IS R

☿ ✶ ♇ 07°♓/♑ 5:32A

"To keep the body in good health is a duty, otherwise we shall not be able to keep our mind strong and clear."
Gautama Buddha

8AM	**2**PM
9AM	**3**PM
10AM	**4**PM
11AM	**5**PM
12PM	**6**PM
1PM	**7**PM

S	M	T	W	T	F	S	S	M	T	W	T	F	S
September 2012						1		1	2	3	4	5	6
2	3	4	5	6	7	8	7	8	9	10	11	12	13
9	10	11	12	13	14	15	14	15	16	17	18	19	20
16	17	18	19	20	21	22	21	22	23	24	25	26	27
23	24	25	26	27	28	29	28	29	30	31	October 2012		
30													

Emotional Wisdom

FRIDAY
09.07.2012

Disseminating

☽ IN ♉
☽ VOC: MIDNIGHT - 12:09A
☽ →♊: 12:09A
HIDDEN 7:7/5:5 STAR GATE

♇ IS R
♆ IS R
♅ IS R
⚷ IS R
♀ IS R

☉ □ ♃ 15°♍/♊ 6:15A

"Of one thing I am certain, the body is not the measure of healing, peace is the measure."

Phyllis McGinley

8ᴬᴹ	2ᴾᴹ
9ᴬᴹ	3ᴾᴹ
10ᴬᴹ	4ᴾᴹ
11ᴬᴹ	5ᴾᴹ
12ᴾᴹ	6ᴾᴹ
1ᴾᴹ	7ᴾᴹ

All times Eastern Daylight Time

Emotional Wisdom

SATURDAY
09.08.2012

Last Quarter

☽ IN ♊: ALL DAY
☽ VOC: NO
HIDDEN 8:8/5:5 STAR GATE

♇ IS R
♆ IS R
♅ IS R
⚷ IS R
♀ IS R

☿ □ ♃ 15° ♍/♊ 8:13P

*"Healing takes courage, and we all have courage,
even if we have to dig a little to find it."*

Tori Amos

8 AM	2 PM
9 AM	3 PM
10 AM	4 PM
11 AM	5 PM
12 PM	6 PM
1 PM	7 PM

S	M	T	W	T	F	S	S	M	T	W	T	F	S
September 2012						1		1	2	3	4	5	6
2	3	4	5	6	7	8	7	8	9	10	11	12	13
9	10	11	12	13	14	15	14	15	16	17	18	19	20
16	17	18	19	20	21	22	21	22	23	24	25	26	27
23	24	25	26	27	28	29	28	29	30	31	October 2012		
30													

Emotional Wisdom		SUNDAY 09.09.2012	

Last Quarter

☽ IN ♊
☽ →♋: 12:48P
☽ VOC: 6:58A - 12:48P { ☽ △ ♄ }
9:9 Star Gate/Hidden 5:5 Star Gate

♇ IS R
♆ IS R
♅ IS R
⚷ IS R
♀ IS R

> *"In order to heal, you must first speak the truth to God.*
> *When you deny you have a problem, it cannot be healed."*
>
> — Derek O'Neill

8ᴀᴍ	2ᴘᴍ
9ᴀᴍ	3ᴘᴍ
10ᴀᴍ	4ᴘᴍ
11ᴀᴍ	5ᴘᴍ
12ᴘᴍ	6ᴘᴍ
1ᴘᴍ	7ᴘᴍ

All times Eastern Daylight Time

MONDAY
09.10.2012

Last Quarter

☽ IN ♋: ALL DAY
☽ VOC: NO
HIDDEN 1:1/5:5 STAR GATE

♇ IS R
♆ IS R
♅ IS R
☄ IS R
♀ IS R

☉ ☌ ☿   18°♍   8:44A

*"There can only be one state of mind
as you approach any profound test; total concentration,
a spirit of togetherness, and strength."*

Pat Riley

8ᴀᴍ	2ᴘᴍ
9ᴀᴍ	3ᴘᴍ
10ᴀᴍ	4ᴘᴍ
11ᴀᴍ	5ᴘᴍ
12ᴘᴍ	6ᴘᴍ
1ᴘᴍ	7ᴘᴍ

S	M	T	W	T	F	S	S	M	T	W	T	F	S
September 2012						1		1	2	3	4	5	6
2	3	4	5	6	7	8	7	8	9	10	11	12	13
9	10	11	12	13	14	15	14	15	16	17	18	19	20
16	17	18	19	20	21	22	21	22	23	24	25	26	27
23	24	25	26	27	28	29	28	29	30	31 October 2012			
30													

TUESDAY
09.11.2012

Emotional Wisdom

Last Quarter

☽ IN ♋
☽ →♌: 11:00p
☽ VOC: 5:58p - 11:00p { ☽ □ ♄ }
HIDDEN 11:11/5:5 STAR GATE

♇ IS R
♆ IS R
♅ IS R
⚷ IS R
♀ IS R

> *"I always try to balance the light with the heavy - a few tears of human spirit in with the sequins and the fringes."*
> — Bette Midler

SEP

8ᴀᴍ	2ᴘᴍ
9ᴀᴍ	3ᴘᴍ
10ᴀᴍ	4ᴘᴍ
11ᴀᴍ	5ᴘᴍ
12ᴘᴍ	6ᴘᴍ
1ᴘᴍ	7ᴘᴍ

All times Eastern Daylight Time

Emotional Wisdom

WEDNESDAY
09.12.2012

Last Quarter

☽ IN ♌: ALL DAY
☽ VOC: NO
12:12/HIDDEN 3:3/5:5 STAR GATE

♇ IS R
♆ IS R
♅ IS R
⚷ IS R
♀ IS R

"Breathe. Let go. And remind yourself that this very moment is the only one you know you have for sure."

Oprah Winfrey

8ᴬᴹ	2ᴾᴹ
9ᴬᴹ	3ᴾᴹ
10ᴬᴹ	4ᴾᴹ
11ᴬᴹ	5ᴾᴹ
12ᴾᴹ	6ᴾᴹ
1ᴾᴹ	7ᴾᴹ

S	M	T	W	T	F	S	S	M	T	W	T	F	S
September 2012						1		1	2	3	4	5	6
2	3	4	5	6	7	8	7	8	9	10	11	12	13
9	10	11	12	13	14	15	14	15	16	17	18	19	20
16	17	18	19	20	21	22	21	22	23	24	25	26	27
23	24	25	26	27	28	29	28	29	30	31	October 2012		
30													

Emotional Wisdom

THURSDAY
09.13.2012

Balsamic

☽ IN ♌: ALL DAY
☽ VOC: NO
9:9 STAR GATE/HIDDEN 4:4/5:5

♇ IS R
♆ IS R
♅ IS R
⚷ IS R
♀ IS R

♀ △ ♅ 07°♌/♈ 12:45A

> "You cannot catch a child's spirit by running after it; you must stand still and for love it will soon itself return."
>
> — Arthur Miller

8ᴀᴍ	2ᴘᴍ
9ᴀᴍ	3ᴘᴍ
10ᴀᴍ	4ᴘᴍ
11ᴀᴍ	5ᴘᴍ
12ᴘᴍ	6ᴘᴍ
1ᴘᴍ	7ᴘᴍ

All times Eastern Daylight Time

FRIDAY
09.14.2012

Balsamic

☽ IN ♌
☽ →♍: 5:31A
☽ VOC: 1:14A - 5:31A { ☽ ✷ ♄ }
5:5 Star Gate/Hidden 5:5 Star Gate

♇ IS R
♆ IS R
♅ IS R
⚷ IS R
♀ IS R

"Bravery leads to the spirit of self-sacrifice. The spirit of self-sacrifice creates trust in the power of love."

Morihei Ueshiba

8ᴬᴹ	2ᴾᴹ
9ᴬᴹ	3ᴾᴹ
10ᴬᴹ	4ᴾᴹ
11ᴬᴹ	5ᴾᴹ
12ᴾᴹ	6ᴾᴹ
1ᴾᴹ	7ᴾᴹ

S	M	T	W	T	F	S	S	M	T	W	T	F	S
September 2012						1		1	2	3	4	5	6
2	3	4	5	6	7	8	7	8	9	10	11	12	13
9	10	11	12	13	14	15	14	15	16	17	18	19	20
16	17	18	19	20	21	22	21	22	23	24	25	26	27
23	24	25	26	27	28	29	28	29	30	31 October 2012			
30													

Emotional Wisdom

SATURDAY
09.15.2012

New Moon

☽ IN ♍: ALL DAY
☽ VOC: NO
♇ IS STATIONING {D}
HIDDEN 6:6/5:5 STAR GATE

♆ IS R
♅ IS R
⚷ IS R
♀ IS R

NEW MOON { ☽ ☌ ☉ }: 10:11P
23° ♍37'

☿ ✶ ☊ 28° ♍/♏ 6:59P
☿ △ ☋ 28° ♍/♉ 6:59P

> "When the belly is empty, the body becomes spirit; and
> when it is full, the spirit becomes body."
>
> Saadi

8 AM	2 PM
9 AM	3 PM
10 AM	4 PM
11 AM	5 PM
12 PM	6 PM
1 PM	7 PM

All times Eastern Daylight Time

| Emotional Wisdom | | SUNDAY
09.16.2012 | *New Moon* |

☽ IN ♍
☽ →♎: 8:56A
☽ VOC: 7:27A - MIDNIGHT { ☽ ☌ ☿ }
♇ IS STATIONING {D}
✷ →♐: 1:50P
☿ →♎: 7:22P
HIDDEN 7:7/5:5 STAR GATE

♆ IS R
♅ IS R
⚷ IS R
♀ IS R

"When you eat, chew well and offer the first mouthful to God, the second mouthful to you as God, and the third mouthful to all the hungry people in the world." Derek O'Neill

8ᴀᴍ	2ᴘᴍ
9ᴀᴍ	3ᴘᴍ
10ᴀᴍ	4ᴘᴍ
11ᴀᴍ	5ᴘᴍ
12ᴘᴍ	6ᴘᴍ
1ᴘᴍ	7ᴘᴍ

S	M	T	W	T	F	S		S	M	T	W	T	F	S
September 2012						1				1	2	3	4	5	6
2	3	4	5	6	7	8		7	8	9	10	11	12	13
9	10	11	12	13	14	15		14	15	16	17	18	19	20
16	17	18	19	20	21	22		21	22	23	24	25	26	27
23	24	25	26	27	28	29		28	29	30	31	October 2012		
30														

| Emotional Wisdom | | **MONDAY**
09.17.2012 |
New Moon |

☽ IN ♎: ALL DAY
☽ VOC: NO
♇ IS STATIONING {D}
HIDDEN 8:8/5:5 STAR GATE

♆ IS R
♅ IS R
⚷ IS R
♀ IS R

"I believe in walking in the spirit."
David Wilkerson

8ᴀᴍ	2ᴘᴍ
9ᴀᴍ	3ᴘᴍ
10ᴀᴍ	4ᴘᴍ
11ᴀᴍ	5ᴘᴍ
12ᴘᴍ	6ᴘᴍ
1ᴘᴍ	7ᴘᴍ

Rosh Hashanah

All times Eastern Daylight Time

TUESDAY
09.18.2012

Crescent

Emotional Wisdom

☽ IN ♎
☽ →♏: 10:46A
☽ VOC: 7:31A - 10:46A { ☽ ☌ ♄ }
♇ STATION: 1:07A
♇ TURNS D: 07° ♑
9:9 STAR GATE/HIDDEN 5:5

♆ IS R
♅ IS R
⚷ IS R
♀ IS R

> *"The spirit can assert itself only through the medium of clear form."*
>
> Gustav Mahler

8AM	**2**PM
9AM	**3**PM
10AM	**4**PM
11AM	**5**PM
12PM	**6**PM
1PM	**7**PM

S	M	T	W	T	F	S	S	M	T	W	T	F	S
September 2012						1		1	2	3	4	5	6
2	3	4	5	6	7	8	7	8	9	10	11	12	13
9	10	11	12	13	14	15	14	15	16	17	18	19	20
16	17	18	19	20	21	22	21	22	23	24	25	26	27
23	24	25	26	27	28	29	28	29	30	31	October 2012		
30													

Emotional Wisdom

WEDNESDAY
09.19.2012

Crescent

☽ IN ♏: ALL DAY
☽ VOC: NO
♇ HAS STATIONED {D}
HIDDEN 1:1/5:5 STAR GATE

♆ IS R
♅ IS R
♄ IS R
♀ IS R

♅ □ ♇ 07°♈/♑ 1:27A

> "Self-esteem is as important to our well-being
> as legs are to a table."
>
> Louise Hart

8 AM	2 PM
9 AM	3 PM
10 AM	4 PM
11 AM	5 PM
12 PM	6 PM
1 PM	7 PM

Ganesh Chaturthi

All times Eastern Daylight Time

Emotional Wisdom		THURSDAY 09.20.2012	

Crescent

☽ IN ♏
☽ →♐: 12:34P
☽ VOC: 9:11A - 12:34P {☽ ✶ ☉}
HIDDEN 2:2/5:5 STAR GATE

♆ IS R
♅ IS R
♄ IS R
♀ IS R

☉ ✶ ☊   28°♍/♏   4:53A
☉ △ ♃   28°♍/♉   4:53A
☿ ☍ ♅   07°♎/♈   6:23P
☿ □ ♇   07°♎/♑   7:21P
♀ ✶ ♃   16°♍/♊   11:45P

> *"It is health that is real wealth and not pieces of gold and silver."*
>
> Mohandas Gandhi

8AM	**2**PM
9AM	**3**PM
10AM	**4**PM
11AM	**5**PM
12PM	**6**PM
1PM	**7**PM

September 2012

S	M	T	W	T	F	S
						1
2	3	4	5	6	7	8
9	10	11	12	13	14	15
16	17	18	19	20	21	22
23	24	25	26	27	28	29
30						

October 2012

S	M	T	W	T	F	S
	1	2	3	4	5	6
7	8	9	10	11	12	13
14	15	16	17	18	19	20
21	22	23	24	25	26	27
28	29	30	31			

Emotional Wisdom

FRIDAY
09.21.2012

Crescent

☽ IN ♐: ALL DAY
☽ VOC: NO
HIDDEN 3:3/5:5 STAR GATE

♆ IS R
♅ IS R
⚷ IS R
♀ IS R

"Man needs difficulties; they are necessary for health."

Carl Jung

8 AM	2 PM
9 AM	3 PM
10 AM	4 PM
11 AM	5 PM
12 PM	6 PM
1 PM	7 PM

UN International Day of Peace

LIBRA

Physical Power

Symbol: The Mirrored Self
Master: Mighty Victory
Quality: Highest Realization
Ray: 9th Ray, Blue/Green
Trine: Air
Hour: 9
Rulers: ♀ ♆ ♂

9 10 11 12

I AM YOU & YOU ARE ME

Physical Power

9 O'Clock Hour
Main Purpose:

Where you experience the true relationship you have with your Self through the mirrored self.

SEPTEMBER 22 – OCTOBER 21

In the Cosmic Astrology system, Libra is the sign of **Highest Realization**. It is also the first of the three signs that embraces the physical body. If it were not for the physical body there would be no such thing as separation and duality. Separation engenders the idea that there is a world 'out there.' The Highest Realization a soul can have is the awareness that there is nothing 'out there' it is all your own reflection. The whole world, including the universe, is your own projection. It is nothing more than the reflection of your own consciousness. Every relationship you ever form is your Higher Self's decision to know itself better. In Libra we move from the scale, which measures the self with everything else, to the mirror, which provides us with no choice but to realize the Self in everything.

Libra is the 9 o'clock hour on the cosmic clock, which corresponds to the 12th house of the birth chart. Since the 12th house speaks to the ways in which we sabotage ourselves, and also contains our entire past within it, it is easy to see the affinity here. This is the experience of Physical Power on the cosmic clock, where, if we are not yet conscious, we experience the power others have over us until we realize we are giving them that power. And if we are conscious we understand the power of the physical world to offer us the experience of duality. Duality is required to experience Love. This is why we are here in this physical form.

Wherever Libra is in your birth chart you have the opportunity to connect with and understand your own reflection through the relationships you attract. Here you can rediscover yourself through the mirrored reflection that allows you to look more closely at the parts of yourself you still refuse to acknowledge. The more fully you take responsibility for your own experience the more comfortable you will be in your own skin. If your Sun sign is Libra, you are here to master the concept of the mirrored self, allowing your authentic Self to shine through and transmute duality and the effects of valuing others more than your Self. Every Libra is here to learn that there is nothing 'out there' at all.

FAMOUS LIBRAS

Jimmy Carter, Mother Amma, John Lennon, Sting, Donna Karan, Annie Besant, Gwyneth Paltrow, Margaret Thatcher, David Ben-Gurion, Stephanie Azaria, Wyclef Jean, Christopher Reeve, Jesse Jackson, Bruce Springsteen, Barbara Walters, Mahatma Gandhi, Alfred Nobel, Oscar Wilde, Will Smith, Paul Strand

SATURDAY
09.22.2012

First Quarter

Physical Power

☽ IN ♐
☽ →♑: 3:20P
☽ VOC: 12:45P - 3:20P {☽ ✶ ♄}
☉→♎: 10:49A
9:9 Star Gate/Hidden 4:4/5:5 Star Gate

♆ IS R
♅ IS R
♂ IS R
♀ IS R

> *"In the faces of men and women I see God."*
>
> Walt Whitman

8ᴬᴹ	2ᴾᴹ
9ᴬᴹ	3ᴾᴹ
10ᴬᴹ	4ᴾᴹ
11ᴬᴹ	5ᴾᴹ
12ᴾᴹ	6ᴾᴹ
1ᴾᴹ	7ᴾᴹ

Fall Equinox
Mabon

All times Eastern Daylight Time

Physical Power

SUNDAY
09.23.2012

First Quarter

☽ IN ♑: ALL DAY
☽ VOC: NO
5:5 STAR GATE/HIDDEN 5:5 STAR GATE

♆ IS R
♅ IS R
⚷ IS R
♀ IS R

*"God is always whispering to us
'it is because you think you are separate.'"*
— Derek O'Neill

8 AM	2 PM
9 AM	3 PM
10 AM	4 PM
11 AM	5 PM
12 PM	6 PM
1 PM	7 PM

S	M	T	W	T	F	S		S	M	T	W	T	F	S
September 2012						1			1	2	3	4	5	6
2	3	4	5	6	7	8		7	8	9	10	11	12	13
9	10	11	12	13	14	15		14	15	16	17	18	19	20
16	17	18	19	20	21	22		21	22	23	24	25	26	27
23	24	25	26	27	28	29		28	29	30	31	October 2012		
30														

Physical Power

MONDAY
09.24.2012

First Quarter

☽ IN ♑
☽ →♒: 7:32P
☽ VOC: 5:19P - 7:32P { ☽ □ ♄ }
HIDDEN 6:6/5:5 STAR GATE

♆ IS R
♅ IS R
⚷ IS R
♀ IS R

"It's not what you look at that matters, it's what you see."
Henry David Thoreau

8 AM	2 PM
9 AM	3 PM
10 AM	4 PM
11 AM	5 PM
12 PM	6 PM
1 PM	7 PM

All times Eastern Daylight Time

TUESDAY
09.25.2012

First Quarter

Physical Power

☽ IN ♒: ALL DAY
☽ VOC: NO
HIDDEN 7:7/5:5 STAR GATE

♆ IS R
♅ IS R
⚷ IS R
♀ IS R

*"I don't need anyone to rectify my existence.
The most profound relationship we will ever have
is the one with ourselves."*

Shirley MacLaine

8ᴀᴍ	2ᴘᴍ
9ᴀᴍ	3ᴘᴍ
10ᴀᴍ	4ᴘᴍ
11ᴀᴍ	5ᴘᴍ
12ᴘᴍ	6ᴘᴍ
1ᴘᴍ	7ᴘᴍ

S	M	T	W	T	F	S	S	M	T	W	T	F	S
September 2012						1		1	2	3	4	5	6
2	3	4	5	6	7	8	7	8	9	10	11	12	13
9	10	11	12	13	14	15	14	15	16	17	18	19	20
16	17	18	19	20	21	22	21	22	23	24	25	26	27
23	24	25	26	27	28	29	28	29	30	31	October 2012		
30													

WEDNESDAY
09.26.2012

Gibbous

Physical Power

☽ IN ♒: ALL DAY
☽ VOC: 11:33P - MIDNIGHT {☽ △ ♄}
♀ →♋: 3:00A
HIDDEN 8:8/5:5 STAR GATE

♆ IS R
♅ IS R
⚷ IS R
♀ IS R

☿ △ ♃ 16°♎/Ⅱ 12:08P

"Life is a mirror and will reflect back to the thinker what he thinks into it."

Ernest Holmes

8ᴀᴍ	2ᴘᴍ
9ᴀᴍ	3ᴘᴍ
10ᴀᴍ	4ᴘᴍ
11ᴀᴍ	5ᴘᴍ
12ᴘᴍ	6ᴘᴍ
1ᴘᴍ	7ᴘᴍ

Yom Kippur

All times Eastern Daylight Time

Physical Power

THURSDAY
09.27.2012

Gibbous

☽ IN ♒
☽ →♓: 1:23A
☽ VOC: MIDNIGHT - 1:23A
HIDDEN 5:5 STAR GATE

♆ IS R
♅ IS R
⚷ IS R
♀ IS R

♀ □ ♂   23° ♌/♏ 4:48A

"Without reflection, we go blindly on our way, creating more unintended consequences, and failing to achieve anything useful."

Margaret J. Wheatley

8 AM	2 PM
9 AM	3 PM
10 AM	4 PM
11 AM	5 PM
12 PM	6 PM
1 PM	7 PM

Physical Power

FRIDAY
09.28.2012

Gibbous

☽ IN ♓: ALL DAY
☽ VOC: 10:24P - MIDNIGHT {☽ △ ♂}
HIDDEN 1:1/5:5 STAR GATE

♆ IS R
♅ IS R
⚷ IS R
♀ IS R

> *"When you live in reaction, you give your power away.*
> *Then you get to experience what you gave your power to."*
> — N. Smith

8AM	**2**PM
9AM	**3**PM
10AM	**4**PM
11AM	**5**PM
12PM	**6**PM
1PM	**7**PM

All times Eastern Daylight Time

Physical Power

SATURDAY
09.29.2012

Full Moon

☽ IN ♓
☽ →♈: 9:14A
☽ VOC: MIDNIGHT - 9:14A
HIDDEN 2:2/5:5 STAR GATE

♆ IS R
♅ IS R
♄ IS R
♀ IS R

FULL MOON { ☽ ☍ ☉ }: 11:19P
07° ♈22'

☉ ☍ ♅ 07°♎/♈ 3:15A
☉ □ ♇ 07°♎/♑ 1:55A

"The relationship of self to other is the complete realization that loving yourself is impossible without loving everything defined as other than yourself."

Alan Watts

8ᴀᴍ	2ᴘᴍ
9ᴀᴍ	3ᴘᴍ
10ᴀᴍ	4ᴘᴍ
11ᴀᴍ	5ᴘᴍ
12ᴘᴍ	6ᴘᴍ
1ᴘᴍ	7ᴘᴍ

S	M	T	W	T	F	S		S	M	T	W	T	F	S
September 2012						1			1	2	3	4	5	6
2	3	4	5	6	7	8		7	8	9	10	11	12	13
9	10	11	12	13	14	15		14	15	16	17	18	19	20
16	17	18	19	20	21	22		21	22	23	24	25	26	27
23	24	25	26	27	28	29		28	29	30	31	October 2012		
30														

SUNDAY
09.30.2012

Full Moon

Physical Power

☽ IN ♈: ALL DAY
☽ VOC: NO
HIDDEN 3:3/5:5 STAR GATE

♆ IS R
♅ IS R
⚷ IS R
♀ IS R

♀ □ ☊ 27° ♌/♏ 12:42P
♀ □ ☋ 27° ♌/♉ 12:42P

"When you don't need anything from anyone else you can love them without attachment."

Derek O'Neill

8ᴬᴹ	2ᴾᴹ
9ᴬᴹ	3ᴾᴹ
10ᴬᴹ	4ᴾᴹ
11ᴬᴹ	5ᴾᴹ
12ᴾᴹ	6ᴾᴹ
1ᴾᴹ	7ᴾᴹ

Lantern Festival

Physical Power

MONDAY
10.01.2012

Full Moon

☽ IN ♈
☽ →♉: 7:26P
☽ VOC: 6:32P - 7:26P { ☽ ☍ ♄ }
1:1 STAR GATE

♆ IS R
♅ IS R
⚷ IS R
♀ IS R

> *"If you want to make the world a better place,
> take a look at yourself and make the change."*
>
> Michael Jackson

8ᴀᴍ	**2**ᴘᴍ
9ᴀᴍ	**3**ᴘᴍ
10ᴀᴍ	**4**ᴘᴍ
11ᴀᴍ	**5**ᴘᴍ
12ᴘᴍ	**6**ᴘᴍ
1ᴘᴍ	**7**ᴘᴍ

Sukkot

S	M	T	W	T	F	S		S	M	T	W	T	F	S
	1	2	3	4	5	6		November 2012			1	2	3
7	8	9	10	11	12	13		4	5	6	7	8	9	10
14	15	16	17	18	19	20		11	12	13	14	15	16	17
21	22	23	24	25	26	27		18	19	20	21	22	23	24
28	29	30	31	October 2012				25	26	27	28	29	30	

Physical Power

♎

TUESDAY
10.02.2012

Full Moon

☽ IN ♉: ALL DAY
☽ VOC: NO

♆ IS R
♅ IS R
⚷ IS R
♀ IS R

♂ ☌ ☊ 27° ♏ 11:06A
♂ ☍ ☋ 27°♏/♉ 11:06A
♀ ✶ ♄ 29°♉/♎ 8:05P

"I salute the light within your eyes where the whole universe dwells. For when you are at the center within yourself and I within mine we shall be as one."

Crazy Horse

OCT

8AM	2PM
9AM	3PM
10AM	4PM
11AM	5PM
12PM	6PM
1PM	7PM

Mahatma Gandhi Jayanthi

All times Eastern Daylight Time

Physical Power

WEDNESDAY
10.03.2012

Full Moon

☽ IN ♉: ALL DAY
☽ VOC: NO
♃ IS STATIONING {R}
♀ →♍: 2:59A
♀ →♓: 6:17P

♆ IS R
♅ IS R
⚷ IS R
♀ IS R

♀ ☍ ♆ 01° ♍/♓ 6:26P

"If you wish to be loved, love."
                                             Seneca

8ᴀᴍ	2ᴘᴍ
9ᴀᴍ	3ᴘᴍ
10ᴀᴍ	4ᴘᴍ
11ᴀᴍ	5ᴘᴍ
12ᴘᴍ	6ᴘᴍ
1ᴘᴍ	7ᴘᴍ

S	M	T	W	T	F	S	S	M	T	W	T	F	S
	1	2	3	4	5	6	November 2012			1	2	3
7	8	9	10	11	12	13	4	5	6	7	8	9	10
14	15	16	17	18	19	20	11	12	13	14	15	16	17
21	22	23	24	25	26	27	18	19	20	21	22	23	24
28	29	30	31 October 2012				25	26	27	28	29	30	

Physical Power

THURSDAY
10.04.2012

Disseminating

☽ IN ♉
☽ →♊: 7:46P
☽ VOC: 3:44A - 7:46A { ☽ ☍ ♂ }
♃ STATION: 9:18A
♃ TURNS R: 16° ♊

♆ IS R
♅ IS R
⚷ IS R
♀ IS R

5:5 Star Gate/Hidden 1:1 Star Gate

> *"How very close is your soul with mine, I know for sure everything you think goes through my mind."*
> — Rumi

8ᴀᴍ	2ᴘᴍ
9ᴀᴍ	3ᴘᴍ
10ᴀᴍ	4ᴘᴍ
11ᴀᴍ	5ᴘᴍ
12ᴘᴍ	6ᴘᴍ
1ᴘᴍ	7ᴘᴍ

All times Eastern Daylight Time

Physical Power

FRIDAY
10.05.2012

Disseminating

☽ IN ♊: ALL DAY
☽ VOC: 5:08P - MIDNIGHT { ☽ ☌ ♃ }
♄ → ♏: 4:34P
♃ HAS STATIONED {R}
☿ → ♏: 6:35A
5:5 STAR GATE

♆ IS R
♅ IS R
⚷ IS R
♀ IS R

☿ ☌ ♄   29° ♎   5:44A
☿ △ ♆   01° ♏/♓ 6:06P

> *"Each relationship nurtures a strength
> or weakness within you."*
>
> Mike Murdoch

....
....
....
....
....
....
....
....

8ᴀᴍ	2ᴘᴍ
9ᴀᴍ	3ᴘᴍ
10ᴀᴍ	4ᴘᴍ
11ᴀᴍ	5ᴘᴍ
12ᴘᴍ	6ᴘᴍ
1ᴘᴍ	7ᴘᴍ

S	M	T	W	T	F	S	S	M	T	W	T	F	S
	1	2	3	4	5	6	November 2012			1	2	3
7	8	9	10	11	12	13	4	5	6	7	8	9	10
14	15	16	17	18	19	20	11	12	13	14	15	16	17
21	22	23	24	25	26	27	18	19	20	21	22	23	24
28	29	30	31	October 2012			25	26	27	28	29	30	

Physical Power

SATURDAY
10.06.2012

Disseminating

☽ in ♊
☽ →♋: 8:45p
☽ voc: Midnight - 8:45p
♂ →♐: 11:21p

♆ is R
♅ is R
♃ is R
♄ is R
♀ is R

"Be the love you wish to see in the world."
Mohandas Gandhi

8ᴀᴍ	2ᴘᴍ
9ᴀᴍ	3ᴘᴍ
10ᴀᴍ	4ᴘᴍ
11ᴀᴍ	5ᴘᴍ
12ᴘᴍ	6ᴘᴍ
1ᴘᴍ	7ᴘᴍ

All times Eastern Daylight Time

Physical Power

SUNDAY
10.07.2012

Disseminating

☽ IN ♋: ALL DAY
☽ VOC: NO

♆ IS R
♅ IS R
♃ IS R
⚷ IS R
♀ IS R

♂ □ ♆ 01° ♐/♓ 10:10P
♀ ☍ ⚷ 06° ♍/♓ 11:05P

> *"God gives us experiences so we can love and have fun."*
>
> Derek O'Neill

8ᴀᴍ	2ᴘᴍ
9ᴀᴍ	3ᴘᴍ
10ᴀᴍ	4ᴘᴍ
11ᴀᴍ	5ᴘᴍ
12ᴘᴍ	6ᴘᴍ
1ᴘᴍ	7ᴘᴍ

S	M	T	W	T	F	S	S	M	T	W	T	F	S
	1	2	3	4	5	6	November 2012			1	2	3
7	8	9	10	11	12	13	4	5	6	7	8	9	10
14	15	16	17	18	19	20	11	12	13	14	15	16	17
21	22	23	24	25	26	27	18	19	20	21	22	23	24
28	29	30	31	October 2012			25	26	27	28	29	30	

Physical Power

♎

MONDAY
10.08.2012

Last Quarter

☽ IN ♋: ALL DAY
☽ VOC: 3:33A - MIDNIGHT { ☽ □ ☉ }
HIDDEN 5:5 STAR GATE

♆ IS R
♅ IS R
♃ IS R
⚷ IS R
♀ IS R

"Are we not like two volumes of one book?"

Marceline Desbordes-Valmore

OCT

8ᴬᴹ	2ᴾᴹ
9ᴬᴹ	3ᴾᴹ
10ᴬᴹ	4ᴾᴹ
11ᴬᴹ	5ᴾᴹ
12ᴾᴹ	6ᴾᴹ
1ᴾᴹ	7ᴾᴹ

Columbus Day
Thanksgiving Day (Canada)
Shemini Atzeret

All times Eastern Daylight Time

Physical Power

TUESDAY
10.09.2012

Last Quarter

☽ IN ♋
☽ →♌: 7:54A
☽ VOC: MIDNIGHT - 7:54A
HIDDEN 1:1/5:5/6:6 STAR GATE

♆ IS R
♅ IS R
♃ IS R
♄ IS R
♀ IS R

☉ △ ♃ 16°♎/Ⅱ 1:52A
☿ △ ♄ 06°♏/♓ 2:48A
♀ △ ♇ 07°♍/♑ 4:04A

*"And ever has it been known that love knows not
its own depth until the hour of separation."*

Kahlil Gibran

8ᴀᴍ	2ᴘᴍ
9ᴀᴍ	3ᴘᴍ
10ᴀᴍ	4ᴘᴍ
11ᴀᴍ	5ᴘᴍ
12ᴘᴍ	6ᴘᴍ
1ᴘᴍ	7ᴘᴍ

Simhat Torah

S	M	T	W	T	F	S	S	M	T	W	T	F	S
	1	2	3	4	5	6	November 2012			1	2	3
7	8	9	10	11	12	13	4	5	6	7	8	9	10
14	15	16	17	18	19	20	11	12	13	14	15	16	17
21	22	23	24	25	26	27	18	19	20	21	22	23	24
28	29	30	31	October 2012			25	26	27	28	29	30	

Physical Power

♎

WEDNESDAY
10.10.2012

Last Quarter

☽ IN ♌: ALL DAY
☽ VOC: 5:40P - MIDNIGHT { ☽ ✶ ☉ }
10:10 STAR GATE

♆ IS R
♅ IS R
♃ IS R
⚷ IS R
♀ IS R

♄ △ ♆ 01° ♏/ ♓ 10:38P
☿ ✶ ♇ 07° ♏/ ♑ 3:31A

"But let there be spaces in your togetherness and let the winds of the heavens dance between you."

Kahlil Gibran

8ᴬᴹ	2ᴾᴹ
9ᴬᴹ	3ᴾᴹ
10ᴬᴹ	4ᴾᴹ
11ᴬᴹ	5ᴾᴹ
12ᴾᴹ	6ᴾᴹ
1ᴾᴹ	7ᴾᴹ

All times Eastern Daylight Time

THURSDAY
10.11.2012

Last Quarter

Physical Power

☽ IN ♌
☽ → ♍: 3:23P
☽ VOC: MIDNIGHT - 3:23P

♆ IS R
♅ IS R
♃ IS R
⚷ IS R
♀ IS R

> *"Setting an example is not the main means of influencing another, it is the only means."*
>
> Albert Einstein

8ᴀᴍ	**2**ᴘᴍ
9ᴀᴍ	**3**ᴘᴍ
10ᴀᴍ	**4**ᴘᴍ
11ᴀᴍ	**5**ᴘᴍ
12ᴘᴍ	**6**ᴘᴍ
1ᴘᴍ	**7**ᴘᴍ

S	M	T	W	T	F	S	S	M	T	W	T	F	S
	1	2	3	4	5	6	November 2012				1	2	3
7	8	9	10	11	12	13	4	5	6	7	8	9	10
14	15	16	17	18	19	20	11	12	13	14	15	16	17
21	22	23	24	25	26	27	18	19	20	21	22	23	24
28	29	30	31	October 2012			25	26	27	28	29	30	

Physical Power

FRIDAY
10.12.2012

Last Quarter

☽ IN ♍: ALL DAY
☽ VOC: 7:48P - MIDNIGHT { ☽ □ ♃ }
12:12 STAR GATE

♆ IS R
♅ IS R
♃ IS R
⚷ IS R
♀ IS R

*"I cleansed the mirror of my heart.
Now it reflects the Moon."*

Renseki

8ᴀᴍ	2ᴘᴍ
9ᴀᴍ	3ᴘᴍ
10ᴀᴍ	4ᴘᴍ
11ᴀᴍ	5ᴘᴍ
12ᴘᴍ	6ᴘᴍ
1ᴘᴍ	7ᴘᴍ

All times Eastern Daylight Time

Physical Power

SATURDAY
10.13.2012

Balsamic

☽ IN ♍
☽ →♎: 7:02P
☽ VOC: MIDNIGHT - 7:02P
5:5 STAR GATE/HIDDEN 1:1 STAR GATE

♆ IS R
♅ IS R
♃ IS R
☿ IS R
♀ IS R

> *"Every relationship you have ever formed is you having a closer look at yourself."*
>
> Stephanie Azaria

8 AM	2 PM
9 AM	3 PM
10 AM	4 PM
11 AM	5 PM
12 PM	6 PM
1 PM	7 PM

S	M	T	W	T	F	S
	1	2	3	4	5	6
7	8	9	10	11	12	13
14	15	16	17	18	19	20
21	22	23	24	25	26	27
28	29	30	31	October 2012		

S	M	T	W	T	F	S
November 2012				1	2	3
4	5	6	7	8	9	10
11	12	13	14	15	16	17
18	19	20	21	22	23	24
25	26	27	28	29	30	

Physical Power ♎

SUNDAY
10.14.2012

Balsamic

☽ IN ♎: ALL DAY
☽ VOC: NO
5:5/1:1 STAR GATE

♆ IS R
♅ IS R
♃ IS R
⚷ IS R
♀ IS R

♂ □ ⚷ 05°♐/♓ 2:47P

> *"We are only mirrors."*
> Derek O'Neill

8 AM	2 PM
9 AM	3 PM
10 AM	4 PM
11 AM	5 PM
12 PM	6 PM
1 PM	7 PM

All times Eastern Daylight Time

Physical Power

MONDAY
10.15.2012

New Moon

☽ IN ♎
☽ →♏: 8:06P
☽ VOC: 8:03A - 8:06P { ☽ ☌ ☉ }

♆ IS R
♅ IS R
♃ IS R
⚷ IS R
♀ IS R

NEW MOON { ☽ ☌ ☉ }: 8:02A
22° ♎ 32'

♂ △ ♅ 06° ♐/♈ 6:33A

*"The fault is in the blamer.
Spirit sees nothing to criticize."*
Rumi

8<small>AM</small>	**2**<small>PM</small>
9<small>AM</small>	**3**<small>PM</small>
10<small>AM</small>	**4**<small>PM</small>
11<small>AM</small>	**5**<small>PM</small>
12<small>PM</small>	**6**<small>PM</small>
1<small>PM</small>	**7**<small>PM</small>

S	M	T	W	T	F	S	S	M	T	W	T	F	S
	1	2	3	4	5	6	November 2012			1	2	3
7	8	9	10	11	12	13	4	5	6	7	8	9	10
14	15	16	17	18	19	20	11	12	13	14	15	16	17
21	22	23	24	25	26	27	18	19	20	21	22	23	24
28	29	30	31	October 2012			25	26	27	28	29	30	

Physical Power

TUESDAY
10.16.2012

New Moon

☽ IN ♏: ALL DAY
☽ VOC: 10:23P - MIDNIGHT { ☽ ☌ ☿ }

♆ IS R
♅ IS R
♃ IS R
♄ IS R
♀ IS R

☿ ✶ ♀   16°♏/♍ 8:32A
♀ □ ♃   16°♍/♊ 7:34P

"If you are distressed by anything external, the pain is not due to the thing itself, but to your estimate of it, and this you have the power to revoke at any moment."

Marcus Aurelius

8ᴀᴍ	2ᴘᴍ
9ᴀᴍ	3ᴘᴍ
10ᴀᴍ	4ᴘᴍ
11ᴀᴍ	5ᴘᴍ
12ᴘᴍ	6ᴘᴍ
1ᴘᴍ	7ᴘᴍ

All times Eastern Daylight Time

Physical Power

WEDNESDAY
10.17.2012

Crescent

☽ IN ♏
☽ →♐: 8:26P
☽ VOC: MIDNIGHT - 8:26P
HIDDEN 5:5 STAR GATE

♆ IS R
♅ IS R
♃ IS R
⚷ IS R
♀ IS R

"There is a treasury of joy within you, why do you keep knocking door to door?"

Sufi saying

8ᴀᴍ	**2**ᴘᴍ
9ᴀᴍ	**3**ᴘᴍ
10ᴀᴍ	**4**ᴘᴍ
11ᴀᴍ	**5**ᴘᴍ
12ᴘᴍ	**6**ᴘᴍ
1ᴘᴍ	**7**ᴘᴍ

S	M	T	W	T	F	S	S	M	T	W	T	F	S
	1	2	3	4	5	6	November 2012				1	2	3
7	8	9	10	11	12	13	4	5	6	7	8	9	10
14	15	16	17	18	19	20	11	12	13	14	15	16	17
21	22	23	24	25	26	27	18	19	20	21	22	23	24
28	29	30	31	October 2012			25	26	27	28	29	30	

THURSDAY
10.18.2012

Crescent

Physical Power

☽ IN ♐: ALL DAY
☽ VOC: NO
HIDDEN 1:1/5:5 STAR GATE

♆ IS R
♅ IS R
♃ IS R
⚷ IS R
♀ IS R

> *"If you want to learn to love better, you should start with a friend who you hate."*
>
> Nikka - age 6

8 AM	2 PM
9 AM	3 PM
10 AM	4 PM
11 AM	5 PM
12 PM	6 PM
1 PM	7 PM

All times Eastern Daylight Time

Physical Power

FRIDAY
10.19.2012

Crescent

☽ IN ♐
☽ →♑: 9:41P
☽ VOC: 4:27P - 9:41P {☽ ✶ ☉}
☿ →R SHADOW
1:1 STAR GATE

♆ IS R
♅ IS R
♃ IS R
⚷ IS R
♀ IS R

*"The whole moon and the entire sky
are reflected in one dewdrop on the grass."*
                                           Dogen

8ᴬᴹ	2ᴾᴹ
9ᴬᴹ	3ᴾᴹ
10ᴬᴹ	4ᴾᴹ
11ᴬᴹ	5ᴾᴹ
12ᴾᴹ	6ᴾᴹ
1ᴾᴹ	7ᴾᴹ

S	M	T	W	T	F	S	S	M	T	W	T	F	S
	1	2	3	4	5	6	November 2012			1	2	3
7	8	9	10	11	12	13	4	5	6	7	8	9	10
14	15	16	17	18	19	20	11	12	13	14	15	16	17
21	22	23	24	25	26	27	18	19	20	21	22	23	24
28	29	30	31	October 2012			25	26	27	28	29	30	

Physical Power

SATURDAY
10.20.2012

Crescent

☽ IN ♑: ALL DAY
☽ VOC: NO
⚳ IS STATIONING {R}
☿ IN R SHADOW

♆ IS R
♅ IS R
♃ IS R
⚷ IS R
♀ IS R

> *"Who sees all beings in his own self and his own self in all beings loses all fear."*
> Upanishads

8ᴬᴹ	2ᴾᴹ
9ᴬᴹ	3ᴾᴹ
10ᴬᴹ	4ᴾᴹ
11ᴬᴹ	5ᴾᴹ
12ᴾᴹ	6ᴾᴹ
1ᴾᴹ	7ᴾᴹ

All times Eastern Daylight Time

Physical Power

SUNDAY
10.21.2012

Crescent

- ☽ IN ♑: ALL DAY
- ☽ VOC: 11:32P - MIDNIGHT { ☽ □ ☉ }
- ⚝ STATION: 2:34A
- ⚝ TURNS R: 26° ♊
- ☿ IN R SHADOW

- ♆ IS R
- ♅ IS R
- ♃ IS R
- ♄ IS R
- ♀ IS R

"Unlearn the duality right and wrong, good and evil because it is all God. When you see God in everything, you will understand the beauty of the world."

Derek O'Neill

8^{AM}	2^{PM}
9^{AM}	3^{PM}
10^{AM}	4^{PM}
11^{AM}	5^{PM}
12^{PM}	6^{PM}
1^{PM}	7^{PM}

S	M	T	W	T	F	S	S	M	T	W	T	F	S
	1	2	3	4	5	6	November 2012			1	2	3
7	8	9	10	11	12	13	4	5	6	7	8	9	10
14	15	16	17	18	19	20	11	12	13	14	15	16	17
21	22	23	24	25	26	27	18	19	20	21	22	23	24
28	29	30	31	October 2012			25	26	27	28	29	30	

SCORPIO

Physical Love

Symbol: The Alchemist
Master: Mighty Cyclopea
Quality: Highest Vision
Ray: 10th Ray, Pearl White
Trine: Water
Hour: 10
Rulers: ♇ ♅ ♇ & beyond

9 10 11 12

I AM ONE WITH SOURCE

Physical Love

10 O'Clock Hour
Main Purpose:

Where you perfect the alchemy of manifestation.

OCTOBER 22 - NOVEMBER 20

In Cosmic Astrology, Scorpio is the sign of **Highest Vision**, representing your capacity to manifest into the physical realm exactly what you envision. Scorpio is the sign of Physical Love, because it is Love that manifests everything and in this aspect of our consciousness we come to realize that we are the co-creators of the world we live in. Scorpio has always been a sign of 'vision,' whether sensory or intuitive, and for the 5D consciousness the symbolism shifts from the Scorpion or the Eagle (or even the Phoenix) to the Alchemist. Here you understand that you co-create with Source everything that you experience. Once it is understood that you are one with Source, you move from co-creator to Creator of your world. Until that awakening comes, however, it is imperative to turn yourself over to Source at all times, sacrificing your lower beliefs and desires, refining your capacity to focus on the Higher Self with undiluted attention.

Scorpio is the 10 o'clock hour on the cosmic clock, which corresponds to the 11th house of the birth chart. The 11th house can be thought of as the support structure in your life, and it is the place where we find our connection with humanity. Humanity is, taken collectively, the one creation of Source, and so it is here that we realize the Highest Vision, the capacity to create in the image of the Creator. Manifestation is truly an alchemical process, whereby the lower attributes of your consciousness, those associated with the lower self's desires, are relinquished in a truly devoted surrender to the Higher Self, where the highest good can be manifested.

Wherever Scorpio is in your chart, you have the capacity to focus with great discipline to purify your desires and intentions and ultimately become the conduit for Source to act through you and manifest your highest good. Where Scorpio hosts your energy field, great strength and fortitude are required in order to bring about the elements necessary for alchemical purification to take place. If your Sun sign is Scorpio you have chosen this lifetime to undertake this alchemy of the soul, experiencing little deaths in order to cleanse your consciousness and fill yourself with Light. True transformation belongs to every Scorpio soul.

FAMOUS SCORPIOS

Hillary Clinton, Edwin Hubble, Michael Crichton, Leonardo DiCaprio, Carl Sagan, Indira Gandhi, Bill Gates, Whoopi Goldberg, Billy Graham, Goldie Hawn, Pablo Picasso, John Keats, John Adams, Marie Curie, Dan Rather, Ted Turner

Physical Love

MONDAY
10.22.2012

First Quarter

☽ IN ♑
☽ →♒: 1:02A
☽ VOC: MIDNIGHT - 1:02A
⚷ HAS STATIONED {R}
☿ IN R SHADOW
☉ →♏: 8:13P
HIDDEN 1:1 STAR GATE

♆ IS R
♅ IS R
♃ IS R
⚷ IS R
♀ IS R

"Every thought we think is creating our future."

Louise L. Hay

8ᴬᴹ	2ᴾᴹ
9ᴬᴹ	3ᴾᴹ
10ᴬᴹ	4ᴾᴹ
11ᴬᴹ	5ᴾᴹ
12ᴾᴹ	6ᴾᴹ
1ᴾᴹ	7ᴾᴹ

Physical Love

TUESDAY
10.23.2012

First Quarter

☽ IN ♒: ALL DAY
☽ VOC: 9:27P - MIDNIGHT { ☽ □ ☿ }
☿ IN R SHADOW
5:5 STAR GATE

♆ IS R
♅ IS R
♃ IS R
⚷ IS R
⚵ IS R
♀ IS R

☉ △ ♆   00°♏/♓ 7:15A

"Life isn't about finding yourself. Life is about creating yourself."

George Bernard Shaw

8ᴬᴹ	2ᴾᴹ
9ᴬᴹ	3ᴾᴹ
10ᴬᴹ	4ᴾᴹ
11ᴬᴹ	5ᴾᴹ
12ᴾᴹ	6ᴾᴹ
1ᴾᴹ	7ᴾᴹ

S	M	T	W	T	F	S		S	M	T	W	T	F	S
	1	2	3	4	5	6	November 2012				1	2	3
7	8	9	10	11	12	13		4	5	6	7	8	9	10
14	15	16	17	18	19	20		11	12	13	14	15	16	17
21	22	23	24	25	26	27		18	19	20	21	22	23	24
28	29	30	31	October 2012			25	26	27	28	29	30	

Physical Love

WEDNESDAY
10.24.2012

First Quarter

☽ IN ♒
☽ → ♓: 7:00A
☽ VOC: MIDNIGHT - 7:00A
☿ IN R SHADOW
6:6 STAR GATE

♆ IS R
♅ IS R
♃ IS R
⚷ IS R
⚳ IS R
♀ IS R

"The best vision is insight."
Malcolm Forbes

8 AM	2 PM
9 AM	3 PM
10 AM	4 PM
11 AM	5 PM
12 PM	6 PM
1 PM	7 PM

Vijaya Dashami

All times Eastern Daylight Time

Physical Love

THURSDAY
10.25.2012

Gibbous

☽ IN ♓: ALL DAY
☽ VOC: NO
☿ IN R SHADOW

♆ IS R
♅ IS R
♃ IS R
♄ IS R
♇ IS R
♀ IS R

☉ ☌ ♄ 02° ♏ 4:32A
☿ ☌ ☊ 26° ♏ 6:04A
☿ ☍ ☋ 26° ♏/♉ 6:04A
♀ ⚹ ☊ 26° ♍/♏ 6:55A
♀ △ ☋ 26° ♍/♉ 6:55A
☿ ⚹ ♀ 27° ♏/♍ 1:07P

"Your destiny is in your hands. Creating the life you want is only, and always, up to you."

Darren L. Johnson

8 AM	2 PM
9 AM	3 PM
10 AM	4 PM
11 AM	5 PM
12 PM	6 PM
1 PM	7 PM

S	M	T	W	T	F	S		S	M	T	W	T	F	S
	1	2	3	4	5	6	November 2012				1	2	3
7	8	9	10	11	12	13		4	5	6	7	8	9	10
14	15	16	17	18	19	20		11	12	13	14	15	16	17
21	22	23	24	25	26	27		18	19	20	21	22	23	24
28	29	30	31	October 2012				25	26	27	28	29	30	

Physical Love

FRIDAY
10.26.2012

Gibbous

☽ IN ♓: ALL DAY
☽ → ♈: 3:31P
☽ VOC: 11:04A - 3:31P { ☽ ☍ ♀ }
☿ IN R SHADOW
HIDDEN 5:5 STAR GATE

♆ IS R
♅ IS R
♃ IS R
⚷ IS R
⚴ IS R
♀ IS R

"Knowledge is love and light and vision."
Helen Keller

OCT

8ᴬᴹ	2ᴾᴹ
9ᴬᴹ	3ᴾᴹ
10ᴬᴹ	4ᴾᴹ
11ᴬᴹ	5ᴾᴹ
12ᴾᴹ	6ᴾᴹ
1ᴾᴹ	7ᴾᴹ

All times Eastern Daylight Time

Physical Love

SATURDAY
10.27.2012

Gibbous

☽ IN ♈: ALL DAY
☽ VOC: 9:32P - MIDNIGHT { ☽ ✶ ♃ }
☿ IN R SHADOW
HIDDEN 1:1/5:5 STAR GATE

♆ IS R
♅ IS R
♃ IS R
♄ IS R
⚷ IS R
♀ IS R

"We waste time looking for the perfect lover, instead of creating the perfect love."

Tom Robbins

8ᴬᴹ	2ᴾᴹ
9ᴬᴹ	3ᴾᴹ
10ᴬᴹ	4ᴾᴹ
11ᴬᴹ	5ᴾᴹ
12ᴾᴹ	6ᴾᴹ
1ᴾᴹ	7ᴾᴹ

S	M	T	W	T	F	S	S	M	T	W	T	F	S
	1	2	3	4	5	6	November 2012			1	2	3
7	8	9	10	11	12	13	4	5	6	7	8	9	10
14	15	16	17	18	19	20	11	12	13	14	15	16	17
21	22	23	24	25	26	27	18	19	20	21	22	23	24
28	29	30	31	October 2012			25	26	27	28	29	30	

Physical Love ♏

SUNDAY
10.28.2012

Gibbous

☽ IN ♈: ALL DAY
☽ VOC: ALL DAY
♀ → ♎: 9:04A
☿ IN R SHADOW
1:1 STAR GATE

♆ IS R
♅ IS R
♃ IS R
⚷ IS R
⚶ IS R
⚳ IS R

☉ △ ⚷ 05° ♏/♓ 11:50P
♂ ☍ ♃ 15° ♐/♊ 8:54A

"Your last thought creates your next manifestation."

Derek O'Neill

8ᴬᴹ	2ᴾᴹ
9ᴬᴹ	3ᴾᴹ
10ᴬᴹ	4ᴾᴹ
11ᴬᴹ	5ᴾᴹ
12ᴾᴹ	6ᴾᴹ
1ᴾᴹ	7ᴾᴹ

All times Eastern Daylight Time

Physical Love

MONDAY
10.29.2012

Full Moon

☽ IN ♈
☽ →♉: 2:15A
☽ VOC: MIDNIGHT - 2:15A { ☽ △ ♇ }
☿ IN R SHADOW
☿ →♐: 2:19A
HIDDEN 5:5 STAR GATE

♆ IS R
♅ IS R
♃ IS R
⚷ IS R
⚶ IS R
♀ IS R

FULL MOON { ☽ ☍ ☉ }: 3:49P
06° ♉48'

☿ □ ♆ 00°♏/♓ 1:40P

> *"We are constantly creating ourselves by what we move toward or away from."*
>
> George Weinberg

8ᴀᴍ	**2**ᴘᴍ
9ᴀᴍ	**3**ᴘᴍ
10ᴀᴍ	**4**ᴘᴍ
11ᴀᴍ	**5**ᴘᴍ
12ᴘᴍ	**6**ᴘᴍ
1ᴘᴍ	**7**ᴘᴍ

S	M	T	W	T	F	S		S	M	T	W	T	F	S
	1	2	3	4	5	6		November 2012			1	2	3
7	8	9	10	11	12	13		4	5	6	7	8	9	10
14	15	16	17	18	19	20		11	12	13	14	15	16	17
21	22	23	24	25	26	27		18	19	20	21	22	23	24
28	29	30	31	October 2012				25	26	27	28	29	30	

Physical Love ♏

TUESDAY
10.30.2012

Full Moon

☽ IN ♉: ALL DAY
☽ VOC: ALL DAY
♀ IS STATIONING {R}
☿ IN R SHADOW

♆ IS R
♅ IS R
♃ IS R
⚷ IS R
⚶ IS R
♀ IS R

☉ ✶ ♇ 07°♏/♑ 6:30A

> "Your vision will become clear only when you can look into your own heart. Who looks outside, dreams; who looks inside, awakens."
>
> Carl Jung

8ᴀᴍ	2ᴘᴍ
9ᴀᴍ	3ᴘᴍ
10ᴀᴍ	4ᴘᴍ
11ᴀᴍ	5ᴘᴍ
12ᴘᴍ	6ᴘᴍ
1ᴘᴍ	7ᴘᴍ

All times Eastern Daylight Time

Physical Love

WEDNESDAY
10.31.2012

Full Moon

- ☽ IN ♉
- ☽ → ♊: 2:40P
- ☽ VOC: MIDNIGHT - 2:40P
- ♃ STATIONS: 11:46A
- ♃ TURNS R: 04° ♋
- ☿ IN R SHADOW

- ♆ IS R
- ♅ IS R
- ♃ IS R
- ⚷ IS R
- ⚹ IS R
- ♀ IS R

5:5 STAR GATE/HIDDEN 1:1

> *"To exist is to change, to change is to mature, to mature is to go on creating oneself endlessly."*
>
> Henri Bergson

8ᴀᴍ	2ᴘᴍ
9ᴀᴍ	3ᴘᴍ
10ᴀᴍ	4ᴘᴍ
11ᴀᴍ	5ᴘᴍ
12ᴘᴍ	6ᴘᴍ
1ᴘᴍ	7ᴘᴍ

Halloween

| Physical Love | ♏ | THURSDAY
11.01.2012 |
Full Moon |

☽ IN ♊: ALL DAY　　　♆ IS R　　　♀ ☍ ♅ 05°♎/♈ 6:05P
☽ VOC: NO　　　　　　♅ IS R
⚴ HAS STATIONED {R}　♃ IS R
☿ IN R SHADOW　　　　⚷ IS R
　　　　　　　　　　　⚳ IS R
　　　　　　　　　　　⚵ IS R

> *"We are all dreamers creating the next world, the next beautiful world for ourselves and for our children."*
>
> Yoko Ono

NOV

8ᴀᴍ	2ᴘᴍ
9ᴀᴍ	3ᴘᴍ
10ᴀᴍ	4ᴘᴍ
11ᴀᴍ	5ᴘᴍ
12ᴘᴍ	6ᴘᴍ
1ᴘᴍ	7ᴘᴍ

All Saint's Day
Samhain

FRIDAY
11.02.2012

Disseminating

Physical Love

☽ IN ♊: ALL DAY
☽ VOC: 5:21A - MIDNIGHT { ☽ ☌ ♂ }
☿ IN R SHADOW
2:2 STAR GATE

♆ IS R
♅ IS R
♃ IS R
⚷ IS R
? IS R
⚸ IS R
♀ IS R

"Not creating delusions is enlightenment."
Bodhidharma

....
....
....
....
....
....
....

8ᴀᴍ	2ᴘᴍ
9ᴀᴍ	3ᴘᴍ
10ᴀᴍ	4ᴘᴍ
11ᴀᴍ	5ᴘᴍ
12ᴘᴍ	6ᴘᴍ
1ᴘᴍ	7ᴘᴍ

All Soul's Day

S	M	T	W	T	F	S
November 2012				1	2	3
4	5	6	7	8	9	10
11	12	13	14	15	16	17
18	19	20	21	22	23	24
25	26	27	28	29	30	

S	M	T	W	T	F	S
December 2012						1
2	3	4	5	6	7	8
9	10	11	12	13	14	15
16	17	18	19	20	21	22
23	24	25	26	27	28	29
30	31					

Physical Love

SATURDAY
11.03.2012

Disseminating

☽ IN ♊
☽ → ♋: 3:43A
☽ VOC: MIDNIGHT - 3:43A
☿ IN R SHADOW
5:5 STAR GATE

♆ IS R
♅ IS R
♃ IS R
⚷ IS R
⚴ IS R
⚸ IS R
♀ IS R

♀ □ ♇ 07°♎/♑ 1:27P

"In creating, the only hard thing is to begin: a grass blade's no easier to make than an oak."

James Russell Lowell

8ᴀᴍ	2ᴘᴍ
9ᴀᴍ	3ᴘᴍ
10ᴀᴍ	4ᴘᴍ
11ᴀᴍ	5ᴘᴍ
12ᴘᴍ	6ᴘᴍ
1ᴘᴍ	7ᴘᴍ

All times Eastern Daylight Time

Physical Love

SUNDAY
11.04.2012

Disseminating

☽ IN ♋: ALL DAY
☽ VOC: 3:37A - MIDNIGHT { ☽ △ ☉ }
♆ IS STATIONING {D}
☿ IN R SHADOW
HIDDEN 2:2 STAR GATE

♅ IS R
♃ IS R
♆ IS R
♇ IS R
⚷ IS R
♀ IS R

"What you focus on is what you are manifesting."

Derek O'Neill

8ᴀᴍ	2ᴘᴍ
9ᴀᴍ	3ᴘᴍ
10ᴀᴍ	4ᴘᴍ
11ᴀᴍ	5ᴘᴍ
12ᴘᴍ	6ᴘᴍ
1ᴘᴍ	7ᴘᴍ

Daylight Savings Time
Ends - 2:00am
(North America)

S	M	T	W	T	F	S
November 2012				1	2	3
4	5	6	7	8	9	10
11	12	13	14	15	16	17
18	19	20	21	22	23	24
25	26	27	28	29	30	

S	M	T	W	T	F	S
December 2012						1
2	3	4	5	6	7	8
9	10	11	12	13	14	15
16	17	18	19	20	21	22
23	24	25	26	27	28	29
30	31					

Physical Love

MONDAY
11.05.2012

Disseminating

☽ IN ♋
☽ → ♌: 2:39P
☽ VOC: MIDNIGHT - 2:39P
♆ IS STATIONING {D}
☿ IN R SHADOW
5:5 Star Gate

♅ IS R
♃ IS R
⚷ IS R
? IS R
⚶ IS R
♀ IS R

"You can't depend on your eyes when your imagination is out of focus."

Mark Twain

8 AM	2 PM
9 AM	3 PM
10 AM	4 PM
11 AM	5 PM
12 PM	6 PM
1 PM	7 PM

TUESDAY
11.06.2012

Disseminating

Physical Love

☽ IN ♌: ALL DAY
☽ VOC: NO
♆ IS STATIONING {D}
☿ STATION: 6:04P
☿ TURNS R: 04° ♐
11:11 STAR GATE

♅ IS R
♃ IS R
♄ IS R
⚷ IS R
⯝ IS R
♀ IS R

"Concentrate all your thoughts upon the work at hand. The sun's rays do not burn until brought to a focus."

Alexander Graham Bell

8ᴬᴹ	2ᴾᴹ
9ᴬᴹ	3ᴾᴹ
10ᴬᴹ	4ᴾᴹ
11ᴬᴹ	5ᴾᴹ
12ᴾᴹ	6ᴾᴹ
1ᴾᴹ	7ᴾᴹ

S	M	T	W	T	F	S
November 2012				1	2	3
4	5	6	7	8	9	10
11	12	13	14	15	16	17
18	19	20	21	22	23	24
25	26	27	28	29	30	

S	M	T	W	T	F	S
December 2012						1
2	3	4	5	6	7	8
9	10	11	12	13	14	15
16	17	18	19	20	21	22
23	24	25	26	27	28	29
30	31					

Physical Love

WEDNESDAY
11.07.2012

Last Quarter

☽ IN ♌
☽ → ♍: 11:35p
☽ VOC: 10:27a - 11:35p { ☽ △ ♂ }
♆ IS STATIONING {D}
☿ HAS STATIONED {R}
HIDDEN 5:5 STAR GATE

♅ IS R
♃ IS R
♄ IS R
? IS R
⚳ IS R
♀ IS R

"Where there is no vision, there is no hope."

George Washington Carver

8ᴀᴍ	2ᴘᴍ
9ᴀᴍ	3ᴘᴍ
10ᴀᴍ	4ᴘᴍ
11ᴀᴍ	5ᴘᴍ
12ᴘᴍ	6ᴘᴍ
1ᴘᴍ	7ᴘᴍ

All times Eastern Standard Time

Physical Love

THURSDAY
11.08.2012

Last Quarter

☽ IN ♍: ALL DAY
☽ VOC: NO
♆ IS STATIONING {D}

♅ IS R
♃ IS R
⚷ IS R
⚴ IS R
⚸ IS R
♀ IS R
☿ IS R

"Leaders must invoke an alchemy of great vision."
                                Henry A. Kissinger

8^{AM}	2^{PM}
9^{AM}	3^{PM}
10^{AM}	4^{PM}
11^{AM}	5^{PM}
12^{PM}	6^{PM}
1^{PM}	7^{PM}

S	M	T	W	T	F	S		S	M	T	W	T	F	S
November 2012				1	2	3		December 2012						1
4	5	6	7	8	9	10		2	3	4	5	6	7	8
11	12	13	14	15	16	17		9	10	11	12	13	14	15
18	19	20	21	22	23	24		16	17	18	19	20	21	22
25	26	27	28	29	30			23	24	25	26	27	28	29
								30	31					

Physical Love

FRIDAY
11.09.2012

Last Quarter

☽ IN ♍: ALL DAY
☽ VOC: 7:27P - MIDNIGHT { ☽ □ ♂ }
♆ IS STATIONING {D}
HIDDEN 2:2/5:5 STAR GATE

♅ IS R
♃ IS R
⚷ IS R
? IS R
⚹ IS R
♀ IS R
☿ IS R

♀ △ ♃ 14° ♎/ Ⅱ 2:26A

"When the divine vision is attained, all appear equal; and there remains no distinction of good and bad, or of high and low." Ramakrishna

8ᴀᴍ	2ᴘᴍ
9ᴀᴍ	3ᴘᴍ
10ᴀᴍ	4ᴘᴍ
11ᴀᴍ	5ᴘᴍ
12ᴘᴍ	6ᴘᴍ
1ᴘᴍ	7ᴘᴍ

All times Eastern Standard Time

SATURDAY
11.10.2012

Last Quarter

Physical Love

- ☽ IN ♍
- ☽ → ♎: 4:35A
- ☽ VOC: MIDNIGHT - 4:35A
- ♆ IS STATIONING {D}
- ⚷ IS STATIONING {D}

- ♅ IS R
- ♃ IS R
- ♄ IS R
- ♇ IS R
- ♀ IS R
- ☿ IS R

"Every creator painfully experiences the chasm between his inner vision and its ultimate expression."

Isaac Bashevis Singer

8ᴀᴍ	2ᴘᴍ
9ᴀᴍ	3ᴘᴍ
10ᴀᴍ	4ᴘᴍ
11ᴀᴍ	5ᴘᴍ
12ᴘᴍ	6ᴘᴍ
1ᴘᴍ	7ᴘᴍ

S	M	T	W	T	F	S		S	M	T	W	T	F	S
November 2012				1	2	3		December 2012						1
4	5	6	7	8	9	10		2	3	4	5	6	7	8
11	12	13	14	15	16	17		9	10	11	12	13	14	15
18	19	20	21	22	23	24		16	17	18	19	20	21	22
25	26	27	28	29	30			23	24	25	26	27	28	29
								30	31					

Physical Love | ♏ | # SUNDAY
11.11.2012

Balsamic

☽ IN ♎: ALL DAY
☽ VOC: NO
♆ STATION: 2:52A
♆ TURNS D: 00° ♓
⚷ IS STATIONING {D}
11:11 STAR GATE

♅ IS R
♃ IS R
? IS R
⚵ IS R
♀ IS R
☿ IS R

> "If we sit still, we will become agitated. When we become agitated, the world is created."
>
> Derek O'Neill

8ᴬᴹ	2ᴾᴹ
9ᴬᴹ	3ᴾᴹ
10ᴬᴹ	4ᴾᴹ
11ᴬᴹ	5ᴾᴹ
12ᴾᴹ	6ᴾᴹ
1ᴾᴹ	7ᴾᴹ

Veteran's Day
Diwali

All times Eastern Standard Time

Physical Love

MONDAY
11.12.2012

Balsamic

- ☽ IN ♎
- ☽ → ♏: 6:11A
- ☽ VOC: 12:14A - 6:11A {☽ ✶ ♂}
- ♆ HAS STATIONED {D}
- ⚷ IS STATIONING {D}
- **12:12 STAR GATE**

- ♅ IS R
- ♃ IS R
- ⚴ IS R
- ⚸ IS R
- ♀ IS R
- ☿ IS R

"The point of vision and desire are the same."
Wallace Stevens

8ᴀᴍ	2ᴘᴍ
9ᴀᴍ	3ᴘᴍ
10ᴀᴍ	4ᴘᴍ
11ᴀᴍ	5ᴘᴍ
12ᴘᴍ	6ᴘᴍ
1ᴘᴍ	7ᴘᴍ

S	M	T	W	T	F	S	S	M	T	W	T	F	S
November 2012			1	2	3					December 2012	1
4	5	6	7	8	9	10	2	3	4	5	6	7	8
11	12	13	14	15	16	17	9	10	11	12	13	14	15
18	19	20	21	22	23	24	16	17	18	19	20	21	22
25	26	27	28	29	30		23	24	25	26	27	28	29
							30	31					

Physical Love ♏

TUESDAY
11.13.2012

New Moon

☽ IN ♏: ALL DAY
☽ VOC: NO
⚷ IS STATIONING {D}
HIDDEN 2:2 STAR GATE

♅ IS R
♃ IS R
⚷ IS R
⚳ IS R
♀ IS R
☿ IS R

NEW MOON { ☽ ☌ ☉ }: 5:08P
21° ♏ 57'
TOTAL SOLAR ECLIPSE

☿ □ ♆ 00° ♐ / ♓ 7:02P

> *"Vision without action is merely a dream. Action without vision just passes the time. Vision with action can change the world."* — Joel A. Barker

8ᴀᴍ	2ᴘᴍ
9ᴀᴍ	3ᴘᴍ
10ᴀᴍ	4ᴘᴍ
11ᴀᴍ	5ᴘᴍ
12ᴘᴍ	6ᴘᴍ
1ᴘᴍ	7ᴘᴍ

All times Eastern Standard Time

Physical Love

WEDNESDAY
11.14.2012

New Moon

☽ IN ♏
☽ →♐: 5:53A
☽ VOC: 5:39A - 5:53A {☽ ☌ ☿}
⚷ STATION: 3:37P
⚷ TURNS D: 05° ♓
☿ →♏: 2:44A
5:5 STAR GATE

♅ IS R
♃ IS R
⚴ IS R
⚵ IS R
♀ IS R
☿ IS R

"Vision is the true creative rhythm."
Robert Delaunay

8AM	2PM
9AM	3PM
10AM	4PM
11AM	5PM
12PM	6PM
1PM	7PM

S	M	T	W	T	F	S	S	M	T	W	T	F	S
November 2012				1	2	3							December 2012 1
4	5	6	7	8	9	10	2	3	4	5	6	7	8
11	12	13	14	15	16	17	9	10	11	12	13	14	15
18	19	20	21	22	23	24	16	17	18	19	20	21	22
25	26	27	28	29	30		23	24	25	26	27	28	29
							30	31					

Physical Love

THURSDAY
11.15.2012

Crescent

☽ IN ♐: ALL DAY
☽ VOC: NO
⚷ HAS STATIONED {D}
2:2 STAR GATE

♅ IS R
♃ IS R
? IS R
⚴ IS R
♀ IS R
☿ IS R

> *"Every great work, every big accomplishment, has been brought into manifestation through holding to the vision."*
>
> Florence Scovel Shinn

8 AM	2 PM
9 AM	3 PM
10 AM	4 PM
11 AM	5 PM
12 PM	6 PM
1 PM	7 PM

Al-Hijira (Islamic New Year)

Physical Love

FRIDAY
11.16.2012

Crescent

☽ IN ♐
☽ →♑: 5:36A
☽ VOC: 4:45A - 5:36A { ☽ ☌ ♂ }
♂ →♑: 9:36P
HIDDEN 5:5 STAR GATE

♅ IS R
♃ IS R
⚷ IS R
♆ IS R
♀ IS R
☿ IS R

♄ △ ♐ 05°♏/♓ 6:26A

"Longing is like the rosy dawn. After the dawn out comes the sun. Longing is followed by the vision of God."
Ramakrishna

8ᴬᴹ	2ᴾᴹ
9ᴬᴹ	3ᴾᴹ
10ᴬᴹ	4ᴾᴹ
11ᴬᴹ	5ᴾᴹ
12ᴾᴹ	6ᴾᴹ
1ᴾᴹ	7ᴾᴹ

S	M	T	W	T	F	S
November 2012				1	2	3
4	5	6	7	8	9	10
11	12	13	14	15	16	17
18	19	20	21	22	23	24
25	26	27	28	29	30	

S	M	T	W	T	F	S
December 2012						1
2	3	4	5	6	7	8
9	10	11	12	13	14	15
16	17	18	19	20	21	22
23	24	25	26	27	28	29
30	31					

Physical Love

SATURDAY
11.17.2012

Crescent

☽ IN ♐: ALL DAY
☽ VOC: NO

♅ IS R
♃ IS R
? IS R
⚸ IS R
♀ IS R
☿ IS R

☿ ☌ ☊ 26°♏ 4:36A
☿ ☍ ☋ 26°♏/♉ 4:36A
♂ ⚹ ♆ 00°♑/♓ 9:22A
☉ ☌ ☿ 26°♏ 10:48A
☉ ☌ ☊ 26°♏ 7:08P
☉ ☍ ☋ 26°♏/♉ 7:08P

*"Standing in the inspiring vision of my future,
I boldly take every step with courage and intent."*
                                Jonathan Lockwood Huie

8ᴀᴍ	2ᴘᴍ
9ᴀᴍ	3ᴘᴍ
10ᴀᴍ	4ᴘᴍ
11ᴀᴍ	5ᴘᴍ
12ᴘᴍ	6ᴘᴍ
1ᴘᴍ	7ᴘᴍ

All times Eastern Standard Time

Physical Love

SUNDAY
11.18.2012

Crescent

☽ IN ♐
☽ → ♒: 7:10A
☽ VOC: 12:54A - 7:10A { ☽ ✳ ☉ }
HIDDEN 2:2/5:5 STAR GATE

♅ IS R
♃ IS R
⚷ IS R
⚵ IS R
♀ IS R
☿ IS R

"We are not the doer until we understand that we created everything."

Derek O'Neill

8ᴀᴍ	2ᴘᴍ
9ᴀᴍ	3ᴘᴍ
10ᴀᴍ	4ᴘᴍ
11ᴀᴍ	5ᴘᴍ
12ᴘᴍ	6ᴘᴍ
1ᴘᴍ	7ᴘᴍ

S	M	T	W	T	F	S		S	M	T	W	T	F	S
November 2012				1	2	3		December 2012						1
4	5	6	7	8	9	10		2	3	4	5	6	7	8
11	12	13	14	15	16	17		9	10	11	12	13	14	15
18	19	20	21	22	23	24		16	17	18	19	20	21	22
25	26	27	28	29	30			23	24	25	26	27	28	29
								30	31					

Physical Love ♏

MONDAY
11.19.2012

Crescent

☽ IN ♒: ALL DAY
☽ VOC: NO
♀ IS STATIONING {D}

♅ IS R
♃ IS R
⚷ IS R
⚳ IS R
☿ IS R

> *"Go confidently in the direction of your dreams. Live the life you have imagined."*
> Henry David Thoreau

8ᴬᴹ	**2**ᴾᴹ
9ᴬᴹ	**3**ᴾᴹ
10ᴬᴹ	**4**ᴾᴹ
11ᴬᴹ	**5**ᴾᴹ
12ᴾᴹ	**6**ᴾᴹ
1ᴾᴹ	**7**ᴾᴹ

All times Eastern Standard Time

Physical Love

TUESDAY
11.20.2012

First Quarter

☽ IN ♒
☽ →♓: 11:55A
☽ VOC: 9:31A - 11:55A {☽ □ ☉}
♀ STATION: 8:24P
♀ TURNS D: 22° ♓
2:2 STAR GATE

♅ IS R
♃ IS R
♄ IS R
⚴ IS R
☿ IS R

"If you can dream it, you can do it."
Walt Disney

8AM	2PM
9AM	3PM
10AM	4PM
11AM	5PM
12PM	6PM
1PM	7PM

S	M	T	W	T	F	S	S	M	T	W	T	F	S
November 2012				1	2	3							December 2012 1
4	5	6	7	8	9	10	2	3	4	5	6	7	8
11	12	13	14	15	16	17	9	10	11	12	13	14	15
18	19	20	21	22	23	24	16	17	18	19	20	21	22
25	26	27	28	29	30		23	24	25	26	27	28	29
							30	31					

SAGITTARIUS

Physical Wisdom

Symbol: The Truth Seeker
Master: Maitreya
Quality: Highest Victory
Ray: 11th Ray, Peach-Apricot
Trine: Fire
Hour: 11
Rulers: ♃ ♄ ⚷

I AM THE WAY

11 O'Clock Hour
Main Purpose:
Where you resolve the habits that keep you from evolving.

NOVEMBER 21 - DECEMBER 20

In Cosmic Astrology, Sagittarius is the sign of **Highest Victory**. It speaks to the triumph of the Higher Self over the lower self. That sounds fantastic, but the reality is much starker. Here we are asked to deal with all the physical evidence that our fears and other misqualified fear-based reactions have brought forth in our lives. This is the final aspect of consciousness in our energy field, after which we spiral up to the next go around. Hopefully we spiral up, but we can only do so if we have successfully cleared the issues that are preventing the expression of the Higher Self. Surrender is pre-requisite here. This is the sign of Physical Wisdom, which implies that we have literally been around the block a time or two and we know just what to do. Face the devil and end the game... the ego's game, that is. Here the archer becomes the Truth–Seeker, moving from shooting in the dark to knowing exactly what the target is. Sagittarius has always been a sign of consciousness, and that is exactly the case here.

Sagittarius is the 11 o'clock hour, corresponding to the 10th house in the birth chart. Triumph over the physical constructs you have created through the realization that by aligning with your Higher Self you can create an entirely different world speaks very directly to the ultimate 10th house goal. This sign features the ending of one cycle and the inevitable beginning of a new one. It is here that your diligence can get you to the opportunity to spiral up instead of going around the wheel again.

Wherever Sagittarius is in your birth chart, there are old habits that must be experienced over and over and then triumphed over. The adventurous truth-seeking nature of Sagittarius gives way to the crystal clear awareness that we are creatures of habit until we awaken to that fact. When we realize we have not surrendered to our higher calling, we have no choice but to get ourselves there. If your Sun sign is Sagittarius you have chosen to spend this lifetime cleaning up your act and getting yourself to higher ground. You may even manage to spiral up off the wheel all together.

FAMOUS SAGITTARIUS

Jane Austin, C.S. Lewis, Brad Pitt, Mark Twain, Woody Allen, Winston Churchill, Walt Disney, Rainer Maria Rilke, Jane Fonda, L.V. Beethovan, Jimi Hendrix, Bruce Lee, Jim Morrison, Steven Spielberg, Nostradamus, Sri Sathya Sai Baba

Physical Wisdom

WEDNESDAY
11.21.2012

First Quarter

☽ IN ♓: ALL DAY
☽ VOC: NO
♀ HAS STATIONED {D}
♀ → ♏: 8:20P
☉ → ♐: 4:50P
5:5 STAR GATE

♅ IS R
♃ IS R
? IS R
⚸ IS R
☿ IS R

"Love is the outreach of self toward completion."
Ralph W. Sockman

8ᴀᴍ	2ᴘᴍ
9ᴀᴍ	3ᴘᴍ
10ᴀᴍ	4ᴘᴍ
11ᴀᴍ	5ᴘᴍ
12ᴘᴍ	6ᴘᴍ
1ᴘᴍ	7ᴘᴍ

All times Eastern Standard Time

Physical Wisdom   # THURSDAY
11.22.2012

First Quarter

☽ IN ♓
☽ → ♈: 8:11P
☽ VOC: 1:32A - 8:11P { ☽ △ ☿ }
HIDDEN 2:2 STAR GATE

♅ IS R
♃ IS R
⚴ IS R
⚸ IS R
♀ IS R

☉ □ ♆   00°♐/♓ 2:11A
♀ △ ♆   00°♏/♓ 3:59A

> *"The human soul, as a part of the movement of life,*
> *is endowed with the ability to participate in the uplift,*
> *elevation, perfection, and completion."*
>
> Alfred Adler

8ᴬᴹ	2ᴾᴹ
9ᴬᴹ	3ᴾᴹ
10ᴬᴹ	4ᴾᴹ
11ᴬᴹ	5ᴾᴹ
12ᴾᴹ	6ᴾᴹ
1ᴾᴹ	7ᴾᴹ

Thanksgiving Day

S	M	T	W	T	F	S
November 2012			1	2	3
4	5	6	7	8	9	10
11	12	13	14	15	16	17
18	19	20	21	22	23	24
25	26	27	28	29	30	

S	M	T	W	T	F	S
December 2012						1
2	3	4	5	6	7	8
9	10	11	12	13	14	15
16	17	18	19	20	21	22
23	24	25	26	27	28	29
30	31					

Physical Wisdom

FRIDAY
11.23.2012

First Quarter

☽ IN ♈: ALL DAY
☽ VOC: 8:34P - MIDNIGHT {☽ ✷ ♃}
5:5 STAR GATE

♅ IS R
♃ IS R
♀ IS R
⚵ IS R
☿ IS R

♂ □ ♅ 05°♑/♈ 5:05A
♂ ✷ ♄ 05°♑/♓ 12:29P

> "By prevailing over all obstacles and distractions, one may unfailingly arrive at his chosen goal or destination."
>
> Christopher Columbus

8 AM	2 PM
9 AM	3 PM
10 AM	4 PM
11 AM	5 PM
12 PM	6 PM
1 PM	7 PM

All times Eastern Standard Time

Physical Wisdom

SATURDAY
11.24.2012

Gibbous

☽ IN ♈: ALL DAY
☽ VOC: NO
11:11 STAR GATE

♅ IS R
♃ IS R
♇ IS R
⚳ IS R
♀ IS R

♂ ✱ ♄ 06°♑/♏ 5:51P

"Courage and perseverance have a magical talisman, before which difficulties disappear and obstacles vanish into air."

John Quincy Adams

8AM	**2**PM
9AM	**3**PM
10AM	**4**PM
11AM	**5**PM
12PM	**6**PM
1PM	**7**PM

Physical Wisdom

SUNDAY
11.25.2012

Gibbous

☽ IN ♈
☽ → ♉: 7:18A
☽ VOC: MIDNIGHT - 7:18A
☿ IS STATIONING {D}
HIDDEN 5:5 STAR GATE

♅ IS R
♃ IS R
⚷ IS R
⯛ IS R

♀ △ ♄ 05° ♏/ ♓ 10:11P

"Face the devil and end the game."
                             Derek O'Neill

8ᴀᴍ	2ᴘᴍ
9ᴀᴍ	3ᴘᴍ
10ᴀᴍ	4ᴘᴍ
11ᴀᴍ	5ᴘᴍ
12ᴘᴍ	6ᴘᴍ
1ᴘᴍ	7ᴘᴍ

All times Eastern Standard Time

Physical Wisdom

MONDAY
11.26.2012

Gibbous

☽ IN ♉: ALL DAY
☽ VOC: 7:57P - MIDNIGHT { ☽ ☌ ☿ }
☿ STATION: 5:48P
☿ TURNS D: 18° ♏

♅ IS R
♃ IS R
? IS R
⚳ IS R

☉ △ ♅ 05° ♐/♈ 9:15A
☉ □ ♇ 05° ♐/♓ 4:45P
♀ ☌ ♄ 06° ♏   8:19P

"Imaginary obstacles are insurmountable. Real ones aren't."
Barbara Sher

8 AM	2 PM
9 AM	3 PM
10 AM	4 PM
11 AM	5 PM
12 PM	6 PM
1 PM	7 PM

S	M	T	W	T	F	S
November 2012			1	2	3	
4	5	6	7	8	9	10
11	12	13	14	15	16	17
18	19	20	21	22	23	24
25	26	27	28	29	30	

S	M	T	W	T	F	S
December 2012						1
2	3	4	5	6	7	8
9	10	11	12	13	14	15
16	17	18	19	20	21	22
23	24	25	26	27	28	29
30	31					

Physical Wisdom

TUESDAY
11.27.2012

Gibbous

☽ IN ♉
☽ →♊: 7:58P
☽ VOC: MIDNIGHT - 7:58P
☿ HAS STATIONED {D}
HIDDEN 2:2/5:5 STAR GATE

♅ IS R
♃ IS R
♄ IS R
♆ IS R

♂ ☌ ♇ 09°♑   3:17P

> *"If you can find a path with no obstacles,*
> *it probably doesn't lead anywhere."*
>
> Frank Howard Clark

8 AM	2 PM
9 AM	3 PM
10 AM	4 PM
11 AM	5 PM
12 PM	6 PM
1 PM	7 PM

All times Eastern Standard Time

WEDNESDAY
11.28.2012

Full Moon

☽ IN ♊: ALL DAY
☽ VOC: 8:04P - MIDNIGHT { ☽ ☌ ♃ }
☿ IN D SHADOW
5:5 STAR GATE

♅ IS R
♃ IS R
♄ IS R
♆ IS R

FULL MOON { ☽ ☍ ☉ }: 9:46A
06° ♊47'
PENUMBRAL LUNAR ECLIPSE

♀ ✶ ♇ 08°♏/♑ 11:01A

"Yesterday I dared to struggle.
Today I dare to win."
Bernadette Devlin

8ᴀᴍ	2ᴘᴍ
9ᴀᴍ	3ᴘᴍ
10ᴀᴍ	4ᴘᴍ
11ᴀᴍ	5ᴘᴍ
12ᴘᴍ	6ᴘᴍ
1ᴘᴍ	7ᴘᴍ

Guru Nanak Jayanthi

S	M	T	W	T	F	S
November 2012				1	2	3
4	5	6	7	8	9	10
11	12	13	14	15	16	17
18	19	20	21	22	23	24
25	26	27	28	29	30	

S	M	T	W	T	F	S
December 2012						1
2	3	4	5	6	7	8
9	10	11	12	13	14	15
16	17	18	19	20	21	22
23	24	25	26	27	28	29
30	31					

Physical Wisdom

THURSDAY
11.29.2012

Full Moon

☽ IN ♊: ALL DAY
☽ VOC: NO
☿ IN D SHADOW
11:11 STAR GATE

♅ IS R
♃ IS R
♄ IS R
⚵ IS R

♀ ✷ ♂ 10° ♏/♑ 5:33P

"Our greatest glory is not in never falling, but in getting up every time we do."

Confucius

8ᴀᴍ	2ᴘᴍ
9ᴀᴍ	3ᴘᴍ
10ᴀᴍ	4ᴘᴍ
11ᴀᴍ	5ᴘᴍ
12ᴘᴍ	6ᴘᴍ
1ᴘᴍ	7ᴘᴍ

All times Eastern Standard Time

FRIDAY
11.30.2012

Full Moon

☽ IN ♊
☽ → ♋: 8:54A
☽ VOC: MIDNIGHT - 8:54A
☿ IN D SHADOW
5:5 STAR GATE

♅ IS R
♃ IS R
♆ IS R
⚷ IS R

"Out of difficulties grow miracles."

Jean De La Bruyere

8ᴀᴍ	2ᴘᴍ
9ᴀᴍ	3ᴘᴍ
10ᴀᴍ	4ᴘᴍ
11ᴀᴍ	5ᴘᴍ
12ᴘᴍ	6ᴘᴍ
1ᴘᴍ	7ᴘᴍ

Physical Wisdom

Physical Wisdom

SATURDAY
12.01.2012

Full Moon

☽ IN ♋: ALL DAY
☽ VOC: NO
☿ IN D SHADOW

♅ IS R
♃ IS R
⚴ IS R
⚳ IS R

> *"Stop worrying about the potholes in the road and celebrate the journey!"*
>
> Barbara Hoffman

8ᴀᴍ	2ᴘᴍ
9ᴀᴍ	3ᴘᴍ
10ᴀᴍ	4ᴘᴍ
11ᴀᴍ	5ᴘᴍ
12ᴘᴍ	6ᴘᴍ
1ᴘᴍ	7ᴘᴍ

All times Eastern Standard Time

Physical Wisdom

SUNDAY
12.02.2012

Disseminating

☽ IN ♋
☽ →♌: 8:57P
☽ VOC: 1:54A - 8:45P
☿ IN D SHADOW
5:5 STAR GATE

♅ IS R
♄ IS R
? IS R
⚷ IS R

☉ ☍ ♃ 11° ♐/♊ 8:45P

"The easiest way to step into your power is to let go of the past."

Derek O'Neill

8AM	2PM
9AM	3PM
10AM	4PM
11AM	5PM
12PM	6PM
1PM	7PM

S	M	T	W	T	F	S	S	M	T	W	T	F	S
			December 2012			1	January		1	2	3	4	5
2	3	4	5	6	7	8	6	7	8	9	10	11	12
9	10	11	12	13	14	15	13	14	15	16	17	18	19
16	17	18	19	20	21	22	20	21	22	23	24	25	26
23	24	25	26	27	28	29	27	28	29	30	31		2013
30	31												

| Physical Wisdom  | **MONDAY** **12.03.2012** | *Disseminating* |

☽ IN ♌: ALL DAY
☽ VOC: NO
☿ IN D SHADOW
3:3 STAR GATE

♅ IS R
♃ IS R
♀ IS R
⚚ IS R

> "Joy is of the will which labours, which overcomes obstacles, which knows triumph."
>
> William Butler Yeats

8ᴬᴹ	2ᴾᴹ
9ᴬᴹ	3ᴾᴹ
10ᴬᴹ	4ᴾᴹ
11ᴬᴹ	5ᴾᴹ
12ᴾᴹ	6ᴾᴹ
1ᴾᴹ	7ᴾᴹ

All times Eastern Standard Time

Physical Wisdom

TUESDAY
12.04.2012

Disseminating

☽ IN ♌: ALL DAY
☽ VOC: 5:07P - MIDNIGHT {☽ □ ☿}
♀ → ♊
☿ IN D SHADOW
HIDDEN 3:3 STAR GATE

♅ IS R
♃ IS R
♀ IS R
⚳ IS R

"It still holds true that man is most uniquely human when he turns obstacles into opportunities."

Eric Hoffer

8ᴀᴍ	2ᴘᴍ
9ᴀᴍ	3ᴘᴍ
10ᴀᴍ	4ᴘᴍ
11ᴀᴍ	5ᴘᴍ
12ᴘᴍ	6ᴘᴍ
1ᴘᴍ	7ᴘᴍ

S	M	T	W	T	F	S	S	M	T	W	T	F	S
		December 2012				1	January		1	2	3	4	5
2	3	4	5	6	7	8	6	7	8	9	10	11	12
9	10	11	12	13	14	15	13	14	15	16	17	18	19
16	17	18	19	20	21	22	20	21	22	23	24	25	26
23	24	25	26	27	28	29	27	28	29	30	31		2013
30	31												

Physical Wisdom

WEDNESDAY
12.05.2012

Disseminating

☽ IN ♌
☽ → ♍: 6:51A
☽ VOC: MIDNIGHT - 6:51A
☿ IN D SHADOW
5:5 STAR GATE

♅ IS R
♃ IS R
♄ IS R
⚷ IS R

"Man will encounter many difficulties and obstacles, and they are the very experiences he needs to encourage and complete the cleansing process."

Sri Sathya Sai Baba

8ᴀᴍ	2ᴘᴍ
9ᴀᴍ	3ᴘᴍ
10ᴀᴍ	4ᴘᴍ
11ᴀᴍ	5ᴘᴍ
12ᴘᴍ	6ᴘᴍ
1ᴘᴍ	7ᴘᴍ

All times Eastern Standard Time

Physical Wisdom

THURSDAY
12.06.2012

Last Quarter

☽ IN ♍: ALL DAY
☽ VOC: NO
☿ IN D SHADOW
HIDDEN 5:5 STAR GATE

♅ IS R
♃ IS R
♀ IS R
⚶ IS R

"Think of using all obstacles as stepping stones to build the life you want."

Marsha Sinetar

8ᴬᴹ	2ᴾᴹ
9ᴬᴹ	3ᴾᴹ
10ᴬᴹ	4ᴾᴹ
11ᴬᴹ	5ᴾᴹ
12ᴾᴹ	6ᴾᴹ
1ᴾᴹ	7ᴾᴹ

S	M	T	W	T	F	S	S	M	T	W	T	F	S
			December 2012			1	January		1	2	3	4	5
2	3	4	5	6	7	8	6	7	8	9	10	11	12
9	10	11	12	13	14	15	13	14	15	16	17	18	19
16	17	18	19	20	21	22	20	21	22	23	24	25	26
23	24	25	26	27	28	29	27	28	29	30	31		2013
30	31												

Physical Wisdom

FRIDAY
12.07.2012

Last Quarter

☽ IN ♍
☽ → ♎: 1:35P
☽ VOC: 5:35A - 1:35P { ☽ ✶ ☿ }
☿ IN D SHADOW
HIDDEN 3:3 STAR GATE

♅ IS R
♃ IS R
? IS R
♥ IS R

☿ ☌ ♋ 26° ♏ 2:02P
♀ ☍ ♑ 26° ♏/♉ 2:02P

"Courage doesn't always roar. Sometimes courage is the quiet voice at the end of the day saying, I will try again tomorrow."

Mary Anne Radmacher

8ᴀᴍ	2ᴘᴍ
9ᴀᴍ	3ᴘᴍ
10ᴀᴍ	4ᴘᴍ
11ᴀᴍ	5ᴘᴍ
12ᴘᴍ	6ᴘᴍ
1ᴘᴍ	7ᴘᴍ

SATURDAY
12.08.2012

Last Quarter

☽ IN ♎: ALL DAY
☽ VOC: 7:37P - MIDNIGHT { ☽ ✶ ☉ }
☿ IN D SHADOW

♅ IS R
♃ IS R
? IS R
⚵ IS R

> *"Circumstances are the rulers of the weak;
> they are but the instruments of the wise."*
>
> — Samuel Lover

8^{AM}	**2**^{PM}
9^{AM}	**3**^{PM}
10^{AM}	**4**^{PM}
11^{AM}	**5**^{PM}
12^{PM}	**6**^{PM}
1^{PM}	**7**^{PM}

Hanukkah Begins (at sundown)
Bodhi Day

S	M	T	W	T	F	S		S	M	T	W	T	F	S
			December 2012			1		January		1	2	3	4	5
2	3	4	5	6	7	8		6	7	8	9	10	11	12
9	10	11	12	13	14	15		13	14	15	16	17	18	19
16	17	18	19	20	21	22		20	21	22	23	24	25	26
23	24	25	26	27	28	29		27	28	29	30	31		2013
30	31													

| Physical Wisdom | ♐ | **SUNDAY** **12.09.2012** | *Last Quarter* |

☽ IN ♎
☽ →♏: 4:51P
☽ VOC: MIDNIGHT - 4:51P
☿ IN D SHADOW
HIDDEN 3:3/5:5 STAR GATE

♅ IS R
♃ IS R
♀ IS R
⚷ IS R

> "You have never been lost. You will never be lost.
> Nobody was ever lost. That is a big illusion."
> — Derek O'Neill

8ᴬᴹ	2ᴾᴹ
9ᴬᴹ	3ᴾᴹ
10ᴬᴹ	4ᴾᴹ
11ᴬᴹ	5ᴾᴹ
12ᴾᴹ	6ᴾᴹ
1ᴾᴹ	7ᴾᴹ

DEC

All times Eastern Standard Time

Physical Wisdom

MONDAY
12.10.2012

Last Quarter

☽ IN ♏: ALL DAY
☽ VOC: NO
☿ IN D SHADOW
☿ → ♐: 8:40P
HIDDEN 5:5 STAR GATE

♅ IS R
♃ IS R
? IS R
⚷ IS R

*"I don't really think in terms of obstacles.
My biggest obstacle is always myself."*

Steve Earle

8ᴀᴍ	2ᴘᴍ
9ᴀᴍ	3ᴘᴍ
10ᴀᴍ	4ᴘᴍ
11ᴀᴍ	5ᴘᴍ
12ᴘᴍ	6ᴘᴍ
1ᴘᴍ	7ᴘᴍ

	S	M	T	W	T	F	S		S	M	T	W	T	F	S
				December 2012			1		January		1	2	3	4	5
	2	3	4	5	6	7	8		6	7	8	9	10	11	12
	9	10	11	12	13	14	15		13	14	15	16	17	18	19
	16	17	18	19	20	21	22		20	21	22	23	24	25	26
	23	24	25	26	27	28	29		27	28	29	30	31		2013
	30	31													

Physical Wisdom

TUESDAY
12.11.2012

Balsamic

☽ IN ♏
☽ → ♐: 5:22P
☽ VOC: 8:09A - 5:22P {☽ ☌ ♀}
♅ IS STATIONING {D}
☿ IN D SHADOW
5:5 STAR GATE

♃ IS R
♆ IS R
⚷ IS R

☿ □ ♆ 01° ♐/♓ 7:57A

> *"I can see clearly now, the rain is gone. I can see all obstacles in my way."*
>
> Johnny Nash

8 AM	2 PM
9 AM	3 PM
10 AM	4 PM
11 AM	5 PM
12 PM	6 PM
1 PM	7 PM

All times Eastern Standard Time

WEDNESDAY
12.12.2012

Balsamic

- ☽ IN ♐: ALL DAY
- ☽ VOC: NO
- ♅ IS STATIONING {D}
- ☿ IN D SHADOW
- **3:3 STAR GATE**

- ♃ IS R
- ♆ IS R
- ⚷ IS R

- ♀ ☌ ☊ 26°♏ 5:54P
- ♀ ☍ ☋ 26°♏/♉ 5:54P

> *"The most authentic thing about us is our capacity to create, to overcome, to endure, to transform, to love and to be greater than our suffering."*
>
> Ben Okri

8ᴀᴍ	2ᴘᴍ
9ᴀᴍ	3ᴘᴍ
10ᴀᴍ	4ᴘᴍ
11ᴀᴍ	5ᴘᴍ
12ᴘᴍ	6ᴘᴍ
1ᴘᴍ	7ᴘᴍ

S	M	T	W	T	F	S	S	M	T	W	T	F	S
			December 2012			1	January		1	2	3	4	5
2	3	4	5	6	7	8	6	7	8	9	10	11	12
9	10	11	12	13	14	15	13	14	15	16	17	18	19
16	17	18	19	20	21	22	20	21	22	23	24	25	26
23	24	25	26	27	28	29	27	28	29	30	31		2013
30	31												

Physical Wisdom

THURSDAY
12.13.2012

New Moon

☽ IN ♐
☽ → ♑: 4:43P
☽ VOC: 3:42A - 4:43P { ☽ ☌ ☉ }
♅ STATION: 7:02A
♅ TURNS D: 05° ♈
☿ IN D SHADOW
5:5 STAR GATE

♃ IS R
♀ IS R
⚴ IS R

NEW MOON { ☽ ☌ ☉ }: 3:42A
21° ♐ 45'

"Life's challenges are not supposed to paralyze you, they're supposed to help you discover who you are."

Bernice Johnson Reagon

8 AM	2 PM
9 AM	3 PM
10 AM	4 PM
11 AM	5 PM
12 PM	6 PM
1 PM	7 PM

All times Eastern Standard Time

Physical Wisdom

FRIDAY
12.14.2012

New Moon

- ☽ IN ♐: ALL DAY
- ☽ VOC: NO
- ♅ HAS STATIONED {D}
- ☿ LEAVES D SHADOW
- **3:3 STAR GATE**

♃ IS R
♀ IS R
⚴ IS R

☿ △ ♅   05°♐/♈   6:24A
☿ □ ☋   05°♐/♓   8:20P

"Pain is inevitable, Suffering is optional."
                                    Buddhist proverb

8ᴀᴍ	2ᴘᴍ
9ᴀᴍ	3ᴘᴍ
10ᴀᴍ	4ᴘᴍ
11ᴀᴍ	5ᴘᴍ
12ᴘᴍ	6ᴘᴍ
1ᴘᴍ	7ᴘᴍ

S	M	T	W	T	F	S	S	M	T	W	T	F	S
			December 2012			1	January		1	2	3	4	5
2	3	4	5	6	7	8	6	7	8	9	10	11	12
9	10	11	12	13	14	15	13	14	15	16	17	18	19
16	17	18	19	20	21	22	20	21	22	23	24	25	26
23	24	25	26	27	28	29	27	28	29	30	31		2013
30	31												

Physical Wisdom

SATURDAY
12.15.2012

Crescent

☽ IN ♑
☽ → ♒: 4:53P
☽ VOC: 4:15P - 4:53P { ☽ ✶ ♀ }
♀ → ♐: 11:38P
HIDDEN 5:5 STAR GATE

♃ IS R
♀ IS R
☿ IS R

> "In the practice of tolerance, one's enemy is the best teacher."
>
> 14th Dalai Lama

8ᴀᴍ	2ᴘᴍ
9ᴀᴍ	3ᴘᴍ
10ᴀᴍ	4ᴘᴍ
11ᴀᴍ	5ᴘᴍ
12ᴘᴍ	6ᴘᴍ
1ᴘᴍ	7ᴘᴍ

All times Eastern Standard Time

SUNDAY
12.16.2012

Crescent

☽ IN ♒: ALL DAY
☽ VOC: NO
HIDDEN 3:3 STAR GATE

♃ IS R
♄ IS R
⚷ IS R

♀ □ ♆   01° ♐/♓ 1:23P

*"Pain is the space between two pleasures;
pleasure is the space between two pains."*
— Derek O'Neill

8ᴀᴍ	2ᴘᴍ
9ᴀᴍ	3ᴘᴍ
10ᴀᴍ	4ᴘᴍ
11ᴀᴍ	5ᴘᴍ
12ᴘᴍ	6ᴘᴍ
1ᴘᴍ	7ᴘᴍ

Last day of Hanukkah.

S	M	T	W	T	F	S	S	M	T	W	T	F	S
			December 2012			1	January		1	2	3	4	5
2	3	4	5	6	7	8	6	7	8	9	10	11	12
9	10	11	12	13	14	15	13	14	15	16	17	18	19
16	17	18	19	20	21	22	20	21	22	23	24	25	26
23	24	25	26	27	28	29	27	28	29	30	31		2013
30	31												

Physical Wisdom

MONDAY
12.17.2012

Crescent

☽ IN ♒
☽ →♓: 7:48P
☽ VOC: 1:13P - 7:48P {☽ ✶ ☉}

♃ IS R
♀ IS R
⚷ IS R

☿ ☌ ♃ 09°♐/♊ 2:22P

> "Your worst enemy cannot harm you as much as your own unguarded thoughts."
>
> — Gautama Buddha

8 AM	2 PM
9 AM	3 PM
10 AM	4 PM
11 AM	5 PM
12 PM	6 PM
1 PM	7 PM

All times Eastern Standard Time

TUESDAY
12.18.2012

Crescent

☽ IN ♓: ALL DAY
☽ VOC: NO
☿ → ♑
HIDDEN 3:3/5:5 STAR GATE

♃ IS R
♄ IS R
♆ IS R

"Remedy it, or welcome it: a wise man's only two choices."
Terri Guillemets

8ᴀᴍ	2ᴘᴍ
9ᴀᴍ	3ᴘᴍ
10ᴀᴍ	4ᴘᴍ
11ᴀᴍ	5ᴘᴍ
12ᴘᴍ	6ᴘᴍ
1ᴘᴍ	7ᴘᴍ

S	M	T	W	T	F	S	S	M	T	W	T	F	S
			December 2012			1	January		1	2	3	4	5
2	3	4	5	6	7	8	6	7	8	9	10	11	12
9	10	11	12	13	14	15	13	14	15	16	17	18	19
16	17	18	19	20	21	22	20	21	22	23	24	25	26
23	24	25	26	27	28	29	27	28	29	30	31		2013
30	31												

Physical Wisdom

WEDNESDAY
12.19.2012

Crescent

☽ IN ♓: ALL DAY
☽ VOC: NO

♃ IS R
♆ IS R
⚴ IS R

♀ △ ♅ 05°♐/♈ 4:38P

"When you lose, don't lose the lesson."
Author Unknown

8 AM	2 PM
9 AM	3 PM
10 AM	4 PM
11 AM	5 PM
12 PM	6 PM
1 PM	7 PM

All times Eastern Standard Time

Physical Wisdom

THURSDAY
12.20.2012

First Quarter

☽ IN ♓
☽ →♈: 2:43A
☽ VOC: 12:19A - 2:43A { ☽ □ ☉ }
5:5 STAR GATE

♃ IS R
♀ IS R
⚷ IS R

♀ □ ♄ 06°♐/♓ 11:19A
♂ ✶ ☊ 26°♑/♏ 4:32A
♂ △ ☋ 26°♑/♉ 4:32A

"The biggest problem in the world could have been solved when it was small."

Witter Bynner

8ᴀᴍ	2ᴘᴍ
9ᴀᴍ	3ᴘᴍ
10ᴀᴍ	4ᴘᴍ
11ᴀᴍ	5ᴘᴍ
12ᴘᴍ	6ᴘᴍ
1ᴘᴍ	7ᴘᴍ

S	M	T	W	T	F	S	S	M	T	W	T	F	S
			December 2012			1	January		1	2	3	4	5
2	3	4	5	6	7	8	6	7	8	9	10	11	12
9	10	11	12	13	14	15	13	14	15	16	17	18	19
16	17	18	19	20	21	22	20	21	22	23	24	25	26
23	24	25	26	27	28	29	27	28	29	30	31		2013
30	31												

Spiritual Power

FRIDAY
12.21.2012

First Quarter

☽ IN ♈: ALL DAY
☽ VOC: NO
☉→♑: 6:12A
3:3 STAR GATE

♃ IS R
♀ IS R
⚷ IS R

"Don't wait for the Last Judgment. It happens every day."
— Albert Camus

8ᴀᴍ	2ᴘᴍ
9ᴀᴍ	3ᴘᴍ
10ᴀᴍ	4ᴘᴍ
11ᴀᴍ	5ᴘᴍ
12ᴘᴍ	6ᴘᴍ
1ᴘᴍ	7ᴘᴍ

Winter Solstice
Yule

All times Eastern Standard Time

Spiritual Power

SATURDAY
12.22.2012

First Quarter

☽ IN ♈
☽ →♉: 1:25P
☽ VOC: 7:57A - 1:25P { ☽ □ ♂ }
HIDDEN 3:3 STAR GATE

♃ IS R
♄ IS R
⚷ IS R

☉ ✶ ♆   01° ♑ / ♓ 1:48A
♀ ☍ ♃   09° ♐ / ♊ 10:50P

"Whatever you are, be a good one."
Abraham Lincoln

8ᴀᴍ	2ᴘᴍ
9ᴀᴍ	3ᴘᴍ
10ᴀᴍ	4ᴘᴍ
11ᴀᴍ	5ᴘᴍ
12ᴘᴍ	6ᴘᴍ
1ᴘᴍ	7ᴘᴍ

S	M	T	W	T	F	S	S	M	T	W	T	F	S
			December 2012			1	January		1	2	3	4	5
2	3	4	5	6	7	8	6	7	8	9	10	11	12
9	10	11	12	13	14	15	13	14	15	16	17	18	19
16	17	18	19	20	21	22	20	21	22	23	24	25	26
23	24	25	26	27	28	29	27	28	29	30	31		2013
30	31												

| Spiritual Power | 10 | **SUNDAY**
12.23.2012 |
First Quarter |

☽ IN ♉: ALL DAY
☽ VOC: NO
5:5 STAR GATE

♃ IS R
♄ IS R
⚳ IS R

> *"You are not on a journey to find God.*
> *God is on a journey to find you."*
> — Derek O'Neill

8 AM	2 PM
9 AM	3 PM
10 AM	4 PM
11 AM	5 PM
12 PM	6 PM
1 PM	7 PM

All times Eastern Standard Time

Spiritual Power

MONDAY
12.24.2012

Gibbous

☾ IN ♉: ALL DAY
☾ VOC: NO
HIDDEN 5:5 STAR GATE

♃ IS R
♀ IS R
♅ IS R

> *"With our thoughts, we make the world."*
> Gautama Buddha

8AM	**2**PM
9AM	**3**PM
10AM	**4**PM
11AM	**5**PM
12PM	**6**PM
1PM	**7**PM

S	M	T	W	T	F	S		S	M	T	W	T	F	S
			December 2012			1		January		1	2	3	4	5
2	3	4	5	6	7	8		6	7	8	9	10	11	12
9	10	11	12	13	14	15		13	14	15	16	17	18	19
16	17	18	19	20	21	22		20	21	22	23	24	25	26
23	24	25	26	27	28	29		27	28	29	30	31		2013
30	31													

Spiritual Power

TUESDAY
12.25.2012

Gibbous

☽ IN ♉
☽ →♊: 2:13A
☽ VOC: 12:58A - 2:13A {☽ △ ♂}
♂ →♒: 7:49P

♃ IS R
♀ IS R
⚷ IS R

☉ □ ♅ 05°♑/♈ 8:31P
☉ ✶ ♆ 06°♑/♓ 11:53P

"Love all beings; that is enough."
Sri Sathya Sai Baba

8ᴬᴹ	2ᴾᴹ
9ᴬᴹ	3ᴾᴹ
10ᴬᴹ	4ᴾᴹ
11ᴬᴹ	5ᴾᴹ
12ᴾᴹ	6ᴾᴹ
1ᴾᴹ	7ᴾᴹ

Christmas Day

All times Eastern Standard Time

Spiritual Power

WEDNESDAY
12.26.2012

Gibbous

☽ IN ♊: ALL DAY ♃ IS R ♄ ✶ ♇ 09°♏/♑ 8:41P
☽ VOC: NO ♀ IS R
8:8 STAR GATE ⚶ IS R

"If you do not make it empty, how will you fill it up again?"
Neem Karoli Baba

8ᴬᴹ	2ᴾᴹ
9ᴬᴹ	3ᴾᴹ
10ᴬᴹ	4ᴾᴹ
11ᴬᴹ	5ᴾᴹ
12ᴾᴹ	6ᴾᴹ
1ᴾᴹ	7ᴾᴹ

Boxing Day
Kwanzaa begins
St. Stephen's Day

S	M	T	W	T	F	S	S	M	T	W	T	F	S
			December 2012			1	January		1	2	3	4	5
2	3	4	5	6	7	8	6	7	8	9	10	11	12
9	10	11	12	13	14	15	13	14	15	16	17	18	19
16	17	18	19	20	21	22	20	21	22	23	24	25	26
23	24	25	26	27	28	29	27	28	29	30	31		2013
30	31												

Spiritual Power

THURSDAY
12.27.2012

Gibbous

☽ IN ♊
☽ → ♋: 3:06P
☽ VOC: 1:50A - 3:06P { ☽ ☌ ☿ }
HIDDEN 5:5/3:3 STAR GATE

♃ IS R
♄ IS R
♅ IS R

> *"The spirit down here in man and the spirit up there in the sun, in reality are only one spirit, and there is no other one."*
>
> Upanishads

8ᴬᴹ	2ᴾᴹ
9ᴬᴹ	3ᴾᴹ
10ᴬᴹ	4ᴾᴹ
11ᴬᴹ	5ᴾᴹ
12ᴾᴹ	6ᴾᴹ
1ᴾᴹ	7ᴾᴹ

All times Eastern Standard Time

| Spiritual Power | | **FRIDAY**
12.28.2012 |
Full Moon |

☽ IN ♋: ALL DAY
☽ VOC: 9:43A - MIDNIGHT { ☽ △ ♄ }

♃ IS R
♀ IS R
⚷ IS R

FULL MOON { ☽ ☍ ☉ }: 5:21A
07° ♋06'

> *"Everything in your life is there as a vehicle for your transformation. Use it."*
>
> — Ram Dass

8ᴀᴍ	2ᴘᴍ
9ᴀᴍ	3ᴘᴍ
10ᴀᴍ	4ᴘᴍ
11ᴀᴍ	5ᴘᴍ
12ᴘᴍ	6ᴘᴍ
1ᴘᴍ	7ᴘᴍ

S	M	T	W	T	F	S		S	M	T	W	T	F	S
			December 2012			1		January	1	2	3	4	5	
2	3	4	5	6	7	8		6	7	8	9	10	11	12
9	10	11	12	13	14	15		13	14	15	16	17	18	19
16	17	18	19	20	21	22		20	21	22	23	24	25	26
23	24	25	26	27	28	29		27	28	29	30	31		2013
30	31													

Spiritual Power

10

SATURDAY
12.29.2012

Full Moon

☽ IN ♋: ALL DAY
☽ VOC: NO
5:5 STAR GATE

♃ IS R
♄ IS R
⚷ IS R

> *"When you know God as peace within, you will realize Him as peace existing in the universal harmony of all things without."*
>
> Paramahansa Yogananda

8ᴀᴍ	2ᴘᴍ
9ᴀᴍ	3ᴘᴍ
10ᴀᴍ	4ᴘᴍ
11ᴀᴍ	5ᴘᴍ
12ᴘᴍ	6ᴘᴍ
1ᴘᴍ	7ᴘᴍ

All times Eastern Standard Time

Spiritual Power

SUNDAY
12.30.2012

Full Moon

☽ IN ♋
☽ →♌: 2:45A
☽ VOC: MIDNIGHT - 2:45A
3:3 STAR GATE

♃ IS R
♀ IS R
☿ IS R

☉ ☌ ♇ 09°♑ 8:39A
☉ ✶ ♄ 09°♑/♏ 12:45P

"When you believe you are in a state of Grace, you start to eat at the big buffet line of abundance."

Derek O'Neill

8AM	2PM
9AM	3PM
10AM	4PM
11AM	5PM
12PM	6PM
1PM	7PM

S	M	T	W	T	F	S	S	M	T	W	T	F	S
			December 2012			1	January	1	2	3	4	5
2	3	4	5	6	7	8	6	7	8	9	10	11	12
9	10	11	12	13	14	15	13	14	15	16	17	18	19
16	17	18	19	20	21	22	20	21	22	23	24	25	26
23	24	25	26	27	28	29	27	28	29	30	31		2013
30	31												

MONDAY
12.31.2012

Spiritual Power 10

Full Moon

☽ IN ♌: ALL DAY
☽ VOC: 4:52P - MIDNIGHT {☽ △ ♀}
☿ →♑: 9:03A
HIDDEN 3:3 STAR GATE

♃ IS R
♀ IS R (?)
⚷ IS R

♂ ✷ ♅ 05°♒/♈ 9:31P

> "We are in the perfect circumstances for our Souls to learn whatever they designed this whole game to learn."
>
> — Ram Dass

8ᴬᴹ	2ᴾᴹ
9ᴬᴹ	3ᴾᴹ
10ᴬᴹ	4ᴾᴹ
11ᴬᴹ	5ᴾᴹ
12ᴾᴹ	6ᴾᴹ
1ᴾᴹ	7ᴾᴹ

New Years Eve

All times Eastern Standard Time

2012

CALENDAR YEAR AT A GLANCE

DECEMBER 2011

S	M	T	W	T	F	S
				1	2	3
4	5	6	7	8	9	10
11	12	13	14	15	16	17
18	19	20	21	22	23	24
25	26	27	28	29	30	31

JANUARY 2012

S	M	T	W	T	F	S
1	2	3	4	5	6	7
8	9	10	11	12	13	14
15	16	17	18	19	20	21
22	23	24	25	26	27	28
29	30	31				

FEBRUARY 2012

S	M	T	W	T	F	S
			1	2	3	4
5	6	7	8	9	10	11
12	13	14	15	16	17	18
19	20	21	22	23	24	25
26	27	28	29			

MARCH 2012

S	M	T	W	T	F	S
				1	2	3
4	5	6	7	8	9	10
11	12	13	14	15	16	17
18	19	20	21	22	23	24
25	26	27	28	29	30	31

APRIL 2012

S	M	T	W	T	F	S
1	2	3	4	5	6	7
8	9	10	11	12	13	14
15	16	17	18	19	20	21
22	23	24	25	26	27	28
29	30					

MAY 2012

S	M	T	W	T	F	S
		1	2	3	4	5
6	7	8	9	10	11	12
13	14	15	16	17	18	19
20	21	22	23	24	25	26
27	28	29	30	31		

JUNE 2012

S	M	T	W	T	F	S
					1	2
3	4	5	6	7	8	9
10	11	12	13	14	15	16
17	18	19	20	21	22	23
24	25	26	27	28	29	30

JULY 2012

S	M	T	W	T	F	S
1	2	3	4	5	6	7
8	9	10	11	12	13	14
15	16	17	18	19	20	21
22	23	24	25	26	27	28
29	30	31				

AUGUST 2012

S	M	T	W	T	F	S
			1	2	3	4
5	6	7	8	9	10	11
12	13	14	15	16	17	18
19	20	21	22	23	24	25
26	27	28	29	30	31	

SEPTEMBER 2012

S	M	T	W	T	F	S
						1
2	3	4	5	6	7	8
9	10	11	12	13	14	15
16	17	18	19	20	21	22
23	24	25	26	27	28	29
30						

OCTOBER 2012

S	M	T	W	T	F	S
	1	2	3	4	5	6
7	8	9	10	11	12	13
14	15	16	17	18	19	20
21	22	23	24	25	26	27
28	29	30	31			

NOVEMBER 2012

S	M	T	W	T	F	S
				1	2	3
4	5	6	7	8	9	10
11	12	13	14	15	16	17
18	19	20	21	22	23	24
25	26	27	28	29	30	

DECEMBER 2012

S	M	T	W	T	F	S
						1
2	3	4	5	6	7	8
9	10	11	12	13	14	15
16	17	18	19	20	21	22
23	24	25	26	27	28	29
30	31					

JANUARY 2013

S	M	T	W	T	F	S
		1	2	3	4	5
6	7	8	9	10	11	12
13	14	15	16	17	18	19
20	21	22	23	24	25	26
27	28	29	30	31		

MOON ASPECTS | DECEMBER 2011

All times Eastern Time

Day	Time	Aspect
Thu 01	1:37 A	☽ △ ♄
	6:26 A	☽ ☌ ♆
	11:24 A	☽ ☌ ⚷
	12:23 P	☽ ⚹ ♃
	9:54 P	☽ ⚹ ♇
	11:19 P	☽ ⚹ ♀
Fri 02	4:52 A	☽ □ ☉
	5:02 A	☽ ☍ ♂
	11:29 A	☽ △ ⚵
	1:06 P	☽ □ ☿
	9:51 P	☽ ☌ ⚸
Sat 03	10:11 P	☽ ☌ ♅
Sun 04	9:40 A	☽ □ ♇
	1:56 P	☽ ⚹ ⚴
	5:56 P	☽ □ ♀
	7:00 P	☽ △ ☿
	10:20 P	☽ △ ☉
Mon 05	10:11 P	☽ ⚹ ⚶
Tue 06	1:56 A	☽ ☍ ♄
	6:13 A	☽ ⚹ ♆
	11:33 A	☽ ⚹ ⚷
	11:36 A	☽ ☌ ♃
	10:38 P	☽ △ ♇
Wed 07	4:08 A	☽ □ ⚴
	10:02 A	☽ △ ♂
	1:47 P	☽ △ ♀
	3:45 P	☽ ☍ ⚵
Thu 08	12:31 A	☽ ⚹ ⚸
	12:41 P	☽ □ ⚶
	6:39 P	☽ □ ♆
	11:09 P	☽ ⚹ ♅
	11:56 P	☽ □ ⚷
Fri 09	9:07 A	☽ ☍ ☿
	5:22 P	☽ △ ⚴
	11:44 P	☽ □ ♂
Sat 10	9:36 A	☽ ☍ ☉
	12:40 P	☽ □ ⚸
Sun 11	1:28 A	☽ △ ⚶
	2:05 A	☽ △ ♄
	5:24 A	☽ △ ♆
	9:40 A	☽ □ ♅
	9:49 A	☽ ⚹ ♃
	10:34 A	☽ △ ⚷
	9:04 P	☽ ☍ ♇
Mon 12	11:08 A	☽ ⚹ ♂
	3:48 P	☽ △ ⚵
	10:39 P	☽ △ ⚸
	11:27 P	☽ ☍ ♀
Tue 13	11:05 A	☽ □ ♄
	5:56 P	☽ □ ♃
	6:00 P	☽ △ ♅
	11:53 P	☽ △ ☿
Wed 14	1:20 P	☽ ☍ ⚴
Thu 15	12:18 A	☽ □ ⚵
	11:06 A	☽ △ ☉
	5:50 P	☽ ⚹ ♄
	7:54 P	☽ ☍ ⚶
	8:20 P	☽ ☍ ♆
	11:55 P	☽ △ ♃
Fri 16	1:12 A	☽ ☍ ⚷
	6:36 A	☽ □ ☿
	10:55 A	☽ △ ♇
Sat 17	2:34 A	☽ ☌ ♂
	6:30 A	☽ ⚹ ⚵
	11:54 A	☽ ☍ ⚸
	7:48 P	☽ □ ☉
	9:29 P	☽ △ ♀
Sun 18	4:15 A	☽ ☍ ♅
	12:24 P	☽ ⚹ ☿
	2:45 P	☽ □ ♇
Mon 19	12:19 A	☽ △ ⚴
Tue 20	1:19 A	☽ ☌ ♄
	2:17 A	☽ ⚹ ☉
	3:13 A	☽ △ ♆
	4:49 A	☽ □ ♀
	5:38 A	☽ △ ⚶
	6:14 A	☽ ☍ ♃
	7:54 A	☽ △ ⚷
	5:01 P	☽ ⚹ ♇
Wed 21	3:17 A	☽ □ ⚴
	9:57 A	☽ ⚹ ♂
	1:31 P	☽ ☌ ⚵
	6:01 P	☽ △ ⚸
Thu 22	4:49 A	☽ □ ♆
	8:12 A	☽ △ ♅
	8:34 A	☽ □ ⚶
	9:30 A	☽ □ ⚷
	10:53 A	☽ ⚹ ♀
	10:10 P	☽ ☌ ☿
Fri 23	5:45 A	☽ ⚹ ⚴
	12:30 P	☽ □ ♂
	8:22 P	☽ □ ⚸
Sat 24	5:03 A	☽ ⚹ ♄
	6:36 A	☽ ⚹ ♆
	9:24 A	☽ △ ♃
	10:00 A	☽ □ ♅
	11:26 A	☽ ⚹ ⚷
	11:49 A	☽ ⚹ ⚶
	1:06 P	☽ ☌ ☉
	8:42 P	☽ ☌ ♇
Sun 25	4:11 P	☽ △ ♂
	7:56 P	☽ ⚹ ⚵
Mon 26	12:09 A	☽ ⚹ ⚸
	8:36 A	☽ □ ♄
	12:53 P	☽ □ ♃
	1:34 P	☽ ⚹ ♅
Tue 27	2:33 A	☽ ☌ ♀
	2:01 P	☽ ⚹ ☿
	3:12 P	☽ ☌ ⚴
Wed 28	2:39 A	☽ □ ⚵
	3:10 P	☽ △ ♄
	4:31 P	☽ ☌ ♆
	7:28 P	☽ ⚹ ♃
	10:05 P	☽ ☌ ⚷
Thu 29	1:47 A	☽ ☌ ⚶
	8:27 A	☽ ⚹ ♇
	8:56 A	☽ ⚹ ☉
Fri 30	4:40 A	☽ □ ☿
	8:37 A	☽ ☍ ♂
	1:09 P	☽ △ ⚵
	5:30 P	☽ ☌ ⚸
Sat 31	6:28 A	☽ ☌ ♅
	7:25 P	☽ □ ♇

Additional Monthly Ephemerides

Centaurs

2011	Pholus	Nessus	Asbolus	Chariklo	Hylon.
Dec					
01	16°♐43′	20°♒17′	23°♉15′R	6°♐49′	17°♐06′
06	16° 57′	20° 24′	23° 00′R	7° 15′	17° 22′
11	17° 11′	20° 32′	22° 45′R	7° 41′	17° 38′
16	17° 25′	20° 40′	22° 32′R	8° 07′	17° 54′
21	17° 39′	20° 50′	22° 19′R	8° 32′	18° 10′
26	17° 53′	21° 00′	22° 07′R	8° 57′	18° 25′
31	18° 07′	21° 11′	21° 57′R	9° 22′	18° 41′

01	25°♈21'R	11	27°♈35'	21	26°♉03'R
02	23° 42'R	12	01°♉07'	22	24° 28'R
03	22° 55'R	13	06° 03'	23	23° 08'R
04	22° 47'	14	11° 56'	24	21° 50'R
05	23° 01'	15	18° 02'	25	20° 07'R
06	23° 20'	16	23° 22'	26	17° 41'R
07	23° 35'	17	27° 09'	27	14° 33'R
08	23° 50'	18	28° 57'	28	11° 00'R
09	24° 18'	19	28° 57'R	29	07° 31'R
10	25° 25'	20	27° 44'R	30	04° 32'R
Black Moon Lilith ⚸				31	02° 17'R

DECEMBER 2011 EPHEMERIS

Ephemeris calculated for 12 Midnight GMT.

DAY	☉	☽	☊T.N.	☿	♀	♂	♃	♄	⚷	♅	♆	♇	⚳	⚴	⚵	⚶
01 Th	08°♐26'	22°♒15'	14°♐18'	16°♐14'R	05°♑33'	09°♍20'	01°♉25'R	25°♎43'	00°♓51'	00°♈41'R	28°♒16'	06°♑15'	18°♓10'	07°♒29'	12°♏40'	22°♒27'
02 Fr	09° 27'	04°♓47'	14° 18'	15° 02'R	06° 47'	09° 46'	01° 21'R	25° 49'	00° 52'	00° 40'R	28° 17'	06° 17'	18° 19'	07° 44'	13° 00'	22° 49'
03 Sa	10° 27'	17°♓02'	14° 18'R	13° 43'R	08° 02'	10° 11'	01° 16'R	25° 55'	00° 53'	00° 40'R	28° 17'	06° 19'	18° 27'	08° 00'	13° 20'	23° 12'
04 Su	11° 28'	29°♓05'	14° 18'R	12° 21'R	09° 16'	10° 37'	01° 11'R	26° 01'	00° 55'	00° 40'R	28° 18'	06° 21'	18° 37'	08° 16'	13° 40'	23° 34'
05 Mo	12° 29'	10°♈59'	14° 18'R	10° 59'R	10° 30'	11° 02'	01° 07'R	26° 06'	00° 56'	00° 39'R	28° 19'	06° 23'	18° 46'	08° 32'	14° 00'	23° 57'
06 Tu	13° 30'	22°♈49'	14° 18'R	09° 38'R	11° 45'	11° 26'	01° 03'R	26° 12'	00° 57'	00° 39'R	28° 20'	06° 25'	18° 56'	08° 48'	14° 19'	24° 20'
07 We	14° 31'	04°♉39'	14° 18'	08° 21'R	12° 59'	11° 51'	00° 59'R	26° 18'	00° 59'	00° 39'R	28° 21'	06° 27'	19° 06'	09° 04'	14° 39'	24° 43'
08 Th	15° 32'	16°♉33'	14° 18'	07° 12'R	14° 13'	12° 15'	00° 55'R	26° 24'	01° 01'	00° 39'R	28° 22'	06° 29'	19° 16'	09° 21'	14° 59'	25° 06'
09 Fr	16° 33'	28°♉33'	14° 18'	06° 12'R	15° 28'	12° 39'	00° 52'R	26° 29'	01° 02'	00° 39'R	28° 23'	06° 31'	19° 26'	09° 37'	15° 18'	25° 29'
10 Sa	17° 34'	10°♊42'	14° 18'	05° 21'R	16° 42'	13° 02'	00° 48'R	26° 35'	01° 04'	00° 39'R	28° 24'	06° 33'	19° 37'	09° 54'	15° 37'	25° 52'
11 Su	18° 35'	23°♊01'	14° 18'R	04° 42'R	17° 56'	13° 26'	00° 45'R	26° 40'	01° 06'	00° 39'	28° 25'	06° 35'	19° 48'	10° 10'	15° 57'	26° 16'
12 Mo	19° 36'	05°♋32'	14° 18'R	04° 14'R	19° 10'	13° 48'	00° 42'R	26° 45'	01° 07'	00° 39'	28° 26'	06° 37'	19° 59'	10° 27'	16° 16'	26° 40'
13 Tu	20° 36'	18°♋15'	14° 17'R	03° 57'R	20° 24'	14° 11'	00° 39'R	26° 51'	01° 09'	00° 39'	28° 27'	06° 39'	20° 11'	10° 44'	16° 35'	27° 03'
14 We	21° 37'	01°♌12'	14° 16'R	03° 51'R	21° 39'	14° 33'	00° 37'R	26° 56'	01° 11'	00° 39'	28° 28'	06° 41'	20° 23'	11° 01'	16° 55'	27° 27'
15 Th	22° 38'	14°♌22'	14° 15'R	03° 56'	22° 53'	14° 55'	00° 34'R	27° 01'	01° 13'	00° 39'	28° 29'	06° 43'	20° 35'	11° 18'	17° 14'	27° 51'
16 Fr	23° 40'	27°♌46'	14° 14'R	04° 09'	24° 07'	15° 17'	00° 32'R	27° 06'	01° 15'	00° 39'	28° 30'	06° 45'	20° 47'	11° 35'	17° 33'	28° 15'
17 Sa	24° 41'	11°♍24'	14° 13'R	04° 32'	25° 21'	15° 38'	00° 30'R	27° 11'	01° 17'	00° 40'	28° 32'	06° 47'	20° 59'	11° 52'	17° 52'	28° 39'
18 Su	25° 42'	25°♍16'	14° 13'R	05° 02'	26° 35'	15° 59'	00° 28'R	27° 16'	01° 19'	00° 40'	28° 33'	06° 49'	21° 12'	12° 10'	18° 10'	29° 03'
19 Mo	26° 43'	09°♎22'	14° 13'	05° 39'	27° 49'	16° 19'	00° 27'R	27° 21'	01° 22'	00° 40'	28° 34'	06° 52'	21° 25'	12° 27'	18° 29'	29° 28'
20 Tu	27° 44'	23°♎40'	14° 14'	06° 22'	29° 03'	16° 39'	00° 26'R	27° 26'	01° 24'	00° 41'	28° 35'	06° 54'	21° 38'	12° 45'	18° 48'	29° 52'
21 We	28° 45'	08°♏07'	14° 15'	07° 11'	00°♒17'	16° 59'	00° 24'R	27° 31'	01° 26'	00° 41'	28° 37'	06° 56'	21° 52'	13° 02'	19° 07'	00°♓17'
22 Th	29° 46'	22°♏41'	14° 16'	08° 05'	01° 31'	17° 18'	00° 23'R	27° 35'	01° 28'	00° 42'	28° 38'	06° 58'	22° 05'	13° 20'	19° 25'	00° 41'
23 Fr	00°♑47'	07°♐15'	14° 17'	09° 03'	02° 45'	17° 37'	00° 23'R	27° 40'	01° 31'	00° 43'	28° 40'	07° 00'	22° 19'	13° 38'	19° 44'	01° 06'
24 Sa	01° 48'	21°♐45'	14° 17'R	10° 04'	03° 59'	17° 56'	00° 22'R	27° 44'	01° 33'	00° 43'	28° 41'	07° 02'	22° 33'	13° 56'	20° 02'	01° 31'
25 Su	02° 49'	06°♑04'	14° 16'R	11° 09'	05° 13'	18° 14'	00° 22'R	27° 49'	01° 36'	00° 44'	28° 42'	07° 04'	22° 48'	14° 13'	20° 20'	01° 56'
26 Mo	03° 51'	20°♑07'	14° 14'R	12° 17'	06° 27'	18° 31'	00° 22'	27° 53'	01° 38'	00° 45'	28° 44'	07° 07'	23° 02'	14° 31'	20° 39'	02° 21'
27 Tu	04° 52'	03°♒50'	14° 11'R	13° 28'	07° 41'	18° 48'	00° 22'	27° 57'	01° 41'	00° 46'	28° 45'	07° 09'	23° 17'	14° 50'	20° 57'	02° 46'
28 We	05° 53'	17°♒10'	14° 08'R	14° 41'	08° 54'	19° 05'	00° 22'	28° 02'	01° 43'	00° 47'	28° 47'	07° 11'	23° 32'	15° 08'	21° 15'	03° 11'
29 Th	06° 54'	00°♓08'	14° 04'R	15° 56'	10° 08'	19° 21'	00° 23'	28° 06'	01° 46'	00° 48'	28° 49'	07° 13'	23° 47'	15° 26'	21° 33'	03° 37'
30 Fr	07° 55'	12°♓44'	14° 01'R	17° 12'	11° 22'	19° 37'	00° 24'	28° 10'	01° 49'	00° 49'	28° 50'	07° 15'	24° 02'	15° 44'	21° 51'	04° 02'
31 Sa	08° 56'	25°♓03'	13° 59'R	18° 30'	12° 36'	19° 52'	00° 25'	28° 14'	01° 51'	00° 50'	28° 52'	07° 17'	24° 18'	16° 03'	22° 08'	04° 27'

MOON ASPECTS | JANUARY 2012

All times Eastern Time

Sun 01	1:15 A ☽ □ ☉		7:23 A ☽ △ ⚷		5:05 P ☽ △ ♀	Mon 23	12:27 A ☽ ✶ ♅
	6:44 A ☽ △ ☊	Mon 09	2:30 A ☽ ☍ ☉	Tue 17	12:58 A ☽ ✶ ♇		12:56 A ☽ □ ♃
	10:03 A ☽ ✶ ♀		8:48 A ☽ ✶ ♂		8:05 A ☽ △ ⚷		2:39 A ☽ ☌ ☉
	2:05 P ☽ ✶ ♀		2:26 P ☽ △ ⚶		11:24 A ☽ ✶ ☿		6:52 P ☽ ✶ ☊
	11:56 P ☽ △ ☿		6:14 P ☽ △ ⚴	Wed 18	12:32 A ☽ □ ♀	Tue 24	5:02 P ☽ ☌ ♀
Mon 02	2:01 P ☽ ☍ ♄		9:25 P ☽ □ ♄		2:24 A ☽ ✶ ♂	Wed 25	2:18 A ☽ □ ⚶
	3:07 P ☽ ✶ ♆	Tue 10	12:58 A ☽ □ ♃		9:55 A ☽ ☌ ⚶		2:59 A ☽ △ ♄
	6:14 P ☽ ☌ ♃		1:29 A ☽ △ ♅		11:00 A ☽ ✶ ☉		3:33 A ☽ ☌ ♆
	9:20 P ☽ ✶ ⚷		9:52 P ☽ △ ☊		1:31 P ☽ □ ♆		7:47 A ☽ ✶ ♃
Tue 03	5:17 A ☽ ✶ ⚹	Wed 11	10:40 A ☽ ☍ ♀		1:57 P ☽ △ ⚴		10:13 A ☽ ☌ ⚷
	8:19 A ☽ △ ♇		9:00 P ☽ □ ⚶		4:41 P ☽ △ ♅		7:30 P ☽ ✶ ♇
	7:43 P ☽ △ ☉	Thu 12	12:28 A ☽ ☍ ♀		7:19 P ☽ □ ⚷	Thu 26	2:02 A ☽ □ ☊
Wed 04	4:30 A ☽ □ ♀		2:49 A ☽ ✶ ♄	Thu 19	12:47 A ☽ □ ♀		8:12 A ☽ ☌ ♀
	5:49 A ☽ □ ♀		3:23 A ☽ ☍ ♆		10:53 A ☽ ☌ ☊		10:40 A ☽ ☌ ⚹
	11:38 A ☽ △ ♂		6:18 A ☽ △ ♃		12:43 P ☽ □ ⚹		11:52 P ☽ ☍ ♂
	4:54 P ☽ ☍ ⚶		9:04 A ☽ ☍ ⚷	Fri 20	4:48 A ☽ ✶ ♀	Fri 27	12:37 P ☽ △ ⚶
	9:05 P ☽ ✶ ⚴		4:33 P ☽ △ ☿		5:42 A ☽ □ ♂		1:30 P ☽ ✶ ☿
Thu 05	3:46 A ☽ □ ♆		6:12 P ☽ △ ♇		4:21 P ☽ ✶ ♄		4:39 P ☽ ☌ ♅
	7:36 A ☽ ✶ ♅		10:21 P ☽ ☍ ⚹		4:49 P ☽ ✶ ♆		6:40 P ☽ ☌ ⚴
	9:58 A ☽ □ ⚷	Fri 13	2:07 A ☽ □ ☊		6:19 P ☽ □ ⚴	Sat 28	5:01 A ☽ ✶ ☉
	7:41 P ☽ □ ⚹		7:36 P ☽ ☌ ♂		8:02 P ☽ □ ♅		5:47 A ☽ □ ♇
Fri 06	6:45 A ☽ ☍ ☊		8:58 P ☽ △ ☉		8:17 P ☽ △ ♃		12:14 P ☽ △ ☊
	5:28 P ☽ △ ♀	Sat 14	1:55 A ☽ ✶ ⚶		10:47 P ☽ ✶ ⚷	Sun 29	4:33 P ☽ ✶ ♀
	11:40 P ☽ △ ♀		5:40 A ☽ ☍ ⚴	Sat 21	7:31 A ☽ ☌ ♇	Mon 30	12:21 A ☽ ☍ ♄
	11:44 P ☽ □ ♂		10:28 A ☽ ☍ ♅		9:00 A ☽ ✶ ♀		1:08 A ☽ ✶ ♆
Sat 07	9:10 A ☽ □ ⚴		9:50 P ☽ □ ♇		5:57 P ☽ ✶ ⚹		6:29 A ☽ ☌ ♃
	1:35 P ☽ △ ♄	Sun 15	2:15 A ☽ □ ☿	Sun 22	7:02 A ☽ ☌ ☿		8:40 A ☽ ✶ ⚷
	2:21 P ☽ △ ♆		5:19 A ☽ ✶ ☊		9:42 A ☽ △ ♂		11:14 A ☽ □ ☿
	2:52 P ☽ ☍ ☿		8:25 P ☽ △ ♀		7:06 P ☽ ✶ ⚶		6:25 P ☽ △ ♇
	5:20 P ☽ ✶ ♃	Mon 16	4:08 A ☽ □ ☉		8:38 P ☽ □ ♄		11:10 P ☽ □ ☉
	5:58 P ☽ □ ♅		10:00 A ☽ ☌ ♄		11:48 P ☽ ✶ ⚹	Tue 31	3:04 P ☽ ✶ ⚹
	8:21 P ☽ △ ⚹		10:28 A ☽ △ ♆				9:08 P ☽ ✶ ♀
Sun 08	6:23 A ☽ ☍ ♇		1:34 P ☽ ☍ ♃				11:28 P ☽ △ ♂

ADDITIONAL MONTHLY EPHEMERIDES

CENTAURS

2012	PHOLUS	NESSUS	ASBOLUS	CHARIKLO	HYLON.
JAN					
5	18° ♐ 20'	21° ♒ 23'	21° ♉ 48'R	9° ♐ 45'	18° ♐ 56'
10	18° 32'	21° 35'	21° 41'R	10° 08'	19° 10'
15	18° 45'	21° 48'	21° 35'R	10° 29'	19° 24'
20	18° 56'	22° 01'	21° 31'R	10° 50'	19° 38'
25	19° 07'	22° 15'	21° 28'R	11° 09'	19° 51'
30	19° 18'	22° 29'	21° 27'R	11° 27'	20° 03'

BLACK MOON LILITH ⚸

01	00°♉44'R	11	21° 35'	21	21°♉50'
02	29°♈40'R	12	25° 07'	22	22° 34'
03	28° 45'R	13	29° 41'	23	22° 17'R
04	27° 39'R	14	04°♉31'	24	20° 52'R
05	26° 11'R	15	08° 53'	25	18° 29'R
06	24° 19'R	16	12° 23'	26	15° 32'R
07	22° 13'R	17	15° 00'	27	12° 32'R
08	20° 22'R	18	17° 02'	28	09° 54'R
09	19° 19'R	19	18° 49'	29	07° 51'R
10	19° 37'	20	20° 28'	30	06° 19'R
				31	05° 06'R

JANUARY 2012 EPHEMERIS

Ephemeris calculated for 12 Midnight GMT.

DAY	☉	☽	☊T.N.	☿	♀	♂	♃	♄	⚷	♅	♆	♇	⚳	⚴	⚵	⚶
01 Su	09°♑57'	07°♈07'	13°♐58'R	19°♐50'	13°♒49'	20°♍07'	00°♉26'	28°♎17'	01°♓54'	00°♈51'	28°♒53'	07°♑19'	24°♓34'	16°♒21'	22°♏26'	04°♓53'
02 Mo	10° 59'	19°♈01'	13° 59'	21° 11'	15° 03'	20° 21'	00° 27'	28° 21'	01° 57'	00° 52'	28° 55'	07° 22'	24° 50'	16° 40'	22° 44'	05° 19'
03 Tu	12° 00'	00°♉51'	14° 00'	22° 33'	16° 17'	20° 35'	00° 29'	28° 25'	02° 00'	00° 53'	28° 57'	07° 24'	25° 06'	16° 58'	23° 01'	05° 44'
04 We	13° 01'	12°♉42'	14° 02'	23° 56'	17° 30'	20° 48'	00° 30'	28° 28'	02° 03'	00° 54'	28° 58'	07° 26'	25° 22'	17° 17'	23° 18'	06° 10'
05 Th	14° 02'	24°♉37'	14° 04'	25° 20'	18° 44'	21° 01'	00° 32'	28° 32'	02° 06'	00° 55'	29° 00'	07° 28'	25° 38'	17° 35'	23° 36'	06° 36'
06 Fr	15° 03'	06°♊42'	14° 05'	26° 44'	19° 57'	21° 13'	00° 35'	28° 35'	02° 09'	00° 57'	29° 02'	07° 30'	25° 55'	17° 54'	23° 53'	07° 02'
07 Sa	16° 04'	18°♊59'	14° 05'R	28° 10'	21° 10'	21° 24'	00° 37'	28° 38'	02° 12'	00° 58'	29° 04'	07° 32'	26° 12'	18° 13'	24° 10'	07° 28'
08 Su	17° 05'	01°♋32'	14° 04'R	29° 36'	22° 24'	21° 35'	00° 40'	28° 42'	02° 15'	01° 00'	29° 05'	07° 34'	26° 29'	18° 32'	24° 27'	07° 54'
09 Mo	18° 07'	14°♋22'	14° 00'R	01°♑03'	23° 37'	21° 46'	00° 42'	28° 45'	02° 18'	01° 01'	29° 07'	07° 36'	26° 46'	18° 51'	24° 43'	08° 20'
10 Tu	19° 08'	27°♋28'	13° 56'R	02° 31'	24° 50'	21° 56'	00° 45'	28° 48'	02° 21'	01° 03'	29° 09'	07° 39'	27° 03'	19° 10'	25° 00'	08° 46'
11 We	20° 09'	10°♌50'	13° 50'R	03° 59'	26° 03'	22° 05'	00° 49'	28° 51'	02° 24'	01° 04'	29° 11'	07° 41'	27° 21'	19° 29'	25° 17'	09° 12'
12 Th	21° 10'	24°♌26'	13° 43'R	05° 28'	27° 16'	22° 14'	00° 52'	28° 53'	02° 27'	01° 06'	29° 13'	07° 43'	27° 38'	19° 48'	25° 33'	09° 39'
13 Fr	22° 11'	08°♍13'	13° 37'R	06° 57'	28° 29'	22° 22'	00° 56'	28° 56'	02° 31'	01° 07'	29° 15'	07° 45'	27° 56'	20° 07'	25° 49'	10° 05'
14 Sa	23° 12'	22°♍08'	13° 32'R	08° 27'	29° 42'	22° 29'	00° 59'	28° 59'	02° 34'	01° 09'	29° 17'	07° 47'	28° 14'	20° 26'	26° 06'	10° 31'
15 Su	24° 13'	06°♎10'	13° 29'R	09° 58'	00° 55'	22° 36'	01° 03'	29° 01'	02° 37'	01° 11'	29° 19'	07° 49'	28° 32'	20° 45'	26° 22'	10° 58'
16 Mo	25° 14'	20°♎15'	13° 27'R	11° 29'	02° 08'	22° 42'	01° 07'	29° 04'	02° 41'	01° 13'	29° 20'	07° 51'	28° 50'	21° 04'	26° 38'	11° 24'
17 Tu	26° 16'	04°♏23'	13° 27'	13° 00'	03° 21'	22° 47'	01° 12'	29° 06'	02° 44'	01° 14'	29° 22'	07° 53'	29° 08'	21° 24'	26° 53'	11° 51'
18 We	27° 17'	18°♏32'	13° 29'	14° 32'	04° 34'	22° 52'	01° 16'	29° 08'	02° 47'	01° 16'	29° 24'	07° 55'	29° 27'	21° 43'	27° 09'	12° 18'
19 Th	28° 18'	02°♐40'	13° 30'	16° 05'	05° 46'	22° 56'	01° 21'	29° 10'	02° 51'	01° 18'	29° 26'	07° 57'	29° 45'	22° 02'	27° 25'	12° 44'
20 Fr	29° 19'	16°♐45'	13° 30'R	17° 38'	06° 59'	23° 00'	01° 26'	29° 12'	02° 54'	01° 20'	29° 28'	07° 59'	00°♈04'	22° 22'	27° 40'	13° 11'
21 Sa	00°♒20'	00°♑46'	13° 29'R	19° 12'	08° 12'	23° 02'	01° 31'	29° 14'	02° 58'	01° 22'	29° 31'	08° 01'	00° 23'	22° 41'	27° 55'	13° 38'
22 Su	01° 21'	14°♑40'	13° 25'R	20° 46'	09° 24'	23° 04'	01° 36'	29° 16'	03° 01'	01° 24'	29° 33'	08° 03'	00° 42'	23° 01'	28° 10'	14° 05'
23 Mo	02° 22'	28°♑22'	13° 19'R	22° 21'	10° 36'	23° 05'	01° 42'	29° 18'	03° 05'	01° 26'	29° 35'	08° 05'	01° 01'	23° 20'	28° 25'	14° 32'
24 Tu	03° 23'	11°♒50'	13° 11'R	23° 56'	11° 49'	23° 06'	01° 47'	29° 19'	03° 08'	01° 29'	29° 37'	08° 07'	01° 21'	23° 40'	28° 40'	14° 59'
25 We	04° 24'	25°♒02'	13° 01'R	25° 32'	13° 01'	23° 05'R	01° 53'	29° 21'	03° 12'	01° 31'	29° 39'	08° 09'	01° 40'	23° 59'	28° 55'	15° 26'
26 Th	05° 25'	07°♓55'	12° 52'R	27° 09'	14° 13'	23° 04'R	01° 59'	29° 22'	03° 16'	01° 33'	29° 41'	08° 11'	02° 00'	24° 19'	29° 09'	15° 53'
27 Fr	06° 26'	20°♓30'	12° 42'R	28° 46'	15° 25'	23° 02'R	02° 05'	29° 23'	03° 19'	01° 35'	29° 43'	08° 13'	02° 19'	24° 39'	29° 24'	16° 20'
28 Sa	07° 27'	02°♈49'	12° 35'R	00°♒24'	16° 37'	23° 00'R	02° 12'	29° 25'	03° 23'	01° 37'	29° 45'	08° 15'	02° 39'	24° 58'	29° 38'	16° 47'
29 Su	08° 28'	14°♈54'	12° 29'R	02° 02'	17° 49'	22° 56'R	02° 18'	29° 26'	03° 27'	01° 40'	29° 47'	08° 17'	02° 59'	25° 18'	29° 52'	17° 14'
30 Mo	09° 29'	26°♈48'	12° 26'R	03° 41'	19° 01'	22° 52'R	02° 25'	29° 27'	03° 30'	01° 42'	29° 49'	08° 19'	03° 19'	25° 38'	00°♐06'	17° 41'
31 Tu	10° 30'	08°♉38'	12° 25'R	05° 21'	20° 13'	22° 47'R	02° 32'	29° 27'	03° 34'	01° 45'	29° 52'	08° 21'	03° 39'	25° 57'	00° 19'	18° 08'

MOON ASPECTS | FEBRUARY 2012

All times Eastern Time

Wed 01	7:06 A	☽ □ ⚴	Wed 08	10:32 A	☽ ☍ ⚴		1:50 A	☽ ☌ ⚵		9:03 P	☽ □ ⚵
	2:06 P	☽ □ ♆		11:42 A	☽ ⚹ ♄		3:47 A	☽ □ ⚷		9:55 P	☽ ☌ ⚷
	3:43 P	☽ ☍ ⚵		12:51 P	☽ ☍ ♆		10:53 A	☽ △ ♀		11:09 P	☽ ⚹ ♃
	5:54 P	☽ ⚹ ♅		4:18 P	☽ □ ⚵		11:39 A	☽ △ ⚸	Wed 22	5:23 A	☽ ⚹ ♇
	9:39 P	☽ □ ⚷		6:45 P	☽ △ ♃		2:08 P	☽ ☌ ☊		7:43 A	☽ □ ☊
	11:01 P	☽ ⚹ ⚸		7:34 P	☽ ☍ ⚷	Thu 16	5:47 A	☽ □ ♂		7:35 P	☽ ☌ ☿
Thu 02	9:41 A	☽ △ ☿	Thu 09	3:08 A	☽ △ ♇		4:50 P	☽ □ ⚶		9:24 P	☽ ☍ ♂
	12:39 P	☽ ☍ ☊		6:56 A	☽ □ ☊		8:08 P	☽ ⚹ ☉	Thu 23	8:13 P	☽ ☌ ⚶
	5:01 P	☽ △ ☉	Fri 10	12:11 A	☽ ☌ ♂		11:03 P	☽ ⚹ ♄	Fri 24	3:26 A	☽ ☌ ♅
Fri 03	5:13 A	☽ □ ⚶		2:59 A	☽ ☍ ⚶	Fri 17	12:57 A	☽ ⚹ ♆		7:24 A	☽ △ ⚵
	10:24 A	☽ □ ♂		6:36 P	☽ ☍ ♅		3:03 A	☽ ⚹ ⚴		3:31 P	☽ □ ♇
	3:03 P	☽ □ ♀		7:18 P	☽ ⚹ ⚵		4:30 A	☽ □ ♅		5:35 P	☽ △ ☊
	7:53 P	☽ △ ⚴		8:24 P	☽ ☍ ♀		8:21 A	☽ ⚹ ⚷		10:35 P	☽ ☌ ⚸
Sat 04	12:06 A	☽ △ ♄	Sat 11	3:31 A	☽ ☍ ⚸		8:44 A	☽ △ ♃	Sat 25	2:00 P	☽ ☌ ♀
	1:06 A	☽ △ ♆		5:23 A	☽ □ ♇		11:51 A	☽ ⚹ ☿	Sun 26	7:52 A	☽ ☍ ♄
	4:44 A	☽ □ ♅		8:52 A	☽ ⚹ ☊		3:41 P	☽ ☌ ♇		11:14 A	☽ ⚹ ♆
	6:53 A	☽ ⚹ ♃	Sun 12	5:27 A	☽ △ ☉		5:36 P	☽ □ ⚸		7:29 P	☽ ⚹ ⚴
	8:23 A	☽ △ ⚷		12:59 P	☽ △ ☿		8:17 P	☽ □ ♀		8:18 P	☽ ⚹ ⚷
	10:59 A	☽ □ ⚸		4:09 P	☽ ☌ ♄	Sat 18	9:33 A	☽ △ ♂		10:43 P	☽ ☌ ♃
	5:07 P	☽ ☍ ♇		5:25 P	☽ △ ⚴		11:58 P	☽ ⚹ ⚶	Mon 27	1:53 A	☽ ⚹ ☉
Sun 05	3:50 P	☽ △ ⚶		5:36 P	☽ △ ♆	Sun 19	4:22 A	☽ □ ♄		3:55 A	☽ △ ♇
	6:01 P	☽ ⚹ ♂	Mon 13	12:12 A	☽ ☍ ♃		10:15 A	☽ ⚹ ♅		5:08 P	☽ △ ♂
Mon 06	4:28 A	☽ △ ♀		12:27 A	☽ △ ⚷		1:02 P	☽ ⚹ ⚵	Tue 28	2:46 P	☽ ⚹ ☿
	7:31 A	☽ □ ♄		7:45 A	☽ ⚹ ♇		3:02 P	☽ □ ♃	Wed 29	12:23 A	☽ □ ♆
	11:33 A	☽ △ ⚵	Tue 14	3:07 A	☽ ⚹ ♂	Mon 20	12:12 A	☽ ⚹ ☊		1:44 A	☽ ⚹ ⚶
	12:00 P	☽ △ ♅		11:07 A	☽ △ ⚶		1:02 A	☽ ⚹ ⚸		4:49 A	☽ ⚹ ♅
	2:23 P	☽ □ ♃		12:04 P	☽ □ ☉		7:28 A	☽ ⚹ ♀		9:35 A	☽ □ ⚷
	7:07 P	☽ △ ⚸		8:40 P	☽ □ ♆	Tue 21	11:17 A	☽ △ ♄		9:44 A	☽ ☍ ⚵
Tue 07	3:49 A	☽ △ ☊		9:36 P	☽ □ ⚴		1:47 P	☽ ☌ ♆		10:11 A	☽ □ ⚴
	4:54 P	☽ ☍ ☉		11:28 P	☽ □ ☿		5:35 P	☽ ☌ ☉		6:14 P	☽ ☍ ☊
	5:41 P	☽ ☍ ☿	Wed 15	12:06 A	☽ △ ♅		6:37 P	☽ ☌ ⚴		8:21 P	☽ □ ☉

ADDITIONAL MONTHLY EPHEMERIDES

CENTAURS

2012	PHOLUS	NESSUS	ASBOLUS	CHARIKLO	HYLON.
FEB					
4	19°♐27′	22°♒43′	21°♉28′	11°♐43′	20°♐14′
9	19° 36′	22° 57′	21° 30′	11° 58′	20° 24′
14	19° 43′	23° 11′	21° 34′	12° 11′	20° 33′
19	19° 50′	23° 26′	21° 40′	12° 23′	20° 42′
24	19° 56′	23° 40′	21° 47′	12° 33′	20° 49′
29	20° 00′	23° 54′	21° 56′	12° 41′	20° 55′

BLACK MOON LILITH ⚸

01	03°♉50'R	11	13°♈28'R	21	13°♉12'
02	02° 10'R	12	13° 10'R	22	14° 56'
03	29°♈51'R	13	12° 59'R	23	15° 13'R
04	26° 53'R	14	13° 22'	24	14° 34'R
05	23° 31'R	15	14° 58'	25	13° 32'R
06	20° 10'R	16	18° 12'	26	12° 33'R
07	17° 21'R	17	23° 01'	27	11° 49'R
08	15° 22'R	18	28° 50'	28	11° 19'R
09	14° 16'R	19	04°♉44'	29	10° 51'R
10	13° 45'R	20	09° 44'		

FEBRUARY 2012 EPHEMERIS

Ephemeris calculated for 12 Midnight GMT.

DAY	☉	☽	☊T.N.	☿	♀	♂	♃	♄	⚷	♅	♆	♇	⚳	⚴	⚵	⚶
01 We	11°♒31'	20°♉27'	12°♐26'	07°♒02'	21°♓24'	22°♍41'R	02°♉38'	29°♎28'	03°♓38'	01°♈47'	29°♒54'	08°♑23'	03°♈59'	26°♒17'	00°♐33'	18°♓36'
02 Th	12° 32'	02°♊22'	12° 26'	08° 43'	22° 36'	22° 35'R	02° 46'	29° 29'	03° 42'	01° 50'	29° 56'	08° 25'	04° 19'	26° 37'	00° 46'	19° 03'
03 Fr	13° 33'	14°♊28'	12° 27'R	10° 25'	23° 47'	22° 27'R	02° 53'	29° 29'	03° 46'	01° 52'	29° 58'	08° 26'	04° 40'	26° 57'	00° 59'	19° 30'
04 Sa	14° 34'	26°♊50'	12° 26'R	12° 07'	24° 58'	22° 19'R	03° 00'	29° 30'	03° 49'	01° 55'	00°♓00'	08° 28'	05° 00'	27° 17'	01° 12'	19° 58'
05 Su	15° 35'	09°♋31'	12° 22'R	13° 51'	26° 09'	22° 10'R	03° 08'	29° 30'	03° 53'	01° 57'	00° 03'	08° 30'	05° 21'	27° 36'	01° 25'	20° 25'
06 Mo	16° 35'	22°♋33'	12° 16'R	15° 35'	27° 21'	22° 00'R	03° 16'	29° 30'	03° 57'	02° 00'	00° 05'	08° 32'	05° 42'	27° 56'	01° 38'	20° 52'
07 Tu	17° 36'	05°♌59'	12° 08'R	17° 19'	28° 31'	21° 50'R	03° 24'	29° 30'	04° 01'	02° 02'	00° 07'	08° 34'	06° 03'	28° 16'	01° 50'	21° 20'
08 We	18° 37'	19°♌45'	11° 57'R	19° 05'	29° 42'	21° 39'R	03° 32'	29° 30'R	04° 05'	02° 05'	00° 09'	08° 35'	06° 24'	28° 36'	02° 02'	21° 47'
09 Th	19° 38'	03°♍49'	11° 46'R	20° 51'	00°♈53'	21° 27'R	03° 40'	29° 30'R	04° 09'	02° 08'	00° 12'	08° 37'	06° 45'	28° 56'	02° 14'	22° 15'
10 Fr	20° 38'	18°♍05'	11° 35'R	22° 38'	02° 04'	21° 14'R	03° 48'	29° 30'R	04° 13'	02° 11'	00° 14'	08° 39'	07° 06'	29° 16'	02° 26'	22° 42'
11 Sa	21° 39'	02°♎28'	11° 26'R	24° 26'	03° 14'	21° 00'R	03° 57'	29° 30'R	04° 16'	02° 13'	00° 16'	08° 41'	07° 27'	29° 36'	02° 38'	23° 10'
12 Su	22° 40'	16°♎51'	11° 19'R	26° 14'	04° 24'	20° 46'R	04° 05'	29° 29'R	04° 20'	02° 16'	00° 18'	08° 42'	07° 48'	29° 56'	02° 49'	23° 37'
13 Mo	23° 40'	01°♏11'	11° 14'R	28° 03'	05° 34'	20° 31'R	04° 14'	29° 29'R	04° 24'	02° 19'	00° 21'	08° 44'	08° 09'	00° 16'	03° 01'	24° 05'
14 Tu	24° 41'	15°♏23'	11° 12'R	29° 53'	06° 44'	20° 15'R	04° 23'	29° 28'R	04° 28'	02° 22'	00° 23'	08° 45'	08° 31'	00° 36'	03° 12'	24° 33'
15 We	25° 42'	29°♏27'	11° 12'	01°♓43'	07° 54'	19° 59'R	04° 32'	29° 28'R	04° 32'	02° 25'	00° 25'	08° 47'	08° 52'	00° 56'	03° 23'	25° 00'
16 Th	26° 42'	13°♐22'	11° 12'R	03° 33'	09° 04'	19° 42'R	04° 41'	29° 27'R	04° 36'	02° 28'	00° 27'	08° 49'	09° 14'	01° 16'	03° 33'	25° 28'
17 Fr	27° 43'	27°♐07'	11° 11'R	05° 24'	10° 14'	19° 24'R	04° 50'	29° 26'R	04° 40'	02° 31'	00° 30'	08° 50'	09° 36'	01° 36'	03° 44'	25° 56'
18 Sa	28° 44'	10°♑44'	11° 09'R	07° 14'	11° 23'	19° 06'R	05° 00'	29° 25'R	04° 44'	02° 33'	00° 32'	08° 52'	09° 57'	01° 56'	03° 54'	26° 23'
19 Su	29° 44'	24°♑11'	11° 03'R	09° 05'	12° 33'	18° 47'R	05° 09'	29° 24'R	04° 48'	02° 36'	00° 34'	08° 53'	10° 19'	02° 16'	04° 04'	26° 51'
20 Mo	00°♓45'	07°♒28'	10° 54'R	10° 56'	13° 42'	18° 27'R	05° 19'	29° 22'R	04° 52'	02° 39'	00° 37'	08° 55'	10° 41'	02° 36'	04° 13'	27° 19'
21 Tu	01° 45'	20°♒34'	10° 42'R	12° 46'	14° 51'	18° 07'R	05° 29'	29° 21'R	04° 56'	02° 43'	00° 39'	08° 56'	11° 03'	02° 56'	04° 23'	27° 47'
22 We	02° 46'	03°♓28'	10° 29'R	14° 35'	16° 00'	17° 46'R	05° 39'	29° 20'R	05° 00'	02° 46'	00° 41'	08° 58'	11° 25'	03° 16'	04° 32'	28° 14'
23 Th	03° 46'	16°♓08'	10° 15'R	16° 24'	17° 08'	17° 25'R	05° 49'	29° 18'R	05° 04'	02° 49'	00° 43'	08° 59'	11° 47'	03° 36'	04° 41'	28° 42'
24 Fr	04° 47'	28°♓34'	10° 01'R	18° 11'	18° 17'	17° 03'R	05° 59'	29° 16'R	05° 08'	02° 52'	00° 46'	09° 00'	12° 10'	03° 56'	04° 50'	29° 10'
25 Sa	05° 47'	10°♈47'	09° 49'R	19° 56'	19° 25'	16° 41'R	06° 09'	29° 15'R	05° 12'	02° 55'	00° 48'	09° 02'	12° 32'	04° 16'	04° 59'	29° 38'
26 Su	06° 47'	22°♈49'	09° 40'R	21° 39'	20° 33'	16° 19'R	06° 19'	29° 13'R	05° 16'	02° 58'	00° 50'	09° 03'	12° 54'	04° 36'	05° 07'	00°♈06'
27 Mo	07° 48'	04°♉42'	09° 34'R	23° 19'	21° 41'	15° 56'R	06° 30'	29° 11'R	05° 20'	03° 01'	00° 53'	09° 05'	13° 17'	04° 56'	05° 15'	00° 34'
28 Tu	08° 48'	16°♉30'	09° 31'R	24° 56'	22° 49'	15° 33'R	06° 40'	29° 09'R	05° 24'	03° 04'	00° 55'	09° 06'	13° 39'	05° 16'	05° 23'	01° 01'
29 We	09° 48'	28°♉18'	09° 29'R	26° 29'	23° 57'	15° 10'R	06° 51'	29° 07'R	05° 28'	03° 08'	00° 57'	09° 07'	14° 02'	05° 36'	05° 30'	01° 29'

MOON ASPECTS — MARCH 2012

All times Eastern Time

Thu 01	3:43 A ☽ ✶ ⚷	Thu 08	4:39 A ☽ ☍ ☉		10:18 P ☽ △ ♂		1:17 P ☽ ☍ ♄
	3:53 A ☽ □ ♂	Fri 09	5:45 A ☽ ☍ ♅		11:00 P ☽ ☌ ♇		9:27 P ☽ ✶ ♆
Fri 02	3:29 A ☽ ✶ ♀		9:29 A ☽ ☍ ⚶	Fri 16	12:00 A ☽ △ ♃	Sun 25	6:13 A ☽ △ ♂
	8:14 A ☽ △ ♄		10:01 A ☽ ☍ ☿		1:48 A ☽ ✶ ♀		8:05 A ☽ ✶ ⚷
	10:33 A ☽ □ ☿		10:20 A ☽ ✶ ⚴		3:11 A ☽ △ ♀		12:58 P ☽ △ ♇
	12:11 P ☽ △ ♆		2:53 P ☽ □ ♇		6:58 P ☽ □ ⚷		6:02 P ☽ ☌ ♃
	3:35 P ☽ □ ⚵		2:57 P ☽ ✶ ☊	Sat 17	7:12 A ☽ ✶ ☉		10:29 P ☽ ✶ ♀
	4:29 P ☽ □ ♅	Sat 10	4:56 A ☽ ☍ ⚷		9:00 A ☽ □ ♄	Mon 26	3:26 P ☽ ☌ ♀
	9:04 P ☽ △ ⚸		10:09 P ☽ ☌ ♄		7:45 P ☽ ✶ ♅	Tue 27	12:35 A ☽ ✶ ☿
	10:56 P ☽ △ ♀	Sun 11	3:38 A ☽ △ ♆		8:46 P ☽ ✶ ☿		10:39 A ☽ □ ♆
Sat 03	12:27 A ☽ ✶ ♃		11:33 A ☽ △ ⚸	Sun 18	1:02 A ☽ ✶ ⚴		4:16 P ☽ ✶ ♅
	3:46 A ☽ ☍ ♇		12:31 P ☽ ☍ ♀		4:32 A ☽ ✶ ☊		6:04 P ☽ □ ♂
	11:58 A ☽ △ ☉		4:13 P ☽ ☍ ♃		6:44 A ☽ ✶ ⚶		9:07 P ☽ ☍ ⚷
	12:18 P ☽ ✶ ♂		4:38 P ☽ ✶ ♇		7:23 A ☽ □ ♃		9:27 P ☽ □ ⚸
	3:39 P ☽ □ ⚷		4:57 P ☽ △ ♀		2:39 P ☽ □ ♀		10:38 P ☽ ✶ ☉
Sun 04	4:20 P ☽ □ ♄		6:33 P ☽ ✶ ♂	Mon 19	3:58 A ☽ ✶ ⚷		11:43 P ☽ ☍ ☊
	5:17 P ☽ □ ♀	Mon 12	2:30 P ☽ △ ☉		4:31 P ☽ △ ♄	Wed 28	12:49 P ☽ ✶ ⚴
	11:57 P ☽ △ ☿	Tue 13	5:19 A ☽ □ ♆		11:17 P ☽ ☌ ♆		1:11 P ☽ □ ♀
Mon 05	12:25 A ☽ △ ♅		9:25 A ☽ △ ♅	Tue 20	9:01 A ☽ ☌ ⚸	Thu 29	10:05 A ☽ □ ☿
	1:21 A ☽ △ ⚴		1:37 P ☽ □ ⚸		9:31 A ☽ □ ⚶		10:12 A ☽ ✶ ⚷
	5:13 A ☽ △ ⚶		2:09 P ☽ △ ☿		10:25 A ☽ ☍ ♂		2:05 P ☽ △ ♄
	8:20 A ☽ □ ♃		2:19 P ☽ ☌ ⚶		12:47 P ☽ □ ☊		11:05 P ☽ △ ♆
	11:18 A ☽ △ ☊		4:17 P ☽ △ ⚴		2:06 P ☽ ✶ ♇	Fri 30	4:38 A ☽ □ ♅
	11:12 P ☽ △ ⚷		6:18 P ☽ ☌ ☊		4:55 P ☽ ✶ ♃		5:06 A ☽ ✶ ♂
Tue 06	8:27 P ☽ ✶ ♄		7:23 P ☽ □ ♂		8:00 P ☽ ☌ ♀		9:38 A ☽ △ ⚷
Wed 07	12:30 A ☽ ☍ ♆		8:12 P ☽ □ ♀	Wed 21	4:39 A ☽ ✶ ♀		1:48 P ☽ ☍ ♇
	1:52 A ☽ △ ♀	Wed 14	12:21 P ☽ △ ⚷	Thu 22	7:50 A ☽ ☌ ☿		3:41 P ☽ □ ☉
	8:25 A ☽ ☍ ⚷		9:25 P ☽ □ ☉		10:37 A ☽ ☌ ☉		8:41 P ☽ ✶ ♃
	9:00 A ☽ □ ⚴	Thu 15	3:34 A ☽ ✶ ♄		2:36 P ☽ ☌ ♅	Sat 31	1:56 A ☽ △ ♀
	12:04 P ☽ ☍ ♀		9:04 A ☽ ✶ ♆		7:56 P ☽ △ ⚴		2:18 A ☽ □ ⚸
	12:17 P ☽ △ ♃		1:26 P ☽ □ ⚸		10:58 P ☽ △ ☊		6:12 P ☽ △ ☿
	1:55 P ☽ △ ♇		4:53 P ☽ □ ☿	Fri 23	12:38 A ☽ □ ♇		10:05 P ☽ □ ⚷
	2:12 P ☽ □ ☊		5:52 P ☽ ✶ ⚷		6:26 A ☽ ☌ ⚸		11:33 P ☽ □ ♄
	6:28 P ☽ ☌ ♂		10:15 P ☽ □ ⚸	Sat 24	4:29 A ☽ ☌ ⚷		

ADDITIONAL MONTHLY EPHEMERIDES

CENTAURS

2012	PHOLUS	NESSUS	ASBOLUS	CHARIKLO	HYLON.
MAR					
5	20°♐04'	24°♒07'	22°♉06'	12°♐47'	21°♐01'
10	20° 07'	24° 21'	22° 17'	12° 52'	21° 05'
15	20° 08'	24° 34'	22° 30'	12° 54'	21° 08'
20	20° 09'	24° 46'	22° 44'	12° 55'	21° 09'
25	20° 08'R	24° 58'	22° 59'	12° 54'R	21° 10'
30	20° 06'R	25° 09'	23° 15'	12° 51'R	21° 09'R

BLACK MOON LILITH ⚸

01	10°♉08'R	11	16° 53'R	21	04°♉18'
02	08° 53'R	12	15° 01'R	22	08° 08'
03	06° 52'R	13	13° 05'R	23	11° 00'
04	04° 05'R	14	11° 33'R	24	13° 01'
05	00° 48'R	15	11° 05'	25	14° 27'
06	27°♈25'R	16	12° 10'	26	15° 34'
07	24° 23'R	17	14° 59'	27	16° 35'
08	21° 56'R	18	19° 15'	28	17° 31'
09	20° 05'R	19	24° 21'	29	18° 16'
10	18° 31'R	20	29° 34'	30	18° 35'
				31	18° 10'R

MARCH 2012 EPHEMERIS

Ephemeris calculated for 12 Midnight GMT.

DAY	☉	☽	☊T.N.	☿	♀	♂	♃	♄	⚷	♅	♆	♇	⚳	⚴	⚵	⚶
01 Th	10°♓48'	10°♊11'	09°♐29'	27°♓58'	25°♈04'	14°♍47'R	07°♉02'	29°♎04'R	05°♓32'	03°♈11'	00°♓59'	09°♑08'	14°♈24'	05°♓56'	05°♐38'	01°♈57'
02 Fr	11° 49'	22°♊15'	09° 29'R	29° 21'	26° 11'	14° 23'R	07° 13'	29° 02'R	05° 36'	03° 14'	01° 02'	09° 10'	14° 47'	06° 15'	05° 45'	02° 25'
03 Sa	12° 49'	04°♋36'	09° 28'R	00°♈39'	27° 18'	13° 59'R	07° 24'	29° 00'R	05° 40'	03° 17'	01° 04'	09° 11'	15° 10'	06° 35'	05° 51'	02° 53'
04 Su	13° 49'	17°♋17'	09° 24'R	01° 51'	28° 25'	13° 36'R	07° 35'	28° 57'R	05° 44'	03° 21'	01° 06'	09° 12'	15° 32'	06° 55'	05° 58'	03° 21'
05 Mo	14° 49'	00°♌24'	09° 18'R	02° 57'	29° 31'	13° 12'R	07° 46'	28° 55'R	05° 48'	03° 24'	01° 08'	09° 13'	15° 55'	07° 15'	06° 04'	03° 49'
06 Tu	15° 49'	13°♌57'	09° 10'R	03° 55'	00°♉37'	12° 48'R	07° 57'	28° 52'R	05° 52'	03° 27'	01° 11'	09° 14'	16° 18'	07° 35'	06° 10'	04° 17'
07 We	16° 49'	27°♌57'	08° 59'R	04° 45'	01° 43'	12° 25'R	08° 09'	28° 49'R	05° 56'	03° 30'	01° 13'	09° 15'	16° 41'	07° 55'	06° 16'	04° 45'
08 Th	17° 49'	12°♍21'	08° 47'R	05° 27'	02° 49'	12° 01'R	08° 20'	28° 46'R	05° 59'	03° 34'	01° 15'	09° 16'	17° 04'	08° 15'	06° 21'	05° 13'
09 Fr	18° 49'	27°♍01'	08° 35'R	06° 01'	03° 55'	11° 38'R	08° 32'	28° 44'R	06° 03'	03° 37'	01° 17'	09° 17'	17° 27'	08° 35'	06° 26'	05° 40'
10 Sa	19° 49'	11°♎51'	08° 25'R	06° 26'	05° 00'	11° 14'R	08° 43'	28° 41'R	06° 07'	03° 40'	01° 19'	09° 18'	17° 50'	08° 55'	06° 31'	06° 08'
11 Su	20° 49'	26°♎41'	08° 17'R	06° 42'	06° 05'	10° 52'R	08° 55'	28° 37'R	06° 11'	03° 44'	01° 22'	09° 19'	18° 13'	09° 14'	06° 35'	06° 36'
12 Mo	21° 49'	11°♏23'	08° 12'R	06° 49'	07° 10'	10° 29'R	09° 07'	28° 34'R	06° 15'	03° 47'	01° 24'	09° 20'	18° 36'	09° 34'	06° 40'	07° 04'
13 Tu	22° 49'	25°♏53'	08° 10'R	06° 47'R	08° 14'	10° 07'R	09° 19'	28° 31'R	06° 19'	03° 51'	01° 26'	09° 21'	19° 00'	09° 54'	06° 44'	07° 32'
14 We	23° 49'	10°♐07'	08° 10'	06° 37'R	09° 18'	09° 45'R	09° 31'	28° 28'R	06° 23'	03° 54'	01° 28'	09° 22'	19° 23'	10° 14'	06° 47'	08° 00'
15 Th	24° 48'	24°♐03'	08° 10'	06° 19'R	10° 22'	09° 23'R	09° 43'	28° 24'R	06° 27'	03° 57'	01° 30'	09° 23'	19° 46'	10° 33'	06° 50'	08° 28'
16 Fr	25° 48'	07°♑42'	08° 09'R	05° 53'R	11° 25'	09° 02'R	09° 55'	28° 21'R	06° 30'	04° 01'	01° 32'	09° 24'	20° 09'	10° 53'	06° 54'	08° 56'
17 Sa	26° 48'	21°♑06'	08° 07'R	05° 21'R	12° 29'	08° 41'R	10° 07'	28° 17'R	06° 34'	04° 04'	01° 34'	09° 24'	20° 33'	11° 13'	06° 56'	09° 24'
18 Su	27° 48'	04°♒15'	08° 02'R	04° 42'R	13° 31'	08° 21'R	10° 20'	28° 14'R	06° 38'	04° 08'	01° 36'	09° 25'	20° 56'	11° 33'	06° 59'	09° 52'
19 Mo	28° 47'	17°♒12'	07° 54'R	03° 57'R	14° 34'	08° 02'R	10° 32'	28° 10'R	06° 42'	04° 11'	01° 39'	09° 26'	21° 20'	11° 52'	07° 01'	10° 20'
20 Tu	29° 47'	29°♒57'	07° 44'R	03° 09'R	15° 36'	07° 42'R	10° 44'	28° 06'R	06° 45'	04° 14'	01° 41'	09° 26'	21° 43'	12° 12'	07° 03'	10° 48'
21 We	00°♈47'	12°♓31'	07° 32'R	02° 18'R	16° 38'	07° 24'R	10° 57'	28° 03'R	06° 49'	04° 18'	01° 43'	09° 27'	22° 07'	12° 31'	07° 04'	11° 16'
22 Th	01° 46'	24°♓55'	07° 20'R	01° 24'R	17° 40'	07° 06'R	11° 09'	27° 59'R	06° 53'	04° 21'	01° 45'	09° 28'	22° 30'	12° 51'	07° 05'	11° 43'
23 Fr	02° 46'	07°♈08'	07° 08'R	00° 30'R	18° 41'	06° 49'R	11° 22'	27° 55'R	06° 56'	04° 25'	01° 47'	09° 28'	22° 54'	13° 10'	07° 06'	12° 11'
24 Sa	03° 45'	19°♈12'	06° 57'R	29°♓36'R	19° 41'	06° 33'R	11° 35'	27° 51'R	07° 00'	04° 28'	01° 49'	09° 29'	23° 18'	13° 30'	07° 06'	12° 39'
25 Su	04° 45'	01°♉08'	06° 49'R	28° 44'R	20° 42'	06° 17'R	11° 48'	27° 47'R	07° 04'	04° 32'	01° 51'	09° 29'	23° 41'	13° 49'	07° 07'R	13° 07'
26 Mo	05° 44'	12°♉58'	06° 44'R	27° 54'R	21° 42'	06° 02'R	12° 00'	27° 43'R	07° 07'	04° 35'	01° 53'	09° 30'	24° 05'	14° 09'	07° 06'R	13° 35'
27 Tu	06° 44'	24°♉44'	06° 41'R	27° 07'R	22° 41'	05° 47'R	12° 13'	27° 39'R	07° 11'	04° 38'	01° 55'	09° 30'	24° 29'	14° 28'	07° 06'R	14° 03'
28 We	07° 43'	06°♊32'	06° 40'R	26° 25'R	23° 40'	05° 34'R	12° 26'	27° 35'R	07° 14'	04° 42'	01° 57'	09° 31'	24° 52'	14° 48'	07° 05'R	14° 31'
29 Th	08° 42'	18°♊24'	06° 40'	25° 47'R	24° 39'	05° 21'R	12° 39'	27° 30'R	07° 18'	04° 45'	01° 59'	09° 31'	25° 16'	15° 07'	07° 04'R	14° 59'
30 Fr	09° 42'	00°♋27'	06° 41'	25° 14'R	25° 37'	05° 09'R	12° 52'	27° 26'R	07° 22'	04° 49'	02° 00'	09° 32'	25° 40'	15° 26'	07° 02'R	15° 26'
31 Sa	10° 41'	12°♋45'	06° 42'R	24° 46'R	26° 35'	04° 57'R	13° 06'	27° 22'R	07° 25'	04° 52'	02° 02'	09° 32'	26° 04'	15° 45'	07° 01'R	15° 54'

MOON ASPECTS

APRIL 2012

All times Eastern Time

Day	Time	Aspect
Sun 01	12:20 A	☽ ⚹ ♀
	1:43 P	☽ △ ♅
	5:18 P	☽ △ ⚵
	7:25 P	☽ △ ☊
Mon 02	4:11 A	☽ △ ☉
	5:18 A	☽ □ ♃
	11:32 A	☽ △ ⚶
Tue 03	4:57 A	☽ ⚹ ♄
	5:27 A	☽ △ ⚳
	9:47 A	☽ □ ♀
	1:33 P	☽ ☍ ♆
	5:16 P	☽ ☌ ♂
	9:27 P	☽ □ ⚵
	10:50 P	☽ ☍ ⚷
	11:25 P	☽ □ ☊
Wed 04	2:01 A	☽ △ ♇
	9:35 A	☽ △ ♃
	2:50 P	☽ ☍ ⚴
Thu 05	1:37 A	☽ ☍ ☿
	2:41 P	☽ △ ♀
	7:54 P	☽ ☍ ♅
	10:18 P	☽ ⚹ ⚵
Fri 06	12:11 A	☽ ⚹ ☊
	2:51 A	☽ □ ♇
	3:19 P	☽ ☍ ☉
	6:02 P	☽ ☍ ⚶
Sat 07	6:15 A	☽ ☌ ♄
	9:51 A	☽ ☍ ⚳
	2:53 P	☽ △ ♆
	5:31 P	☽ ⚹ ♂
	11:46 P	☽ △ ⚷
Sun 08	2:27 A	☽ ⚹ ♇
	11:08 A	☽ ☍ ♃
	4:48 P	☽ △ ⚴
Mon 09	2:56 A	☽ △ ☿
	2:59 P	☽ □ ♆
	5:22 P	☽ □ ♂
	8:02 P	☽ △ ♅
	8:27 P	☽ ☍ ♀
	9:37 P	☽ ☌ ⚵
	11:43 P	☽ ☌ ☊
Tue 10	12:12 A	☽ □ ⚷
	6:49 P	☽ □ ⚴
	9:51 P	☽ △ ⚶
	10:51 P	☽ △ ☉
Wed 11	6:06 A	☽ □ ☿
	7:05 A	☽ ⚹ ♄
	2:20 P	☽ △ ⚳
	5:07 P	☽ ⚹ ♆
	7:23 P	☽ △ ♂
	10:33 P	☽ □ ♅
Thu 12	2:56 A	☽ ⚹ ⚷
	5:30 A	☽ ☌ ♇
	4:44 P	☽ △ ♃
	11:40 P	☽ ⚹ ⚴
Fri 13	3:31 A	☽ □ ⚶
	6:50 A	☽ □ ☉
	11:12 A	☽ □ ♄
	1:05 P	☽ ⚹ ☿
	8:50 P	☽ □ ⚳
Sat 14	4:07 A	☽ ⚹ ♅
	4:40 A	☽ ⚹ ⚵
	7:23 A	☽ ⚹ ☊
	11:10 A	☽ △ ♀
Sun 15	12:10 A	☽ □ ♃
	12:38 P	☽ ⚹ ⚶
	6:20 P	☽ △ ♄
	6:42 P	☽ ⚹ ☉
Mon 16	6:25 A	☽ ☌ ♆
	6:41 A	☽ ⚹ ⚳
	8:44 A	☽ ☍ ♂
	12:31 P	☽ □ ⚵
	3:40 P	☽ □ ☊
	5:35 P	☽ ☌ ⚷
	7:58 P	☽ ⚹ ♇
	11:40 P	☽ □ ♀
Tue 17	10:34 A	☽ ⚹ ♃
	6:59 P	☽ ☌ ⚴
Wed 18	3:28 P	☽ ☌ ☿
	10:38 P	☽ △ ⚵
	11:45 P	☽ ☌ ♅
Thu 19	2:16 A	☽ △ ☊
	6:57 A	☽ □ ♇
	2:40 P	☽ ⚹ ♀
Fri 20	2:58 P	☽ ☌ ⚶
	3:35 P	☽ ☍ ♄
Sat 21	3:18 A	☽ ☌ ☉
	5:24 A	☽ ⚹ ♆
	8:12 A	☽ △ ♂
	9:38 A	☽ ☌ ⚳
	5:25 P	☽ ⚹ ⚷
	7:25 P	☽ △ ♇
Sun 22	1:10 P	☽ ☌ ♃
	10:41 P	☽ ⚹ ⚴
Mon 23	6:33 P	☽ □ ♆
	9:46 P	☽ □ ♂
	10:30 P	☽ ☍ ⚵
Tue 24	1:42 A	☽ ⚹ ♅
	3:10 A	☽ ☍ ☊
	5:17 A	☽ ⚹ ☿
	6:42 A	☽ □ ⚷
	11:36 P	☽ ☌ ♀
Wed 25	1:06 P	☽ □ ⚴
	4:31 P	☽ △ ♄
	9:30 P	☽ ⚹ ⚶
Thu 26	7:09 A	☽ △ ♆
	10:50 A	☽ ⚹ ♂
	2:17 P	☽ □ ♅
	3:15 P	☽ ⚹ ⚳
	3:31 P	☽ ⚹ ☉
	7:05 P	☽ △ ⚷
	8:31 P	☽ ☍ ♇
Fri 27	12:34 A	☽ □ ☿
	3:59 P	☽ ⚹ ♃
Sat 28	1:35 A	☽ △ ⚴
	3:05 A	☽ □ ♄
	10:22 A	☽ □ ⚶
	7:20 P	☽ △ ⚵
Sun 29	12:18 A	☽ △ ♅
	12:43 A	☽ △ ☊
	2:52 A	☽ □ ⚳
	5:57 A	☽ □ ☉
	4:31 P	☽ △ ☿
Mon 30	12:55 A	☽ ⚹ ♀
	1:14 A	☽ □ ♃
	10:17 A	☽ ⚹ ♄
	7:15 P	☽ △ ⚶

Additional Monthly ephemerides

Centaurs

2012 Apr	Pholus	Nessus	Asbolus	Chariklo	Hylon.
4	20°♐03'R	25°♒20'	23°♉32'	12°♐46'R	21°♐08'R
9	20° 00'R	25° 30'	23° 50'	12° 39'R	21° 05'R
14	19° 55'R	25° 39'	24° 09'	12° 31'R	21° 01'R
19	19° 49'R	25° 47'	24° 28'	12° 21'R	20° 56'R
24	19° 42'R	25° 54'	24° 47'	12° 10'R	20° 50'R
29	19° 35'R	26° 00'	25° 08'	11° 57'R	20° 44'R

01	16°♉52'R	11	24° 00'R	21	11° 50'
02	14° 44'R	12	22° 00'R	22	14° 54'
03	12° 02'R	13	20° 49'R	23	17° 43'
04	09° 11'R	14	20° 45'	24	20° 21'
05	06° 33'R	15	21° 57'	25	22° 51'
06	04° 19'R	16	24° 17'	26	25° 11'
07	02° 25'R	17	27° 26'	27	27° 12'
08	00° 34'R	18	01°♉04'	28	28° 38'
09	28°♈34'R	19	04° 49'	29	29° 12'
10	26° 19'R	20	08° 27'	30	28° 44'R

Black Moon Lilith ⚸

APRIL 2012 EPHEMERIS

Ephemeris calculated for 12 Midnight GMT.

DAY	☉	☽	☊T.N.	☿	♀	♂	♃	♄	⚷	♅	♆	♇	⚳	⚴	⚵	⚶
01 Su	11°♈40'	25°♋23'	06°♐41'R	24°♓24'R	27°♉32'	04°♍47'R	13°♉19'	27°♎18'R	07°♓28'	04°♈56'	02°♓04'	09°♑32'	26°♈28'	16°♓04'	06°♐58'R	16°♈22'
02 Mo	12° 39'	08°♌26'	06° 38'R	24° 07'R	28° 28'	04° 37'R	13° 32'	27° 13'R	07° 32'	04° 59'	02° 06'	09° 33'	26° 52'	16° 24'	06° 56'R	16° 50'
03 Tu	13° 39'	21°♌57'	06° 32'R	23° 57'R	29° 25'	04° 28'R	13° 45'	27° 09'R	07° 35'	05° 02'	02° 08'	09° 33'	27° 15'	16° 43'	06° 53'R	17° 18'
04 We	14° 38'	05°♍58'	06° 26'R	23° 51'R	00°♊20'	04° 20'R	13° 59'	27° 04'R	07° 39'	05° 06'	02° 10'	09° 33'	27° 39'	17° 02'	06° 50'R	17° 45'
05 Th	15° 37'	20°♍26'	06° 18'R	23° 52'	01° 15'	04° 13'R	14° 12'	27° 00'R	07° 42'	05° 09'	02° 12'	09° 33'	28° 03'	17° 21'	06° 46'R	18° 13'
06 Fr	16° 36'	05°♎16'	06° 10'R	23° 58'	02° 09'	04° 06'R	14° 25'	26° 55'R	07° 45'	05° 12'	02° 13'	09° 33'	28° 27'	17° 40'	06° 43'R	18° 41'
07 Sa	17° 35'	20°♎21'	06° 03'R	24° 09'	03° 03'	04° 00'R	14° 39'	26° 51'R	07° 48'	05° 16'	02° 15'	09° 34'	28° 51'	17° 59'	06° 38'R	19° 09'
08 Su	18° 34'	05°♏30'	05° 58'R	24° 25'	03° 56'	03° 55'R	14° 52'	26° 46'R	07° 52'	05° 19'	02° 17'	09° 34'	29° 15'	18° 17'	06° 34'R	19° 36'
09 Mo	19° 33'	20°♏34'	05° 55'R	24° 46'	04° 49'	03° 51'R	15° 06'	26° 42'R	07° 55'	05° 23'	02° 18'	09° 34'	29° 39'	18° 36'	06° 29'R	20° 04'
10 Tu	20° 32'	05°♐24'	05° 54'R	25° 11'	05° 40'	03° 47'R	15° 20'	26° 37'R	07° 58'	05° 26'	02° 20'	09° 34'	00°♉03'	18° 55'	06° 24'R	20° 32'
11 We	21° 30'	19°♐56'	05° 54'	25° 41'	06° 31'	03° 45'R	15° 33'	26° 33'R	08° 01'	05° 29'	02° 22'	09° 34'R	00° 27'	19° 14'	06° 19'R	20° 59'
12 Th	22° 29'	04°♑04'	05° 56'	26° 16'	07° 22'	03° 43'R	15° 47'	26° 28'R	08° 04'	05° 33'	02° 23'	09° 34'R	00° 52'	19° 32'	06° 13'R	21° 27'
13 Fr	23° 28'	17°♑50'	05° 57'	26° 54'	08° 11'	03° 41'R	16° 01'	26° 24'R	08° 07'	05° 36'	02° 25'	09° 34'R	01° 16'	19° 51'	06° 07'R	21° 55'
14 Sa	24° 27'	01°♒13'	05° 57'R	27° 36'	09° 00'	03° 41'R	16° 14'	26° 19'R	08° 10'	05° 39'	02° 27'	09° 34'R	01° 40'	20° 10'	06° 00'R	22° 22'
15 Su	25° 26'	14°♒16'	05° 55'R	28° 21'	09° 48'	03° 41'	16° 28'	26° 14'R	08° 13'	05° 42'	02° 28'	09° 33'R	02° 04'	20° 28'	05° 53'R	22° 50'
16 Mo	26° 24'	27°♒03'	05° 51'R	29° 11'	10° 35'	03° 42'	16° 42'	26° 10'R	08° 16'	05° 46'	02° 30'	09° 33'R	02° 28'	20° 47'	05° 46'R	23° 17'
17 Tu	27° 23'	09°♓34'	05° 46'R	00°♈03'	11° 21'	03° 44'	16° 56'	26° 05'R	08° 19'	05° 49'	02° 31'	09° 33'R	02° 52'	21° 05'	05° 39'R	23° 45'
18 We	28° 22'	21°♓53'	05° 40'R	00° 58'	12° 06'	03° 46'	17° 10'	26° 00'R	08° 22'	05° 52'	02° 33'	09° 33'R	03° 16'	21° 23'	05° 31'R	24° 13'
19 Th	29° 20'	04°♈03'	05° 33'R	01° 57'	12° 51'	03° 49'	17° 24'	25° 56'R	08° 25'	05° 55'	02° 34'	09° 33'R	03° 40'	21° 41'	05° 23'R	24° 40'
20 Fr	00°♉19'	16°♈04'	05° 27'R	02° 58'	13° 34'	03° 53'	17° 38'	25° 51'R	08° 28'	05° 59'	02° 36'	09° 32'R	04° 05'	22° 00'	05° 15'R	25° 08'
21 Sa	01° 18'	27°♈59'	05° 21'R	04° 02'	14° 16'	03° 58'	17° 51'	25° 47'R	08° 30'	06° 02'	02° 37'	09° 32'R	04° 29'	22° 18'	05° 06'R	25° 35'
22 Su	02° 16'	09°♉49'	05° 17'R	05° 09'	14° 58'	04° 03'	18° 05'	25° 42'R	08° 33'	06° 05'	02° 38'	09° 32'R	04° 53'	22° 36'	04° 57'R	26° 02'
23 Mo	03° 15'	21°♉37'	05° 14'R	06° 18'	15° 38'	04° 09'	18° 19'	25° 38'R	08° 36'	06° 08'	02° 40'	09° 31'R	05° 17'	22° 54'	04° 48'R	26° 30'
24 Tu	04° 13'	03°♊24'	05° 14'R	07° 30'	16° 17'	04° 15'	18° 34'	25° 33'R	08° 38'	06° 11'	02° 41'	09° 31'R	05° 41'	23° 12'	04° 39'R	26° 57'
25 We	05° 12'	15°♊13'	05° 14'	08° 43'	16° 55'	04° 22'	18° 48'	25° 29'R	08° 41'	06° 14'	02° 42'	09° 31'R	06° 06'	23° 30'	04° 29'R	27° 25'
26 Th	06° 10'	27°♊09'	05° 15'	10° 00'	17° 31'	04° 30'	19° 02'	25° 24'R	08° 44'	06° 17'	02° 44'	09° 30'R	06° 30'	23° 47'	04° 19'R	27° 52'
27 Fr	07° 08'	09°♋14'	05° 17'	11° 18'	18° 07'	04° 39'	19° 16'	25° 20'R	08° 46'	06° 21'	02° 45'	09° 30'R	06° 54'	24° 05'	04° 09'R	28° 19'
28 Sa	08° 07'	21°♋32'	05° 19'	12° 39'	18° 41'	04° 48'	19° 30'	25° 15'R	08° 48'	06° 24'	02° 46'	09° 29'R	07° 18'	24° 23'	03° 58'R	28° 47'
29 Su	09° 05'	04°♌09'	05° 19'	14° 01'	19° 13'	04° 57'	19° 44'	25° 11'R	08° 51'	06° 27'	02° 47'	09° 29'R	07° 43'	24° 40'	03° 47'R	29° 14'
30 Mo	10° 03'	17°♌08'	05° 19'R	15° 26'	19° 45'	05° 08'	19° 58'	25° 06'R	08° 53'	06° 30'	02° 48'	09° 28'R	08° 07'	24° 58'	03° 37'R	29° 41'

MOON ASPECTS | MAY 2012

All times Eastern Time

Day	Time	Aspect
Tue 01	12:00 A	☽ ☍ ♆
	4:27 A	☽ ☌ ♂
	6:29 A	☽ □ ☊
	10:18 A	☽ △ ⚳
	10:38 A	☽ ☍ ⚷
	11:30 A	☽ △ ♇
	3:34 P	☽ △ ☉
Wed 02	6:21 A	☽ △ ♃
	6:58 A	☽ □ ♀
	3:04 P	☽ ☍ ⚴
Thu 03	2:57 A	☽ ⚹ ⚵
	8:36 A	☽ ⚹ ☊
	8:58 A	☽ ☍ ♅
	1:27 P	☽ □ ♇
Fri 04	9:16 A	☽ △ ♀
	10:10 A	☽ ☍ ☿
	2:02 P	☽ ☌ ♄
Sat 05	1:34 A	☽ ☍ ⚶
	2:55 A	☽ △ ♆
	8:10 A	☽ ⚹ ♂
	12:41 P	☽ △ ⚷
	1:10 P	☽ ⚹ ♇
	2:49 P	☽ ☍ ⚳
	11:35 P	☽ ☍ ☉
Sun 06	8:14 A	☽ ☍ ♃
	4:47 P	☽ △ ⚴
Mon 07	1:07 A	☽ ☌ ⚵
	2:18 A	☽ □ ♆
	7:32 A	☽ ☌ ☊
	8:18 A	☽ □ ♂
	8:32 A	☽ △ ♅
	12:13 P	☽ □ ⚷
Tue 08	10:39 A	☽ ☍ ♀
	12:58 P	☽ ⚹ ♄
	5:53 P	☽ □ ⚴
	9:34 P	☽ △ ☿
Wed 09	2:54 A	☽ ⚹ ♆
	4:27 A	☽ △ ⚶
	9:32 A	☽ □ ♅
	9:59 A	☽ △ ♂
	1:21 P	☽ ⚹ ⚷
	1:34 P	☽ ☌ ♇
	6:14 P	☽ △ ⚳
Thu 10	8:03 A	☽ △ ☉
	11:57 A	☽ △ ♃
	3:11 P	☽ □ ♄
	9:42 P	☽ ⚹ ⚴
Fri 11	3:22 A	☽ ⚹ ⚵
	8:12 A	☽ □ ☿
	9:42 A	☽ □ ⚶
	11:41 A	☽ ⚹ ☊
	1:33 P	☽ ⚹ ♅
Sat 12	12:19 A	☽ □ ⚳
	5:47 P	☽ □ ☉
	6:40 P	☽ □ ♃
	8:13 P	☽ △ ♀
	8:52 P	☽ △ ♄
Sun 13	9:15 A	☽ □ ⚵
	1:24 P	☽ ☌ ♆
	6:51 P	☽ □ ☊
	6:59 P	☽ ⚹ ⚶
	11:48 P	☽ ☍ ♂
Mon 14	12:50 A	☽ ⚹ ☿
	1:21 A	☽ ⚹ ♇
	1:29 A	☽ ☌ ⚷
	10:26 A	☽ ⚹ ⚳
Tue 15	5:09 A	☽ ⚹ ♃
	5:54 A	☽ □ ♀
	7:59 A	☽ ⚹ ☉
	4:33 P	☽ ☌ ⚴
	6:21 P	☽ △ ⚵
Wed 16	5:12 A	☽ △ ☊
	8:11 A	☽ ☌ ♅
	12:10 P	☽ □ ♇
Thu 17	5:40 P	☽ ⚹ ♀
	5:44 P	☽ ☍ ♄
Fri 18	12:18 P	☽ ⚹ ♆
	10:50 P	☽ ☌ ⚶
Sat 19	12:46 A	☽ △ ♇
	1:20 A	☽ ⚹ ⚷
	2:32 A	☽ △ ♂
	2:48 P	☽ ☌ ⚳
Sun 20	12:37 A	☽ ☌ ☿
	8:35 A	☽ ☌ ♃
	5:26 P	☽ ☍ ⚵
	7:47 P	☽ ☌ ☉
	8:35 P	☽ ⚹ ⚴
Mon 21	1:22 A	☽ □ ♆
	6:14 A	☽ ☍ ☊
	10:13 A	☽ ⚹ ♅
	2:25 P	☽ □ ⚷
	5:17 P	☽ □ ♂
Tue 22	5:24 P	☽ ☌ ♀
	6:51 P	☽ △ ♄
Wed 23	10:18 A	☽ □ ⚴
	1:42 P	☽ △ ♆
	10:30 P	☽ □ ♅
Thu 24	1:34 A	☽ ☍ ♇
	2:30 A	☽ △ ⚷
	4:26 A	☽ ⚹ ⚶
	6:59 A	☽ ⚹ ♂
	7:21 P	☽ ⚹ ⚳
Fri 25	5:44 A	☽ □ ♄
	10:34 A	☽ ⚹ ♃
	2:31 P	☽ △ ⚵
	10:02 P	☽ △ ⚴
Sat 26	1:32 A	☽ ⚹ ☿
	4:09 A	☽ △ ☊
	4:41 A	☽ ⚹ ☉
	8:44 A	☽ △ ♅
	4:17 P	☽ □ ⚶
Sun 27	6:16 A	☽ □ ⚳
	9:57 A	☽ ⚹ ♀
	2:07 P	☽ ⚹ ♄
	7:54 P	☽ □ ♃
	9:42 P	☽ □ ⚵
Mon 28	7:46 A	☽ ☍ ♆
	11:18 A	☽ □ ☊
	4:16 P	☽ □ ☉
	6:16 P	☽ △ ♇
	7:25 P	☽ ☍ ⚷
	7:53 P	☽ □ ☿
Tue 29	12:46 A	☽ △ ⚶
	2:29 A	☽ ☌ ♂
	1:42 P	☽ △ ⚳
	1:44 P	☽ □ ♀
Wed 30	1:49 A	☽ ⚹ ⚵
	1:50 A	☽ △ ♃
	12:04 P	☽ ☍ ⚴
	3:13 P	☽ ⚹ ☊
	7:57 P	☽ ☍ ♅
	9:54 P	☽ □ ♇
	11:48 P	☽ △ ☉
Thu 31	8:44 A	☽ △ ☿
	2:30 P	☽ △ ♀
	9:31 P	☽ ☌ ♄

ADDITIONAL MONTHLY EPHEMERIDES

CENTAURS

2012	PHOLUS	NESSUS	ASBOLUS	CHARIKLO	HYLON.
May					
4	19°♐27′R	26°♒06′	25°♉28′	11°♐44′R	20°♐36′R
9	19° 18′R	26° 10′	25° 49′	11° 29′R	20° 28′R
14	19° 08′R	26° 13′	26° 10′	11° 14′R	20° 19′R
19	18° 58′R	26° 16′	26° 30′	10° 57′R	20° 09′R
24	18° 48′R	26° 17′	26° 51′	10° 41′R	20° 00′R
29	18° 37′R	26° 17′R	27° 12′	10° 24′R	19° 49′R

BLACK MOON LILITH ⚸

Day	Position	Day	Position	Day	Position
01	27°♉17′R	11	05° 14′R	21	18° 34′
02	25° 08′R	12	03° 32′R	22	21° 45′
03	22° 41′R	13	02° 45′R	23	25° 13′
04	20° 18′R	14	02° 58′	24	28° 51′
05	18° 12′R	15	04° 04′	25	02°♊29′
06	16° 19′R	16	05° 51′	26	05° 47′
07	14° 27′R	17	08° 01′	27	08° 23′
08	12° 23′R	18	10° 25′	28	09° 57′
09	10° 02′R	19	12° 57′	29	10° 18′R
10	07° 32′R	20	15° 39′	30	09° 28′R
				31	07° 46′R

MAY 2012 EPHEMERIS

Ephemeris calculated for 12 Midnight GMT.

DAY	☉	☽	☊T.N.	☿	♀	♂	♃	♄	⚷	♅	♆	♇	⚳	⚴	⚵	⚶
01 Tu	11°♉02'	00°♍33'	05°♐18'R	16°♈53'	20°♊14'	05°♍18'	20°♉12'	25°♎02'R	08°♓56'	06°♈33'	02°♓49'	09°♑27'R	08°♉31'	25°♓15'	03°♐25'R	00°♉08'
02 We	12° 00'	14°♍25'	05° 16'R	18° 21'	20° 42'	05° 30'	20° 26'	24° 58'R	08° 58'	06° 36'	02° 51'	09° 27'R	08° 55'	25° 32'	03° 14'R	00° 35'
03 Th	12° 58'	28°♍45'	05° 13'R	19° 52'	21° 09'	05° 42'	20° 41'	24° 53'R	09° 00'	06° 38'	02° 52'	09° 26'R	09° 20'	25° 50'	03° 02'R	01° 02'
04 Fr	13° 56'	13°♎29'	05° 10'R	21° 25'	21° 34'	05° 54'	20° 55'	24° 49'R	09° 02'	06° 41'	02° 53'	09° 26'R	09° 44'	26° 07'	02° 50'R	01° 30'
05 Sa	14° 54'	28°♎32'	05° 08'R	22° 59'	21° 57'	06° 07'	21° 09'	24° 45'R	09° 04'	06° 44'	02° 54'	09° 25'R	10° 08'	26° 24'	02° 38'R	01° 57'
06 Su	15° 52'	13°♏45'	05° 06'R	24° 36'	22° 18'	06° 21'	21° 23'	24° 41'R	09° 06'	06° 47'	02° 55'	09° 24'R	10° 32'	26° 41'	02° 26'R	02° 24'
07 Mo	16° 51'	28°♏58'	05° 05'R	26° 15'	22° 37'	06° 35'	21° 37'	24° 37'R	09° 08'	06° 50'	02° 56'	09° 23'R	10° 56'	26° 58'	02° 14'R	02° 51'
08 Tu	17° 49'	14°♐01'	05° 05'	27° 55'	22° 55'	06° 49'	21° 52'	24° 33'R	09° 10'	06° 53'	02° 57'	09° 23'R	11° 21'	27° 14'	02° 01'R	03° 18'
09 We	18° 47'	28°♐47'	05° 06'	29° 37'	23° 10'	07° 04'	22° 06'	24° 29'R	09° 12'	06° 55'	02° 57'	09° 22'R	11° 45'	27° 31'	01° 49'R	03° 45'
10 Th	19° 45'	13°♑10'	05° 07'	01°♉22'	23° 24'	07° 20'	22° 20'	24° 25'R	09° 14'	06° 58'	02° 58'	09° 21'R	12° 09'	27° 48'	01° 36'R	04° 12'
11 Fr	20° 43'	27°♑07'	05° 08'	03° 08'	23° 35'	07° 36'	22° 34'	24° 21'R	09° 16'	07° 01'	02° 59'	09° 20'R	12° 33'	28° 04'	01° 23'R	04° 38'
12 Sa	21° 40'	10°♒38'	05° 09'	04° 56'	23° 45'	07° 52'	22° 49'	24° 17'R	09° 18'	07° 04'	03° 00'	09° 19'R	12° 57'	28° 21'	01° 10'R	05° 05'
13 Su	22° 38'	23°♒45'	05° 09'R	06° 46'	23° 52'	08° 09'	23° 03'	24° 13'R	09° 19'	07° 06'	03° 01'	09° 18'R	13° 22'	28° 37'	00° 57'R	05° 32'
14 Mo	23° 36'	06°♓30'	05° 09'R	08° 39'	23° 57'	08° 26'	23° 17'	24° 09'R	09° 21'	07° 09'	03° 01'	09° 17'R	13° 46'	28° 53'	00° 44'R	05° 59'
15 Tu	24° 34'	18°♓56'	05° 08'R	10° 33'	23° 59'	08° 44'	23° 31'	24° 06'R	09° 23'	07° 11'	03° 02'	09° 16'R	14° 10'	29° 09'	00° 30'R	06° 26'
16 We	25° 32'	01°♈08'	05° 07'R	12° 29'	23° 59'R	09° 02'	23° 45'	24° 02'R	09° 24'	07° 14'	03° 03'	09° 15'R	14° 34'	29° 25'	00° 17'R	06° 52'
17 Th	26° 30'	13°♈09'	05° 06'R	14° 26'	23° 57'R	09° 21'	24° 00'	23° 59'R	09° 26'	07° 16'	03° 03'	09° 14'R	14° 58'	29° 41'	00° 04'R	07° 19'
18 Fr	27° 28'	25°♈03'	05° 05'R	16° 26'	23° 53'R	09° 40'	24° 14'	23° 55'R	09° 27'	07° 19'	03° 04'	09° 13'R	15° 22'	29° 57'	29°♏50'R	07° 46'
19 Sa	28° 25'	06°♉52'	05° 04'R	18° 28'	23° 46'R	09° 59'	24° 28'	23° 52'R	09° 29'	07° 21'	03° 04'	09° 12'R	15° 47'	00°♈13'	29° 37'R	08° 12'
20 Su	29° 23'	18°♉39'	05° 03'R	20° 31'	23° 37'R	10° 19'	24° 42'	23° 48'R	09° 30'	07° 24'	03° 05'	09° 11'R	16° 11'	00° 28'	29° 23'R	08° 39'
21 Mo	00°♊21'	00°♎27'	05° 03'R	22° 36'	23° 25'R	10° 39'	24° 56'	23° 45'R	09° 31'	07° 26'	03° 06'	09° 10'R	16° 35'	00° 44'	29° 09'R	09° 05'
22 Tu	01° 19'	12°♊18'	05° 03'	24° 42'	23° 11'R	11° 00'	25° 11'	23° 42'R	09° 32'	07° 29'	03° 06'	09° 09'R	16° 59'	00° 59'	28° 56'R	09° 32'
23 We	02° 16'	24°♊14'	05° 03'	26° 50'	22° 54'R	11° 20'	25° 25'	23° 39'R	09° 34'	07° 31'	03° 06'	09° 08'R	17° 23'	01° 15'	28° 42'R	09° 58'
24 Th	03° 14'	06°♋17'	05° 03'	28° 59'	22° 35'R	11° 42'	25° 39'	23° 36'R	09° 35'	07° 33'	03° 07'	09° 07'R	17° 47'	01° 30'	28° 29'R	10° 25'
25 Fr	04° 12'	18°♋31'	05° 04'	01°♊10'	22° 14'R	12° 03'	25° 53'	23° 33'R	09° 36'	07° 35'	03° 07'	09° 06'R	18° 11'	01° 45'	28° 16'R	10° 51'
26 Sa	05° 09'	00°♌57'	05° 04'R	03° 21'	21° 51'R	12° 25'	26° 07'	23° 30'R	09° 37'	07° 38'	03° 08'	09° 05'R	18° 35'	02° 00'	28° 02'R	11° 17'
27 Su	06° 07'	13°♌38'	05° 04'R	05° 32'	21° 25'R	12° 48'	26° 21'	23° 27'R	09° 38'	07° 40'	03° 08'	09° 03'R	18° 59'	02° 14'	27° 49'R	11° 43'
28 Mo	07° 05'	26°♌38'	05° 03'R	07° 44'	20° 58'R	13° 10'	26° 35'	23° 25'R	09° 39'	07° 42'	03° 08'	09° 02'R	19° 23'	02° 29'	27° 36'R	12° 10'
29 Tu	08° 02'	09°♍59'	05° 03'	09° 56'	20° 28'R	13° 33'	26° 49'	23° 22'R	09° 39'	07° 44'	03° 08'	09° 01'R	19° 47'	02° 43'	27° 22'R	12° 36'
30 We	09° 00'	23°♍43'	05° 04'	12° 08'	19° 57'R	13° 57'	27° 03'	23° 19'R	09° 40'	07° 46'	03° 09'	09° 00'R	20° 11'	02° 58'	27° 09'R	13° 02'
31 Th	09° 57'	07°♎50'	05° 04'	14° 19'	19° 24'R	14° 20'	27° 18'	23° 17'R	09° 41'	07° 48'	03° 09'	08° 58'R	20° 35'	03° 12'	26° 57'R	13° 28'

MOON ASPECTS | JUNE 2012

All times Eastern Time

Fri 01	1:37 P ☽ △ ♆		10:49 A ☽ △ ♀		8:09 A ☽ △ ♂	Sun 24	8:06 A ☽ □ ?
	10:55 P ☽ ✶ ♇		4:22 P ☽ □ ⚷		12:48 P ☽ ☍ ⚴		1:00 P ☽ □ ♃
Sat 02	12:10 A ☽ △ ⚷		6:35 P ☽ △ ☉		7:55 P ☽ ☌ ?		1:15 P ☽ ☍ ♆
	7:55 A ☽ ☍ ⚵	Sat 09	2:35 A ☽ △ ♄	Sun 17	3:58 A ☽ ☌ ♃		2:18 P ☽ ✶ ☉
	9:14 A ☽ ✶ ♂		4:59 A ☽ □ ?		7:42 A ☽ □ ♆		2:23 P ☽ □ ☊
	7:27 P ☽ ☍ ?		6:19 A ☽ □ ⚴		9:37 A ☽ ☍ ☊		9:32 P ☽ □ ♀
Sun 03	2:35 A ☽ ☌ ⚴		2:33 P ☽ □ ♃		3:35 P ☽ ✶ ♀		10:54 P ☽ △ ♇
	5:29 A ☽ ☍ ♃		9:09 P ☽ ☌ ♆		6:09 P ☽ ✶ ♅	Mon 25	1:14 A ☽ ☍ ⚷
	1:33 P ☽ □ ♆		11:34 P ☽ □ ☊		8:13 P ☽ ☌ ♀	Tue 26	12:08 A ☽ ✶ ♃
	3:01 P ☽ △ ♀	Sun 10	1:11 A ☽ △ ⚵		9:06 P ☽ □ ⚷		3:45 A ☽ △ ⚵
	4:08 P ☽ ☌ ☊		7:34 A ☽ ✶ ♇	Mon 18	11:11 P ☽ □ ♂		6:53 A ☽ ☌ ♂
	9:09 P ☽ △ ♅		9:28 A ☽ ☌ ⚷		11:16 P ☽ △ ♄		2:40 P ☽ ✶ ⚵
Mon 04	12:00 A ☽ □ ⚷		3:16 P ☽ □ ♀	Tue 19	11:02 A ☽ ☌ ☉		3:10 P ☽ △ ?
	7:12 A ☽ ☍ ☉	Mon 11	1:40 A ☽ ✶ ⚵		7:40 P ☽ △ ♆		7:10 P ☽ △ ⚵
	10:22 A ☽ □ ♂		3:16 A ☽ ☍ ♂	Wed 20	4:16 A ☽ □ ♀		7:27 P ☽ ✶ ☊
	11:02 A ☽ ☍ ♀		6:41 A ☽ □ ☉		5:57 A ☽ □ ♅		11:30 P ☽ □ ☉
	9:23 P ☽ ✶ ♄		1:52 P ☽ △ ⚵		6:16 A ☽ ☍ ♇	Wed 27	2:16 A ☽ △ ♀
Tue 05	1:08 A ☽ ☍ ⚵		3:06 P ☽ ✶ ?		8:40 A ☽ △ ⚷		3:42 A ☽ □ ♇
	1:38 P ☽ ✶ ♆	Tue 12	12:34 A ☽ ✶ ♃	Thu 21	9:40 A ☽ ✶ ⚵		3:54 A ☽ ☍ ♅
	3:53 P ☽ □ ♀		8:51 A ☽ △ ☊		9:58 A ☽ □ ♄		4:16 A ☽ ☍ ♀
	9:31 P ☽ □ ♅		12:09 P ☽ ☌ ♀		10:34 A ☽ △ ⚵	Thu 28	4:22 A ☽ ☌ ♄
	10:55 P ☽ ☌ ♇		4:28 P ☽ ☌ ♅		12:18 P ☽ ✶ ♂		9:33 P ☽ △ ♆
Wed 06	12:23 A ☽ ✶ ⚷		5:29 P ☽ □ ♇		12:48 P ☽ ☌ ⚵		10:13 P ☽ □ ⚵
	11:16 A ☽ △ ⚵		9:05 P ☽ □ ⚵		10:25 P ☽ ✶ ?	Fri 29	5:59 A ☽ △ ☉
	12:33 P ☽ △ ♂		11:09 P ☽ ✶ ♀	Fri 22	4:19 A ☽ ✶ ♃		6:20 A ☽ ✶ ♇
	10:29 P ☽ □ ♄	Wed 13	9:55 P ☽ ☍ ♄		6:59 A ☽ △ ☊		8:34 A ☽ △ ⚷
	11:07 P ☽ △ ?		11:09 P ☽ ✶ ☉		2:45 P ☽ △ ♀	Sat 30	5:10 A ☽ ☌ ⚵
Thu 07	2:33 A ☽ ✶ ⚵	Thu 14	6:42 P ☽ ✶ ♆		2:50 P ☽ ✶ ♀		12:05 P ☽ ☍ ⚵
	8:38 A ☽ △ ♃	Fri 15	5:53 A ☽ △ ♇		3:38 P ☽ △ ♅		3:46 P ☽ ✶ ♂
	6:07 P ☽ ✶ ☊		8:11 A ☽ ✶ ⚷	Sat 23	6:26 P ☽ ✶ ♄		10:32 P ☽ ☍ ?
	6:52 P ☽ ✶ ♀		8:00 P ☽ ✶ ⚵		6:29 P ☽ □ ⚵		10:54 P ☽ □ ♆
Fri 08	12:09 A ☽ ✶ ♅	Sat 16	6:02 A ☽ ☌ ⚵		8:01 P ☽ □ ⚵		11:30 P ☽ ☌ ☊

ADDITIONAL MONTHLY EPHEMERIDES

CENTAURS

2012	PHOLUS	NESSUS	ASBOLUS	CHARIKLO	HYLON.
Jun					
3	18°♐26'R	26°♒17'R	27°♉32'	10°♐07'R	19°♐39'R
8	18° 15'R	26° 15'R	27° 52'	9° 50'R	19° 28'R
13	18° 04'R	26° 12'R	28° 12'	9° 33'R	19° 17'R
18	17° 53'R	26° 08'R	28° 31'	9° 17'R	19° 07'R
23	17° 43'R	26° 03'R	28° 49'	9° 02'R	18° 56'R
28	17° 32'R	25° 58'R	29° 07'	8° 47'R	18° 46'R

01	05°♊37'R	11	13° 59'R	21	26° 06'
02	03° 27'R	12	13° 22'R	22	00°♊15'
03	01° 29'R	13	13° 31'	23	04° 56'
04	29°♉43'R	14	14° 10'	24	09° 40'
05	27° 54'R	15	15° 05'	25	13° 48'
06	25° 48'R	16	16° 06'	26	16° 46'
07	23° 17'R	17	17° 12'	27	18° 13'
08	20° 29'R	18	18° 31'	28	18° 11'R
09	17° 45'R	19	20° 18'	29	17° 04'R
10	15° 29'R	20	22° 47'	30	15° 24'R
BLACK MOON LILITH ⚸					

JUNE 2012 EPHEMERIS

Ephemeris calculated for 12 Midnight GMT.

DAY	☉	☽	☊T.N.	☿	♀	♂	♃	♄	⚷	♅	♆	♇	⚳	⚴	⚵	⚶
01 Fr	10°♊55'	22°♎19'	05°♐04'	16°♊29'	18°♊50'R	14°♍44'	27°♉32'	23°♎15'R	09°♓42'	07°♈50'	03°♓09'	08°♑57'R	20°♉59'	03°♈26'	26°♏44'R	13°♉54'
02 Sa	11° 52'	07°♏07'	05° 05'	18° 39'	18° 15'R	15° 09'	27° 45'	23° 12'R	09° 42'	07° 52'	03° 09'	08° 56'R	21° 23'	03° 40'	26° 31'R	14° 20'
03 Su	12° 50'	22°♏07'	05° 05'	20° 47'	17° 39'R	15° 33'	27° 59'	23° 10'R	09° 43'	07° 54'	03° 09'	08° 54'R	21° 47'	03° 54'	26° 19'R	14° 46'
04 Mo	13° 47'	07°♐12'	05° 05'R	22° 54'	17° 02'R	15° 58'	28° 13'	23° 08'R	09° 43'	07° 56'	03° 09'	08° 53'R	22° 10'	04° 08'	26° 06'R	15° 12'
05 Tu	14° 45'	22°♐14'	05° 05'R	24° 59'	16° 24'R	16° 23'	28° 27'	23° 06'R	09° 44'	07° 57'	03° 09'R	08° 52'R	22° 34'	04° 21'	25° 54'R	15° 37'
06 We	15° 42'	07°♑04'	05° 04'R	27° 02'	15° 47'R	16° 48'	28° 41'	23° 04'R	09° 44'	07° 59'	03° 09'R	08° 50'R	22° 58'	04° 34'	25° 42'R	16° 03'
07 Th	16° 39'	21°♑34'	05° 03'R	29° 04'	15° 09'R	17° 14'	28° 55'	23° 02'R	09° 44'	08° 01'	03° 09'R	08° 49'R	23° 22'	04° 48'	25° 30'R	16° 29'
08 Fr	17° 37'	05°♒40'	05° 02'R	01°♋03'	14° 31'R	17° 40'	29° 09'	23° 01'R	09° 45'	08° 03'	03° 09'R	08° 48'R	23° 46'	05° 01'	25° 19'R	16° 55'
09 Sa	18° 34'	19°♒19'	05° 00'R	03° 00'	13° 54'R	18° 06'	29° 23'	22° 59'R	09° 45'	08° 04'	03° 09'R	08° 46'R	24° 09'	05° 14'	25° 08'R	17° 20'
10 Su	19° 32'	02°♓31'	04° 59'R	04° 55'	13° 18'R	18° 33'	29° 36'	22° 57'R	09° 45'	08° 06'	03° 09'R	08° 45'R	24° 33'	05° 26'	24° 56'R	17° 46'
11 Mo	20° 29'	15°♓19'	04° 58'R	06° 47'	12° 43'R	18° 59'	29° 50'	22° 56'R	09° 45'	08° 07'	03° 08'R	08° 43'R	24° 57'	05° 39'	24° 45'R	18° 11'
12 Tu	21° 26'	27°♓46'	04° 58'	08° 37'	12° 09'R	19° 26'	00°♊04'	22° 55'R	09° 45'	08° 09'	03° 08'R	08° 42'R	25° 20'	05° 51'	24° 35'R	18° 37'
13 We	22° 24'	09°♈57'	04° 59'	10° 25'	11° 36'R	19° 54'	00° 17'	22° 53'R	09° 45'R	08° 10'	03° 08'R	08° 41'R	25° 44'	06° 04'	24° 24'R	19° 02'
14 Th	23° 21'	21°♈55'	05° 00'	12° 10'	11° 05'R	20° 21'	00° 31'	22° 52'R	09° 45'R	08° 12'	03° 08'R	08° 39'R	26° 07'	06° 16'	24° 14'R	19° 27'
15 Fr	24° 18'	03°♉46'	05° 02'	13° 52'	10° 35'R	20° 49'	00° 45'	22° 51'R	09° 45'R	08° 13'	03° 07'R	08° 38'R	26° 31'	06° 28'	24° 04'R	19° 53'
16 Sa	25° 16'	15°♉33'	05° 03'	15° 33'	10° 08'R	21° 17'	00° 58'	22° 50'R	09° 45'R	08° 14'	03° 07'R	08° 36'R	26° 54'	06° 39'	23° 54'R	20° 18'
17 Su	26° 13'	27°♉20'	05° 04'	17° 10'	09° 42'R	21° 45'	01° 12'	22° 49'R	09° 45'R	08° 16'	03° 07'R	08° 35'R	27° 18'	06° 51'	23° 45'R	20° 43'
18 Mo	27° 10'	09°♊12'	05° 04'R	18° 45'	09° 18'R	22° 13'	01° 25'	22° 48'R	09° 44'R	08° 17'	03° 06'R	08° 33'R	27° 41'	07° 02'	23° 36'R	21° 08'
19 Tu	28° 07'	21°♊09'	05° 03'R	20° 18'	08° 57'R	22° 42'	01° 39'	22° 48'R	09° 44'R	08° 18'	03° 06'R	08° 32'R	28° 05'	07° 13'	23° 27'R	21° 33'
20 We	29° 05'	03°♋16'	05° 01'R	21° 48'	08° 38'R	23° 10'	01° 52'	22° 47'R	09° 44'R	08° 19'	03° 05'R	08° 30'R	28° 28'	07° 24'	23° 18'R	21° 58'
21 Th	00°♋02'	15°♋32'	04° 58'R	23° 15'	08° 21'R	23° 39'	02° 05'	22° 47'R	09° 43'R	08° 20'	03° 05'R	08° 29'R	28° 51'	07° 35'	23° 10'R	22° 23'
22 Fr	00° 59'	28°♋01'	04° 54'R	24° 40'	08° 07'R	24° 09'	02° 19'	22° 46'R	09° 43'R	08° 21'	03° 04'R	08° 27'R	29° 15'	07° 46'	23° 02'R	22° 48'
23 Sa	01° 57'	10°♌42'	04° 50'R	26° 02'	07° 54'R	24° 38'	02° 32'	22° 46'R	09° 42'R	08° 22'	03° 04'R	08° 26'R	29° 38'	07° 56'	22° 54'R	23° 13'
24 Su	02° 54'	23°♌37'	04° 46'R	27° 22'	07° 45'R	25° 08'	02° 45'	22° 46'R	09° 41'R	08° 23'	03° 03'R	08° 24'R	00°♊01'	08° 07'	22° 47'R	23° 37'
25 Mo	03° 51'	06°♍46'	04° 43'R	28° 39'	07° 37'R	25° 38'	02° 58'	22° 46'R	09° 41'R	08° 24'	03° 03'R	08° 23'R	00° 24'	08° 17'	22° 40'R	24° 02'
26 Tu	04° 48'	20°♍11'	04° 41'R	29° 53'	07° 32'R	26° 08'	03° 11'	22° 46'	09° 40'R	08° 25'	03° 02'R	08° 21'R	00° 47'	08° 26'	22° 33'R	24° 27'
27 We	05° 46'	03°♎53'	04° 40'R	01°♌04'	07° 30'R	26° 38'	03° 24'	22° 46'	09° 39'R	08° 26'	03° 01'R	08° 20'R	01° 10'	08° 36'	22° 26'R	24° 51'
28 Th	06° 43'	17°♎50'	04° 40'	02° 12'	07° 29'	27° 09'	03° 37'	22° 46'	09° 38'R	08° 27'	03° 01'R	08° 18'R	01° 33'	08° 45'	22° 20'R	25° 15'
29 Fr	07° 40'	02°♏04'	04° 41'	03° 18'	07° 31'	27° 39'	03° 50'	22° 46'	09° 37'R	08° 27'	03° 00'R	08° 17'R	01° 56'	08° 54'	22° 14'R	25° 40'
30 Sa	08° 37'	16°♏32'	04° 43'	04° 20'	07° 36'	28° 10'	04° 03'	22° 47'	09° 36'R	08° 28'	02° 59'R	08° 15'R	02° 19'	09° 03'	22° 09'R	26° 04'

MOON ASPECTS | JULY 2012

All times Eastern Time

Day	Time	Aspect
Sun 01	1:05 A	☽ ☍ ♃
	3:11 A	☽ △ ☿
	6:42 A	☽ ☍ ♀
	7:52 A	☽ △ ♅
	9:10 A	☽ △ ⚴
	9:39 A	☽ □ ⚷
Mon 02	7:08 A	☽ ✶ ♄
	6:21 P	☽ □ ♂
	11:39 P	☽ ✶ ♆
Tue 03	8:12 A	☽ ☌ ♇
	8:45 A	☽ □ ♅
	10:27 A	☽ ✶ ⚷
	10:29 A	☽ □ ⚴
	2:52 P	☽ ☍ ☉
Wed 04	6:43 A	☽ ✶ ⚵
	8:25 A	☽ □ ♄
	5:06 P	☽ △ ⚶
	9:49 P	☽ △ ♂
Thu 05	1:42 A	☽ ✶ ☊
	3:46 A	☽ △ ⚳
	5:12 A	☽ △ ♃
	10:53 A	☽ ✶ ♅
	11:08 A	☽ △ ♀
	12:00 P	☽ ☍ ☿
	1:08 P	☽ ✶ ⚴
Fri 06	9:43 A	☽ □ ⚵
	11:48 A	☽ △ ♄
	10:32 P	☽ □ ⚶
Sat 07	5:39 A	☽ ☌ ♆
	5:53 A	☽ □ ☊
	9:51 A	☽ □ ⚳
	10:40 A	☽ □ ♃
	3:04 P	☽ ✶ ♇
	5:29 P	☽ □ ♀
	5:37 P	☽ ☌ ⚷
Sun 08	6:59 A	☽ △ ☉
	4:10 P	☽ △ ⚵
Mon 09	7:56 A	☽ ✶ ⚶
	1:47 P	☽ △ ☊
	2:41 P	☽ ☍ ♂
	8:02 P	☽ ✶ ⚳
	8:06 P	☽ ✶ ♃
	11:44 P	☽ □ ♇
Tue 10	12:47 A	☽ ☌ ♅
	4:18 A	☽ ✶ ♀
	4:22 A	☽ ☌ ⚴
	6:59 A	☽ △ ☿
	9:48 P	☽ □ ☉
Wed 11	5:23 A	☽ ☍ ♄
Thu 12	1:09 A	☽ ✶ ♆
	11:34 A	☽ △ ♇
	2:23 P	☽ ✶ ⚷
	8:35 P	☽ □ ☿
Fri 13	3:02 P	☽ ☍ ⚵
	3:46 P	☽ ✶ ☉
Sat 14	12:12 P	☽ ☌ ⚶
	1:45 P	☽ ☍ ☊
	2:01 P	☽ □ ♆
	9:05 P	☽ △ ♂
	10:56 P	☽ ☌ ♃
Sun 15	12:41 A	☽ ☌ ⚳
	1:43 A	☽ ✶ ♅
	3:10 A	☽ □ ⚷
	6:21 A	☽ ✶ ⚴
	9:46 A	☽ ✶ ☿
	10:30 A	☽ ☌ ♀
Mon 16	6:56 A	☽ △ ♄
Tue 17	1:49 A	☽ △ ♆
	11:34 A	☽ □ ♂
	11:48 A	☽ ☍ ♇
	1:12 P	☽ □ ♅
	2:27 P	☽ △ ⚷
	6:02 P	☽ □ ⚴
Wed 18	2:00 P	☽ △ ⚵
	5:24 P	☽ □ ♄
Thu 19	12:24 A	☽ ☌ ☉
	10:38 A	☽ △ ☊
	1:17 P	☽ ✶ ⚶
	9:22 P	☽ ✶ ♃
	10:08 P	☽ △ ♅
	11:12 P	☽ ✶ ♂
Fri 20	12:35 A	☽ ✶ ⚳
	3:03 A	☽ △ ⚴
	3:34 A	☽ ☌ ☿
	11:51 A	☽ ✶ ♀
	9:57 P	☽ □ ⚵
Sat 21	1:17 A	☽ ✶ ♄
	5:26 P	☽ □ ☊
	6:05 P	☽ ☍ ♆
	9:46 P	☽ □ ⚶
Sun 22	3:14 A	☽ △ ♇
	4:44 A	☽ □ ♃
	5:35 A	☽ ☍ ⚷
	8:33 A	☽ □ ⚳
	8:44 P	☽ □ ♀
Mon 23	3:47 A	☽ ✶ ⚵
	9:23 P	☽ ✶ ☉
	10:20 P	☽ ✶ ☊
Tue 24	4:13 A	☽ △ ⚶
	7:59 A	☽ □ ♇
	9:26 A	☽ ☍ ♅
	10:15 A	☽ △ ♃
	10:32 A	☽ ✶ ☿
	2:27 P	☽ ☍ ⚴
	2:38 P	☽ △ ⚳
	3:09 P	☽ ☌ ♂
Wed 25	3:56 A	☽ △ ♀
	11:22 A	☽ ☌ ♄
Thu 26	2:46 A	☽ △ ♆
	4:56 A	☽ □ ☉
	11:28 A	☽ ✶ ♇
	11:38 A	☽ □ ☿
	1:36 P	☽ △ ⚷
Fri 27	11:24 A	☽ ☌ ⚵
Sat 28	4:29 A	☽ ☌ ☊
	5:25 A	☽ □ ♆
	11:16 A	☽ △ ☉
	11:47 A	☽ △ ☿
	1:10 P	☽ ☍ ⚶
	3:28 P	☽ △ ♅
	4:02 P	☽ □ ⚷
	5:37 P	☽ ☍ ♃
	8:32 P	☽ △ ⚴
	11:08 P	☽ ☍ ⚳
Sun 29	1:23 A	☽ ✶ ♂
	3:07 P	☽ ☍ ♀
	5:01 P	☽ ✶ ♄
Mon 30	7:30 A	☽ ✶ ♆
	4:04 P	☽ ☌ ♇
	5:34 P	☽ □ ♅
	6:03 P	☽ ✶ ⚷
	10:43 P	☽ □ ⚴
Tue 31	5:43 A	☽ □ ♂
	4:26 P	☽ ✶ ⚵
	7:30 P	☽ □ ♄

ADDITIONAL MONTHLY EPHEMERIDES

CENTAURS

2012	PHOLUS	NESSUS	ASBOLUS	CHARIKLO	HYLON.
JUL					
3	17°♐22'R	25°♒51'R	29°♉23'	8°♐34'R	18°♐36'R
8	17° 13'R	25° 44'R	29° 39'	8° 21'R	18° 27'R
13	17° 04'R	25° 36'R	29° 54'	8° 10'R	18° 18'R
18	16° 55'R	25° 28'R	0°♊08'	8° 01'R	18° 10'R
23	16° 48'R	25° 19'R	0° 21'	7° 52'R	18° 02'R
28	16° 41'R	25° 09'R	0° 32'	7° 46'R	17° 56'R

01	13°♊41'R	11	21° 40'R	21	22° 56'
02	12° 06'R	12	20° 54'R	22	27° 27'
03	10° 35'R	13	20° 26'R	23	02°♊49'
04	08° 50'R	14	20° 03'R	24	08° 07'
05	06° 37'R	15	19° 33'R	25	12° 30'
06	03° 51'R	16	18° 54'R	26	15° 22'
07	00° 44'R	17	18° 13'R	27	16° 41'
08	27°♉40'R	18	17° 49'R	28	16° 51'R
09	25° 00'R	19	18° 12'	29	16° 28'R
10	22° 59'R	20	19° 49'	30	16° 03'R
BLACK MOON LILITH ⚸				31	15° 44'R

JULY 2012 EPHEMERIS

Ephemeris calculated for 12 Midnight GMT.

DAY	☉	☽	☊T.N.	☿	♀	♂	♃	♄	⚷	♅	♆	♇	⚳	⚴	⚵	⚶
01 Su	09°♋34'	01°♐11'	04°♐44'	05°♌19'	07°♊42'	28°♍41'	04°♊16'	22°♎47'	09°♓35'R	08°♈29'	02°♓58'R	08°♑14'R	02°♊42'	09°♈12'	22°♏04'R	26°♉28'
02 Mo	10° 32'	15°♐57'	04° 43'R	06° 15'	07° 51'	29° 12'	04° 28'	22° 48'	09° 34'R	08° 29'	02° 57'R	08° 12'R	03° 05'	09° 20'	21° 59'R	26° 52'
03 Tu	11° 29'	00°♑42'	04° 41'R	07° 07'	08° 01'	29° 44'	04° 41'	22° 49'	09° 33'R	08° 30'	02° 57'R	08° 11'R	03° 28'	09° 29'	21° 54'R	27° 16'
04 We	12° 26'	15°♑21'	04° 37'R	07° 56'	08° 14'	00°♎15'	04° 54'	22° 50'	09° 32'R	08° 30'	02° 56'R	08° 09'R	03° 51'	09° 37'	21° 50'R	27° 40'
05 Th	13° 23'	29°♑45'	04° 32'R	08° 42'	08° 29'	00° 47'	05° 06'	22° 50'	09° 31'R	08° 31'	02° 55'R	08° 08'R	04° 13'	09° 44'	21° 46'R	28° 04'
06 Fr	14° 20'	13°♒49'	04° 26'R	09° 24'	08° 46'	01° 19'	05° 19'	22° 51'	09° 29'R	08° 31'	02° 54'R	08° 06'R	04° 36'	09° 52'	21° 43'R	28° 28'
07 Sa	15° 17'	27°♒29'	04° 20'R	10° 02'	09° 04'	01° 51'	05° 31'	22° 53'	09° 28'R	08° 31'	02° 53'R	08° 05'R	04° 58'	09° 59'	21° 39'R	28° 52'
08 Su	16° 15'	10°♓45'	04° 15'R	10° 36'	09° 25'	02° 23'	05° 44'	22° 54'	09° 27'R	08° 32'	02° 52'R	08° 03'R	05° 21'	10° 06'	21° 37'R	29° 16'
09 Mo	17° 12'	23°♓36'	04° 10'R	11° 06'	09° 47'	02° 55'	05° 56'	22° 55'	09° 25'R	08° 32'	02° 51'R	08° 02'R	05° 43'	10° 13'	21° 34'R	29° 39'
10 Tu	18° 09'	06°♈05'	04° 08'R	11° 31'	10° 11'	03° 28'	06° 08'	22° 56'	09° 24'R	08° 32'	02° 50'R	08° 00'R	06° 06'	10° 20'	21° 32'R	00°♊03'
11 We	19° 06'	18°♈16'	04° 07'R	11° 53'	10° 37'	04° 00'	06° 20'	22° 58'	09° 22'R	08° 32'	02° 49'R	07° 59'R	06° 28'	10° 26'	21° 30'R	00° 26'
12 Th	20° 03'	00°♉15'	04° 07'	12° 10'	11° 04'	04° 33'	06° 32'	23° 00'	09° 21'R	08° 32'	02° 48'R	07° 57'R	06° 50'	10° 32'	21° 28'R	00° 49'
13 Fr	21° 01'	12°♉05'	04° 09'	12° 22'	11° 33'	05° 06'	06° 44'	23° 01'	09° 19'R	08° 32'	02° 47'R	07° 56'R	07° 13'	10° 38'	21° 27'R	01° 12'
14 Sa	21° 58'	23°♉53'	04° 10'	12° 30'	12° 03'	05° 39'	06° 56'	23° 03'	09° 17'R	08° 32'R	02° 46'R	07° 54'R	07° 35'	10° 43'	21° 26'R	01° 36'
15 Su	22° 55'	05°♊42'	04° 10'R	12° 33'	12° 34'	06° 13'	07° 08'	23° 05'	09° 16'R	08° 32'R	02° 44'R	07° 53'R	07° 57'	10° 48'	21° 25'R	01° 59'
16 Mo	23° 52'	17°♊38'	04° 09'R	12° 31'R	13° 07'	06° 46'	07° 20'	23° 07'	09° 14'R	08° 32'R	02° 43'R	07° 51'R	08° 19'	10° 53'	21° 25'R	02° 22'
17 Tu	24° 50'	29°♊44'	04° 06'R	12° 24'R	13° 41'	07° 20'	07° 32'	23° 09'	09° 12'R	08° 32'R	02° 42'R	07° 50'R	08° 41'	10° 58'	21° 25'	02° 44'
18 We	25° 47'	12°♋03'	04° 01'R	12° 12'R	14° 17'	07° 54'	07° 43'	23° 11'	09° 10'R	08° 32'R	02° 41'R	07° 48'R	09° 03'	11° 02'	21° 25'	03° 07'
19 Th	26° 44'	24°♋35'	03° 54'R	11° 56'R	14° 54'	08° 28'	07° 55'	23° 13'	09° 08'R	08° 32'R	02° 40'R	07° 47'R	09° 25'	11° 06'	21° 26'	03° 30'
20 Fr	27° 42'	07°♌23'	03° 45'R	11° 35'R	15° 31'	09° 02'	08° 06'	23° 16'	09° 06'R	08° 31'R	02° 38'R	07° 46'R	09° 47'	11° 10'	21° 27'	03° 52'
21 Sa	28° 39'	20°♌24'	03° 36'R	11° 10'R	16° 10'	09° 36'	08° 17'	23° 18'	09° 04'R	08° 31'R	02° 37'R	07° 44'R	10° 08'	11° 13'	21° 28'	04° 15'
22 Su	29° 36'	03°♍40'	03° 27'R	10° 40'R	16° 51'	10° 10'	08° 29'	23° 21'	09° 02'R	08° 31'R	02° 36'R	07° 43'R	10° 30'	11° 16'	21° 30'	04° 37'
23 Mo	00°♌33'	17°♍08'	03° 19'R	10° 07'R	17° 32'	10° 45'	08° 40'	23° 23'	09° 00'R	08° 30'R	02° 35'R	07° 41'R	10° 51'	11° 19'	21° 32'	04° 59'
24 Tu	01° 31'	00°♎47'	03° 13'R	09° 31'R	18° 14'	11° 19'	08° 51'	23° 26'	08° 58'R	08° 30'R	02° 33'R	07° 40'R	11° 13'	11° 21'	21° 34'	05° 22'
25 We	02° 28'	14°♎35'	03° 09'R	08° 52'R	18° 57'	11° 54'	09° 02'	23° 29'	08° 56'R	08° 29'R	02° 32'R	07° 39'R	11° 34'	11° 23'	21° 36'	05° 44'
26 Th	03° 25'	28°♎33'	03° 08'R	08° 10'R	19° 41'	12° 29'	09° 13'	23° 32'	08° 54'R	08° 29'R	02° 30'R	07° 37'R	11° 56'	11° 25'	21° 39'	06° 06'
27 Fr	04° 23'	12°♏38'	03° 08'	07° 28'R	20° 26'	13° 04'	09° 24'	23° 35'	08° 52'R	08° 28'R	02° 29'R	07° 36'R	12° 17'	11° 27'	21° 42'	06° 27'
28 Sa	05° 20'	26°♏51'	03° 09'	06° 44'R	21° 11'	13° 39'	09° 34'	23° 38'	08° 49'R	08° 27'R	02° 28'R	07° 35'R	12° 38'	11° 28'	21° 46'	06° 49'
29 Su	06° 17'	11°♐09'	03° 09'R	06° 00'R	21° 58'	14° 14'	09° 45'	23° 41'	08° 47'R	08° 27'R	02° 26'R	07° 33'R	12° 59'	11° 29'	21° 50'	07° 11'
30 Mo	07° 15'	25°♐31'	03° 07'R	05° 17'R	22° 45'	14° 50'	09° 55'	23° 44'	08° 45'R	08° 26'R	02° 25'R	07° 32'R	13° 20'	11° 29'	21° 54'	07° 32'
31 Tu	08° 12'	09°♑52'	03° 02'R	04° 36'R	23° 33'	15° 25'	10° 06'	23° 48'	08° 42'R	08° 25'R	02° 23'R	07° 31'R	13° 41'	11° 29'R	21° 58'	07° 53'

MOON ASPECTS | AUGUST 2012

All times Eastern Time

Day	Time	Aspect
Wed 01	8:47 A	☽ ✶ ☊
	11:58 A	☽ ☍ ☿
	8:15 P	☽ ✶ ♅
	8:38 P	☽ △ ⚶
	11:27 P	☽ ☍ ☉
	11:50 P	☽ △ ♃
Thu 02	1:34 A	☽ ✶ ⚴
	6:50 A	☽ △ ⚸
	11:06 A	☽ △ ♂
	8:13 P	☽ □ ⚵
	11:19 P	☽ △ ♄
Fri 03	3:24 A	☽ △ ♀
	12:44 P	☽ □ ☊
	2:04 P	☽ ☌ ♆
	11:16 P	☽ ✶ ♇
Sat 04	1:16 A	☽ ☌ ⚷
	2:49 A	☽ □ ⚶
	5:27 A	☽ □ ♃
	1:36 P	☽ □ ⚸
Sun 05	2:44 A	☽ △ ⚵
	1:56 P	☽ □ ♀
	7:42 P	☽ △ ☊
	8:11 P	☽ △ ☿
Mon 06	7:04 A	☽ □ ♇
	8:51 A	☽ ☌ ♅
	12:31 P	☽ ✶ ⚶
	2:29 P	☽ ✶ ♃
	2:43 P	☽ ☌ ⚴
	9:45 P	☽ △ ☉
Tue 07	12:02 A	☽ ✶ ⚸
	7:27 A	☽ ☍ ♂
	4:04 P	☽ ☍ ♄
Wed 08	4:54 A	☽ ✶ ♀
	6:19 A	☽ □ ☿
	7:49 A	☽ ✶ ♆
	6:12 P	☽ △ ♇
	8:12 P	☽ ✶ ⚷
Thu 09	2:55 P	☽ □ ☉
Fri 10	1:52 A	☽ ☍ ⚵
	6:34 P	☽ ☍ ☊
	7:58 P	☽ ✶ ☿
	8:28 P	☽ □ ♆
Sat 11	8:50 A	☽ ✶ ♅
	8:51 A	☽ □ ⚷
	2:38 P	☽ ✶ ⚴
	4:23 P	☽ ☌ ⚶
	4:32 P	☽ ☌ ♃
Sun 12	4:16 A	☽ ☌ ⚸
	9:01 A	☽ ✶ ☉
	2:55 P	☽ △ ♂
	5:49 P	☽ △ ♄
Mon 13	8:29 A	☽ △ ♆
	3:45 P	☽ ☌ ♀
	6:41 P	☽ ☍ ♇
	8:20 P	☽ △ ⚷
	8:26 P	☽ □ ♅
Tue 14	1:44 A	☽ □ ⚴
Wed 15	2:05 A	☽ △ ⚵
	4:15 A	☽ □ ♂
	4:21 A	☽ □ ♄
	3:47 P	☽ △ ☊
	11:24 P	☽ ☌ ☿
Thu 16	5:04 A	☽ △ ♅
	9:46 A	☽ △ ⚴
	1:32 P	☽ ✶ ♃
	3:00 P	☽ ✶ ⚶
Fri 17	1:40 A	☽ ✶ ⚸
	9:47 A	☽ □ ⚵
	11:39 A	☽ ✶ ♄
	11:54 A	☽ ☌ ☉
	1:55 P	☽ ✶ ♂
	9:58 P	☽ □ ☊
	11:57 P	☽ ☍ ♆
Sat 18	9:13 A	☽ △ ♇
	10:27 A	☽ ☍ ⚷
	3:05 P	☽ ✶ ♀
	7:26 P	☽ □ ♃
	9:32 P	☽ □ ⚶
Sun 19	7:46 A	☽ □ ⚸
	2:56 P	☽ ✶ ⚵
Mon 20	1:55 A	☽ ✶ ☊
	1:00 P	☽ □ ♇
	2:25 P	☽ ☍ ♅
	6:08 P	☽ ☍ ⚴
	6:53 P	☽ ✶ ☿
	10:42 P	☽ □ ♀
	11:32 P	☽ △ ♃
Tue 21	2:15 A	☽ △ ⚶
	12:17 P	☽ △ ⚸
	8:00 P	☽ ☌ ♄
Wed 22	2:24 A	☽ ☌ ♂
	3:13 A	☽ ✶ ☉
	6:57 A	☽ △ ♆
	4:00 P	☽ ✶ ♇
	4:57 P	☽ △ ⚷
Thu 23	3:54 A	☽ □ ☿
	5:34 A	☽ △ ♀
	10:21 P	☽ ☌ ⚵
Fri 24	7:37 A	☽ ☌ ☊
	9:48 A	☽ □ ♆
	9:54 A	☽ □ ☉
	7:44 P	☽ □ ⚷
	8:12 P	☽ △ ♅
	11:06 P	☽ △ ⚴
Sat 25	6:25 A	☽ ☍ ♃
	10:25 A	☽ ☍ ⚶
	1:44 P	☽ △ ☿
	8:32 P	☽ ☍ ⚸
Sun 26	2:39 A	☽ ✶ ♄
	12:51 P	☽ ✶ ♆
	1:21 P	☽ ✶ ♂
	4:50 P	☽ △ ☉
	10:06 P	☽ ☌ ♇
	10:48 P	☽ ✶ ⚷
	11:19 P	☽ □ ♅
Mon 27	1:47 A	☽ □ ⚴
	8:02 P	☽ ☍ ♀
Tue 28	6:20 A	☽ ✶ ⚵
	6:33 A	☽ □ ♄
	2:02 P	☽ ✶ ☊
	7:37 P	☽ □ ♂
Wed 29	3:06 A	☽ ✶ ♅
	5:05 A	☽ ✶ ⚴
	2:44 P	☽ △ ♃
	8:11 P	☽ △ ⚶
Thu 30	6:46 A	☽ △ ⚸
	11:34 A	☽ △ ♄
	11:45 A	☽ □ ⚵
	1:48 P	☽ ☍ ☿
	6:43 P	☽ □ ☊
	9:20 P	☽ ☌ ♆
Fri 31	3:25 A	☽ △ ♂
	7:12 A	☽ ✶ ♇
	7:38 A	☽ ☌ ⚷
	9:58 A	☽ ☍ ☉
	8:58 P	☽ □ ♃

ADDITIONAL MONTHLY EPHEMERIDES

CENTAURS

2012 Aug	Pholus	Nessus	Asbolus	Chariklo	Hylon.
2	16°♐35′R	24°♒59′R	0°♊43′	7°♐41′R	17°♐50′R
7	16° 30′R	24° 49′R	0° 51′	7° 37′R	17° 45′R
12	16° 25′R	24° 39′R	0° 59′	7° 36′R	17° 42′R
17	16° 22′R	24° 28′R	1° 05′	7° 36′	17° 39′R
22	16° 20′R	24° 17′R	1° 10′	7° 38′	17° 37′R
27	16° 19′R	24° 07′R	1° 13′	7° 42′	17° 37′R

01	15°♊18′R	11	24° 46′R	21	14° 47′
02	14° 22′R	12	23° 24′R	22	16° 58′
03	12° 38′R	13	21° 36′R	23	19° 07′
04	10° 04′R	14	19° 19′R	24	21° 15′
05	06° 58′R	15	16° 45′R	25	23° 36′
06	03° 47′R	16	14° 16′R	26	26° 27′
07	00° 57′R	17	12° 20′R	27	29° 54′
08	28°♉44′R	18	11° 23′R	28	03°♊40′
09	27° 07′R	19	11° 36′	29	07° 11′
10	25° 54′R	20	12° 51′	30	09° 51′
Black Moon Lilith ⚸				31	11° 12′

AUGUST 2012 EPHEMERIS

Ephemeris calculated for 12 Midnight GMT.

DAY	☉	☽	☊T.N.	☿	♀	♂	♃	♄	⚷	♅	♆	♇	⚳	⚴	⚵	⚶
01 We	09°♌09'	24°♑08'	02°♐56'R	03°♌57'R	24°♊22'	16°♎01'	10°♊16'	23°♎51'	08°♓40'R	08°♈24'R	02°♓22'R	07°♑30'R	14°♊02'	11°♈29'R	22°♏02'	08°♊15'
02 Th	10° 07'	08°♒14'	02° 47'R	03° 21'R	25° 12'	16° 37'	10° 26'	23° 54'	08° 38'R	08° 23'R	02° 20'R	07° 28'R	14° 22'	11° 29'R	22° 07'	08° 36'
03 Fr	11° 04'	22°♒05'	02° 36'R	02° 49'R	26° 02'	17° 13'	10° 36'	23° 58'	08° 35'R	08° 22'R	02° 19'R	07° 27'R	14° 43'	11° 28'R	22° 12'	08° 57'
04 Sa	12° 02'	05°♓37'	02° 25'R	02° 21'R	26° 53'	17° 49'	10° 46'	24° 02'	08° 33'R	08° 21'R	02° 17'R	07° 26'R	15° 04'	11° 26'R	22° 18'	09° 17'
05 Su	12° 59'	18°♓47'	02° 15'R	01° 59'R	27° 44'	18° 25'	10° 56'	24° 05'	08° 30'R	08° 20'R	02° 16'R	07° 25'R	15° 24'	11° 25'R	22° 23'	09° 38'
06 Mo	13° 57'	01°♈36'	02° 06'R	01° 42'R	28° 37'	19° 01'	11° 06'	24° 09'	08° 28'R	08° 19'R	02° 14'R	07° 24'R	15° 44'	11° 23'R	22° 29'	09° 59'
07 Tu	14° 54'	14°♈04'	02° 00'R	01° 31'R	29° 30'	19° 38'	11° 16'	24° 13'	08° 25'R	08° 18'R	02° 13'R	07° 23'R	16° 05'	11° 21'R	22° 36'	10° 19'
08 We	15° 51'	26°♈15'	01° 57'R	01° 26'R	00°♋23'	20° 14'	11° 25'	24° 17'	08° 22'R	08° 17'R	02° 11'R	07° 21'R	16° 25'	11° 18'R	22° 42'	10° 40'
09 Th	16° 49'	08°♉14'	01° 55'R	01° 28'	01° 17'	20° 51'	11° 35'	24° 21'	08° 20'R	08° 16'R	02° 10'R	07° 20'R	16° 45'	11° 15'R	22° 49'	11° 00'
10 Fr	17° 47'	20°♉04'	01° 55'	01° 36'	02° 12'	21° 27'	11° 44'	24° 25'	08° 17'R	08° 15'R	02° 08'R	07° 19'R	17° 05'	11° 11'R	22° 56'	11° 20'
11 Sa	18° 44'	01°♊53'	01° 55'	01° 52'	03° 07'	22° 04'	11° 53'	24° 30'	08° 14'R	08° 13'R	02° 07'R	07° 18'R	17° 25'	11° 08'R	23° 03'	11° 40'
12 Su	19° 42'	13°♊44'	01° 54'R	02° 14'	04° 02'	22° 41'	12° 02'	24° 34'	08° 12'R	08° 12'R	02° 05'R	07° 17'R	17° 44'	11° 03'R	23° 11'	11° 59'
13 Mo	20° 39'	25°♊44'	01° 52'R	02° 44'	04° 58'	23° 18'	12° 11'	24° 38'	08° 09'R	08° 11'R	02° 03'R	07° 16'R	18° 04'	10° 59'R	23° 18'	12° 19'
14 Tu	21° 37'	07°♋56'	01° 48'R	03° 20'	05° 55'	23° 56'	12° 20'	24° 43'	08° 06'R	08° 09'R	02° 02'R	07° 15'R	18° 23'	10° 54'R	23° 26'	12° 38'
15 We	22° 35'	20°♋24'	01° 41'R	04° 03'	06° 52'	24° 33'	12° 29'	24° 47'	08° 04'R	08° 08'R	02° 00'R	07° 14'R	18° 43'	10° 49'R	23° 35'	12° 58'
16 Th	23° 32'	03°♌11'	01° 31'R	04° 54'	07° 49'	25° 10'	12° 37'	24° 52'	08° 01'R	08° 06'R	01° 59'R	07° 13'R	19° 02'	10° 43'R	23° 43'	13° 17'
17 Fr	24° 30'	16°♌17'	01° 20'R	05° 50'	08° 47'	25° 48'	12° 46'	24° 57'	07° 58'R	08° 05'R	01° 57'R	07° 12'R	19° 21'	10° 37'R	23° 52'	13° 36'
18 Sa	25° 28'	29°♌41'	01° 07'R	06° 54'	09° 46'	26° 25'	12° 54'	25° 01'	07° 55'R	08° 03'R	01° 55'R	07° 12'R	19° 40'	10° 31'R	24° 01'	13° 55'
19 Su	26° 25'	13°♍21'	00° 55'R	08° 03'	10° 44'	27° 03'	13° 02'	25° 06'	07° 52'R	08° 02'R	01° 54'R	07° 11'R	19° 59'	10° 24'R	24° 10'	14° 13'
20 Mo	27° 23'	27°♍14'	00° 45'R	09° 19'	11° 44'	27° 41'	13° 10'	25° 11'	07° 49'R	08° 00'R	01° 52'R	07° 10'R	20° 18'	10° 17'R	24° 19'	14° 32'
21 Tu	28° 21'	11°♎15'	00° 37'R	10° 40'	12° 43'	28° 19'	13° 18'	25° 16'	07° 47'R	07° 58'R	01° 50'R	07° 09'R	20° 36'	10° 09'R	24° 29'	14° 50'
22 We	29° 19'	25°♎21'	00° 31'R	12° 06'	13° 43'	28° 57'	13° 26'	25° 21'	07° 44'R	07° 57'R	01° 49'R	07° 08'R	20° 55'	10° 01'R	24° 39'	15° 08'
23 Th	00°♍17'	09°♏29'	00° 29'R	13° 37'	14° 43'	29° 35'	13° 33'	25° 26'	07° 41'R	07° 55'R	01° 47'R	07° 07'R	21° 13'	09° 53'R	24° 49'	15° 26'
24 Fr	01° 14'	23°♏37'	00° 28'R	15° 13'	15° 44'	00°♏14'	13° 41'	25° 31'	07° 38'R	07° 53'R	01° 45'R	07° 07'R	21° 31'	09° 44'R	24° 59'	15° 44'
25 Sa	02° 12'	07°♐44'	00° 28'R	16° 53'	16° 45'	00° 52'	13° 48'	25° 36'	07° 35'R	07° 51'R	01° 44'R	07° 06'R	21° 50'	09° 35'R	25° 10'	16° 02'
26 Su	03° 10'	21°♐49'	00° 27'R	18° 36'	17° 46'	01° 31'	13° 55'	25° 42'	07° 32'R	07° 49'R	01° 42'R	07° 05'R	22° 08'	09° 26'R	25° 20'	16° 19'
27 Mo	04° 08'	05°♑51'	00° 25'R	20° 23'	18° 48'	02° 09'	14° 02'	25° 47'	07° 29'R	07° 48'R	01° 41'R	07° 05'R	22° 25'	09° 16'R	25° 31'	16° 36'
28 Tu	05° 06'	19°♑49'	00° 20'R	22° 12'	19° 50'	02° 48'	14° 09'	25° 52'	07° 27'R	07° 46'R	01° 39'R	07° 04'R	22° 43'	09° 06'R	25° 42'	16° 53'
29 We	06° 04'	03°♒39'	00° 12'R	24° 04'	20° 52'	03° 27'	14° 16'	25° 58'	07° 24'R	07° 44'R	01° 37'R	07° 03'R	23° 00'	08° 55'R	25° 54'	17° 10'
30 Th	07° 02'	17°♒21'	00° 01'R	25° 57'	21° 54'	04° 06'	14° 23'	26° 03'	07° 21'R	07° 42'R	01° 36'R	07° 03'R	23° 18'	08° 45'R	26° 05'	17° 27'
31 Fr	08° 00'	00°♓50'	29°♏49'R	27° 52'	22° 57'	04° 45'	14° 29'	26° 09'	07° 18'R	07° 40'R	01° 34'R	07° 02'R	23° 35'	08° 33'R	26° 17'	17° 43'

MOON ASPECTS | SEPTEMBER 2012

All times Eastern Time

Day	Time	Aspect
Sat 01	3:23 A	☽ □ ⚶
	2:32 P	☽ □ ⚳
	4:02 P	☽ △ ♀
	7:23 P	☽ △ ⚵
Sun 02	1:36 A	☽ △ ☊
	2:55 P	☽ □ ♇
	3:59 P	☽ ☌ ♅
	4:48 P	☽ ☌ ⚴
Mon 03	5:57 A	☽ ⚹ ♃
	1:29 P	☽ ⚹ ⚶
Tue 04	1:20 A	☽ ⚹ ⚳
	4:54 A	☽ ☍ ♄
	7:06 A	☽ □ ♀
	2:32 P	☽ ⚹ ♆
Wed 05	1:38 A	☽ △ ♇
	1:44 A	☽ ⚹ ⚷
	4:08 A	☽ ☍ ♂
	4:08 A	☽ △ ☿
	2:54 P	☽ △ ☉
Thu 06	7:33 P	☽ ☍ ⚵
	11:37 P	☽ ☍ ☊
Fri 07	1:31 A	☽ ⚹ ♀
	2:57 A	☽ □ ♆
	2:15 P	☽ □ ⚷
	2:16 P	☽ ⚹ ⚴
	3:12 P	☽ ⚹ ♅
Sat 08	4:49 A	☽ □ ☿
	7:13 A	☽ ☌ ♃
	9:15 A	☽ □ ☉
	4:44 P	☽ ☌ ⚶
Sun 09	5:06 A	☽ ☌ ⚳
	6:59 A	☽ △ ♄
	3:25 P	☽ △ ♆
Mon 10	1:26 A	☽ □ ⚴
	2:19 A	☽ △ ⚷
	2:38 A	☽ ☍ ♇
	3:17 A	☽ □ ♅
	12:05 P	☽ △ ♂
Tue 11	1:54 A	☽ ⚹ ☉
	3:22 A	☽ ⚹ ☿
	5:58 P	☽ □ ♄
	8:54 P	☽ △ ⚵
	10:01 P	☽ △ ☊
Wed 12	9:48 A	☽ △ ⚴
	11:16 A	☽ ☌ ♀
	12:27 P	☽ △ ♅
	11:54 P	☽ □ ♂
Thu 13	3:53 A	☽ ⚹ ♃
	1:44 P	☽ ⚹ ⚶
Fri 14	12:49 A	☽ ⚹ ⚳
	1:14 A	☽ ⚹ ♄
	4:22 A	☽ □ ☊
	4:29 A	☽ □ ⚵
	7:35 A	☽ ☍ ♆
	5:01 P	☽ ☍ ⚷
	5:39 P	☽ △ ♇
Sat 15	7:33 A	☽ ⚹ ♂
	8:52 A	☽ □ ♃
	6:43 P	☽ □ ⚶
	10:11 P	☽ ☌ ☉
Sun 16	5:20 A	☽ □ ⚳
	7:26 A	☽ ☌ ☿
	7:38 A	☽ ⚹ ☊
	8:50 A	☽ ⚹ ⚵
	4:46 P	☽ ☍ ⚴
	8:33 P	☽ □ ♇
	8:42 P	☽ ☍ ♅
Mon 17	4:39 A	☽ ⚹ ♀
	11:27 A	☽ △ ♃
	9:34 P	☽ △ ⚶
Tue 18	7:30 A	☽ ☌ ♄
	8:02 A	☽ △ ⚳
	12:33 P	☽ △ ♆
	9:21 P	☽ △ ⚷
	10:16 P	☽ ⚹ ♇
Wed 19	10:29 A	☽ □ ♀
	4:33 P	☽ ☌ ♂
Thu 20	9:11 A	☽ ⚹ ☉
	10:56 A	☽ ☌ ☊
	2:15 P	☽ ☌ ⚵
	2:18 P	☽ □ ♆
	6:35 P	☽ △ ⚴
	11:09 P	☽ □ ⚷
Fri 21	12:06 A	☽ △ ♅
	12:53 A	☽ ⚹ ☿
	3:41 P	☽ ☍ ♃
	5:00 P	☽ △ ♀
Sat 22	3:04 A	☽ ☍ ⚶
	12:45 P	☽ ⚹ ♄
	2:07 P	☽ ☍ ⚳
	3:41 P	☽ □ ☉
	5:02 P	☽ ⚹ ♆
	8:32 P	☽ □ ⚴
Sun 23	2:02 A	☽ ⚹ ⚷
	3:02 A	☽ □ ♅
	3:19 A	☽ ☌ ♇
	11:02 A	☽ □ ☿
Mon 24	3:49 A	☽ ⚹ ♂
	5:19 P	☽ □ ♄
	5:25 P	☽ ⚹ ☊
	11:20 P	☽ ⚹ ⚵
	11:50 P	☽ ⚹ ⚴
	11:57 P	☽ △ ☉
Tue 25	7:26 A	☽ ⚹ ♅
	11:13 P	☽ △ ☿
Wed 26	12:31 A	☽ △ ♃
	11:27 A	☽ ☍ ♀
	12:05 P	☽ □ ♂
	1:41 P	☽ △ ⚶
	10:58 P	☽ □ ☊
	11:33 P	☽ △ ♄
Thu 27	1:44 A	☽ △ ⚳
	3:00 A	☽ ☌ ♆
	6:26 A	☽ □ ⚵
	12:27 P	☽ ☌ ⚷
	2:11 P	☽ ⚹ ♇
Fri 28	7:30 A	☽ □ ♃
	9:43 P	☽ □ ⚶
	10:34 P	☽ △ ♂
Sat 29	6:29 A	☽ △ ☊
	10:25 A	☽ □ ⚳
	11:29 A	☽ ☌ ⚴
	3:43 P	☽ △ ⚵
	9:41 P	☽ ☌ ♅
	10:35 P	☽ □ ♇
	11:19 P	☽ ☍ ☉
Sun 30	4:40 P	☽ ⚹ ♃

Additional Monthly Ephemerides

Centaurs

2012	Pholus	Nessus	Asbolus	Chariklo	Hylon.
Sep					
1	16°♐19′	23°♒57′R	1°♊14′	7°♐48′	17°♐37′
6	16° 20′	23° 47′R	1° 14′R	7° 55′	17° 39′
11	16° 22′	23° 37′R	1° 13′R	8° 04′	17° 42′
16	16° 25′	23° 28′R	1° 10′R	8° 15′	17° 46′
21	16° 29′	23° 20′R	1° 05′R	8° 27′	17° 51′
26	16° 34′	23° 12′R	0° 59′R	8° 41′	17° 57′

01	11°♊06'R	11	25° 20'R	21	05° 05'R
02	09° 51'R	12	22° 32'R	22	04° 23'R
03	07° 54'R	13	19° 18'R	23	04° 52'
04	05° 46'R	14	15° 59'R	24	07° 03'
05	03° 51'R	15	13° 05'R	25	11° 02'
06	02° 20'R	16	10° 52'R	26	16° 22'
07	01° 09'R	17	09° 23'R	27	22° 13'
08	00° 08'R	18	08° 21'R	28	27° 37'
09	29°♉01'R	19	07° 23'R	29	01°♊52'
10	27° 29'R	20	06° 15'R	30	04° 38'

Black Moon Lilith ⚸

SEPTEMBER 2012 EPHEMERIS

Ephemeris calculated for 12 Midnight GMT.

DAY	☉	☽	☊T.N.	☿	♀	♂	♃	♄	⚷	♅	♆	♇	⚳	⚴	⚵	⚶
01 Sa	08°♍58'	14°♓04'	29°♏37'R	29°♌48'	24°♋00'	05°♏24'	14°♊35'	26°♎15'	07°♓15'R	07°♈38'R	01°♓32'R	07°♑02'R	23°♊52'	08°♈22'R	26°♏29'	17°♊59'
02 Su	09° 56'	27°♓01'	29° 25'R	01°♍44'	25° 04'	06° 03'	14° 41'	26° 20'	07° 12'R	07° 36'R	01° 31'R	07° 01'R	24° 09'	08° 10'R	26° 41'	18° 15'
03 Mo	10° 54'	09°♈40'	29° 15'R	03° 41'	26° 07'	06° 42'	14° 47'	26° 26'	07° 09'R	07° 34'R	01° 29'R	07° 01'R	24° 26'	07° 58'R	26° 53'	18° 31'
04 Tu	11° 52'	22°♈03'	29° 08'R	05° 38'	27° 11'	07° 22'	14° 53'	26° 32'	07° 06'R	07° 32'R	01° 28'R	07° 00'R	24° 42'	07° 46'R	27° 06'	18° 47'
05 We	12° 50'	04°♉11'	29° 03'R	07° 35'	28° 16'	08° 01'	14° 59'	26° 38'	07° 03'R	07° 29'R	01° 26'R	07° 00'R	24° 59'	07° 33'R	27° 18'	19° 02'
06 Th	13° 48'	16°♉08'	29° 00'R	09° 32'	29° 20'	08° 41'	15° 04'	26° 44'	07° 01'R	07° 27'R	01° 24'R	07° 00'R	25° 15'	07° 20'R	27° 31'	19° 17'
07 Fr	14° 47'	27°♉57'	29° 00'R	11° 28'	00°♌25'	09° 21'	15° 09'	26° 50'	06° 58'R	07° 25'R	01° 23'R	06° 59'R	25° 31'	07° 06'R	27° 44'	19° 32'
08 Sa	15° 45'	09°♊45'	29° 00'	13° 24'	01° 30'	10° 00'	15° 14'	26° 56'	06° 55'R	07° 23'R	01° 21'R	06° 59'R	25° 47'	06° 53'R	27° 58'	19° 47'
09 Su	16° 43'	21°♊36'	29° 00'R	15° 18'	02° 35'	10° 40'	15° 19'	27° 02'	06° 52'R	07° 21'R	01° 20'R	06° 59'R	26° 02'	06° 39'R	28° 11'	20° 01'
10 Mo	17° 42'	03°♋37'	28° 59'R	17° 12'	03° 41'	11° 20'	15° 24'	27° 08'	06° 49'R	07° 19'R	01° 18'R	06° 58'R	26° 18'	06° 25'R	28° 24'	20° 16'
11 Tu	18° 40'	15°♋51'	28° 55'R	19° 05'	04° 46'	12° 00'	15° 29'	27° 14'	06° 46'R	07° 16'R	01° 16'R	06° 58'R	26° 33'	06° 10'R	28° 38'	20° 30'
12 We	19° 38'	28°♋24'	28° 50'R	20° 58'	05° 52'	12° 40'	15° 33'	27° 20'	06° 43'R	07° 14'R	01° 15'R	06° 58'R	26° 48'	05° 56'R	28° 52'	20° 43'
13 Th	20° 37'	11°♌19'	28° 42'R	22° 49'	06° 58'	13° 21'	15° 37'	27° 27'	06° 41'R	07° 12'R	01° 13'R	06° 58'R	27° 03'	05° 41'R	29° 06'	20° 57'
14 Fr	21° 35'	24°♌37'	28° 32'R	24° 39'	08° 05'	14° 01'	15° 41'	27° 33'	06° 38'R	07° 10'R	01° 12'R	06° 58'R	27° 18'	05° 25'R	29° 20'	21° 10'
15 Sa	22° 34'	08°♍19'	28° 21'R	26° 28'	09° 11'	14° 42'	15° 45'	27° 39'	06° 35'R	07° 07'R	01° 10'R	06° 57'R	27° 32'	05° 10'R	29° 35'	21° 23'
16 Su	23° 32'	22°♍20'	28° 11'R	28° 16'	10° 18'	15° 22'	15° 49'	27° 46'	06° 32'R	07° 05'R	01° 09'R	06° 57'R	27° 46'	04° 55'R	29° 49'	21° 36'
17 Mo	24° 31'	06°♎37'	28° 02'R	00°♎03'	11° 25'	16° 03'	15° 53'	27° 52'	06° 30'R	07° 03'R	01° 07'R	06° 57'R	28° 00'	04° 39'R	00°♐04'	21° 48'
18 Tu	25° 29'	21°♎04'	27° 55'R	01° 49'	12° 32'	16° 44'	15° 56'	27° 59'	06° 27'R	07° 00'R	01° 06'R	06° 57'R	28° 14'	04° 23'R	00° 19'	22° 00'
19 We	26° 28'	05°♏35'	27° 50'R	03° 34'	13° 39'	17° 24'	15° 59'	28° 05'	06° 24'R	06° 58'R	01° 04'R	06° 57'	28° 28'	04° 07'R	00° 34'	22° 12'
20 Th	27° 26'	20°♏04'	27° 48'R	05° 17'	14° 47'	18° 05'	16° 02'	28° 12'	06° 22'R	06° 55'R	01° 03'R	06° 57'	28° 41'	03° 51'R	00° 49'	22° 24'
21 Fr	28° 25'	04°♐26'	27° 48'	07° 00'	15° 55'	18° 46'	16° 05'	28° 18'	06° 19'R	06° 53'R	01° 02'R	06° 57'	28° 54'	03° 34'R	01° 04'	22° 35'
22 Sa	29° 24'	18°♐40'	27° 49'	08° 42'	17° 02'	19° 27'	16° 07'	28° 25'	06° 16'R	06° 51'R	01° 00'R	06° 57'	29° 07'	03° 18'R	01° 19'	22° 46'
23 Su	00°♎22'	02°♑43'	27° 49'R	10° 23'	18° 10'	20° 09'	16° 10'	28° 32'	06° 14'R	06° 48'R	00° 59'R	06° 58'	29° 20'	03° 02'R	01° 35'	22° 57'
24 Mo	01° 21'	16°♑35'	27° 48'R	12° 03'	19° 19'	20° 50'	16° 12'	28° 38'	06° 11'R	06° 46'R	00° 57'R	06° 58'	29° 32'	02° 45'R	01° 51'	23° 07'
25 Tu	02° 20'	00°♒16'	27° 45'R	13° 41'	20° 27'	21° 31'	16° 14'	28° 45'	06° 09'R	06° 44'R	00° 56'R	06° 58'	29° 45'	02° 28'R	02° 06'	23° 17'
26 We	03° 19'	13°♒45'	27° 39'R	15° 19'	21° 36'	22° 13'	16° 16'	28° 52'	06° 06'R	06° 41'R	00° 55'R	06° 58'	29° 57'	02° 12'R	02° 22'	23° 27'
27 Th	04° 18'	27°♒03'	27° 32'R	16° 56'	22° 44'	22° 54'	16° 17'	28° 59'	06° 04'R	06° 39'R	00° 53'R	06° 58'	00°♋08'	01° 55'R	02° 38'	23° 36'
28 Fr	05° 16'	10°♓08'	27° 23'R	18° 32'	23° 53'	23° 36'	16° 19'	29° 05'	06° 02'R	06° 36'R	00° 52'R	06° 59'	00° 20'	01° 38'R	02° 55'	23° 45'
29 Sa	06° 15'	23°♓00'	27° 14'R	20° 08'	25° 02'	24° 18'	16° 20'	29° 12'	05° 59'R	06° 34'R	00° 51'R	06° 59'	00° 31'	01° 22'R	03° 11'	23° 54'
30 Su	07° 14'	05°♈39'	27° 05'R	21° 42'	26° 11'	24° 59'	16° 21'	29° 19'	05° 57'R	06° 31'R	00° 50'R	06° 59'	00° 42'	01° 05'R	03° 27'	24° 02'

MOON ASPECTS | OCTOBER 2012

All times Eastern Time

Mon 01	7:36 A	☽ ☍ ☿			11:18 A	☽ △ ♂			7:38 A	☽ ⚹ ♇	Wed 24	1:55 A	☽ □ ☊
	8:05 A	☽ ⚹ ⚷			7:34 P	☽ △ ♅			10:16 P	☽ ⚹ ♀		7:49 A	☽ ☌ ♆
	4:06 P	☽ △ ♀			7:55 P	☽ △ ⚶			10:23 P	☽ ☌ ☿		9:53 A	☽ △ ☉
	6:32 P	☽ ☍ ♄			8:36 P	☽ □ ☿	Wed 17	2:45 P	☽ △ ♀		11:09 A	☽ △ ♄
	9:00 P	☽ ⚹ ♆	Wed 10	2:36 P	☽ ⚹ ♃			4:31 P	☽ ☌ ☊		1:36 P	☽ △ ⚴
	9:32 P	☽ ⚹ ⚴			5:40 P	☽ ⚹ ☉			9:16 P	☽ □ ♆		4:37 P	☽ ☌ ⚷
Tue 02	7:04 A	☽ ⚹ ⚷	Thu 11	6:51 A	☽ ⚹ ⚷	Thu 18	5:06 A	☽ □ ⚷		8:32 P	☽ ⚹ ♇
	9:22 A	☽ △ ♇			11:39 A	☽ □ ☊			5:50 A	☽ △ ♅	Thu 25	3:28 A	☽ □ ⚶
Wed 03	N/A				4:29 P	☽ ☍ ♆			9:41 A	☽ ☌ ♂		7:33 A	☽ □ ♂
Thu 04	3:44 A	☽ ☍ ♂			4:39 P	☽ ⚹ ♃			10:54 A	☽ ☌ ⚴		12:09 P	☽ □ ♃
	4:18 A	☽ ☍ ☊			7:51 P	☽ ⚹ ⚴			10:32 P	☽ ☍ ♃	Fri 26	5:27 A	☽ ☌ ♀
	7:28 A	☽ ⚹ ♀			9:36 P	☽ □ ♂	Fri 19	3:15 A	☽ □ ♀		6:50 A	☽ □ ⚷
	9:17 A	☽ □ ♆	Fri 12	1:09 A	☽ ☍ ⚷			2:17 P	☽ ☍ ⚷		9:59 A	☽ △ ☊
	10:56 A	☽ □ ♀			3:45 A	☽ □ ⚴			3:05 P	☽ □ ♀		10:44 A	☽ △ ☿
	5:37 P	☽ ☍ ⚴			3:56 A	☽ △ ♇			4:26 P	☽ ⚹ ☉		11:04 A	☽ ☍ ♀
	7:30 P	☽ □ ⚷			9:23 A	☽ ⚹ ☿			10:31 P	☽ ⚹ ♆		10:34 P	☽ □ ⚴
	8:39 P	☽ ⚹ ♅			10:36 A	☽ ☌ ♀	Sat 20	12:33 A	☽ ⚹ ♄	Sat 27	2:06 A	☽ ☌ ♅
Fri 05	9:41 A	☽ △ ☉			7:48 P	☽ □ ♃			3:14 P	☽ ☍ ⚴		5:43 A	☽ □ ♇
	5:08 P	☽ ☌ ♃	Sat 13	11:16 A	☽ □ ⚹			6:34 A	☽ ⚹ ⚷		2:23 P	☽ △ ⚶
Sat 06	10:18 A	☽ ☌ ⚹			2:44 P	☽ ☍ ♀			7:18 A	☽ □ ♅		8:44 P	☽ △ ♂
	7:06 P	☽ □ ♀			3:20 P	☽ ⚹ ☊			9:50 A	☽ ☌ ♇		9:32 P	☽ ⚹ ♃
	9:02 P	☽ △ ♄			11:37 P	☽ □ ⚴	Sun 21	10:29 A	☽ △ ♀	Sun 28	5:03 P	☽ ⚹ ⚹
	10:09 P	☽ △ ♆	Sun 14	3:31 A	☽ ⚹ ♂			11:05 A	☽ ⚹ ☿	Mon 29	3:04 A	☽ ⚹ ♆
Sun 07	12:31 A	☽ ☌ ⚴			4:55 A	☽ ☍ ♅			5:22 P	☽ ⚹ ♀		7:55 A	☽ ☍ ♄
	2:09 A	☽ △ ☿			6:52 A	☽ □ ♇			8:25 P	☽ ⚹ ☊		9:39 A	☽ ⚹ ⚴
	6:29 A	☽ ⚹ ♀			7:43 A	☽ ⚹ ⚶			11:32 P	☽ □ ☉		12:27 P	☽ ⚹ ⚷
	8:09 A	☽ △ ⚷			9:44 P	☽ △ ♃	Mon 22	4:30 A	☽ □ ♄		3:49 P	☽ ☍ ☉
	9:15 A	☽ □ ♅	Mon 15	8:03 A	☽ ☌ ☉			11:00 A	☽ ⚹ ♅		5:01 P	☽ △ ♇
	10:55 A	☽ ☍ ♇			12:47 P	☽ △ ⚹			7:13 P	☽ ⚹ ⚶	Wed 31	2:25 A	☽ ⚹ ♀
Mon 08	3:33 A	☽ □ ☉			8:59 P	☽ △ ♆			9:16 P	☽ ⚹ ♂		8:17 A	☽ ☍ ☊
Tue 09	4:08 A	☽ △ ☊			10:04 P	☽ ☌ ♄	Tue 23	5:06 A	☽ △ ♃		3:28 P	☽ □ ♆
	5:07 A	☽ △ ♀	Tue 16	12:53 A	☽ △ ⚶			9:27 P	☽ □ ☿		6:55 P	☽ ☍ ☿
	8:45 A	☽ □ ♄			4:48 A	☽ △ ⚷			10:49 P	☽ △ ⚹		11:33 P	☽ △ ♀

ADDITIONAL MONTHLY EPHEMERIDES

2012	PHOLUS	NESSUS	ASBOLUS	CHARIKLO	HYLON.
OCT					
1	16°♐40'	23°♒05'R	0°♊52'R	8°♐57'	18°♐04'
6	16° 46'	22° 59'R	0° 43'R	9° 13'	18° 12'
11	16° 54'	22° 54'R	0° 33'R	9° 31'	18° 21'
16	17° 03'	22° 49'R	0° 22'R	9° 51'	18° 31'
21	17° 12'	22° 46'R	0° 09'R	10° 11'	18° 42'
26	17° 22'	22° 43'R	29°♉56'R	10° 32'	18° 54'
31	17° 33'	22° 42'R	29° 42'R	10° 55'	19° 06'

01	06°♊03'	11	00° 37'R	21	07° 48'R		
02	06° 30'	12	27°♉33'R	22	07° 04'R		
03	06° 28'R	13	24° 23'R	23	07° 43'		
04	06° 21'R	14	21° 31'R	24	09° 52'		
05	06° 20'	15	19° 08'R	25	13° 21'		
06	06° 25'	16	17° 11'R	26	17° 43'		
07	06° 24'R	17	15° 26'R	27	22° 25'		
08	06° 02'R	18	13° 35'R	28	26° 57'		
09	05° 01'R	19	11° 32'R	29	00°♊58'		
10	03° 12'R	20	09° 28'R	30	04° 18'		
BLACK MOON LILITH ⚸					31	07° 00'	

OCTOBER 2012 EPHEMERIS

Ephemeris calculated for 12 Midnight GMT.

DAY	☉	☽	☊T.N.	☿	♀	♂	♃	♄	⚷	♅	♆	♇	⚳	⚴	⚵	⚶
01 Mo	08°♎13'	18°♈04'	26°♏57'R	23°♎15'	27°♌21'	25°♏41	16°♊22'	29°♎26	05°♓54'R	06°♈29'R	00°♓48'R	07°♑00	00°♋52	00°♈48'R	03°♐44	24°♊11'
02 Tu	09° 12'	00°♉17'	26° 52'R	24° 48'	28° 30'	26° 23'	16° 22'	29° 33'	05° 52'R	06° 27'R	00° 47'R	07° 00'	01° 03'	00° 32'R	04° 01'	24° 18'
03 We	10° 11'	12°♉19'	26° 49'R	26° 20'	29° 40'	27° 05'	16° 23'	29° 40'	05° 50'R	06° 24'R	00° 46'R	07° 01'	01° 13'	00° 15'R	04° 18'	24° 26'
04 Th	11° 10'	24°♉12'	26° 47'R	27° 50'	00°♍49'	27° 47'	16° 23'	29° 47'	05° 48'R	06° 22'R	00° 45'R	07° 01'	01° 23'	29° 59'R	04° 35'	24° 33'
05 Fr	12° 09'	06°♊00'	26° 48'	29° 21'	01° 59'	28° 29'	16° 23'R	29° 54'	05° 46'R	06° 19'R	00° 44'R	07° 02'	01° 32'	29° 43'R	04° 52'	24° 40'
06 Sa	13° 09'	17°♊47'	26° 49'	00°♏50'	03° 09'	29° 12'	16° 23'R	00°♏01	05° 43'R	06° 17'R	00° 43'R	07° 02'	01° 42'	29° 26'R	05° 09'	24° 46'
07 Su	14° 08'	29°♊38'	26° 51'	02° 18'	04° 20'	29° 54'	16° 22'R	00° 08'	05° 41'R	06° 15'R	00° 42'R	07° 03'	01° 50'	29° 10'R	05° 26'	24° 52'
08 Mo	15° 07'	11°♋37'	26° 52'	03° 46'	05° 30'	00°♐37	16° 22'R	00° 15'	05° 39'R	06° 12'R	00° 40'R	07° 03'	01° 59'	28° 54'R	05° 43'	24° 58'
09 Tu	16° 06'	23°♋49'	26° 51'R	05° 12'	06° 40'	01° 19'	16° 21'R	00° 22'	05° 37'R	06° 10'R	00° 39'R	07° 04'	02° 07'	28° 39'R	06° 01'	25° 03'
10 We	17° 05'	06°♌21'	26° 49'R	06° 38'	07° 51'	02° 02'	16° 20'R	00° 29'	05° 35'R	06° 07'R	00° 38'R	07° 05'	02° 15'	28° 23'R	06° 19'	25° 08'
11 Th	18° 05'	19°♌16'	26° 46'R	08° 03'	09° 02'	02° 44'	16° 19'R	00° 37'	05° 33'R	06° 05'R	00° 37'R	07° 05'	02° 23'	28° 08'R	06° 36'	25° 12'
12 Fr	19° 04'	02°♍36'	26° 41'R	09° 27'	10° 13'	03° 27'	16° 17'R	00° 44'	05° 32'R	06° 03'R	00° 36'R	07° 06'	02° 30'	27° 52'R	06° 54'	25° 16'
13 Sa	20° 04'	16°♍23'	26° 35'R	10° 50'	11° 24'	04° 10'	16° 16'R	00° 51'	05° 30'R	06° 00'R	00° 36'R	07° 07'	02° 38'	27° 37'R	07° 12'	25° 20'
14 Su	21° 03'	00°♎35'	26° 29'R	12° 12'	12° 35'	04° 53'	16° 14'R	00° 58'	05° 28'R	05° 58'R	00° 35'R	07° 08'	02° 44'	27° 23'R	07° 30'	25° 23'
15 Mo	22° 02'	15°♎08'	26° 24'R	13° 33'	13° 46'	05° 36'	16° 12'R	01° 05'	05° 26'R	05° 56'R	00° 34'R	07° 08'	02° 51'	27° 08'R	07° 48'	25° 26'
16 Tu	23° 02'	29°♎56'	26° 21'R	14° 53'	14° 57'	06° 19'	16° 10'R	01° 12'	05° 24'R	05° 54'R	00° 33'R	07° 09'	02° 57'	26° 54'R	08° 07'	25° 28'
17 We	24° 02'	14°♏51'	26° 19'R	16° 12'	16° 09'	07° 02'	16° 07'R	01° 20'	05° 23'R	05° 51'R	00° 32'R	07° 10'	03° 02'	26° 40'R	08° 25'	25° 30'
18 Th	25° 01'	29°♏44'	26° 18'	17° 30'	17° 20'	07° 45'	16° 05'R	01° 27'	05° 21'R	05° 49'R	00° 31'R	07° 11'	03° 08'	26° 26'R	08° 43'	25° 32'
19 Fr	26° 01'	14°♐29'	26° 19'	18° 46'	18° 32'	08° 29'	16° 02'R	01° 34'	05° 20'R	05° 47'R	00° 30'R	07° 12'	03° 13'	26° 13'R	09° 02'	25° 33'
20 Sa	27° 00'	29°♐00'	26° 21'	20° 01'	19° 43'	09° 12'	15° 59'R	01° 41'	05° 18'R	05° 45'R	00° 30'R	07° 13'	03° 17'	26° 00'R	09° 21'	25° 34'
21 Su	28° 00'	13°♑13'	26° 22'	21° 14'	20° 55'	09° 56'	15° 56'R	01° 49'	05° 17'R	05° 42'R	00° 29'R	07° 14'	03° 21'	25° 47'R	09° 39'	25° 34'
22 Mo	29° 00'	27°♑07'	26° 23'	22° 26'	22° 07'	10° 39'	15° 52'R	01° 56'	05° 15'R	05° 40'R	00° 28'R	07° 15'	03° 25'	25° 35'R	09° 58'	25° 34'R
23 Tu	29° 59'	10°♒43'	26° 22'R	23° 36'	23° 19'	11° 23'	15° 49'R	02° 03'	05° 14'R	05° 38'R	00° 28'R	07° 16'	03° 29'	25° 23'R	10° 17'	25° 34'R
24 We	00°♏59'	24°♒00'	26° 21'R	24° 44'	24° 31'	12° 06'	15° 45'R	02° 10'	05° 13'R	05° 36'R	00° 27'R	07° 17'	03° 32'	25° 11'R	10° 36'	25° 33'R
25 Th	01° 59'	07°♓01'	26° 18'R	25° 49'	25° 43'	12° 50'	15° 41'R	02° 18'	05° 12'R	05° 34'R	00° 27'R	07° 18'	03° 35'	25° 00'R	10° 55'	25° 31'R
26 Fr	02° 59'	19°♓47'	26° 14'R	26° 53'	26° 56'	13° 34'	15° 37'R	02° 25'	05° 10'R	05° 32'R	00° 26'R	07° 19'	03° 37'	24° 49'R	11° 14'	25° 30'R
27 Sa	03° 59'	02°♈20'	26° 11'R	27° 54'	28° 08'	14° 18'	15° 32'R	02° 32'	05° 09'R	05° 30'R	00° 25'R	07° 20'	03° 39'	24° 38'R	11° 33'	25° 27'R
28 Su	04° 58'	14°♈41'	26° 07'R	28° 52'	29° 21'	15° 02'	15° 28'R	02° 39'	05° 08'R	05° 28'R	00° 25'R	07° 22'	03° 41'	24° 28'R	11° 53'	25° 25'R
29 Mo	05° 58'	26°♈51'	26° 04'R	29° 46'	00°♎33'	15° 46'	15° 23'R	02° 47'	05° 07'R	05° 26'R	00° 24'R	07° 23'	03° 42'	24° 18'R	12° 12'	25° 21'R
30 Tu	06° 58'	08°♉53'	26° 02'R	00°♐37'	01° 46'	16° 30'	15° 18'R	02° 54'	05° 06'R	05° 24'R	00° 24'R	07° 24'	03° 43'	24° 09'R	12° 32'	25° 18'R
31 We	07° 58'	20°♉48'	26° 01'R	01° 24'	02° 58'	17° 14'	15° 13'R	03° 01'	05° 05'R	05° 22'R	00° 24'R	07° 25'	03° 43'	24° 00'R	12° 51'	25° 14'R

MOON ASPECTS | NOVEMBER 2012

All times Eastern Time

Thu 01	1:30 A ☽ ✶ ♅	Fri 09	1:23 A ☽ □ ♃		6:37 P ☽ ☍ ⚷		5:43 A ☽ ☌ ♀
	6:07 P ☽ ☍ ⚶		4:17 A ☽ □ ⚶	Fri 16	4:44 A ☽ ☌ ♂		11:53 A ☽ △ ☊
	9:18 P ☽ ☌ ♃		6:57 A ☽ ✶ ☉		6:11 A ☽ ✶ ♆		10:37 P ☽ △ ☉
Fri 02	5:21 A ☽ ☍ ♂		4:21 P ☽ ☍ ♀		10:13 A ☽ ☍ ⚸	Fri 23	12:04 A ☽ □ ⚸
	2:45 P ☽ □ ♀		6:33 P ☽ □ ⚷		1:32 P ☽ □ ♅		5:27 A ☽ ☌ ♅
	5:33 P ☽ ☌ ⚷		7:27 P ☽ □ ♂		1:39 P ☽ ✶ ♆ (☊?)		5:29 A ☽ □ ♂
Sat 03	4:29 A ☽ △ ♆		10:20 P ☽ ✶ ☊		1:42 P ☽ ✶ ♄		11:47 A ☽ □ ♇
	10:43 A ☽ △ ♄	Sat 10	10:06 A ☽ ✶ ⚳		6:18 P ☽ ☌ ♇		8:34 P ☽ ✶ ♃
	11:12 A ☽ ☌ ⚸		10:20 A ☽ □ ⚸	Sat 17	6:28 P ☽ ✶ ♀	Sat 24	1:53 P ☽ △ ⚶
	1:55 P ☽ △ ♆ (☊?)		1:09 P ☽ ☍ ♅		10:46 P ☽ ✶ ⚳		2:00 P ☽ ✶ ⚷
	2:20 P ☽ □ ♅		5:33 P ☽ □ ♇		11:03 P ☽ □ ♀	Sun 25	8:08 A ☽ ✶ ♆
	6:54 P ☽ ☍ ♇	Sun 11	4:13 A ☽ △ ♃	Sun 18	12:15 A ☽ ✶ ☊		10:34 A ☽ ✶ ⚸
	7:31 P ☽ □ ♀		8:32 A ☽ ✶ ⚶		12:54 A ☽ ✶ ☉		4:53 P ☽ ☍ ♀
Sun 04	3:37 A ☽ △ ☉		9:13 A ☽ ☌ ♀		3:29 P ☽ ✶ ♅		5:26 P ☽ ✶ ♄ (☽?)
Mon 05	1:30 A ☽ △ ♀		8:12 P ☽ △ ⚷		4:10 P ☽ □ ♄		7:30 P ☽ ☍ ♄
	7:57 A ☽ △ ☊	Mon 12	12:13 A ☽ ✶ ♂	Mon 19	5:47 A ☽ △ ♃		9:00 P ☽ △ ♂
	9:58 P ☽ □ ♄		6:45 A ☽ △ ♆		5:11 P ☽ ✶ ⚶		11:36 P ☽ △ ♇
	10:57 P ☽ △ ⚸		11:22 A ☽ △ ⚸		10:08 P ☽ △ ⚷	Mon 26	7:57 P ☽ ☍ ⚸
Tue 06	12:44 A ☽ △ ♅		1:28 P ☽ ☌ ♄		10:22 P ☽ □ ⚸	Tue 27	4:53 A ☽ ✶ ♀
	12:14 P ☽ ✶ ♀		2:10 P ☽ △ ♇ (☽?)	Tue 20	4:19 A ☽ □ ☊		10:39 A ☽ ☍ ☊
	6:45 P ☽ ✶ ♃		6:34 P ☽ ✶ ♇		8:35 A ☽ △ ♀		8:52 P ☽ □ ♆
	7:36 P ☽ □ ☉	Tue 13	5:08 P ☽ ☌ ☉		9:31 A ☽ □ ☉	Wed 28	5:33 A ☽ ✶ ♅
	7:55 P ☽ △ ⚶		6:12 P ☽ △ ♀		12:37 P ☽ ☌ ♆		6:17 A ☽ □ ♇ (☽?)
Wed 07	10:27 A ☽ △ ♂		11:45 P ☽ ☌ ☊		4:11 P ☽ △ ⚶		9:46 A ☽ ☍ ☉
	1:20 P ☽ ✶ ⚷	Wed 14	5:39 A ☽ ☌ ⚸		5:11 P ☽ ✶ ♂		8:04 P ☽ ☌ ♃
	5:04 P ☽ □ ☊		6:26 A ☽ □ ♆		9:03 P ☽ ☌ ♇ (☽?)	Thu 29	12:55 P ☽ ☌ ⚷
Thu 08	12:15 A ☽ ☍ ♆		1:42 P ☽ △ ♅		10:01 P ☽ △ ♄		6:08 P ☽ □ ♀
	6:00 A ☽ ✶ ⚶		1:44 P ☽ □ ♇ (☽?)	Wed 21	2:31 A ☽ ✶ ♇		6:57 P ☽ ☍ ⚶
	6:57 A ☽ ✶ ♄	Thu 15	3:25 A ☽ ☍ ♃		11:34 A ☽ □ ♃	Fri 30	9:51 A ☽ △ ♆
	7:06 A ☽ □ ⚸ (☽?)		10:32 A ☽ ☌ ⚶	Thu 22	1:32 A ☽ △ ⚸ (☽?)		10:25 A ☽ ☌ ⚸
	8:41 A ☽ ☍ ♄ (☽?)		5:29 P ☽ ✶ ♀		1:49 A ☽ □ ⚶		6:22 P ☽ □ ♅
	1:25 P ☽ △ ♇		5:36 P ☽ □ ♀		4:36 A ☽ □ ⚷		7:14 P ☽ △ ♄ (☽?)
							10:18 P ☽ △ ♄

ADDITIONAL MONTHLY EPHEMERIDES

CENTAURS

2012	PHOLUS	NESSUS	ASBOLUS	CHARIKLO	HYLON.
Nov					
5	17°♐45′	22°♒42′	29°♉27′R	11°♐18′	19°♐19′
10	17° 57′	22° 43′	29° 12′R	11° 42′	19° 33′
15	18° 09′	22° 44′	28° 57′R	12° 06′	19° 47′
20	18° 22′	22° 47′	28° 41′R	12° 31′	20° 02′
25	18° 35′	22° 51′	28° 25′R	12° 56′	20° 17′
30	18° 49′	22° 56′	28° 10′R	13° 22′	20° 32′

01	09°♊09′	11	07° 27′R	21	17° 35′
02	10° 59′	12	04° 43′R	22	18° 22′
03	12° 37′	13	02° 23′R	23	20° 16′
04	14° 07′	14	00° 24′R	24	23° 01′
05	15° 20′	15	28°♉31′R	25	26° 15′
06	16° 04′	16	26° 29′R	26	29° 42′
07	16° 00′R	17	24° 10′R	27	03°♊09′
08	14° 57′R	18	21° 44′R	28	06° 31′
09	12° 58′R	19	19° 32′R	29	09° 50′
10	10° 20′R	20	18° 02′R	30	13° 08′

BLACK MOON LILITH ⚸

NOVEMBER 2012 EPHEMERIS

Ephemeris calculated for 12 Midnight GMT.

DAY	☉	☽	☊T.N.	☿	♀	♂	♃	♄	⚷	♅	♆	♇	⚳	⚴	⚵	⚶
01 Th	08°♏58'	02°♊37'	26°♏01'	02°♐07'	04°♎11'	17°♐58	15°♊08'R	03°♏08	05°♓04R	05°♈20R	00°♓23R	07°♑27	03°♋44'R	23°♓51'R	13°♐11	25°♊09'R
02 Fr	09° 58'	14°♊24'	26° 02'	02° 45'	05° 24'	18° 43'	15° 03'R	03° 16'	05° 04'R	05° 18'R	00° 23'R	07° 28'	03° 43'R	23° 43'R	13° 30'	25° 04'R
03 Sa	10° 58'	26°♊12'	26° 03'	03° 17'	06° 37'	19° 27'	14° 57'R	03° 23'	05° 03'R	05° 16'R	00° 23'R	07° 29'	03° 42'R	23° 35'R	13° 50'	24° 59'R
04 Su	11° 58'	08°♋03'	26° 05'	03° 43'	07° 50'	20° 11'	14° 52'R	03° 30'	05° 02'R	05° 14'R	00° 22'R	07° 31'	03° 41'R	23° 28'R	14° 10'	24° 53'R
05 Mo	12° 59'	20°♋02'	26° 06'	04° 02'	09° 03'	20° 56'	14° 46'R	03° 37'	05° 02'R	05° 13'R	00° 22'R	07° 32'	03° 40'R	23° 21'R	14° 30'	24° 47'R
06 Tu	13° 59'	02°♌14'	26° 07'	04° 14'	10° 16'	21° 41'	14° 40'R	03° 44'	05° 01'R	05° 11'R	00° 22'R	07° 33'	03° 38'R	23° 14'R	14° 50'	24° 40'R
07 We	14° 59'	14°♌42'	26° 07'	04° 18'R	11° 30'	22° 25'	14° 34'R	03° 52'	05° 01'R	05° 09'R	00° 22'R	07° 35'	03° 35'R	23° 08'R	15° 10'	24° 33'R
08 Th	15° 59'	27°♌31'	26° 07'R	04° 13'R	12° 43'	23° 10'	14° 28'R	03° 59'	05° 00'R	05° 08'R	00° 22'R	07° 36'	03° 33'R	23° 02'R	15° 30'	24° 25'R
09 Fr	16° 59'	10°♍44'	26° 06'R	03° 59'R	13° 56'	23° 55'	14° 21'R	04° 06'	05° 00'R	05° 06'R	00° 22'R	07° 38'	03° 29'R	22° 57'R	15° 50'	24° 17'R
10 Sa	18° 00'	24°♍25'	26° 05'R	03° 35'R	15° 10'	24° 39'	14° 15'R	04° 13'	04° 59'R	05° 04'R	00° 22'R	07° 39'	03° 26'R	22° 52'R	16° 10'	24° 09'R
11 Su	19° 00'	08°♎33'	26° 04'R	03° 02'R	16° 23'	25° 24'	14° 08'R	04° 20'	04° 59'R	05° 03'R	00° 22'R	07° 41'	03° 22'R	22° 48'R	16° 31'	24° 00'R
12 Mo	20° 00'	23°♎06'	26° 04'R	02° 18'R	17° 37'	26° 09'	14° 01'R	04° 27'	04° 59'R	05° 01'R	00° 22'	07° 42'	03° 17'R	22° 44'R	16° 51'	23° 51'R
13 Tu	21° 01'	08°♏00'	26° 03'R	01° 24'R	18° 51'	26° 54'	13° 54'R	04° 34'	04° 59'R	05° 00'R	00° 22'	07° 44'	03° 13'R	22° 40'R	17° 11'	23° 41'R
14 We	22° 01'	23°♏07'	26° 03'R	00° 22'R	20° 04'	27° 39'	13° 47'R	04° 41'	04° 59'R	04° 58'R	00° 22'	07° 45'	03° 07'R	22° 37'R	17° 32'	23° 31'R
15 Th	23° 02'	08°♐19'	26° 03'	29°♏12R	21° 18'	28° 25'	13° 40'R	04° 49'	04° 59'	04° 57'R	00° 22'	07° 47'	03° 02'R	22° 34'R	17° 52'	23° 21'R
16 Fr	24° 02'	23°♐24'	26° 03'	27° 56'R	22° 32'	29° 10'	13° 33'R	04° 56'	04° 59'	04° 56'R	00° 22'	07° 49'	02° 56'R	22° 32'R	18° 13'	23° 10'R
17 Sa	25° 03'	08°♑16'	26° 03'	26° 36'R	23° 46'	29° 55'	13° 25'R	05° 03'	04° 59'	04° 54'R	00° 22'	07° 50'	02° 49'R	22° 30'R	18° 34'	22° 58'R
18 Su	26° 03'	22°♑47'	26° 04'	25° 15'R	25° 00'	00°♑40	13° 18'R	05° 09'	04° 59'	04° 53'R	00° 22'	07° 52'	02° 42'R	22° 28'R	18° 54'	22° 47'R
19 Mo	27° 04'	06°♒54'	26° 03'R	23° 55'R	26° 14'	01° 26'	13° 10'R	05° 16'	04° 59'	04° 52'R	00° 23'	07° 54'	02° 35'R	22° 27'R	19° 15'	22° 35'R
20 Tu	28° 04'	20°♒36'	26° 03'R	22° 39'R	27° 28'	02° 11'	13° 03'R	05° 23'	05° 00'	04° 51'R	00° 23'	07° 55'	02° 27'R	22° 27'R	19° 36'	22° 23'R
21 We	29° 05'	03°♓53'	26° 03'	21° 30'R	28° 42'	02° 57'	12° 55'R	05° 30'	05° 00'	04° 50'R	00° 23'	07° 57'	02° 19'R	22° 26'R	19° 57'	22° 10'R
22 Th	00°♐05'	16°♓47'	26° 04'	20° 30'R	29° 56'	03° 42'	12° 47'R	05° 37'	05° 00'	04° 49'R	00° 24'	07° 59'	02° 11'R	22° 26'	20° 18'	21° 57'R
23 Fr	01° 06'	29°♓23'	26° 04'	19° 39'R	01°♏10	04° 28'	12° 39'R	05° 44'	05° 01'	04° 47'R	00° 24'	08° 01'	02° 02'R	22° 27'	20° 39'	21° 44'R
24 Sa	02° 07'	11°♈43'	26° 05'	18° 59'R	02° 24'	05° 14'	12° 31'R	05° 51'	05° 01'	04° 46'R	00° 24'	08° 02'	01° 53'R	22° 28'	21° 00'	21° 30'R
25 Su	03° 07'	23°♈51'	26° 05'	18° 31'R	03° 38'	05° 59'	12° 23'R	05° 57'	05° 02'	04° 46'R	00° 25'	08° 04'	01° 44'R	22° 29'	21° 21'	21° 17'R
26 Mo	04° 08'	05°♉49'	26° 06'	18° 15'R	04° 53'	06° 45'	12° 15'R	06° 04'	05° 02'	04° 45'R	00° 25'	08° 06'	01° 34'R	22° 31'	21° 42'	21° 03'R
27 Tu	05° 09'	17°♉42'	26° 07'	18° 10'	06° 07'	07° 31'	12° 07'R	06° 11'	05° 03'	04° 44'R	00° 26'	08° 08'	01° 24'R	22° 33'	22° 03'	20° 48'R
28 We	06° 09'	29°♉31'	26° 07'R	18° 16'	07° 21'	08° 17'	11° 59'R	06° 17'	05° 04'	04° 43'R	00° 26'	08° 10'	01° 14'R	22° 36'	22° 24'	20° 34'R
29 Th	07° 10'	11°♊19'	26° 06'R	18° 32'	08° 36'	09° 03'	11° 51'R	06° 24'	05° 05'	04° 42'R	00° 27'	08° 12'	01° 03'R	22° 39'	22° 45'	20° 19'R
30 Fr	08° 11'	23°♊08'	26° 05'R	18° 57'	09° 50'	09° 49'	11° 43'R	06° 31'	05° 06'	04° 42'R	00° 28'	08° 14'	00° 52'R	22° 42'	23° 07'	20° 04'R

MOON ASPECTS | DECEMBER 2012

All times Eastern Time

Day	Time	Aspect
Sat 01	1:36 A	☽ ☍ ♇
	7:01 A	☽ ☍ ♂
	8:40 A	☽ △ ♀
Sun 02	1:55 A	☽ △ ☿
	6:50 A	☽ △ ⚴
	11:21 A	☽ △ ☊
Mon 03	6:07 A	☽ △ ♅
	10:30 A	☽ □ ♄
	6:50 P	☽ ⚹ ♃
	9:04 P	☽ △ ☉
Tue 04	2:38 A	☽ □ ♀
	9:45 A	☽ ⚹ ⚶
	5:08 P	☽ □ ☿
	9:16 P	☽ △ ⚵
	9:27 P	☽ □ ☊
Wed 05	6:26 A	☽ ⚹ ⚸
	7:51 A	☽ ☍ ♆
	4:35 P	☽ ☍ ⚷
	8:14 P	☽ ⚹ ♄
	10:35 P	☽ △ ♇
Thu 06	3:04 A	☽ □ ♃
	10:31 A	☽ △ ♂
	10:31 A	☽ □ ☉
	4:39 P	☽ □ ⚶
	4:54 P	☽ ⚹ ♀
Fri 07	1:41 A	☽ ☍ ⚴
	4:32 A	☽ ⚹ ☊
	5:35 A	☽ ⚹ ☿
	6:06 A	☽ □ ⚵
	12:20 P	☽ □ ⚸
	9:43 P	☽ ☍ ♅
Sat 08	4:27 A	☽ □ ♇
	8:00 A	☽ △ ♃
	6:34 P	☽ □ ♂
	7:37 P	☽ ⚹ ☉
	8:16 P	☽ △ ⚶
Sun 09	11:09 A	☽ ⚹ ⚵
	2:54 P	☽ △ ⚸
	5:50 P	☽ △ ♆
Mon 10	1:34 A	☽ △ ⚷
	5:21 A	☽ ☌ ♄
	6:56 A	☽ ⚹ ♇
	10:51 P	☽ ⚹ ♂
Tue 11	7:30 A	☽ △ ⚴
	8:08 A	☽ ☌ ♀
	8:54 A	☽ ☌ ☊
	6:21 P	☽ □ ♆
	7:21 P	☽ ☌ ☿
Wed 12	12:40 A	☽ △ ♅
	1:50 A	☽ □ ⚷
	9:12 A	☽ ☍ ♃
	7:43 P	☽ ☍ ⚶
Thu 13	3:42 A	☽ ☌ ☉
	7:21 A	☽ □ ⚴
	1:25 P	☽ ☍ ⚸
	1:38 P	☽ ☌ ⚵
	5:45 P	☽ ⚹ ♆
Fri 14	12:01 A	☽ □ ♅
	1:16 A	☽ ⚹ ⚷
	5:24 A	☽ ⚹ ♄
	6:31 A	☽ ☌ ♇
Sat 15	3:17 A	☽ ☌ ♂
	7:41 A	☽ ⚹ ⚴
	7:51 A	☽ ⚹ ☊
	4:15 P	☽ ⚹ ♀
Sun 16	12:30 A	☽ ⚹ ♅
	5:03 A	☽ ⚹ ☿
	6:27 A	☽ □ ♄
	8:38 A	☽ △ ♃
	7:01 P	☽ △ ⚶
Mon 17	9:57 A	☽ □ ☊
	1:11 P	☽ ⚹ ☉
	2:29 P	☽ △ ⚸
	7:05 P	☽ ⚹ ⚵
	9:07 P	☽ ☌ ♆
Tue 18	12:17 A	☽ □ ♀
	5:37 A	☽ ☌ ⚷
	10:46 A	☽ △ ♄
	11:34 A	☽ ⚹ ♇
	12:16 P	☽ □ ♃
	3:10 P	☽ □ ☿
	10:57 P	☽ □ ⚶
Wed 19	3:51 P	☽ △ ☊
	5:27 P	☽ ☌ ⚴
	5:44 P	☽ ⚹ ♂
	7:59 P	☽ □ ⚸
Thu 20	12:19 A	☽ □ ☉
	3:34 A	☽ □ ⚵
	11:34 A	☽ ☌ ♅
	1:40 P	☽ △ ♀
	7:52 P	☽ □ ♇
	7:54 P	☽ ⚹ ♃
Fri 21	6:47 A	☽ ⚹ ⚶
	7:13 A	☽ △ ☿
Sat 22	5:11 A	☽ ⚹ ⚸
	7:57 A	☽ □ ♂
	3:07 P	☽ ⚹ ♆
	4:09 P	☽ △ ⚵
	4:19 P	☽ △ ☉
Sun 23	12:52 A	☽ ⚹ ⚷
	7:13 A	☽ ☍ ♄
	7:35 A	☽ △ ♇
Mon 24	1:57 P	☽ ☍ ☊
	6:08 P	☽ ⚹ ⚴
Tue 25	12:58 A	☽ △ ♂
	4:04 A	☽ □ ♆
	11:45 A	☽ ⚹ ♅
	2:01 P	☽ □ ⚷
	7:18 P	☽ ☌ ♃
Wed 26	4:09 A	☽ ☍ ♀
	5:32 A	☽ ☌ ⚶
Thu 27	1:50 A	☽ ☍ ☿
	4:28 A	☽ ☌ ⚸
	8:11 A	☽ □ ⚴
	5:03 P	☽ △ ♆
	9:42 P	☽ ☍ ⚵
Fri 28	12:34 A	☽ □ ♅
	2:56 A	☽ △ ⚷
	5:21 A	☽ ☍ ☉
	9:34 A	☽ ☍ ♇
	9:43 A	☽ △ ♄
Sat 29	2:24 P	☽ △ ☊
	9:06 P	☽ △ ⚴
Sun 30	9:47 A	☽ ☍ ♂
	12:01 P	☽ △ ♅
	6:07 P	☽ ⚹ ♃
	9:14 P	☽ □ ♄
Mon 31	2:56 A	☽ ⚹ ⚶
	4:52 P	☽ △ ♀

ADDITIONAL MONTHLY EPHEMERIDES

CENTAURS

2012	PHOLUS	NESSUS	ASBOLUS	CHARIKLO	HYLON.
DEC					
5	19°♐02′	23°♒02′	27°♉54′R	13°♐47′	20°♐48′
10	19° 16′	23° 09′	27° 40′R	14° 13′	21° 03′
15	19° 30′	23° 17′	27° 26′R	14° 38′	21° 19′
20	19° 43′	23° 25′	27° 13′R	15° 03′	21° 35′
25	19° 57′	23° 35′	27° 00′R	15° 28′	21° 50′
30	20° 10′	23° 45′	26° 49′R	15° 53′	22° 06′

BLACK MOON LILITH ⚸

01	16°♊27'	11	19° 55'R	21	29°♉44'
02	19° 44'	12	17° 42'R	22	00°♊22'
03	22° 52'	13	15° 44'R	23	01° 39'
04	25° 35'	14	13° 48'R	24	03° 17'
05	27° 36'	15	11° 38'R	25	05° 07'
06	28° 35'	16	09° 05'R	26	07° 07'
07	28° 23'R	17	06° 16'R	27	09° 23'
08	27° 04'R	18	03° 32'R	28	12° 06'
09	24° 56'R	19	01° 20'R	29	15° 25'
10	22° 24'R	20	00° 02'R	30	19° 22'
				31	23° 50'

DECEMBER 2012 EPHEMERIS

Ephemeris calculated for 12 Midnight GMT.

DAY	☉	☽	☊T.N.	☿	♀	♂	♃	♄	⚷	♅	♆	♇	⚳	⚴	⚵	⚶
01 Sa	09°♐12'	05°♋00'	26°♏03'R	19°♏30'	11°♏05'	10°♑35'	11°♊35'R	06°♏37'	05°♓07'	04°♈41'R	00°♓28'	08°♑15'	00°♋40'R	22°♓46'	23°♐28'	19°♊49'R
02 Su	10° 13'	16°♋56'	26° 01'R	20° 11'	12° 19'	11° 21'	11° 27'R	06° 44'	05° 08'	04° 40'R	00° 29'	08° 17'	00° 29'R	22° 50'	23° 49'	19° 34'R
03 Mo	11° 13'	29°♋01'	25° 59'R	20° 58'	13° 34'	12° 07'	11° 18'R	06° 50'	05° 09'	04° 40'R	00° 30'	08° 19'	00° 17'R	22° 55'	24° 11'	19° 19'R
04 Tu	12° 14'	11°♌16'	25° 57'R	21° 52'	14° 48'	12° 53'	11° 10'R	06° 56'	05° 10'	04° 39'R	00° 30'	08° 21'	00° 05'R	23° 00'	24° 32'	19° 03'R
05 We	13° 15'	23°♌44'	25° 55'R	22° 50'	16° 03'	13° 39'	11° 02'R	07° 03'	05° 11'	04° 39'R	00° 31'	08° 23'	29°♊52'R	23° 05'	24° 53'	18° 48'R
06 Th	14° 16'	06°♍30'	25° 54'R	23° 53'	17° 18'	14° 25'	10° 54'R	07° 09'	05° 12'	04° 38'R	00° 32'	08° 25'	29° 40'R	23° 11'	25° 15'	18° 32'R
07 Fr	15° 17'	19°♍36'	25° 54'	24° 59'	18° 32'	15° 11'	10° 46'R	07° 15'	05° 13'	04° 38'R	00° 33'	08° 27'	29° 27'R	23° 17'	25° 36'	18° 16'R
08 Sa	16° 18'	03°♎05'	25° 54'	26° 09'	19° 47'	15° 58'	10° 38'R	07° 21'	05° 15'	04° 38'R	00° 34'	08° 29'	29° 14'R	23° 23'	25° 58'	18° 00'R
09 Su	17° 19'	16°♎59'	25° 56'	27° 22'	21° 02'	16° 44'	10° 30'R	07° 28'	05° 16'	04° 37'R	00° 35'	08° 31'	29° 01'R	23° 30'	26° 20'	17° 45'R
10 Mo	18° 20'	01°♏18'	25° 57'	28° 37'	22° 16'	17° 31'	10° 22'R	07° 34'	05° 17'	04° 37'R	00° 36'	08° 33'	28° 47'R	23° 37'	26° 41'	17° 29'R
11 Tu	19° 21'	16°♏01'	25° 58'	29° 55'	23° 31'	18° 17'	10° 14'R	07° 40'	05° 19'	04° 37'R	00° 37'	08° 35'	28° 33'R	23° 44'	27° 03'	17° 13'R
12 We	20° 22'	01°♐02'	25° 58'R	01°♐14'	24° 46'	19° 04'	10° 06'R	07° 46'	05° 20'	04° 37'R	00° 38'	08° 37'	28° 20'R	23° 52'	27° 25'	16° 57'R
13 Th	21° 23'	16°♐14'	25° 57'R	02° 35'	26° 01'	19° 50'	09° 58'R	07° 52'	05° 22'	04° 37'R	00° 39'	08° 39'	28° 06'R	24° 00'	27° 46'	16° 41'R
14 Fr	22° 24'	01°♑27'	25° 55'R	03° 57'	27° 16'	20° 37'	09° 50'R	07° 58'	05° 24'	04° 37'	00° 40'	08° 41'	27° 52'R	24° 09'	28° 08'	16° 26'R
15 Sa	23° 25'	16°♑31'	25° 51'R	05° 21'	28° 31'	21° 23'	09° 42'R	08° 03'	05° 25'	04° 37'	00° 41'	08° 43'	27° 38'R	24° 17'	28° 30'	16° 10'R
16 Su	24° 26'	01°♒17'	25° 47'R	06° 46'	29° 46'	22° 10'	09° 34'R	08° 09'	05° 27'	04° 37'	00° 42'	08° 46'	27° 24'R	24° 26'	28° 51'	15° 55'R
17 Mo	25° 27'	15°♒39'	25° 43'R	08° 11'	01°♐00'	22° 57'	09° 27'R	08° 15'	05° 29'	04° 37'	00° 43'	08° 48'	27° 10'R	24° 36'	29° 13'	15° 39'R
18 Tu	26° 28'	29°♒33'	25° 39'R	09° 37'	02° 15'	23° 43'	09° 19'R	08° 21'	05° 31'	04° 37'	00° 44'	08° 50'	26° 55'R	24° 46'	29° 35'	15° 24'R
19 We	27° 29'	12°♓57'	25° 37'R	11° 05'	03° 30'	24° 30'	09° 12'R	08° 26'	05° 33'	04° 38'	00° 46'	08° 52'	26° 41'R	24° 56'	29° 57'	15° 09'R
20 Th	28° 30'	25°♓55'	25° 36'R	12° 32'	04° 45'	25° 17'	09° 05'R	08° 32'	05° 35'	04° 38'	00° 47'	08° 54'	26° 27'R	25° 06'	00°♑19'	14° 54'R
21 Fr	29° 32'	08°♈29'	25° 36'	14° 01'	06° 00'	26° 04'	08° 57'R	08° 37'	05° 37'	04° 38'	00° 48'	08° 56'	26° 13'R	25° 17'	00° 41'	14° 40'R
22 Sa	00°♑33'	20°♈45'	25° 37'	15° 29'	07° 15'	26° 51'	08° 50'R	08° 43'	05° 39'	04° 39'	00° 50'	08° 58'	25° 59'R	25° 28'	01° 02'	14° 26'R
23 Su	01° 34'	02°♉47'	25° 39'	16° 59'	08° 30'	27° 38'	08° 43'R	08° 48'	05° 41'	04° 39'	00° 51'	09° 00'	25° 44'R	25° 39'	01° 24'	14° 11'R
24 Mo	02° 35'	14°♉40'	25° 41'	18° 28'	09° 45'	28° 24'	08° 36'R	08° 53'	05° 43'	04° 40'	00° 52'	09° 02'	25° 30'R	25° 51'	01° 46'	13° 58'R
25 Tu	03° 36'	26°♉27'	25° 41'R	19° 58'	11° 00'	29° 11'	08° 30'R	08° 58'	05° 46'	04° 40'	00° 54'	09° 04'	25° 17'R	26° 02'	02° 08'	13° 44'R
26 We	04° 37'	08°♊14'	25° 40'R	21° 29'	12° 15'	29° 58'	08° 23'R	09° 03'	05° 48'	04° 41'	00° 55'	09° 07'	25° 03'R	26° 15'	02° 30'	13° 31'R
27 Th	05° 38'	20°♊03'	25° 37'R	23° 00'	13° 30'	00°♒45'	08° 17'R	09° 08'	05° 50'	04° 42'	00° 57'	09° 09'	24° 49'R	26° 27'	02° 52'	13° 18'R
28 Fr	06° 39'	01°♋56'	25° 32'R	24° 31'	14° 45'	01° 32'	08° 10'R	09° 13'	05° 52'	04° 42'	00° 58'	09° 11'	24° 35'R	26° 40'	03° 14'	13° 05'R
29 Sa	07° 40'	13°♋56'	25° 26'R	26° 02'	16° 00'	02° 19'	08° 04'R	09° 18'	05° 55'	04° 43'	01° 00'	09° 13'	24° 22'R	26° 53'	03° 36'	12° 53'R
30 Su	08° 42'	26°♋03'	25° 18'R	27° 34'	17° 16'	03° 07'	07° 58'R	09° 23'	05° 57'	04° 44'	01° 01'	09° 15'	24° 09'R	27° 06'	03° 58'	12° 41'R
31 Mo	09° 43'	08°♌19'	25° 09'R	29° 06'	18° 31'	03° 54'	07° 52'R	09° 28'	06° 00'	04° 45'	01° 03'	09° 17'	23° 56'R	27° 19'	04° 20'	12° 29'R

2011–2012 EPHEMERIS
KUIPER BELT OBJECTS

Ephemeris calculated for 12 Midnight GMT.

	Orcus	Quaoar	Varuna	Haumea	Makemake	Eris	Sedna
2011 Dec							
1	4°♍04′R	22°♐10′	24°♋06′R	19°♎07′R	28°♍41′	21°♈31′	22°♉27′R
12	4° 03′R	22° 27′	23° 56′R	19° 17′R	28° 47′	21° 28′	22° 21′R
23	4° 00′R	22° 44′	23° 45′R	19° 25′R	28° 50′	21° 25′	22° 16′R
2012 Jan							
3	3° 53′R	23° 01′	23° 32′R	19° 30′R	28° 50′R	21° 23′	22° 11′R
14	3° 45′R	23° 17′	23° 19′R	19° 33′R	28° 47′R	21° 23′	22° 08′R
25	3° 35′R	23° 32′	23° 06′R	19° 32′R	28° 42′R	21° 24′	22° 06′R
Feb							
5	3° 23′R	23° 45′	22° 53′R	19° 29′R	28° 34′R	21° 27′	22° 05′R
16	3° 11′R	23° 56′	22° 42′R	19° 23′R	28° 24′R	21° 31′	22° 06′
27	2° 58′R	24° 04′	22° 32′R	19° 15′R	28° 13′R	21° 36′	22° 08′
Mar							
9	2° 45′R	24° 10′	22° 24′R	19° 05′R	28° 01′R	21° 41′	22° 12′
20	2° 33′R	24° 12′	22° 19′R	18° 54′R	27° 48′R	21° 48′	22° 17′
31	2° 23′R	24° 12′	22° 17′R	18° 42′R	27° 36′R	21° 55′	22° 23′
Apr							
11	2° 14′R	24° 09′	22° 17′	18° 29′R	27° 24′R	22° 02′	22° 30′
22	2° 07′R	24° 03′R	22° 20′	18° 16′R	27° 13′R	22° 09′	22° 37′
May							
3	2° 03′R	23° 55′R	22° 26′	18° 04′R	27° 04′R	22° 16′	22° 46′
14	2° 01′R	23° 45′R	22° 34′	17° 53′R	26° 56′R	22° 23′	22° 54′
25	2° 02′	23° 34′R	22° 45′	17° 44′R	26° 51′R	22° 29′	23° 03′
Jun							
5	2° 05′	23° 21′R	22° 57′	17° 37′R	26° 49′R	22° 34′	23° 11′
16	2° 11′	23° 08′R	23° 11′	17° 32′R	26° 49′R	22° 38′	23° 19′
27	2° 20′	22° 56′R	23° 27′	17° 30′R	26° 51′R	22° 41′	23° 26′
Jul							
8	2° 30′	22° 43′R	23° 43′	17° 30′	26° 57′	22° 43′	23° 32′
19	2° 42′	22° 32′R	23° 59′	17° 32′	27° 04′	22° 43′	23° 37′
30	2° 56′	22° 23′R	24° 16′	17° 38′	27° 14′	22° 43′	23° 41′
Aug							
10	3° 11′	22° 16′R	24° 31′	17° 46′	27° 25′	22° 41′	23° 43′
21	3° 26′	22° 11′R	24° 46′	17° 56′	27° 39′	22° 38′	23° 45′
Sep							
1	3° 42′	22° 08′R	25° 00′	18° 07′	27° 53′	22° 34′R	23° 44′R
12	3° 57′	22° 09′R	25° 11′	18° 21′	28° 08′	22° 29′R	23° 43′R
23	4° 12′	22° 12′	25° 21′	18° 36′	28° 24′	22° 23′R	23° 40′R
Oct							
4	4° 25′	22° 18′	25° 28′	18° 51′	28° 39′	22° 17′R	23° 36′R
15	4° 38′	22° 27′	25° 32′	19° 07′	28° 54′	22° 10′R	23° 31′R
26	4° 48′	22° 38′	25° 33′	19° 23′	29° 08′	22° 03′R	23° 25′R
Nov							
6	4° 56′	22° 51′	25° 32′	19° 38′	29° 21′	21° 57′R	23° 18′R
17	5° 01′	23° 06′	25° 28′	19° 52′	29° 31′	21° 51′R	23° 11′R
28	5° 04′	23° 22′	25° 21′	20° 05′	29° 40′	21° 46′R	23° 05′R
Dec							
9	5° 04′R	23° 39′	25° 12′	20° 16′	29° 46′	21° 42′R	22° 58′R
20	5° 02′R	23° 57′	25° 01′	20° 24′	29° 50′	21° 39′R	22° 53′R
31	4° 56′R	24° 14′	24° 49′	20° 30′	29° 51′	21° 37′R	22° 48′R

HEALING MODALITIES

As the new consciousness of Cosmic Astrology emerged, so too did a healing system that focuses specifically on the clearing of our subtle energy bodies, also known as the lower four body system. The Cosmic Path of Initiations is an extraordinary spiritual practice utilizing the new principles of Cosmic Astrology. Here is how it works.

THE COSMIC PATH OF INITIATIONS

THIS IS A SYSTEM OF TRANSMUTATION AND TRANSFORMATION

Using a newly developed astrological tool it is now possible to illuminate your soul's journey at any point in time by following a path of personalized initiations on a regular basis. Using your natal birth information, you can begin right here, right now (anywhere) to comprehend exactly where you are on the path of your evolution. This information allows you to transmute blocked energies in a simple step-by-step process.

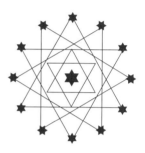

NEW ENERGY FOR NEW ANSWERS

This new Cosmic Astrology system, the Cosmic Path of Initiations (CPI), is an ongoing therapeutic and energetic approach to understanding what you are going through and why, at any given moment. You don't have to feel lost anymore. With this system you can locate where you are on your path and instantly 'get' the lesson that is being offered. You can choose, with great consciousness and confidence, to step into the higher qualities that are always there for your development. You will feel empowered, supported and loved through this process.

Whenever there is a crisis or drama that generates fear or pain there is an amazing opportunity to break through to your highest Self. Imagine being able to pinpoint the very nature of the issue right in the moment it arises and using that awareness to move past your old habitual responses and break the chain of constantly reenacting your old belief systems (BS).

THE COSMIC CLOCK

The natural wheel of the zodiac is actually a series of solar (soular) hierarchies (the signs) that can be overlaid onto your natal birth chart to help with your understanding of the different aspects of higher consciousness. Each month you undertake an initiation, the first step onto the next leg of your journey. This has always been true; it is just that we have not been particularly conscious of it before. Each time you successfully undertake the lessons of the aspect of consciousness you are dealing with you gain momentum toward your ascension process. When done on a monthly basis, the clarity and understanding that is achieved facilitates the evolution of your soul in a most personalized way.

HOW IT WORKS

The initiations are the gateways to your Higher Self. The process begins with a 60 – 90 minute session that delineates your higher purpose, the particular issues you are dealing with in this lifetime, and more specifically at the moment, and the timing with which you personally are able to access your own growth process. This method is explained fully and your own personal path mapped out for you.

After this first session, there are monthly 30-minute sessions that fall around the same time each month, based on your birth date, to focus you in depth on the issues you are working with for the four weeks ahead.

You will work closely together with a certified CPI facilitator for at least one full journey around the clock, or one year, to mobilize you toward your Higher Self by showing you how to release yourself from the gravity of the wheel of life's centrifugal force, which has kept you stuck, going around and around for lifetimes.

All CPI facilitators are trained and certified through a rigorous process by Stephanie herself. Please note that Stephanie is no longer personally offering these sessions to new clients, but has opted instead to oversee and continue to train all of the facilitators she certifies. They all come highly recommended for their great skills as astrologers, counselors and spiritual guides. Please go to **www.Cosmic-Quotient.com/Practitioners** and have a closer look at the facilitators that currently offer the system. Find the one you resonate with and make the connection that will change your life.

The focus is on locating your own personal fear-based habitual responses, clearing them away with specific transmutation tools that are given to you, and moving into your full potential.

THE TIME IS NOW. ARE YOU READY TO MOVE INTO ASCENSION?

Why waste another minute trying to figure out why you cannot get past your old issues. The Cosmic Path of Initiations will take you where you are truly meant to be: co-creating your destiny in a very interactive way. It is time to serve yourself and the planet. You will find information on how to find a facilitator and start your journey at the back of the journal.

HERE'S WHAT PEOPLE ARE SAYING ABOUT THE SYSTEM:

"The information and insight I have received from Stephanie's readings have been hugely transformational. I consider myself as being knowledgeable with astrology and my spiritual path. However, Stephanie's advice and explanations are real and

practical tools, which have helped me tremendously. Her explanations of what is happening in my life are comforting and accurate, and her advice on how to improve my life and understanding of life are spot on! This has been an amazing journey for me and having Stephanie's help and insight are invaluable. You need this!" ~J.R.

"I just want to thank you again for the readings that you provided to me. You are truly amazing! And your presentation of the new astrology is so profound, rich, dense and just beautiful! I am so glad that I stumbled on your website years ago... And I'm very grateful that you have helped me, guided me on so many occasions, in the right direction home (Source). Love to you!" ~L.P.

"I wanted to tell you that if you have ever doubted for one second that your Cosmic Path changes lives - it does. In reading your post yesterday about the mercury retrograde cycle and connecting that to the profound changes in my inner world in the past week I realized just how much change is truly possible.

I have been a control freak all of my life, a child of a mentally ill father. In response I developed a driving need to control every aspect of my life because the world was an unsafe place. In speaking with my husband this morning about the cosmic path and your piece of yesterday I had a profound moment of realization that if all the changes that had happened in my inner world through this past week with the help of the planets, then there truly is a God who watches over us and that perfect orchestration happens every moment of every day without my having to try to control anything....which of course is just one big illusion anyway. I think in that moment it finally became believable to me. For the first time in my almost 53 years I let go of every part of my body - my organs, my skin, every cell...everything and let God drive the bus. It was a feeling I cannot describe adequately with words....

I sincerely doubt I have adequately described any of this to you...how huge of a thing this is...but I do hope that you realize that your work does help people to change their lives....it did mine. Thank you for that Stephanie ...and may God richly bless you the way you bless others with your contributions. Deepest honor and respect and with much love and gratitude." ~J.P.

"A great gift has been given to me through the work of Cosmic SQ and during our last phone conversation ...understanding the tool of 'using the mirror-ed self.' An incredible weapon against the misqualified energies!

It has also been a tremendous value each month getting the feedback that I trust (our planets) to let me know I am right on the track that God intends. Awareness heals thank-you." ~T.M.

PIVOTAL MOMENTS
OTHER OPPORTUNITIES FOR HEALING

Everyone practicing the Cosmic Path of Initiations comes to 4 major turning points throughout the year, and at these critical passages you would benefit greatly from additional healing support. When the 12, 3, 6, and 9 o'clock hours are reached during the course of the year, we each move energetically into the next lower body system, a process that requires integration and clearing. The Rising Star and Prema Birthing healing systems, with their focus on clearing the chakras and cutting the energetic cords of ties that bind, are perfect for these pivotal turning points. Here is a brief introduction to these amazing healing modalities.

ABOUT RISING STAR HEALINGS

The Rising Star can assist in healing unresolved issues, old or blocked energy and physical symptoms, leaving you feeling empowered, lighter, more joyful and energized. The Rising Star healing system even activates DNA, bringing forward your true potential and helping you to become the person you were born to be. The Rising Star is a Source to Source healing – completely pure. Every session is unique.

- During a healing session, all levels of your being are addressed – physical, emotional, psychological, spiritual and etheric (a layer of energy that exists beyond physical matter, not visible to the eye), thus making the Rising Star extraordinarily comprehensive and effective.

- The Rising Star works on the five elements that exist within your being: fire, water, air, earth and ether.

- The Rising Star also brings healing to all seven body systems. The seven body systems are like seven layers of energy around you. As healing is brought to all body systems at once, very deep healing can occur.

- It raises the vibration of the aura (human energy field) and the energy field around every living thing. It also restructures your energy circuits to hold more life-force energy.

- The Rising Star incorporates the energy of your personal lineage (both in this lifetime, as in your ancestral line, and on your soul level) into each session, bringing you the healing most beneficial and effective for your soul in the present moment.

THE RISING STAR SYMBOL

- You may find that the healing also has an effect on family and friends. Since we are all connected and not separate, when you change, so do all around you change.

The Rising Star was channeled by Derek O'Neill. The channeling came through unexpectedly from higher dimensions during a More Truth Will Set You Free workshop in New York City where several hundred people witnessed the transmission.

The Rising Star does not require you to have faith, follow a specific religion, or even believe in it, in order for it to be effective. It merely takes your willingness to heal and transform.

ABOUT PREMA BIRTHING HEALINGS

The Prema Birthing healing system is a loving way to be reborn into your true Self. It is a gentle and powerful way for you to let go of the negative programming and limiting beliefs that keep you stuck.

WIPE THE SLATE CLEAN

Each of us is born with a set of circumstances, or "karmas," that create our experiences. As we live our lives and learn from our surroundings, we accumulate fears, false belief systems and negative programming. As we come into awareness of these things that no longer serve us, we become ready to let go of them.

> THE PREMA BIRTHING PROCESS CAN ELIMINATE DIS-EASE
> FROM ALL LEVELS OF YOUR BEING - MIND, BODY, AND SPIRIT.

If you are aware of the things you are ready to let go of at this time in your life, you can release them during a Prema Birthing session. This transforms the environment or receptors in your body, which in turn change the cells of your biology, and dis-ease has to leave. The results of this technique have amazed countless people around the world who have experienced it.

FIND A PRACTITIONER

For Cosmic Path of Initiations, please refer online to:
www.Cosmic-Quotient.com/practitioners

For Rising Star and Prema Birthing, please refer online to: **www.SQ-Wellness.com/find-a-healer**

ADDITIONAL
RESOURCES

Derek O'Neill is a master spiritual teacher, healer and psychotherapist. With his long anticipated first book, *More Truth Will Set You Free,* Derek shares his incredible healing journey and shows you how you too can heal your life on all levels, emerging as the happy, fulfilled person you were born to be. This book will bring you from doubt to proof that we are more than just what we see ourselves as. This extraordinary "life manual" is an inner and outer journey of great benefit to all walks of life. It is infused with Derek's unsurpassed energy, so as you read the teachings you will receive powerful healing in your own life. Enjoy this powerful step on your spiritual journey.

Available for purchase online at
www.Amazon.com or **www.SQ-Wellness.com**.

Water Drop and Her Friends coloring book is an informative, inspirational teaching tool for children of all ages. Children have fun as they learn the lesson of water conservation, cooperation, and so much more. Simple, easy to understand, and fun to color in whimsical illustrations makes this a great gift for the kids on your list!

Available for purchase online at
www.SQ-Wellness.com.

AN INTRODUCTION TO COSMIC ASTROLOGY
An Interactive Workbook
by Stephanie Azaria

Astrology is a conscious science that is evolving and becoming an increasingly relevant tool for assisting us to expand into our higher awareness. It is Stephanie Azaria's highest goal to bring forth the emerging new consciousness of Cosmic Astrology as soon as possible. She is hard at work on a new publication, an interactive workbook on Cosmic Astrology that will help you merge all your current knowledge about astrology with the newer system that is so relevant to the times we are living in.

LOOK FOR THE WORKBOOK IN 2013.

CQ WEBSITE
WWW.COSMIC-QUOTIENT.COM

The Cosmic-Quotient website, www.Cosmic-Quotient.com, has been created to establish a connection between Stephanie's popular www.TheCosmicPath.com and www.SQ-Wellness.com, which is the website of Spiritual Teacher, Derek O'Neill. The CQ website is primarily focused on expanding human consciousness through a growing awareness of the Cosmic Path of Initiations healing modality, which utilizes Cosmic Astrology.

As we all move more and more fully into 5D consciousness, places like this website connect us with the support we need. It has always been Stephanie's mission to use astrology to gain higher ground. With Cosmic Astrology and the Cosmic Path of Initiations healing modality, the higher path has become so much more accessible.

CONNECT WITH A CPI FACILITATOR

All facilitators of the Cosmic Path of Initiations at the time of this publication have been important contributors to the evolution and development of the Cosmic Astrology system over the past 5 years. They have all been personally trained and certified by Stephanie Azaria, who is not currently taking on new CPI clients, but has opted instead to oversee and guide the expansion of the system. Each facilitator has been trained in the same way.

The Cosmic Path of Initiations is a year-long process (or as long as you like) involving an initial 60-90 minute session that lays the foundation for your journey and orients you powerfully with the tools you will need for transmuting your core issues. Each consecutive month after your initial orientation provides you with a 30-minute session that delineates your focus and discipline for the next 30-31 days. Tools and expansive options change each month and out of the focus and devoted practice that is asked of you during this process, you will develop the spiritual discipline required to move more fully into the ascension journey.

Come to the Cosmic Quotient website and using your intuition, choose a certified CPI facilitator from the list found at **www.Cosmic-Quotient.com.**

Your inner guidance will lead you to the right guide for your personal journey.

MASTER & GODDESS IMAGES

Having a daily practice that fortifies your connection with your higher consciousness is an important part of healing and overall well-being. In an effort to encourage your connection with your Higher Self, we have asked graphic artist Matt Rockman to create 24 brand new, vibrant, energy filled images that represent the masters of the signs on the cosmic clock and their feminine counterparts.

Place them on your altar and use them regularly for inspiration, meditation and to make contact with the master within yourself.

We are honored to bring you these all new, completely accessible renditions of the masters and goddesses of Cosmic Astrology.

These prints are available in many sizes and forms. Please visit **www.Cosmic-Quotient.com** to check them out and make your purchase.